Managing your internet and intranet services

the information professional's
guide to strategy

Second edition

Peter Griffiths

facet publishing

© Peter Griffiths, 2000, 2004

Published by
Facet Publishing
7 Ridgmount Street
London WC1E 7AE

Facet Publishing (formerly Library Association Publishing) is wholly owned by
CILIP: the Chartered Institute of Library and Information Professionals.

First published 2000
This second edition 2004

British Library Cataloguing in Publication Data
A catalogue record for this book is available from the British Library.

ISBN 1-85604-483-1

Peter Griffiths writes in a personal capacity but is grateful for the Home
Office's agreement to publish this book. Nothing in this text should be taken
as a description of official practice and mention of any commercial service or
product does not imply official endorsement.

Typeset in 11/14pt Aldine 401 and Verdana by Facet Publishing.
Printed and made in Great Britain by MPG Books Ltd, Bodmin, Cornwall.

Contents

Introduction:
The everyday internet

It is just three years since the first edition of this book appeared. In that time the internet has gone from being slightly exotic and technical to being a part of everyday life, not just in the UK but in many countries. Where it was unusual for URLs to be found in public, now they appear a dozen times an evening on television stations, in advertisements, on the side of delivery vehicles and in a thousand other places. The public is used to inserting the unquoted 'www' in front of the URLs that companies have purchased to match their names or slogans. Governments have policies for making the internet a part of everyone's life (and libraries have an important part in those policies). The major consumer magazines for the internet are reaching their hundredth editions and are a staple of the news kiosks, although several others have bitten the dust on the way. It's becoming difficult to imagine the way things were before we had the web.

But it has become more complex and difficult to manage a website. Major websites contain a number of features based on advanced software, and although there seem to be fewer 'plug-ins' for the current crop of web browsers, greater skills are needed to create worthwhile content in software such as Flash or Acrobat. More money and time is invested in training staff to work on the web than ever before. So it is still no picnic to be given a website to manage; the sums invested are greater than ever, and the need to manage them well is also greater than ever because of the risks involved.

So, as with the previous edition, this book aims to help library and information science (LIS) professionals whose responsibilities include the management of a website. Much of what it says is true for any discipline, but since the first edition it has become only too obvious that a number of library and information professional skills are indispensable to managing an organization's or a community's web presence, and that it makes eminent sense for those professionals to play a prominent – indeed the most prominent – role in overall management of websites.

The role may be combined with the rather more widely found technical roles that LIS professionals often fulfil in this field. For these roles as editors, designers and creators of websites, or as server and systems managers, there is considerably more guidance available. It comes in printed form as books and periodicals, in electronic form as e-journals and newsletters, and as postings to online discussion groups. Despite some reduction in the number of periodicals, there is a good choice of support materials being available and this is reflected in the reading lists of this book.

However, management of a website or sites in the more conventional sense of the term has got no easier. Not only are some of the turf wars still going on after three or four years but there are new players who have a claim to lead development of either the external website, or the intranet, or both. The collapse of the 'dot com' market has led senior managers to look again at the costs and benefits of having a website. Even though in many areas (such as local government) it is considered indispensable to have one, this is not the same as saying that every chief finance officer is convinced that they justify their cost. The LIS professional responsible for the management of a website or web-based service, and often answerable to senior people in the community, has a difficult task.

- How do you manage an area of work that has technical people doing advanced but exciting things with a medium that develops rapidly, that your colleagues in other departments also want to manage, and that you know only as a search tool?
- How do you – as a more senior manager – take on managing an area that has developed its own advanced technical standards and activities in just a few years, and that therefore could never have been covered in your own training? Your mistakes are going to be very public, so how do you get it right from the start?
- How do you – as a non-technical person – make decisions on the technical questions when there seems to be a new technological development every other week?
- How do you make the business case to senior managers when the numbers never quite add up, but everyone else seems to be able to make the

business justification for spending lots of money?
- Should you – as an information professional – be in this game at all, or should you pass this work to another department and get back to the real job?

The main focus of the book remains the management of websites from the point of view of a library and information professional who is responsible for the management of a website or sites, or has an important role in their management. It is not intended as a technical guide and those who are required not only to act as business managers but as hands-on technicians will need to look for further guidance on technical matters. Similarly it cannot provide a definitive guide to the legal and financial issues that are involved in managing any but the most basic websites, and for this guidance it is essential to consult the appropriate professionals.

The Resource List (page 215) contains a range of materials of differing levels of complexity. It provides information on subjects from the syntax of HTML tags to the way in which you can develop multimedia presentations for your website. The list has been expanded to cover related topics, and one intriguing aspect of the web's development is the continuing relevance of some of the classic texts from pre-web days on branding and other subjects, which have yet to be bettered.

There are a number of technical tasks that are peculiar to library websites, the main one being to make an online catalogue available on the web. Providing comprehensive instructions for the technical processes that are involved in putting a catalogue onto the web would take a considerable space from a book that is not intended to provide that kind of technical depth. The solution in any particular case is likely to be different from that for many others, depending on the catalogue software being used, the network configuration, and whether the intention is for specific users to have access or for worldwide access to be provided via the world wide web. You will probably have to obtain advice from your automated system vendor or catalogue software supplier, although some general remarks can be made. For this kind of task you are likely to have to make specific enquiries once you have absorbed the information in this book.

This book covers a lot of ground. First it examines the reasons for the importance of the internet and explains why LIS professionals have such a strong claim to be involved in its development. Then it looks at a number of aspects of managing websites on the internet, intranets and extranets. Because the book considers management questions more than technical ones, problems of finance and outsourcing are never far away. The book also examines issues such as the business case for developing or outsourcing your site. To conclude there is an attempt to look into the future and identify major future trends.

But the subject is vast and constantly changing, so this book can never be a complete reference work. If it were, it would be ten times the size, and out of date long before it got to you. It aims to point to the issues that you should consider, provide many of the clues and give some of the answers. In many cases, the important thing is that you consider the question, even if you decide that your current answer is (at least) adequate. However the field is changing so your answers may well change too – and the reasons for those changes may well come from the internet medium itself, as you discover what others have done in positions similar to your own.

If there are any lessons to be learned, they could be these:

- Running a website has got too big for it to be a sideline for the library or anyone else. Make the business case to run the service, devote the resources it needs in terms of people, technical facilities and money. Manage the service using all your professional skills and demonstrate the value of our profession.
- The range of areas that need library and information skills is expanding. Metadata is a word on everybody's lips as a smart alternative to classification and cataloguing; and many people can now have a stab at defining a taxonomy for you. Reputation management is yet another development in which LIS professionals have a distinctive and essential role to play.
- We are past the point when it is reasonable for library webmasters to know how to do everything that needs to be done on a website, so complex have they and the technology become. An important skill now is to be able to specify what needs to be done, assess bids and prices and be able to judge that the contractor has done what was asked for or has provided the specified functionality.
- Nothing stands still in this business, whether it is technical progress or pornographers looking for lapsed domain name registrations to take over. Keep your eyes open, keep moving forward and keep up to date.

To do this, readers of this book have access to a companion website, which will signal major new publications and issues of interest. It is continually available to purchasers of this title at www.facetpublishing.co.uk.

You will need to invest some time every week or even every day to monitoring newsletters, bulletins and weblogs, to looking at what your colleagues and competitors are doing on the web, and to sharing your ideas and experiences on mailing lists. That's something library and information professionals are good at doing for other people; do the best job you can on your own behalf and keep on top of the wave. It hasn't stopped being exciting yet.

1

The internet revolution

●●●●●●●●●●●●●●●●●●●●●●●●●●●●●●●●●●●●●●●

This chapter examines:

- why the world wide web has become such an important medium
- the things that people and organizations do on their websites
- some basics about the way the world wide web works.

●●●●●●●●●●●●●●●●●●●●●●●●●●●●●●●●●●●●●●●

The success of the internet has been remarkable. Internet historians will point out that it has a considerable history stretching over more than 30 years in military and academic circles, but to the general public the internet is synonymous with the world wide web. Public awareness is now almost universal and many organizations are starting to regard the internet as a mass medium. They now include it in their strategies just as they plan to use newspapers, magazines, television and radio. How did this come about? And why does it matter to LIS professionals?

The importance of the world wide web

This new generation of interfaces frees users from having to understand a set of protocols developed by scientists more than 20 years ago. Novices no longer have to join a clique of knowledgeable people and go through an apprenticeship. Instead they can concentrate on finding and sharing information and communicating with friends and colleagues. There's an ever-expanding list of services on the internet today to explore . . . . The internet is evolving beyond its anarchistic nature and haphazard interfaces to become the basis for an international information structure. The network is expanding beyond government labs and universities to commercial organizations, local schools, and into homes. Increasing numbers of businesses – large and small – are beginning to make use of the Internet, and the Net is now accessible to anyone with a terminal, modem and phone line.[1]

The sense of wonder is still apparent in that introduction to 'next-generation interfaces' (web browsers to you and me) written in 1994, one year after the Mosaic browser was released and web pages in HTML began to supplant the text-based information retrieved using tools such as Archie and Gopher, and services such as Hytelnet. Some elements of those early days are still important: the Lynx browser popular for text-based services is still going strong. On the other hand, the prediction in the same article that we would all be surfing using verbal commands to a speech-based recognition system by 1997 proved to be a little too far-sighted.

The web has become a mass medium in around five years. We have gone rapidly from expressing surprise when a newspaper or television advertisement includes a web address (or URL) to surprise when it does not. Even on the advertisements in London Underground trains (one place where nobody can yet get a connection to their ISP,[2] companies now include e-mail address and URL in their advertisements as a matter of course. The web has become all pervasive and is the constant subject of media attention and fascination.

This sudden development of the mass medium has had some important effects on the environment that readers of this book are likely to work in.

- Most managers are aware of the web. They know that most companies and many public bodies have a site there. It has been said that the risk of not having a website is now greater than the risk of having one. Companies and their managers feel that a website makes them appear to be modern and progressive, and in tune with their business. Being without one is like being without a telephone in a previous business generation, although many businesses seem unconcerned about the impression the site itself gives to callers. Managers may have some idea about who can run the site – usually they think of the computer department. However, the instinct to give the computer department the first option on creating and managing a website is wrong. A corporate website is no longer an interesting side line for the IT department or for an enthusiastic amateur. It is the place where the organization advertises itself to the world and, as the saying goes, you only get one chance to make a first impression.

- Businesses seem to have got past the stage where they entrust developing a website to a single person who happens to have some kind of technical background or interest, or to the IT section as a purely technical project. But they usually have rather less idea of what should go into a website, of who in the organization is presently sitting on that information, and what should be done to get it onto the web and so to the user community. In recent years organizations have become more aware of the potential of their intranets to provide useful content for the web, although there is also confusion about how this content can be managed. There is an important role for LIS professionals whose training and experience allow them to combine an understanding of the world wide web with a knowledge of the way that information is created, stored and used. The difficulty is likely to be in persuading their own managers that creating a website is a major project that involves a range of management and organizational skills, and that it is their LIS colleagues who have acquired many of those skills through their professional training and experience.

- Managers are constantly being told in their own professional reading that the corporate website is vitally important for the health of the organization. They read that a good site will provide them with a shortcut to addressing current concerns such as knowledge management, although the map of this shortcut is still not very clearly drawn. This leads many organizations to enter areas that they know little about and where few real skills are available to them. The websites that they build can be models of bad navigation and poor content. On the web, they confuse customers; on intranets, they waste not only the resources that developed them but the time of every member of the user community.[3] What organizations and communities desperately need are websites that are managed by people who understand what users do when they visit websites – how they navigate and how they seek information.

- The world wide web has attracted vast amounts of coverage in other media, with the result that there is an awareness of the web and its contents that was never achieved by other information services such as traditional online searching. It is also the first truly democratic medium, because anyone can create a website, either directly or through an agent, at low cost. These personal sites can stand alongside the efforts of transnational corporations and have sometimes shamed those very companies into doing the job properly themselves.

Since around the middle of 1996 the emphasis has been on the rise of commercial sites and the development of sound business reasons for organizations and communities of all sizes to be on the web. This has led to some considerable differences compared with the early days.

- It has become easier to produce websites. A critical mass has been reached so that it is now worthwhile for companies like Microsoft to produce programs that will deliver a half-decent web page with little more skill than it takes to use a word processor.
- Even though there are millions of amateur pages and the numbers continue to swell, the world wide web has become a serious means of communication. Amateur efforts just will not do any longer for an organization that wants to be taken seriously. With the tools available, even many of the 'hobby' sites on the web are of a quality way beyond that of many commercial sites of two years ago.
- The arrival of commercial websites has made it possible to find reliable and authoritative information on the web. Government policies in many countries are now encouraging electronic commerce (e-commerce) and the provision of public terminals to allow access for as many people as possible.

Who uses the internet?

The initial public image of an internet user was of a young male person, either one with inadequate social skills, or one with large amounts of disposable cash to enable him to maintain his computer at the leading edge of technology. As the web has developed and become a serious medium this has greatly changed. Although there are still some references to this type of user, it is clear that an increasing proportion of users are female, that family use in being encouraged, and that serious use of the web for commercial purposes continues to grow.

Information about users has been charted by a number of organizations from the early days of the world wide web as a public service. Perhaps the best known are the surveys by the Graphics, Visualization and Usability Center (GVU) at Georgia Tech, which undertook ten surveys between 1994 and 1998[4] although their planned eleventh survey has not yet taken place. A useful source for information about other surveys is the Nua[5] website, while information on current developments can be gathered from a range of sources to which search directories provide ready access. Official sources such as the office of the UK's e-envoy[6] (with its monthly reports on current official developments) can also be helpful in tracking developments: current issues of internet journals will supply further news. Other long-running surveys include the American Interactive Consumer Survey[7] and A. C. Nielsen.[8]

Commercial use of the internet has led to rapid development of software tools and a wide range of sophisticated uses for the web. Sites have developed quickly from being simple presentations of selections from publicity material for the site owner. This is one way in which the development of websites has been characterized:

Stage 1: Brochureware

The website reflects corporate publicity and structures. There are news updates, copies of corporate documents that often slavishly reflect the printed form, and corporate public relations branding is everywhere.

Stage 2: Interaction

Users can obtain forms by download from the site. It is possible to provide some information back to the site through an interactive process. Information provision on the site is managed through an interface that allows some form of searching.

Stage 3: Advanced interaction

Users can return forms online and enter transactions by e-mail. Information provision on the site is managed through a sophisticated interface that allows advanced searching.

Stage 4: Transaction

Users interact with databases, carry out transactions and are able to discover the state of their order or a process – for example they can track packages in transit.

Stage 5: Advanced transaction

Users can maintain online accounts and the system can respond based on constantly updated information about that account and its history.

Telling or selling?

The events described above have brought about a fundamental change in the nature of the web. Until the mid-1990s it was a tool for research and collaboration, and users were typically academics, researchers or the military (who originally devised it).

Commercial websites came on the scene in around 1994 and 1995. At the same time the level of available interactivity grew as new browsers were launched. Scripts made it possible to interact with the site owner. At first, information went from the website to the user who stored it on disk, often briefly because of the cost of storage. More recently, the information has flowed in two directions and allowed electronic commerce. The cost of storage has also fallen dramatically, leading to expansive websites and increased use of multimedia effects.

Since the arrival of commercial websites, most sites have fallen into one of two broad categories:

- sites that tell people something
- sites that sell people something (or at least collect money in exchange for something).

Much of the literature on web management assumes that these are synonymous, or that selling follows on directly from telling and should occur during the same visit by the user to the website. Telling and selling are not necessarily linked, and especially not in many of the areas where librarians and other information professionals work. While it is certainly true that public services are operating in ways unheard of 20 years ago, they are still essentially in the business of service and of telling people things that help them.

Many early websites (and not a few still) tell people little or nothing of any use to them. Personal home pages (with apologies to readers who maintain one and to the owners of the undoubted good ones) are by and large fairly awful. They serve mainly to present selective information about people's personal hobby-horses and obsessions, and underdeveloped photographs of their relatives, to the world. They may steal other people's copyrights and intellectual property or provide a mass of unsubstantiated opinion masquerading as fact. They clog up the search engines with trivia. Their only saving grace is that just sometimes they show up organizations that should have thought to provide a website by doing the job better than the real owners of the information.

> Because the Web is so new, few companies have dedicated personnel assigned to creating and updating their site. Instead, it's likely to be the enthusiast – the one who browses the Web in his or her spare time, who knows a little bit about the structure of Web sites – who will be asked to manage the Company's site. *PC Magazine*, March 1997

As interest in the web has grown, many organizations have decided that they need a website. What senior managers typically do next is to hand over control of it to one of two people: either the head of the computer section or somebody who is known to use a computer at home. Neither of these is a good idea.

A website built by the computer section may well have every latest bell and whistle attached to it. Technology will drive the site, which will display the combined expertise of the section. It will probably run very slowly because so much has to be downloaded to make it work, and finding information will be difficult because the content will be secondary to the technology.

Somebody who uses a computer at home is likely to use the web and have some idea of what goes on there; they may well have some good ideas on how to achieve it. They will probably have rather less idea about how to get this into a web page, and if they do know they should consider working for the computer section.

A home-grown enthusiast may produce a good-looking website, and may produce an impressively flashy one. He or she is much less likely to produce one that helps people to find information (or the products they want to buy) and finish their transaction by going away with the knowledge they wanted or having placed an order.

The following chapters will examine the case for giving management responsibility for websites to library and information professionals. Although they may need to contract with others inside or outside their employing organization or community in order to obtain all the technical services that are needed, their business and technical skills are sufficiently well developed to manage these contracts effectively. LIS skills are at a premium when it comes to indexing and organizing the information within a website. Suddenly the traditional and sometimes despised library skills are in great demand. Chapter 2 looks at the reasons for this in more detail and suggests why LIS professionals should be involved in the management of websites in many organizations.

Intranets and extranets

Many organizations have developed closed and private internal versions of the internet. These so-called intranets provide information services within organizations – across a global community in the case of some of the major international corporations. In some cases extranets provide important customers with access to selected parts of the intranet, such as ordering systems and other information about the company that supplies them. Because these are information products that are typically limited to users connected to a company network, they tend to be more detailed, more inward-looking and more confidential in nature than much of the world wide web. Because of this, their management and organization often demands a level of skill even greater than for a public website. There is more jargon to be organized into a meaningful structure, and frequently issues of organizational culture to be managed. Information still represents power in many communities, and the fact that the work of LIS professionals is to map and organize this information gives a political as well as a technical and professional dimension to these tasks. Intranets are increasingly being used as a tool to develop internal communication, and they play a pivotal role in the introduction of knowledge management to many organizations.

What is happening to the technology?

This book is avowedly non-technical. However, in order to follow the remainder of the book you need to understand some of the technology and what developments are taking place.

The bulk of websites are made up of linked pages of information or data, which are generally coded in HyperText Mark-up Language (HTML). This tells the browser – software such as Internet Explorer or

Netscape Navigator – how to lay out the various elements of the page. Related pages are connected to each other within the site using hyperlinks. These are live links within the document that, when clicked on by the mouse, take the reader to related information that the writer has identified elsewhere. This may be on another page on the same website or it may be on another site somewhere else on the world wide web.

HTML has evolved through several versions and is about to evolve again into something called eXtensible Mark-up Language (XML). This emerging standard offers greater flexibility and gives you better ways to distinguish between the various content elements on your site. Microsoft's Office software makes considerable use of it, so it will be increasingly easy to output browser compatible XML code even if you are not comfortable writing code. (Surveys consistently find that around 20% of HTML authors prefer using Windows Notepad and coding everything 'by hand'.) New code protocols are constantly being developed for a range of applications – for example Wireless Application Protocol (WAP), which will allow you to send information to suitably equipped mobile tele- phones. Chapter 11 contains a glimpse into the crystal ball and suggests ways to stay ahead of the markup language game.

You can include many other types of document on your website. Doc- uments created for word processors can be included, as can spreadsheets and presentations. Software is available that will produce copies of the pages of a printed document in a format that can be viewed and printed almost like a photograph of the page; many sites use Adobe Acrobat, and although at first many people were wary of introducing a proprietary file format onto their pages, Adobe's Portable Document Format (.pdf) is now a de facto standard on the web.

Software to read .pdf files and for a number of other purposes can be downloaded from the web. The latest versions of browser software are capable of reading many different types of file format, but the earlier ver- sions that many people still use are not. They rely on 'plug-in' software, which is extra programs downloaded from the suppliers' sites and then loaded into the browser so that the user can read files in the format in question. Why are these reader files provided free? Because the vendors make their money from selling software to website owners in order to cre- ate the document or graphics files that they put on the web. Thus in order to create copies of documents in .pdf format, you need a copy of the full Adobe Acrobat software rather than the Acrobat reader that is widely and freely distributed. Similarly, if you are going to provide audio or video files in Real Media formats, you need a copy of the full software package, not just the Real Media player.

Visitors to your website will be using a wide variety of computers. Although many people assume that their readers are using Microsoft software on a PC machine, this is not so. You should remember that people also use Mac, Unix, Linux and a variety of other machines and operating systems. Many people use systems that cannot easily handle graphics, and others deliberately turn them off in order to reduce the time it takes to load web pages. (More about this in Chapter 8, which discusses the things that annoy website users, and questions of accessibility.).

To help to provide every user with the same experience of your site, such techniques as the use of cascading style sheets (CSS) are available. These allow you to specify the way that headings, text and some layout elements appear on screen.

Not everyone has the same software packages as you: think before you issue a file only in Word XP, as you are limiting access to other users of this package. However, offering a text document in a variety of formats is a good way of including longer publications on your site without having to carry out hours of processing to convert it into short HTML files.

There is plenty of help available with the technical issues on the web. A good place to start is the website of the World Wide Web Consortium, otherwise the W3C,[9] where you can read about HTML, XML and related issues.

Summary

In this chapter we looked at the nature and recent history of the internet. We saw that there had been a fundamental change in the nature of the internet with the arrival of the world wide web, which was followed by the introduction of a commercial approach to what had been a research and collaborative tool. More recently the web has caught the public imagination, and government and other official policies are now helping to shape it. We took a first glance at some of the subjects that this book will cover, and recalled some of the basic technology of the web.

References

1   Miller, D. (1994) The Many Faces of the Internet, *Internet World*, **5** (7), (October), 34–8.

2   Or, to be precise, in deep tunnels, although on some cities' metro systems – such as line 14 in Paris – mobile telephones will work even 50m below ground.

3   In 2002 Jakob Nielsen estimated that average US companies could save up to $5 million a year by improving their intranets – see his Intranet Usability: the Trillion Dollar Question, *Alertbox*, 11 November 2002, www.useit.com/alertbox/20021111.html. Neilsen reported that employee time (and therefore company revenue) was being wasted by poor search features, which accounted for 43% of the difference in employee productivity. He found search mechanisms that didn't index all the intranet pages, poorly prioritized search results, poorly written page titles that couldn't be scanned easily and poor page summaries. LIS professionals have skills in handling all these areas and can make a significant contribution to realizing these potential savings.

4   www.gvu.gatech.edu/user_surveys/.

5   www.nua.com/surveys/ or www.nua.ie/surveys, now part of cyberatlas.internet.com.

6   www.e-envoy.gov.uk.

7   Formerly the American Internet User Survey; see www.thedrg.com (Dieringer Research Group) for 2003 surveys onward and www.cyberdialogue.com for earlier surveys.

8   www.acnielsen.com/ and www.nielsen-netratings.com.

9   www.w3c.org.

2

LIS professionals and the web

•••
This chapter examines:

- why LIS professionals have become important in managing websites
- roles that LIS professionals can play
- how the professional skills of LIS professionals can be used in managing websites.

•••

This chapter looks at the opportunities for the LIS professional in managing and operating websites. Quite apart from the chances to do technical services work in compiling HTML and other code, and carrying out technical management of a site, there is much to be undertaken in seeking and organizing information content, creating site architecture, page and site design, and building navigation aids. Many of these tasks call for the abilities of LIS professionals.

Why have LIS professionals become so important?

Librarians and information scientists took quickly to the internet as an information resource. Perhaps this was because the internet – both the older technologies such as Gopher, Archie and Veronica, and the new technologies such as the world wide web – made such a large contribution to their own research resources. Perhaps it was because so many LIS professionals are interested in library technology. Or perhaps it was because so many suppliers turned to the web to deliver their services, and moved away from dial-up online.

End-users continue to be heavy users of the web as suppliers pursue these policies. In many organizations end-users have access to the web through the computers on their desk, via the organization's network. But what they get when they search directly is a disorganized, inconsistent and unreliable collection of information that surrounds what is accurate information with gossip and propaganda masquerading as fact.[1] As a result many librarians have developed a role as trusted advisers, experts at navigating and analysing information on the internet, and at understanding and explaining how and why it was put there. Using their skills in coaching and training they help end-users to separate fact from fiction. By helping users to conduct simple searches alone, they free their own time for work that adds higher value, where their LIS professional skills are essential if a good result is to be achieved.

Many websites have been created in a short time and are indexed very poorly. As a result, the traditional skills of LIS professionals such as indexing and classification have become very important. Although much of the creation of web pages can be automated or made easier with the right software, intellectual effort is needed to add the data to a page that will make it possible for the largest number of people to retrieve it when required. This has made some of the traditional library skills suddenly become much in demand, even if the terminology is now different. But there are other reasons why LIS professionals should get involved.

A natural role for LIS professionals

The role of the LIS professional in these areas of work is nothing new – only the level of interest is anything remarkable. Look at this extract from a 1967 lecture:

> The brave electronic shock troops . . . bring us ever greater core-stores and ever-increasing transfer speed. . . . They can print faster than a man can read!
>
> So, here is a powerful tool: and all around us is good and plentiful material. Whose skill and what skill shall guide the tool?

The problem is not basically new. What is new is its scale. The load, the power, the speed and the unthinking discipline of the new robot create a gear ratio where a false move, or a good move, will have vastly more effect than hitherto. Only the human contribution can decide whether we shall have a Sorcerer's Apprentice or a Fairy Godmother.[2]

This was evidently not a new problem over 30 years ago. Now here is a webmaster of the late 1990s who recognized one role that librarians can play:

Reference librarians have helped tremendously. I highly recommend enlisting the help of your library department reference staff before going down this road alone.[3]

It has taken time for others to recognize the skills of LIS professionals beyond being the providers of reference data for websites. In fact we are well equipped for many aspects of the production and management of websites.

Information management skills

Many LIS professionals have been able to show that their understanding of information management can be given a financial value in this context. When your organization has spent some thousands of pounds – sometimes tens or even hundreds of thousands – on a website, it is money wasted if the product is never found and used again. The major search engines now draw from a pool well in excess of two billion pages. Getting yours to appear at the top of a search among so many items demands industrial strength indexing and an indexer who understands the web – and those are the skills of the library and information professional.

Editorial skills

Some information professionals have been able to take the logical next step from their use of the web in their information work and are involved in editing and publishing their organizations' websites. They are showing how the skills they have learnt in their research can enhance their professional activities on other tasks for the benefit of their community.

Organizing information

Librarians' training provides skills in organizing and navigating documents, while the information scientist brings an understanding of the relationships between the documents. The first requirement must be for a website that helps people to find the information they need through its organization and structure. This of course is exactly what information professionals are trained to do. Their skills will allow them to provide an orderly structure that links relevant information within the sites and provides the necessary signposts and directions to relevant pages.

Louis Rosenfeld and Peter Morville turn this fact on its head:

> Believe it or not, we're all becoming librarians. This quiet yet powerful revolution is being driven by the decentralizing force of the global Internet. . . As [it] provides users with the freedom to publish information, it quietly burdens them with the responsibility to organize that information. . . . As we struggle to meet these challenges we unknowingly adopt the language of librarians. How should we *label* that content? Is there an existing *classification scheme* we can borrow? Who's going to *catalog* all that information?[4]

LIS skills extend not just to creating the information architecture for the website, but also to categorizing and managing the data that drives the site.[5]

Adding value

The websites that are managed by LIS professionals show our worth to the various groups of users and stakeholders that we serve. Intranets form an integral part of the way the information professional communicates to and with the rest of the organization or community, and we should remember that the early and rapid development of the world wide web was based on sites that existed primarily to provide information. Many early webmasters were amateurs who wrote their own sites in order to publish their knowledge – and frequently their quirky views – for public consumption. They led the way for what are now ubiquitous commercial uses of the web. And it was factual sites such as those made available by libraries that showed how useful the web could be in reality, when proper content was made available.

Management skills

The management skills of each of these related disciplines are focused on adding value for the customer. Skills such as project and financial management may be seen as less closely related to the 'workface' in many libraries but are valuable additions to the toolkit of the information professional who manages a website.

Technology skills

Librarians have skills that make them among the best suited people in most organizations to run a website. The need to manage specialist software applications that are often unsupported by corporate IT departments has led LIS professionals to develop a general understanding (and frequently a love) of technology. This makes them well suited to dealing with the technological aspects of creating websites but likely to get over-engrossed in technology to the point of ignoring the organization. But with a proper balance of skills and interests, LIS professionals have the skills needed to manage websites better than almost anyone.

Too much opportunity?

Firms often do not realise the importance of librarians' roles as knowledge workers and managers, and their status and compensation seldom reflect their real value to a firm.

They have familiar ways to quantify the benefits of the library as an information source and information marketplace. Even though they 'know' value exists there, their inability to express it in traditional financial or accounting terms makes them behave as if it didn't.[6]

Unfortunately, as Louis Rosenfeld and Peter Morville pointed out in the first edition of their book on information architecture, librarians reacted slowly and often defensively and negatively to their new opportunities.

The truth is . . . that skills in information organisation and access are more and more necessary in this era of information explosion. We have found that the demand for our skills in classifying and organising information in websites has grown beyond our wildest dreams, so we believe that you, your sites and their users will benefit from [the librarian's] perspective.[7]

It is the librarian's skills of indexing, classifying, structuring information and cataloguing it that allow the user to navigate efficiently within a website. It is the information professional's skill in compiling abstracts that matches the requirements of writing for the web, where the trick is to compile short pages that fit together in a structured system of links and navigation, rather than (in many cases) simply transferring a long document to HTML.

Librarians approach the internet from the point of view of the user. Some commentators overplay this point:

> Librarians don't provide answers; they improve access. Librarians create an invisible gateway to the information you need. You barely notice how they are helping you. Ideally, they want you to be able to help yourself.[8]

Some compilers of web directory sites – including the best known of the big league players like Yahoo! – use or have used teams of librarians to provide their indexing and commentaries on websites. This can only remain a growth industry as the web continues to expand exponentially.

There is another potential call on librarians' skills for managing websites, which is to maintain an archive of your website. In a company, you may well need to keep an archive of your website for legal purposes, particularly if you use the site to carry out any kind of trading or e-commerce. In the public sector, you will need to maintain an archive because the website forms part of the public record. In both these cases you will probably print out the pages and archive them, but you will also need to maintain an electronic archive. This will preserve the links contained within the site and allow you to demonstrate what the users saw on their screens rather than how the pages printed out from the machine that created them.

There is more about archiving your site in Chapter 9.

More skills of the LIS professional

Librarians are likely to posses a wide range of further skills that support website management. Some of these are discussed below.

Project management

Many library professionals become expert project managers in the course of their careers. Library automation tends to demand careful planning and installation, often because the library staff are working with companies that are managing simultaneous technical installations with many interdependent activities. In these circumstances, only by adopting a project management system (of which PRINCE[9] is a widely used example) can the library and information professional hope to keep the project on track. That applies to website development too: it is certainly possible to create and launch a site by simply throwing unco-ordinated resource at it, but it works far better when the resource and timing is planned. That way, corrective action can be taken if the work looks as if it will run out of time or exceed the financial budget. So project management skills are now much sought after among web staff and the LIS professional can stake a strong claim to these roles.

Budgeting

The planning skills needed to set a library budget will also help website management work. The skills needed to prepare business cases for new projects and new library facilities can be brought to bear in calculating the resource requirements and timescales for launching new websites. While the claimed return on investment figures for some web projects still look remarkable when compared with the more normal returns that may be experienced, your management line will be far more inclined to accept the predictions of large returns and savings in return for a modest outlay if the person making those predictions has a sound reputation for forecasting library budgets or balancing information service resources and demand.

People management

Human resources skills will come to the fore increasingly as the website develops. The strong interpersonal skills of modern information and library professionals will be valuable in building the website team. As the profile of the site develops, the demands will grow as departments and related organizations recognize the value of taking part in the project. This is the point at which two distinct interpersonal skills will be needed, especially in handling senior staff and directors. The first is the ability to say 'No' to people; the other is to tell people they are wrong without losing their backing for the project.

You will have to say 'No' to some requests in order to prioritize demands on the time of the web team. Some projects will arrive late into the queue but have strong potential and need to be brought to the front. But if you constantly say 'Yes' to new requests, you will simply extend the length of the waiting queue of projects, and you'll be playing a dangerous game. You might convince managers that you are short of resource, but you may also give the impression of being unable to prioritize. You will have to tell some people that their ideas are valued but inappropriate (if not actually 'wrong') at the particular moment.

People's knowledge about the internet has grown, with routine coverage in the popular press, sufficient for there to be many self-taught 'experts' in web design on the strength of this. In the average corporate organization you are likely to meet senior managers who present confused designs for revising the website, or who insist that what the internet site really needs is the latest plug-in to allow users an interactive multimedia experience when visiting the organization online (at least, if they have a 2.8 GHz clock speed, 512Mb of memory, the latest versions of Flash and RealPlayer, 3-D graphics and fast broadband).

Political skills

Dealing with this kind of well-meant but ultimately unhelpful suggestion needs diplomatic and political skills, and perhaps training skills as you to try to harness the surplus energy that these managers could devote to improving the resources available to the website teams. Those political skills will also be needed to raise awareness of what the website teams are planning to do and what resources they have (or are lacking). They will be needed too in order to know when information on the site seems to be getting out of kilter with the organization's published line, and when it is safe – or even prudent – to delete (or archive) superseded material. A politically skilled website manager will know when to commission new material from a section with a highly visible programme of work that needs to be publicized.

Business skills

Information professionals also tend to be good at committee work. They will need to use that skill in working with the editorial boards that frequently oversee the management of websites. Depending on their role on the board, the information staff will be able to develop their skills as chairperson or committee secretary, and exercise their networking skills among the committee members and clients of the website authoring team. Top-level support will be found and nurtured for the work on the websites through these committees, as well as through the contacts that LIS professionals make in the course of library work.

Information professional skills

As well as the information management skills already mentioned, further skills of the information and library professional are valuable to the website manager and his or her team. These include the expertise that many LIS professionals have in user training: in this case, the training is not just that needed for end-users to become proficient at web searching and retrieval, but also in supporting web awareness and information literacy. The librarian's searching skills are also valuable, and not just for their value in teaching users how to search. Through the librarian's understanding of how people search, the quality of the indexing and the retrievability of the information on the site are improved. This skill also confirms the value of the information professional's skill in determining what information users are seeking, and the use of the reference interview to do this.[10]

Other useful librarian skills include marketing, both in terms of selling the potential audience what benefits are to be gained from the service being offered, and selling involvement with the website project to members of the organization that creates the information.

The LIS professional skill that has come to the fore, however, is the ability to apply metadata. The remark has been widely made that this is in fact a reinvention of cataloguing and classification, but metadata goes wider. Alongside these skills are thesaurus construction, quality control and training.

Technical skills

With the growing ease of constructing web pages using a range of software, the technical skill in constructing good pages is too readily overlooked. Contrary to what the creators and vendors of these programs might want potential users to think, it is not yet possible to write code for websites that is both efficient and compact without some sort of intellectual effort. A number of general office software packages allow the user to output HTML code from a word-processed document or spreadsheet, but even the most recent versions produce over-padded code that needs to be edited down before it is let loose on the public. (There is more about this in Chapter 8.)

An alternative approach is to generate the whole website from a database. If this is done at a very basic level, the result can be a site that has very little variation in its appearance and where navigation can be difficult. In this case, staff are likely to need the skills in order to create additional pages that contain more than just text or tables appearing on a uniform background. Librarians' long-standing technical skills, such as in managing library systems, gives many the background to do this work together with the credibility so necessary where two professional areas overlap.

Understanding service level management

A further useful skill is the understanding of service level agreement (SLA) management. Where an external host is used for the website (or even where this host is in another department, such as a university's computing centre), the guarantees for the supply of the service and of its quality and availability are likely to be enshrined in a service level agreement. Library SLAs are somewhat different from the run of agreements, but it is worth taking the effort to get them right.[11] Many web hosting companies now offer SLAs rather than contracts – often, the cynical might think, in an effort to avoid giving any cast-iron and therefore actionable guarantees about the availability of service. But from the supplier's point of view this is sensible, as some factors such as interruptions to the telephone services of the main telecommunications companies are out of their control. This is particularly true if you deal with one of the smaller companies who resell the connections, with their own support services included as part of the package.

Summary

In this chapter we saw that a number of the professional skills that LIS professionals can offer are relevant to the management of websites. These include technical and business skills as well as the more traditional library skills that are now in great demand by some major national and international organizations to manage the structure and organization of websites, and the categorization and organization of data. However there is a strong case that many more corporate organizations and communities do not understand the contributions that librarians and information scientists can make to the effective management of their websites, and that the profession should be marketing its skills. There is already a sufficient body of evidence to call upon, with examples of successful internet and intranet websites being managed by librarians.

References

1   Mintz, A. A. (ed.) (2002) *Web of Deception: misinformation on the internet*, Medford, New Jersey, Cyberage Books; Griffiths, P. (2001) All that Glitters: the role of the information professional in handling rogue information on the internet, *Online Information 2001, Proceedings*, Learned Information Europe, 2001, 17–23.

2   Batten, W. E. (1967) The future of information work: the ASLIB annual lecture, *Aslib Proceedings*, **19**, 6 June, 163–72 .

3   Comment by the web Doyenne, City of Clearwater, Florida, in response to a request on a discussion list for examples of excellent local government websites. In: Kennedy, S., Posting to Local and State Government Info on the Internet [GOVPUB@LISTSERV.NODAK.EDU], 14 May 1999.

4   Rosenfeld, L. and Morville, P. (2002) *Information Architecture for the World Wide Web*, 2nd edn, USA, O'Reilly, 51–2.

5   Rowbotham, J. (1999) Librarians – architects of the future?, *Aslib Proceedings*, **51** (2), (February), 59–63. See also Haynes, D. (2004) *Metadata for Information Management and Retrieval*, Facet Publishing; and Gilchrist, A. and Mahon, B. (eds) (2004) *Information Architecture: designing information environments for purpose*, Facet Publishing.

6   Davenport, T. H. and Prusak, L. (1998) *Working Knowledge: how organizations manage what they know*, USA, Harvard Business School Press, 29–30.

7   Rosenfeld, L. and Morville, P. (1998) *Information Architecture for the World Wide Web*, USA, O'Reilly, xiv.

8   Dougherty, D. (1997) Librarians get it: how librarians are shaping

the Web, *Web Review*, 4, July,
webreview.com/wr/pub/97/07/04/imho/index.html.

9 PRojects IN Controlled Environments, developed by the Central
Computer and Telecommunications Agency (CCTA) for the United
Kingdom Government, is now a widely used project management
system. Its latest iteration is PRINCE2, which is described at
www.ogc.gov.uk/prince/.

10 Rosenfeld, L. and Morville, P., op cit, (1st edn), 121–2.

11 Guidance on library SLAs is contained in Pantry, S. and Griffiths, P.
(2001) *The Complete Guide to Preparing and Implementing Service Level
Agreements*, 2nd edn, London, Library Association.

3

Getting on the web

● ●
This chapter examines:

- the reasons for an organization having a web presence
- how to identify your audience
- how to identify what are you trying to communicate to your audience
- how to build the web into your communication strategy
- technical matters to take into account
- the resources you will need.

● ●

Many of the websites that were constructed in the early days of the world wide web were there simply as a way of establishing a presence on the web. Often there was no thought of it being part of any kind of communication strategy. Since then the web has become a much more professional place, but some of those sites remain. They look very dated, and compare badly with the many good sites; but designers and suppliers who should know better still sell these one-size-fits-all templates to important organizations who have not troubled to do some basic homework about what they want their website to do. For the vast majority of sites, there needs to be a much more disciplined approach. That is what we shall look at here, before Chapter 4 considers some of the financial and management considerations of managing a website, and at the elements of a business case for using the web as a communications channel.

But first, why do it at all? What is the point of having a website – and does your answer depend on the apparent fact that everyone else has one? If you really must be there, what is the real message that you want to be your permanent presence on the web?

Why have a website?

There is a global audience that is eager for information and equipped to use the web to its fullest extent. It did not exist outside research institutions and universities ten years ago. Now it is something ordinary. Surveys suggest that in many countries half the population has ready access to the web at home or at work, or in both places. The public uses the web as a normal means of finding information. It has become a broadcasting medium, allowing users to listen to the output of radio stations (and, with broadband access, television stations) around the world. If you miss a favourite programme, you can listen to it on the web. The web has become a sophisticated replacement for character-based teletext systems, providing television viewers with additional information about programmes that is not limited to the confines of the television screen and its graphic constraints. The main problem is now sifting rather than finding information: any information search is likely to retrieve far more web pages than most users have time to examine, so that the best page (in terms of content rather than indexing) may not be retrieved in the first two or three pages of results. There is more about what this means to you as an information publisher in Chapters 7 and 8 on website publishing.

The web has turned many of the assumptions about communication on their head. For an outward-facing organization it is remarkable news. People from across the world in effect pay to come and view your information and your advertisements. They read the news that you issue exactly as you issued it, without the intervention of journalists who then rewrite it in ways that convey a different meaning. Site visitors download and print off your brochures and advertisements at their own expense. This can help to reduce the costs of an organization's external communications and commerce, although it will pay to divert some of those savings into making your online presence the best possible. The use of credit cards can bring revenues from across the globe, and the development of secure electronic transactions by various means will encourage this trend. Some of the most successful new companies (and certainly some of the best known) exist only as electronic companies. An entire market has grown up around selling goods on the web (Amazon being the best-known example), auctioning goods (eBay), and selling services at the last minute (LastMinute). Despite the worries and dire predictions, some of these companies are now trading at a profit, and it is becoming easier to cover the costs of running these services as they become more widespread and the costs reduce through economies of scale.

It might be tempting to think that there is no room left for new entrants, but the growth of the web shows no sign of slowing down. The issue of access speed is being solved as broadband connections are rolled out across many countries – certainly in centres of population and in a number of rural areas. The use of new information and communication technologies – such as connection via satellite – open further possibilities for high speed connection to the internet. The problem now is not whether the user can get connected at high speed, but whether your site can be served to a large number of users at high speed. The internet has become a part of daily business across the world and the question is no longer whether you will be part of it or not, but whether you will be an effective part of it, and whether your site will stand out from the welter of others.

Who is your audience?

Many website owners undertake or commission considerable amounts of design and content collection work before they address this simple question, but if you do not know what audience you have in mind when you develop your site, it will lack purpose and cohesion.

Your community, company or organization may by its nature define your primary audience: residents and the working population of a particular local government area, members and potential members of a university and clients and potential clients of its paid-for external services, or clients and customers of a company.

Those people within your organization or community who are going to supply you with information to include on your website will have an audience or audiences in mind. If they do not tell who these site users should be, you must challenge them to identify their audience before you accept any content from them. You need to know from the outset who the intended users of the site will be, because you need to design with them in mind. Do not accept the argument that an intranet is somehow less important than your internet site: the same applies to all kinds of website – identify the intended audience before you start work.

Who are your customers?

Do you know who your customers are for your current information services? What about your potential customers, both those you would like to have as customers and those people who would like to use your services but are unable to do so? Can a website help you to serve those people? Does your organization want to reach these people or other groups using an internet site? Do you want to reach these people with services via your intranet?

Many of the organizations where library webmasters are working will have an obvious customer community, even if the exact boundaries of that group are unclear. For example academic libraries will have common ground with many other academic communities and their common interest is demonstrated by the large number of library catalogues that are available on the world wide web. In local and central government there are obvious user communities among the chargepayers, ratepayers or taxpayers who fund the services.

Internal and external customers

The webmaster may well have internal and external customers, and act as an intermediary in the production chain. This requires a good understanding of the organization's business so that he or she can understand what the internal customer is trying to get across. Fortunate then that a webmaster based in the library and information service is in an excellent position to bring the LIS professional's networking expertise to the task, and improve the end product by maximizing the relevance of the site's proposed content to the activities of the organization.

The guidelines for creating UK government websites [1] suggest that market research or surveys should be undertaken to help to identify the audience for your site. A short consultancy, or even a survey carried out by telephone among known members of the audience, could help you to identify whether your potential audience is the one you thought, and what kind of service that audience might be looking for.

The survey could provide some other information that would influence your decisions about the way that your site develops. For example, you might be considering the inclusion of multimedia content such as video on your website. If this content were intended for older people in your community, your survey might for example show that many members of your potential audience were using their equipment 'out of the box' just as it had been delivered and had not installed a streaming video player (such as Real Player). In that case you would need to think again as that part of the site would be unlikely to reach your intended audience. If you did go ahead, you would ensure that any essential messages that were contained within the video were also spelt out in text in a prominent part of the site. Perhaps you would also decide to include a page explaining in detail what needs to be done to install a suitable video player, and telling people how they would benefit once they had this software available. Or perhaps you intend to include some kind of interactive game to promote a library activity; if so, how will you ensure that all parts of the user community, including the visually impaired or those with motor disability, have access to it?

Once you have identified the audience and the constraints or requirements that are associated with it, your next question is this:

What is the purpose of your site?

Once you have identified the audience and the constraints or requirements that are associated with it you will need to consider what the purpose of your site is. It is probably one of the following:

- publicizing your organization
- doing business
- communicating with customers and other interested users of your site
- providing information
- something else, such as vanity publishing.

Publicizing your organization

Good websites are well known and frequently referred to in the popular media. There is a definite cachet in creating a successful site for a well-known organization and a considerable risk in not having a site rather than in having one, because of the impression that websites give of an organization that is abreast of the times. It is becoming unthinkable that any major organization does not have a site, and in the public sector it is now expected.

Probably the majority of websites are still intended as a sort of shop window for the owner. They give some details of the organization or individual that is responsible for the site and create an impression that can be followed up in a number of ways: for example, further exploration of the website, writing, faxing or telephoning for more details, or by purchasing goods. (In the latter case, purchase can be either by going to a store that sells the organization's products, or by buying online.)

There are various ways of publicizing an organization. A number of sites do little but reproduce paper documents in electronic form. Whether this is an adequate web presence must depend to some extent on what the organization is. A public body could be expected to provide copies of its publications for downloading or reading online, while a commercial organization might be criticized for putting its corporate brochures on the web and in effect asking people to pay via their phone bills to read its advertising.

In this type of material can be included corporate information materials. These documents might be items such as mission statements that are not information in the sense that information professionals understand it, but amount to a corporate advertisement of belief or aspiration. This is a typical mission statement from the Royal College of Physicians' website (see Figure 3.1):

> By maintaining and developing this site, we aim to improve communications with not only our Fellows and Members in the UK and all over the world, but also anyone with an interest in medicine and the work of physicians.[2]

Notice that this is a mission statement for the website, and that the College has a separate over-arching mission statement. A mission statement such as this can provide a helpful starting point in setting down the justification and benefit of your website, and thus contribute to establishing the business case for the site. It is most useful if it expresses a mission that is founded within the parent body – in this example because it contributes to communication with the Fellows and Members of the College.

Fig. 3.1 *The website of the Royal College of Physicians' Library and Information Services*

It is less obviously useful to pitch for a website that attempts to justify its mission purely in terms of its own existence, for example if this had been described only as a 'site for people interested in medicine' without reference to the work of the funding body.

Another way of making it clear who the audience is expected to be – and who the site is intended for – is demonstrated on parts of the London Stock Exchange website, for example the regulation area (www.london-stockexchange.com/regulation/), which includes a note against the links of a number of pages showing who the documents there are aimed at (see Figure 3.2).

Or consider this customer-focused statement from the European Union:

> This website is designed to keep you informed on the ongoing progress being made in the construction of the new European space policy. The site serves as a practical platform and reference point to help European citizens better understand how they can benefit from space-related technology – an area often considered the territory of experts.[3]

Fig. 3.2 *The website of the London Stock Exchange*

Doing business

Libraries will need to consider e-business (that is, business conducted online) in the near future if they are not already doing so. Whatever sector you are in, there are reasons why your website is likely to need facilities to manage ordering and purchasing online. You may for example be responsible for selling from a sales catalogue, or for making documents available from a local or central government department, or simply for managing the ordering and supply of electronic copies of articles and books. How much simpler this would be if the transaction could be carried out using electronic ordering and payment online. It is worth bearing in mind that some of the most successful internet businesses supply publications through electronic searching and ordering facilities, and that these have become global enterprises in a short period of time.

Many organizations now use their site for recruitment. The web offers an instant way of making vacancies known to a wide audience and of removing the notice once the post is filled. A number of recruitment companies run internet-based businesses, and many organizations include details of their current vacancies on their site.

Communicating with customers and other interested people

There are many people who are happy to consult your website in order to discover information about your services, such as when they are open or what exhibitions are talking place in the library gallery at present. Communication with your customers is an important process, and one that needs to be got right. A website will certainly help, and can tell others around the world about your library and its services. It may even produce helpful comments from staff and users of other libraries.

In a wider context the website that you manage may be providing the communications channel from your organization or community to a global audience. If yours is a company website, or belongs to an official body, then you may be charged with carrying information about the organization to potential visitors from anywhere in the world that has access to the web. In this case you will need to agree a policy with the communications managers so that you are all clear about the way that the website fits into overall communications strategies.

Providing information

For libraries, the most obvious function is to provide information on a website in order to complement the conventional services. This is work that forms the library's lifeblood, and it is important to get this area right in order to maintain credibility. The library has a wide range of materials to draw upon, from digitized out-of-copyright works on the one hand to the library catalogue on the other. Many library materials could be suitable for adding to a website, and librarians are easily capable of creating original content to supplement any facsimile copies of library holdings.

Libraries may also be involved in the provision of other kinds of specialist information, for example the travel information services that are now provided by a number of local authorities on the world wide web.[4]

Pitching the level right for your target customers

You have a number of decisions to make about the technical infrastructure of your website before you can really begin work. Even if you contract the site out, you will have similar conversations with your suppliers.

You need first to decide what level of complexity your site will have. What multimedia and other facilities are you likely to think are worth including? There are disadvantages to many of the ways that multimedia content comes down to your computer, and it is no better if you are the supplier of the service than a consumer.

Do you want your visitors to be drawn only from among those with high-powered computers that are equipped with the latest software? If not (as seems likely) you need to ensure that you do not take decisions that will exclude any of your target audience. Features such as streaming audio (using Microsoft's Media Player, or Real Player) are sure-fire attractions on news sites and entertainment pages, but less useful on small corporate sites. Although Media Player and Real Player are fairly commonly found, there are a number of plug-in programs that have hardly been used on any websites, and which it would be as well to avoid. Limit your use of plug-ins to the few well-known formats, as your visitors will not take the time to download a program that is of no other use to them. Make sure that the pages that require plug-ins are still usable by those who do not have the program and either will not or cannot install it. (In this context, ask whether the audience that invests in this kind of equipment and the latest downloads is the target audience you envizage for the presentation in question. If you are thinking of using the latest version of Real Player to show a video of the chairman of your leisure committee reading a message of welcome, ask if it has any real appeal to an audience of leading-edge technical experts.)

You will find many sites around the web that state that they are 'optimized' for one or other software browser. This is because the two main browsers use different conventions to address commands from the user to the software and are based on slightly differing forms of HTML. In a few cases this saves the user from such dreadful features as flashing text – thankfully, Internet Explorer cannot display it – but generally it is an inconvenience to your users if something does not work in their browser on a site that they are looking at.

The user could be working with one of a number of browser programs. Internet Explorer and Netscape Communicator are the most common, and you may see sites with a logo from one or other of these companies highlighting their suitability for viewing through the relevant browser. However only the latest versions of these packages are really welcome – versions 4 and 5 onwards – although earlier versions are still quite commonly in use. There are a number of less well-known browsers on the market, of which Opera[5] is probably the most widely used. This is a small, frill-free package that still fits onto one floppy disk. It has non-English language versions in a number of European languages, with an interesting emphasis on Celtic versions. Other browsers can be found from time to time on magazine cover CDs, but none has caught on to the extent that it can be considered a serious rival to the main contenders.

New versions of browsers are frequently issued in beta versions and can be found on the cover discs of many computer magazines or downloaded. Although they can be risky to run on the machine you use to develop your website, they can be valuable clues to features that you may need to include in your site design in the near future.

Resource issues: recruitment and training

At this stage you will need to start considering resource issues for your website. There is more about this in Chapter 4, where the business plan for the site is examined in detail, and in Chapter 5, which discusses the role of webmaster.

It would pay to begin identifying resources while you assemble the business plan. Do you have any members of staff who are interested in moving to web work? Do they need any training to improve their skills in order to be able to join your team?

Training is not always instantly available. Many of the professional bodies in the library and information sector provide suitable basic training courses in web skills, as do a number of independent consultants. However, you will need to look out for advertisements for these in professional journals and on newsgroups and plan ahead. An alternative is to enquire at local cybercafés but you will need to exercise more care if you do this to ensure that the trainer has suitable skills and preferably some understanding of the context of your work in order to give you training tailored to developing library-based sites. It is possible that trainers could have excellent technical understanding of web technology but be less skilled at training users from a business environment. Identify costs to feed in to your business plan.

You also need to consider whether you are likely to need to recruit externally for suitable staff. There is a lead time to obtain experienced and qualified staff and this period needs to be built into your time scale for developing the site. You may need to consult a specialist employment agency to help you find the staff you need and you should allow for their fees – typically 15% of the annual salary of the successful candidate – or for the cost of advertisements in computer magazines, newspapers and the library and information science press.

You should be aware that good web staff do not come cheaply, and that if your organization uses some kind of standard pay scales there could be a problem attracting the right person.

The web and your business strategy

By now you and your colleagues should be clear about the role that the website will play in the strategy of your organization or community. It should be clear whether it is to be a key communication channel or an additional source of information, whether you are going to use the site as a means of doing business and whether you want the web to provide a two-way interaction between your customers or visitors and yourselves.

In order to looks at the preparation of a business plan for going onto the web in a sensible way, you need to consider how the use of the internet fits into your business strategy overall. By now you will have examined the major reasons for going to the web and considered some of the technical aspects that will affect the way you decide to develop the site.

Consider how your answers to these questions align with your business strategy before moving on to complete a business case.

- What was your primary reason (or reasons) for deciding to have a website? What would you give as your website's mission statement? Does it align with your organization's mission, or with your community's requirements? Is this apparent in the business case?
- Thinking about that mission statement or that community requirement, what kind of content did you decide you wanted to meet your target users' needs? Can it be provided by your plans to obtain, manage and publish information (or will you have to create a new system to deliver content)?
- Thinking about the technical standard (equipment and software) that your website visitors will need to see this content, does your intended audience have access to the kind of equipment and skills needed to view your proposed content? If not, will you expect them to obtain this in order to view your site, or will you simplify the content and presentation?

Using business analysis to keep your strategies aligned

Use business techniques to see how well your website strategy is aligning with your business strategies as it develops. Do a SWOT analysis of your plans and activities on the web by listing its Strengths, Weaknesses, Opportunities and Threats in a table. Use the table to identify the things you are doing right (S), and what you need to change to make things go better (W). What opportunities are there to develop new business paths to your users via your website (O)? And what could make your site fail (T)?

Your list of answers will be unique, and will identify areas of work to take priority. The work is iterative, so you should perform these analyses regularly. You will certainly need to repeat the process as new technologies are announced and new versions of browsers appear. Your assessment of which of them have major importance for the future and which are passing fads will inform the plans for your site and provide strategic direction until the next regular review. The results of your user testing will also help to identify strengths and weaknesses of your site.

Handling e-mail

Do you intend to use e-mail as part of your communication with your customers? If so, you will need to ensure that staff are ready to answer e-mails and to send prompt responses to customers. This is equally true whether those responses are in reply to 'Ask the Librarian' features, to orders for your organization's publications or to interlibrary loan requests. Does this apply equally to all areas of the site – publicity and marketing, publications, enquiries and research, loan and other services, and perhaps even to relations with your suppliers? These questions should be driven by business need.

Just because you can create massive technical solutions to these issues, you do not necessarily need to do so. Ultimately, however powerful the scripts or the database engine on your site, there needs to be a person in a position to ensure that messages move to the right person and are answered promptly. For this type of service, the quality of your site comes down to the level of personal intervention that you build in to its operation.

Summary

In this chapter we have seen that it is not enough simply to want to get your organization onto the web. There has to be a good reason for doing this, starting with knowing your target audience. Identify what you want to say to that audience and the kind of ways that you will say it. Take a level-headed approach to the glut of technical wizardry now available and avoid using it for its own sake. Begin with a businesslike approach and identify requirements such as staff recruitment and training in advance of your business case, so that you can be well on the way to resolving these issues by the time your business case is agreed and you can start work in earnest.

References

1   www.e-envoy.gov.uk/Resources/WebHandbookIndex1/fs/en.

2   www.rcplondon.ac.uk. This website mission statement was removed in mid-2000 but is still accessible in versions of the site on the Wayback Machine (Internet Archive). See www.archive.org/web/ 20000622031538; www.rcplondon.ac.uk; and earlier archived versions.

3   European Union, *Towards a European Space Policy*, http://europa.eu.int/comm/space/organis/mission_statement_en.html.

4   *Netting more passengers: the fundamentals of travel information on the web . . .*, Chartered Institute of Transport, 1999, www.archive.org/web/20000915094908/; www.iolt.org.uk/accreditation/netting.doc; or at www/trg.soton.ac.uk/news-features/ilt-web/report./pdf. Section 140 of the Transport Act 2000 (2000 Chapter 38) places a duty on local authorities to make public transport information available.

5   www.opera.com; details of available language files at www.opera.com/download/languagefiles/.

4

The business case for creating a website

● ●

This chapter examines:

- making the business case for creating a website
- budgeting
- business plans
- selling the service to the organization
- reporting back to the organization.

● ●

When creating a website you will need to present a case to your organization to justify the money and other resources that you intend to devote to the project. While in the early days of the web you might have got away with a fairly sketchy and shaky business plan, the amounts of money now required to run an effective website are so great that you cannot expect to be provided with these resources unless you make a convincing business case. How can you do this? Organizations have a wide style of financial management styles, which makes it impossible to provide a template that will suit every situation, so this chapter can only give a guide to the subjects that need to be included in the business plan. Here the main elements are covered, but you may be charged the full cost of accommodation, telephones, and so on, and in that case you need to add those costs to your plan.

Making the business case

If your managers are easily fooled, you can still find plenty of recent literature that proposes a very large return on investment each year – in other words, that by investing a sum of money in a website, you will make ten times that amount, either by earning it or saving it.

Business cases like this are founded on the premise that having a website (whether on the internet or an intranet) saves you from the cost of printing that same information on paper. The return is in fact not new money generated from new business, but savings on old costs of printing. This is a false benefit. Unless you take the decision that you will no longer deal with any customers or enquirers unless they use your website, you still need to produce your information in the conventional way as print on paper, with all the attendant costs of page composition and printing.

Your costs may even go up. Once you start to publish on the web it is easy to keep information up to date. When a detail changes it is a simple matter to recast the page that contains it. But changing the printed version is a different matter. You can either issue amendment slips – which is messy – or you can reprint the document. You may well find that you are printing smaller runs at more frequent intervals – both of which add to your costs – once you draw attention to the volatility of information by publishing to the web.

So why do organizations spend the money on websites? What kind of business case can be made? There are different factors to be taken into account for web publishing and intranet publishing, and the next sections consider these in turn.

Reasons for creating a website

Chapter 2 looked at some of the reasons that organizations and individuals create websites. These included:

- publicizing the organization
- doing business or carrying out other transactions
- communicating with customers and other stakeholders
- providing information
- other reasons (such as vanity publishing).

Many analyses of return on investment consider the costs of performing an activity (or combination of activities) in the traditional way, and set the costs of using the internet against them in order to establish a balance sheet. The result ought to give you a fair idea of the economics of setting up a website. It used to be evident that some sites had ignored this basic task and had set up a site to perform tasks that did not need doing. Now it seems as likely that corporate websites will be created by agencies who have been given a sketchy brief and have taken large sums of money to create a site heavy on features and light on content. A site that does credit to a library shows a proper balance between content and resources. So now let us examine some of the costs and benefits of setting up a 'shop window' website and a 'marketplace' website.

Publicizing the organization – the 'shop window' website

This kind of basic site still has considerable use for libraries as many potential customers look up basic information about organizations on their websites. What kinds of conventional publicity does your organization use? How much does it currently spend on publicity? How will a website affect these costs?

Elements of the balance sheet will fall under several headings.

The cost of continuing existing publicity

If you opt for this basic level of internet presence, you will need to continue your existing publicity efforts. Not only can you not assume that all your customers have internet access but you will still need printed copies for distribution in your service points and around your community. You will need to assess the new estimated quantities of conventional publicity and add the cost to the cost of your web presence. You also need to know the cost of continuing your existing publicity at current and future levels in order to obtain the true additional costs (or benefits) of your website. These will include:

- the cost of printing updated material (see the note above about shorter print runs)
- the cost of new material
- the cost of postage or other distribution costs
- loss if material is scrapped before stock is exhausted.

The cost of providing new internet-based publicity

Factors to be taken into account include the cost of:

- design and illustration (one-off)
- writing and laying out pages (one off initially, then maintenance and ongoing costs for new information)
- additional material for global audience (if necessary)
- additional functions on the website, e.g. streaming video
- hosting the website (ongoing)
- servicing enquiries via the website.

You will be able to expand this list depending on your situation; for example, there are set-up costs associated with creating a new website, such as domain name registration and server costs. The actual figures will depend on whether you decide to provide these services in-house or use an external supplier, and whether these services are provided by your organization.

Benefits of creating a website

Benefits include:

- the value of additional contacts or business prospects made through the web
- reduced costs of printing (these are effectively transferred to the user)
- reduced costs of postage – especially to overseas destinations
- the ability to amend information instantly as contact names, prices, specifications or other details change – your pages can be always up to the minute
- more business if you respond to e-mail enquiries immediately
- reduced stationery and postage costs when you use e-mail.

Can you give these figures an estimated cash value? Some of them can be reasonably estimated, such as the cost of printing corporate brochures each year. Others, such as the cost of web design, will need to be obtained by asking for estimates or quotations.

These figures will vary: if your existing design lends itself to use on the web, the costs will be lower than if the work needs to be done again from scratch. Designers will give different quotes depending on how easily they can do the work and whether they are interested.

The timing will have an effect on these costs: if your business plan allows you to delay commissioning a new corporate design until you can specify suitability for the web as an element of that design, the overall cost is lower. Adapting your current design for the web when you are going for a corporate makeover in six months is a waste of money unless there are other compelling reasons to do this.

Given the speed with which the web and websites develop, you should certainly project these costs over a short period. Changes in the delivery platform have not taken place as fast as was predicted, but increased uptake of web services via digital television and other devices should still be built into your calculations. You need to charge your costs off over a relatively short period, as you cannot expect your website to remain unchanged for more than a couple of years at most. This can be a problem in the public sector, which is used to charging off its costs over as long as a decade, but this practice makes little sense, especially if you include cash predicted to arrive in later years when you may well want to do something quite different with the money.

You might end up with something like Figure 4.1. It is based on five years' costs and benefits. In this fictional example, the assumptions are:

- that the organization goes on printing 50% of the previous levels of printed material it sends out by post, and
- that it makes savings on the staff who post out brochures and answer telephone requests for information now available on the web, but
- it has to pay for a member of staff to answer e-mail enquiries at £15,000 a year including salary and overheads.

This balance sheet suggests that, if the assumptions are right, then the organization could benefit by around £300,000 on its publicity costs over five years. It also suggests that an internet presence on this scale could save around £116,000 a year. However, there will be other costs that have to be taken into account in your own situation – or indeed other benefits to bring into the equation either for conventional publicity or for the internet presence.

Note that despite the benefit over the five-year period, around £40,000 of the costs in this example fall in the set-up period of the internet presence (for authoring and creating the site) while the benefits accrue steadily

Costs of conventional print (alongside internet)	£	Benefits of conventional print (alongside internet)	£
Cost of printing updated material • 50% of previous print run, set-up cost £10k and £1k per 1000 for 100,000 corporate brochures, reprinted every 2½ years	220,000		
Cost of new material • 2 small brochures per year at £5k set-up plus £500 per 1000 for 10,000 copies	100,000		
Cost of postage or other distribution costs • Average 50 pence on 90% of stock printed	135,000		
Loss on material pulped after 12 months in stock	32,000	Value of waste paper	1,500
Cost of storage (estimate £1k a year)	5,000		
TOTAL COST of conventional print (continued alongside website)	492,000	TOTAL BENEFIT of conventional print (continued alongside website)	1,500

Costs of internet presence	£	Benefits of internet presence	£
Cost of design and illustration (one-off)	20,000		
Cost of writing and laying out pages (one-off initially, then maintenance and ongoing costs for new information)	25,000	Savings on postage (50% of original costs)	67,500
Cost of additional material for global audience (if necessary)	2,500	Additional business from global audience (est.)	50,000
Cost of additional functions on the website, e.g. streaming video (not implemented in this example)	0	Savings on material no longer pulped as out of date (estimated at 50%)	16,000
Cost of hosting the website (ongoing)	5,000	Savings on mailing house contract	10,000
Cost of servicing enquiries via the website (one member of staff, 5 years at £15,000 a year)	75,000	Staff savings from distribution centre	100,000
TOTAL COST of internet presence	127,500	TOTAL BENEFIT of internet presence	243,500

Fig. 4.1   *A basic cost worksheet for a publicity-oriented website* (continued on facing page)

Costs of conventional print (no change)	£	Benefits of conventional print (no change)	£
Cost of printing updated material: • Existing print run set-up cost £10k and £1k per 1000 for 200,000 corporate brochures, reprinted every 2½ years	420,000		
Cost of new material • 2 small brochures per year at £5k set-up plus £500 per 1000 for 20,000 copies	150,000		
Cost of postage or other distribution costs • Average 50 pence on 90% of stock printed	270,000		
Loss on material pulped after 12 months in stock	57,000	Value of waste paper	3,000
Cost of storage (estimate £2k a year)	10,000		
TOTAL COST of conventional print	907,000	TOTAL BENEFIT of conventional print	3,000
Cost of traditional printing (cost less benefit)	904,000		
Cost of 50% traditional print plus internet	606,500		

Fig. 4.1   *A basic cost worksheet for a publicity-oriented website* (continued from previous page)

over the period. Thus there is less benefit in the first years and may be a loss in some cases.

Surprisingly little guidance is published in this field. A reasonable number of titles explain how to project manage websites but assume that the finance has already been taken care of. The first edition of this book included a table from the Center for Technology in Government at Albany University, which included costs in the areas listed below:

General preparation

• training for technology awareness
• planning for internet presence

Access for agency staff and other users

- hardware for end-users
- software for end-users
- network and internet access for end-users
- other vendor services

Human resources
- start-up process for equipment
- procurement
- establishing and managing vendor and ISP contracts

End-user support

- vendor services

Human resources
- establishing and managing vendor contracts
- development and delivery of user training
- user time in training
- help desk for users

Content development and maintenance

- hardware for content developers
- software for content developers
- network and internet access for content developers
- other vendor services

Human resources
- start-up process for equipment procurement
- establishing and managing vendor contracts
- development and delivery of staff training
- staff time in training
- webmaster
- editorial review
- content creation and co-ordination
- website design and development
- staff support for service
- programming support
- database administration

- other clerical support
- management support

Host of site infrastructure

- hardware
- software
- network and internet access
- other vendor services

Human resources
- front-end research and technical evaluation
- start-up process for equipment procurement
- establishing and managing vendor and ISP contracts
- development and delivery of staff training
- staff time in training
- network and systems administration
- web server management
- operations support
- clerical support.

Making the business case for your website is still a comparatively rickety business, yet organizations increasingly expect a clear argument to explain why they should invest significant sums of money in electronic communications. It's probably easier to argue for major outlay in a large organization that expects to make expensive publicity a part of its marketing strategy than it is to make the case for spending a few thousand pounds in a small enterprise.

There is some guidance for public sector web managers in publications by the Office of the e-Envoy. Two business case studies look at the case for information publishing.[1–2] These offer methodologies for assessing the costs of managing content and transactions, respectively, deriving costs for preparing copy and handling interaction with the public. Of particular interest in the first study is the analysis of the relative costs of managing HTML and PDF files, and the conclusion that a growing website with no additional resources will eventually absorb its entire resources for site maintenance (in other words editing pages to refresh links, change outdated information and so on). This will lead to there being a steady decline in the ability to publish new content, which will eventually suffocate the site. The second study examines the savings and costs of handling complaints using the web. Projections demonstrate the cost and benefits of transferring differing proportions of an organization's dealings with the public to the web.

But there is generally little useful guidance available about how to establish return on investment in website development and e-business, and the business plan method described later in this chapter may offer a better approach to the 'soft' and often unpredictable costs involved.[3]

Budgeting

Your budget for the website will include a number of elements, which will depend on the type of site or sites that you are running. Figure 4.1 will provide you with some possible headings under which expenditure will fall.

Your main expense may well be on staff costs. In Chapter 7 some of the staff requirements for managing a website are described and what becomes clear is that the staff you need are likely to be expensive to hire and retain. You will also need to make financial allowance for sufficient staff to manage (or at least monitor) it and the site 24 hours a day, seven days a week. If yours is not a 24/7 organization you will need to make the case for this different approach to operations.

Training is a necessary expense. Your budget sheet will need to reflect the delicate balance between training costs and salary costs for your team. Pay staff too little and they will take their talents elsewhere, effectively wasting the money that you have invested in their training. Fail to train them adequately and you will pay the price through the ineffectiveness of the websites that they produce.

Many companies will provide you with web training of varying quality and effectiveness. Whichever trainer you choose, it is probably true that you will get what you pay for. Consider courses provided for the library and information community, which may be more appropriate for your team than the general IT community courses that tend to focus on the technical issues rather than the information management questions. (After all, if you intend to contract out the technical management, or your IT department insists on doing this work, you only need to know enough to ensure that you are not having the wool pulled over your eyes.)

The unquantifiable benefits of a website

The available analyses do not show the unquantifiable benefits of a website. You might expect to include as balance sheet benefits:

- increased efficiency in handling enquiries, orders or other transactions – you may be asked, or be able, to estimate a percentage of overall costs for this item and assign a cash value (and as the police complaints example[2] shows, you may be able to increase these by driving up the percentage of business transacted on the web)
- improved visibility for the organization, leading to more custom as a result
- an impression of go-ahead modernity that also attracts custom
- custom taken from competitors through the availability to process transactions on the web
- time saved in confirming or cancelling orders when prices or specifications change.

Business plans

If you are responsible for an independent site, you may be called on to provide a full business plan suitable for submission to a bank or other financial institution. Elements that could be included are described below:

- *An executive summary* An executive summary will set out the key elements of the plan, and summarize the arguments that are in the full document into two or three pages. It should be obvious to any potential backer by reading this section what it is you want to do, why you want to do it, how you want to do it, and when you think your new site will make a return sufficient to cover the costs.
- *A description of the organization and the management team* What is this organization and who are the key players? Why does the organization want to undertake this line of business and do it on the web? Who are the people involved and what are their credentials? (This could make or break your proposals.)
- *Market and competition* Who is out there who will use (or better yet, buy) your service? And who else is doing it, and how well are they doing it? What is your unique selling proposition and does it make your site the automatic first choice for every potential user once it is launched?

- *A marketing plan* How are you going to get people to use this site? How much is it going to cost? Of course, this will vary depending on whether you advertise locally, nationally or internationally, and whether you use the web to promote your service or go for printed media, e-mail or text messages, or something altogether grander and more expensive like broadcast advertisements.
- *A schedule* When are you going to do this and will you do it all at once? (So do you need the money all at once or in stages?)
- *Financial forecasts* What are the start-up costs? What is the predicted cashflow? What profit and loss is expected? When (if at all) do you expect to break even?
- *Business forecasts* How many people do you expect to visit the site? How does this translate into your technical plans, and into the need for hardware and software purchase or rental? When will this happen and what resources will be spent or received at these times?
- *Risks and opportunities* What are the possible risks in this plan and how will they be dealt with? What will you be looking for as a sign that further development is sensible and worthwhile? What opportunities are apparent and could be planned for while the site is being set up?
- *Any other information* You could include diagrams showing organizational structures, financial statements or annual reports, or you could decide that the plan already speaks for itself and avoid the possible accusation that you are padding the document with irrelevant but fine-looking detail.

Although this approach will need some hard numerical data to be included, this approach is a useful way to set out the business case for building websites, given the relatively 'soft' nature of the information available compared with, say, the business plan seeking finance for a manufacturing company.[4-6]

Doing business through e-commerce – the 'marketplace' website

If you are doing business via the web rather than simply publicizing your organization your balance sheet should show the comparative costs of trading by conventional and electronic means.

You will need to include charges related to credit and debit card and other electronic transactions if you do not currently accept these. Recent and planned changes to card security may leave you with a choice between upgrading your software or losing customers who are no longer confident in the level of security that you offer.

Your costs of storage and distribution will continue, but the use of electronic ordering means that you can locate the stock anywhere convenient. You may already use a storage and distribution contractor: many of them are ready to accept orders electronically. Orders generated from a website, either by e-mail or through a script, can easily be sent to your mailing house instead of your offices, with a consequent saving in transmission costs.

Analyse the costs and benefits on your balance sheet and consider each item on that sheet carefully. Does it need to be there? Does the internet provide any way of making the business process more efficient? Are there any features of well-known websites that you could emulate?[7] (The core business of Amazon.com is quite similar to that of libraries – getting books to their readers – but the site offers a wide range of much-admired features such as showing related items that customers commonly purchase together.)

Your policy on electronic commerce will need to take account of national and international developments. Authentication – knowing that the customer is who he or she says, and has the right to use the payment card offered – is a key issue that is being tackled by banks and government internationally, and you may need to be aware of your legal liabilities if you intend selling publications, information or services worldwide over the internet. Perhaps you should create an SDI profile or set your agentware running to find news stories from the internet!

If you decide to sell publications or other materials over the web you have a number of choices relating to the management of your site of varying complexity and cost.

Build the application using dedicated e-commerce application writing software, and run it in house

E-commerce software is now widely available for site operators to develop e-commerce operations. An example is Shop@ssistant,[8] which allows the development of complex sites allowing a choice of goods and providing links to a number of financial services that provide secure means of payment in a range of currencies. Software costs from around £200, but of course there are training, set-up and maintenance costs to add to this, besides any fees that your incur with banking services.

Commission a bespoke e-commerce application from an external software house and run it in-house

Costs for this option start at around £3000, and again you will have service charges, training and maintenance to add. If your internal programmers have sufficient experience they may be able to undertake this work for less, but the cost may be justified by the knowledge that a number of external companies specialize in this work and have tried and tested solutions to offer.

Both of these options will involve you in issues of site security, verification and data protection. For example, the level of protection that must be provided to ensure the safety of credit card and other financial details entered by customers requires strong security. PGP (Pretty Good Protection/Privacy) and, particularly, SSL (Secure Socket Layer) are widely used, requiring an e-commerce site to be able to handle these methods and to manage them. Establishing the required certificates (such as those issued by Verisign) for SSL is likely to cost about £1000, not including any management charges levied by your ISP. [9]

Outsource to an ISP or website

Many website managers are finding that the complexity of e-commerce operations and the rapid development of the technology make it sensible to outsource these areas of operation to external suppliers, typically ISPs of websites that provide e-commerce services. You should expect service providers' sites to have the required security levels and certificates, and to host the secure site and handle the e-commerce transactions for you.

Outsource by making use of external systems and servers

For these services the webmaster pays a monthly fee depending on the size of the catalogue and the number of pages in the e-commerce site.

Communicating with customers and other interested users of your site

Electronic mail opens up a vast array of possibilities for communication with your customers and others who form part of your community of interest. In a library and information context, it opens up the possibility of receiving loan requests and suppliers' reports electronically. This saves time in transmission and allows you to copy information to other systems without the need to re-key it.

If this is an important element of your web presence, then you are likely to need to include some of the following items when constructing the headings on your balance sheet:

- the costs of monitoring the incoming e-mail and responding to it: there is an expectation among users of e-mail that they will get a rapid response – e-mail is on a par with the telephone in terms of people's expectations of a rapid reply, even though it produces a record like the conventional letter or form
- any additional costs in linking the incoming messages to your automated system, e.g. to provide coding to 'translate' an incoming bookseller's report into formatted data to update records on the library system
- the costs of additional telephone, ISDN and ADSL connections
- the savings in postage and telephone costs (e.g. on posting requests or ringing other libraries for interlibrary loans).

Providing information

Other costs may need to be considered if you use your library website mainly to provide information. For example, many libraries provide online catalogues. Although there is prestige in doing this (and perhaps some surprise if you do not) as well as a definite value to the research community, there are quantifiable costs.

One of the most likely is the cost of creating a searchable database. Many library automation packages include a module that can produce a browser-based search facility that allows the user to search the catalogue via the world wide web. However, these modules are usually charged at extra cost, so there is a real amount of expenditure to be costed in. The same information may also be routed to internal users on the intranet, but this is likely to raise security issues if there is the slightest possibility of external users being able to hack their way to the internal computer system. So firewalls and other security will need to be included in the calculations. There may be compensating savings such as staff time in dealing with incoming requests that are now handled by self-service over the internet.

Databases can be created for the web using a wide variety of products that are included in office automation suites. Microsoft Access, with its ability to save files as HTML for the web, is a common example, but other integrated packages include similar products and there are a number of standalone databases that can be found on magazine cover discs for little cost. Frequently these are full copies of a superseded version of the software or of an older product (such as FileMaker Pro); support may be lacking but, for a reasonably competent person, good results are possible and can be output for the web.

These simple database programs may be all you need to run an information-based service from your site. Otherwise you may decide to use output from your existing library automation system. If you do this, you can expect a variety of additional costs including licence fees and the technical costs of creating or enabling the web interface.

Other reasons to have a website

Despite the heavy costs that can be involved, there is clearly no lack of people who simply want to publish their ideas and opinions on the web. Many of their websites are unreliable and contain information that varies from the inaccurate to the downright scurrilous and dangerous, but it remains true that the authors seems quite happy to pay for their existence without any thought of financial return for their effort.[10]

Why should this bother the webmaster or web manager of an organization? The costs fall to the authors and keepers of these sites so from that point of view there is little problem. However, you need to be aware of two issues that are looked at in more detail in Chapter 9 relating to acceptable use policies.

- Staff may set up their own websites, which make reference to the fact that they work for your organization, but include material on those sites that is unacceptable for a number of reasons. For example, someone may declare a political opinion when the organization has other public affiliations, or demands neutrality as a condition of employment.

- Parts of your organization may decide to be independent and deliberately ignore the webmaster to publish its own information on the world wide web. This problem has been described as the 'undernet'. These sections of your community may go this way because they think the central web service is too slow, because they want to exert some kind of independence for their 'skunk works' or simply because they are ignorant of the proper procedures. The impression this gives is poor, particularly if they use a sub-domain of their ISP. It is often disruptive to the organization's planned marketing strategy if this kind of site is allowed to continue unregulated.

The website manager therefore needs to keep some kind of political watch on events in the organization, and identify any reasons that members of the community might have for wanting to create unofficial sites, particularly if these are to lobby against the official view.

Selling the service to the organization

It ought to be plain sailing from here on . . . but, of course, it's not. Having constructed the business case to show that it is worth creating a website and having worked out your budget, you now need to present your service to the organization and get its support.

In fact you need several different kinds of support, and need to sell the service in different ways to several audiences. Various parts of the organization want different things from you, and you need different things from them.[11]

- Directors or senior managers will be mainly interested in the business case that we examined earlier, and you want their support, sponsorship . . . and finance.
- Departmental managers want you to deliver the benefits you promise with the minimum disruption and demands on their time and resources, and you want their contributions and support in return.
- IT managers will need to be handled particularly carefully as they may see themselves as being ousted by the information service; they want some kind of involvement, and you will need to negotiate with them, because they control the technical systems that will deliver your

information service. Without their co-operation, you may as well not bother.

- Content owners want the means of sharing information that you are offering them, but they also want you to give them the training they need to create the documents that go on their websites. They need templates and software that can be relied on. They also need to know their contribution is important. As indeed it is; without it you have no content for your website, and if it is of poor quality, it will not serve your requirements.
- Users, finally, also need to be involved. Effective navigation of useful content will suit their needs, and a feedback mechanism will allow them to tell you about their experience. In that way you can ensure that your website visitors return and that your usage figures continue to rise!

A senior champion will make the path smoother. Success stories that involve your best or most senior users will have a positive effect on all concerned.

Reporting back to the organization

It is in your interests to ensure that the organization knows what you achieve with the resources it gives you. As you are managing channels of communication within the organization and beyond, you have the means at hand to provide regular reports on progress and problems.

Adopt a suitable tone for each audience, perhaps in the form of a short report for senior managers and as newspaper articles for wider consumption in the organization or the community at large. Stories about the internet are often given high prominence in the media and you may be able to get good coverage in the local newspaper or in a staff journal.

Be prepared to explain the importance of the story to those who do not understand the web in great detail, and remember to go back to the writer after a period of perhaps two to three months to see if they are interested in a follow-up. That advice would probably apply to a number of your senior management figures and, given that you need them to provide you with a constant flow of funds, it is as well to ensure that they also understand the value of the website – perhaps by putting on a presentation in the information centre for their benefit. Invite your management champion to make the best possible case to senior management. You need them to leave the presentation understanding that even if times are hard they cannot withdraw funding from the website in the way that they can for some other programmes: their entire investment in the site will be put at risk if the site suddenly becomes neglected and out of date. People do not come back three months later to see if you have improved because by then they have usually found an alternative supply of information. On the web, the world is your competitor.

Summary

It is important to prepare a business case, but there is not a good track record of organizations preparing cases that are both convincing and founded in reality. Despite the relative maturity of the web, there has been little real progress in establishing benchmarks for sound business cases and business plans. A wide range of elements needs to be identified and included and these will be found by considering a basic list and adding headings to suit the local situation. It must be clearly understood that considerable investment is needed early in the development cycle before there is any hope of a return on that investment.

References

1   United Kingdom, Office of the e-Envoy (2002) *Business Case Studies for the Web: information publishing, Department of Health*, Quality briefings for UK Government Websites, 3, London, OeE, www. e-envoy.gov.uk/publications/ webqualitybrief/doh.

2   United Kingdom, Office of the e-Envoy (2002) *Business Case Studies for the Web: online transactions, Police Complaints Authority*, Quality Briefings for UK Government Websites, 4, London, OeE, www.e-envoy.gov.uk/publications/webqualitybrief/pca.

3   For a high level and fairly theoretical approach see for example Mogollon, M. and Raisinghani, M. (2003) Measuring ROI in E-business: a practical approach, *Information Systems Management*, **20** (2), (Spring), 63–81.

4   Monroe, J. (2000) *How to Net a Million*, New Jersey, Prentice Hall.

5   Bayne, K. M. (2000) *The Internet Marketing Plan: the complete guide to instant Web presence*, 2nd edn, Chichester, Wiley.

6   Eglash, J. (2000) *How to Write a .com Business Plan: the internet entrepre-

neur's guide to everything you need to know about business plans and financing options, Columbus, OH, McGraw-Hill Education.

7 Starling, A. (2000) Making Shopping Sites Easy to Use, *Internet Magazine*, (June), 139–43.

8 www.floyd.co.uk/. This site includes detailed explanations of the technology and design principles of e-commerce sites using this product and includes a demonstration model of a video store system.

9 For detailed information see Talacko, P. (1999) Who Goes There? Proving Who You are on the Net – Certification, Authentication and Digital Signatures, *Internet Works*, 22, (August), 59–63.

10 For some insights see Osler, F. and Hollis, P. (2001) *The Activist's Guide to the Internet*, Prentice-Hall.

11 See Jones, J. M. (1998) How to Make Employees Buy into your KNOWLedge Management Intranet, *Intranet Communicator*, (November), 21–5 for further commentary.

Software

Web Strategy Pro 4.0. Palo Alto Software. Available for sale or download from amazon.com (but not European Amazon sites).

5

The webmaster and the web team

● ●

This chapter examines:

- the definition of a webmaster
- the skills and qualifications needed to be a webmaster
- the personality and interests needed to be a webmaster
- the typical tasks and roles of webmasters
- how to hang on to your investment in a rapidly moving market.

● ●

What is a webmaster?

If asked, most people would probably say that a webmaster is the person in charge of a website or sites – but now there is much more to it than that. Both the role and the range of titles for the job of webmaster are constantly developing.

In 1997, *Internet Business* magazine noted that webmasters were professionals who 'maintain the technical aspects of the company Internet or intranet site . . . but the position is still evolving.'[1] The job was frequently poorly defined, and the job description written on the fly by managers who did not understand its nature or importance.

By 1998, according to the website of the San Diego chapter of the

World Organization of Webmasters,[2] there was: 'a general agreement, that a Webmaster does one or more of the following duties: design, develop, market, implement, and maintain one or more sites on the Internet. This is in addition to other responsibilities, such as legal and security issues that may come in to play. Webmaster responsibilities also may include Gopher Servers, Web Servers, List Servers, and Intranets.'

A survey carried out through a mailing list in October 1998 discovered the duties that UK academic webmasters were performing.[3-4] The replies showed that there was a wide range of tasks for which webmasters were responsible:

- corporate management
- information management tasks
- quality management
- liaison, training and support to contributors to the website
- design.

By now a growing division was emerging between the management of information technology and information content was also highlighted by some of the exchanges. A list member working in a university noted that someone had been appointed to manage the technology and systems issues while a different person was in charge of the look and design of the site. A number of other contributors reported that they had responsibility for the management of the system that carried the corporate website and therefore had to have computing skills as well as editorial skills in order to manage the service.

CIO magazine commented in 1999:

> We are seeing that the position of Webmaster is becoming seen as a more senior-level position, with the person being responsible for managing the evolution and well-being of the web work, as well as the more traditional HTML and other technical work. In some organizations the Webmaster has a senior level position (e.g. VP/Webmaster), which we expect will become more commonplace as the web becomes critical to the success of a company's information environment.[5]

A number of new titles began to appear in advertisements for jobs in website teams. Terms include not only 'webmaster' but also:

- web editor – concerned primarily with editing and publishing the text content of web pages
- web designer – concerned with layout and appearance, particularly in graphics-intensive sites and on commercial sites
- web manager – a managerial role; a web manager will need to rely on a webmaster and probably a web editor or designer in order to deliver results.

More recently we find titles such as webmaker, webmistress (the feminine of webmaster, we may suppose), world wide web designer and world wide web implementation engineer. Other posts are described as 'web writer', 'web developer' or 'web programmer', emphasizing two requirements for the job: having deep technical knowledge for site operation and having copywriting and editorial skills. By 2003 Amazon.co.uk's copywriter said in a book review that 'today's Webmasters must be literate in a number of different – and ever-evolving – languages and technologies'[6] without mentioning the editorial and content management skills that were once needed for the job. Not only that, but the book that was being reviewed was 576 pages long, dealing only with the technical aspects of the webmaster's role.

Some more fanciful titles have appeared for web-related jobs, including:

- web evangelist – to publicize, promote and update a website
- Minister of Propaganda and Virtual Space Planner – to design online computer system interfaces
- code connoisseur – an expert programmer
- online liaison – to respond to e-mail and online requests.

In 2001 the World Organization of Webmasters (WOW)[7] stated that a webmaster should be able to: write HTML, develop artwork, implement firewalls, manage intranets and write programming scripts. In other cases, the webmaster works at a general management level. WOW's members report that they do all kinds of web-related work, including design, hosting, content creation and production, marketing and much more. Their categorization of the tasks looks like this:

- content developers who create content and adapt others' content for presentation on the web

- technical developers who create web tools and special web functionality
- business managers who set up, market, manage, budget, justify and evaluate websites.

The role varies with the size of the organization that the webmaster works within. In a small company or organization the webmaster would have to perform most or all of the functions on his or her own. He or she would probably also need to identify an internet service provider if the organization did not have its own (or be prepared to be on continuous call if the server was located in the company's computer suite). The webmaster would probably have to take responsibility for managing e-mail feedback arriving in the organization via the website. Thus in a small organization the webmaster will need a combination of technical, editorial, financial, procurement and management skills.

Working in a larger organization may be easier. It may be possible to convince management that additional help would be useful so that the maintenance duties of the webmaster could at least be shared. This would leave sufficient time for the co-ordination work that is needed to manage the contributions of the different departments and sections that should be contributing to the site. The webmaster might be responsible for the organization's intranet and extranet (which are discussed in Chapter 8), and if there is a separate technical management section, some considerable time will be spent co-ordinating with its members over more advanced technical requirements and programming.

These variations can still manifest themselves in a vague or non-existent job description for the post of webmaster. The biggest obstacle to clarity remains the manager who does not understand what the webmaster will do, but still needs to write down a specification of the role so that the job can be advertised. Unless it is clear what the webmaster is expected to achieve, the wrong person might be appointed. The recruiter needs at least to decide whether the person is to be hired for their technical expertise in handling HTML and scripts, for their design and marketing skills, or for their vision of the internet as a management or communication tool. Each of these approaches will demand a different approach and a different set of person specifications accordingly. There is a danger that the description ends up being vague, as this 2002 job advertisement for an American university webmaster was:

JOB SPECIFICATION

JOB TITLE: Internet Services Specialist/Webmaster

Performs a variety of non-routine administrative and technical tasks relating to the technical computing support for Internet Protocol based services and serve as campus webmaster.

1 Serve as system administrator for Internet Protocol based services. Serve as user contact and consultant.

2 Serve as campus Webmaster, system administration, development and maintenance of campus web servers and ensuring their availability.

3 Assist in the coordination of the activities of messaging services ensuring functional operation, including communications, software, equipment and materials.

4 Analyze systems. Design, write, develop, debug, install, modify, configure and maintain software in support of IP-based services.[8]

Building the website team

As work on your website develops it will become increasingly difficult for one person to cope with it all. More people will be needed to ensure that deadlines are met and that the full benefit is gained from the investment in the website. The work of the original webmaster will need to be divided among the additional members of the team and the webmaster's role will become more that of a co-ordinator.

The types of work that team members undertake can be viewed in a number of ways. There is probably no ideal structure for your web team; its mixture will depend on the skills that each individual member brings and on questions such as whether your hosting or other work is outsourced (meaning that one of your team members should have skills in contract management of technology rather than hands-on skills in fixing faulty hardware).

One view is to divide web work into in four broad categories:

- editorial
- managerial
- technical
- design.

Editorial work

Editorial work might be described by such titles as web news editor, interactive editor or online editor, and might demand skills in traditional (paper-based) editorial work, writing and journalism as well as an interest in or experience of new media. (Badly written text is equally bad on the web as in print.)

Managerial work

Managerial staff are called things like corporate web manager, web project manager, or site production manager. They need traditional business expertise such as financial planning and people management skills, because their job is to make the site happen by bringing together the specialist abilities and flair of the creative staff. They need to be good at specifying the services they want, budgeting and controlling finance, negotiation and supplier management. They can see the big picture. And it helps if they have at least some technical skills, so they have the respect of the rest of the team. Even if they cannot roll up their sleeves and stand in for a designer or coder, they need to demonstrate that they understand what these people do and why it matters.

Technical work

The technical staff have titles like website builder or technical leader; or they have quite specific titles and jobs that tell you something about the way the site runs – for example, client and server side web developer. They probably have computer science degrees and will have experience on particular IT systems and platforms. There is a tendency to advertise for specific software or system skills – for a knowledge of Perl or Apache, or experience of Dreamweaver, for example.

Design work

Design staff may have job titles like animator, web designer or creative director. They may come with a degree in graphic design, experience of graphics software (such as Photoshop) or graphics-based website packages (like Dreamweaver). Recruiters often also look for qualities such as creative flair.

Because of the growing complexity of the web there is a growing tendency for web teams to have members taking more specific roles to do with the production cycle for websites. In line with the way that many sites are now developed, the team members will include usability researchers, navigation designers or content designers, content managers, production staff, technical staff such as database integrators or coders, and project managers.

The mixture of skills on the team is important, and so is keeping the team members on board for a sufficient time for everyone to benefit from their presence. However, many web team members are ready for a move within a year or two, so it is important to discover what your team members are learning and to make that knowledge available to all. Making time for effective personnel management in the web team is no more than good management practice and there is nothing in the nature of web work that excuses managers from managing their teams well. Later in this chapter we discuss the reasons why web staff leave their jobs in search of work elsewhere.

The days of the all-singing, all-dancing webmaster are largely gone from all but the smallest sites, because of the depth of skills that are now needed to make sites perform at their best. Instead, posts typically demand a narrow spread of abilities and may have titles such as:

- usability researchers
- navigation, interface or content designers
- production staff
- technical staff – builders, coders, database integrators
- content managers
- project managers.[9]

Freelance work on the web

There is a market for freelance webmasters or web managers. Small organizations may decide that they cannot yet justify the cost of employing a full-time webmaster, but still want to establish their presence on the internet.

As a freelance webmaster you might work for a number of such organizations and split your time between them. Much of the work can be done from a remote computer, especially as it is unlikely that small organizations will want the burden of maintaining a 24-hour, seven-day site on their own computer. So an important task will be selecting the ISP for each website that you are contracted to manage and providing a contact point with those ISPs.

Apart from the usual tasks of creating, maintaining and updating your websites you will probably have a considerable training and representational role to play in the organizations that you work with. In a small business, it will be the senior managers with whom you will work – not least because there will be few other staff there! You will need to demonstrate to them, frequently, exactly what they are getting in return for investing a part of their turnover in the internet.

It may be necessary to educate your clients about the internet. Their knowledge and understanding, unlike yours, will not be based on experience and training but on what they have read in the newspapers and seen on television. They will be thinking as much about the downside of the web as of its positive aspects, and may be convinced that by setting up a website they are laying themselves open to the hackers of the world. They will also be in your hands when you recommend paying another specialist for a particular service, such as setting up the multimedia site they have dreamed of. Your advice might be that this is inappropriate for a small organization, or that it is just the way to be noticed. Whichever it is, you need to be diplomatic, credible and reliable in the advice you give and the way that you give it.

Going freelance is always a serious and potentially risky venture. Many of the issues raised in the chapter 'Going independent – the pitfalls, perils and pleasures' in *Your essential guide to career success*[10] apply here. But there are many opportunities on the internet and the web, and you may well have the combination of knowledge and flair to be able to identify and fill a gap in the market locally, nationally or internationally. An obvious first step, if you are selling your internet knowledge and skills, is to set up a website that will demonstrate your abilities to your audience. The next stage is to make sure that it is well publicized through search engines (see Chapter 7) and through publicity in newspapers, magazines and websites aimed at your target audience.

Skills and qualifications of the webmaster

The role of webmaster first emerged in the mid-1990s with the rapid expansion of the world wide web; it has since become an important function in many organizations.

The webmaster role has developed in a number of different contexts – information technology, new media publishing, and information and library services being three of them.

Information technology departments have taken on this role in many organizations as they were in charge of the equipment on which the service was run. Websites managed by IT-based webmasters tend to be technology focused and the organization of information is a secondary consideration.

Apart from university degrees in computing or information science with relevant modules there are a number of certification schemes for webmasters. Some of the professional bodies such as the World Organization of Webmasters or the International Webmasters' Association[11] offer online courses and certification.

A survey in 2001 for the Association of Research Libraries reported:

> today's library webmasters have acquired skills to do this job as the technology has been developing and in many cases outside traditional academic degree programs. Most library webmasters have a library science degree (70%), but other degrees range from the bachelor- to the Ph.D.-level in subjects as varied as English, history, law, and computer science. Only 57% of these library webmasters handle website responsibility on a full-time basis. Their other responsibilities may include reference, electronic resources management, user education, systems, and collection development.[12]

Holding on to your investment

You will invest considerable resources in recruiting and training your webmaster, but many webmasters move on quickly to other employers, so your benefit from the investment may be short-lived or even entirely wasted. What are the reasons that web staff move on so quickly? The problem is not widely discussed but the following possible reasons have been identified.

Boredom and lack of challenge

Web work can become repetitive, especially in a small team working under constant pressure. Equally, if your site becomes static and fails to develop, boredom is a likely consequence. There tends to be a feeling that once a site is built, the job is done; the webmaster begins to look elsewhere. Maintaining a site is far less interesting than building a new site or carrying out a complete makeover of an existing product. If your staff are feeling stale, then your website is probably feeling stale as well, and it may well be time to look at creating additional sites or revising the existing site.

Limited opportunities for growth or advancement

Web staff tend to form a small group within an organization and to have no opportunities to move into more general management – especially as they have been hired for one specific skill. In the model that this book proposes, the web team will have a number of librarians on it. These librarians need to be encouraged to maintain their general interest in the profession. A posting to a related area – either to the internet enquiry desk or to indexing, for example – would not only be useful for the web staff member's personal development, but would also allow him or her to feed back useful information on the website from a user perspective. Non-librarian staff might benefit from a spell in the IT section or in marketing. If they gain a transfer to a general post elsewhere in the organization they can be a valuable spokesperson who will market the web service within the organization at large.

Lack of appreciation

Make sure that senior management knows what a valuable contribution the web team are making! This is your responsibility as a manager – but you may need to give a basic explanation to the senior partners about the importance of the web.

Low expectations and standards for the position

Lack of understanding of the nature and importance of the webmaster's work leads to low expectations in the organization. Without an organizational culture that understands and values this work, there can be a tendency to accept whatever the webmaster produces, whether or not it is up to scratch. If it becomes apparent to the webmaster that anything will be accepted, no matter how poorly done, then discontent can set in.

Inferior or ineffective co-workers

A single highly skilled webmaster will not give his or her best if the supporting team is not up to scratch.

Lack of leadership or poor supervision

The corporate leadership must be able to provide effective leadership for the web team, which starts with understanding its work. Managers who do not understand or support the role of the web team will be poor supervisors for that team. Although this will not cramp the style of a team that has a creative nature and is not likely to relish close supervision, an anarchic and unsupervised atmosphere is not going to be conducive to the long-term satisfaction of skilled staff.

Pervasive bureaucracy

There is truth in the perception that webmasters are a different breed of employee, which dislikes rules and bureaucracy. In many instances they are hired exactly because they need to be different from the bureaucrats who surround them. They need to think laterally – which may be a desirable feature of new-style bureaucrats – and sometimes break the established rules. They work in a fast-moving field where their networks are as likely to include other webmasters outside the organization as senior managers within it.

It seems that a number of webmasters tire quickly of the kind of rules and conventions in many organizations and move on. There are apocryphal tales of freelance webmasters who travel with a tie in their briefcase and wear it or not according to the client's style. The age and experience profile of webmasters – still young, and often recently in education – makes them more likely to be comfortable in informal surroundings rather than in a bureaucracy.

You can't change your organizational culture over night. You may have to accept that your organization needs to tolerate individuals who have skills that it wants but that these people do not necessarily wish to buy into the organization's bureaucracy and values. Even libraries, which have a fairly free and easy feel about them in many cases, may prove too formal for some of the webbies.

Unreasonable work hours

Long working hours are a feature of much of the work that webmasters do. Often they work long and hard to get a site finished or because the client has a deadline. What drives people away is continual demand and long hours without recognition or reasonable recompense. The organization's culture may prevent it even from seeing what the webmaster has achieved, never mind thanking him or her for the effort. Long hours alone are not sufficient to drive staff away, but unreasonable hours and unreasonable demands are. As a manager, you can help by ensuring that your organization or your community understands what the web team has achieved and how much effort was put into that achievement.

Remuneration packages

Webmasters are worth a fair amount of money and their value is increasing. You should keep an eye on what is being offered in the market and ensure that your offer is a reasonable one. Once again, organizations with a traditional and rigid hierarchy are going to fare worst, because they cannot find ways to make their offer to the webmaster more attractive within the rules. In this case, 'soft' benefits such as the working environment become more important as retention factors. Investing in fast new machines or an office makeover may pay dividends in different ways. It may prove to be money spent that allows you to retain the investment in training your web staff and proves to be a sound investment taken overall.

Commuting time or location of organization

As an example of the 'soft' benefits issues, the length of commuting time to your office and the location of the organization can influence staff decisions to stay or leave. Much of the webmaster's work can be done away from your headquarters building. A good web editor can work as well from a computer in his or her home as from a desk in an office. Indeed, this potential flexibility can save you money if you 'hot-desk' web staff around a limited number of work stations in your offices. Organizations in the centre of large cities may find that web workers will prefer to work over the web for organizations that are prepared to be flexible about work-place locations.

Future prospects for webmasters

There is little doubt that webmasters and workers in jobs related to them have a good future. There is demand for their skills on a level that is exceeding many estimates and has become steady and established. Web-masters have become valuable and valued employees in many organizations. Those who can combine the technical and strategic aspects of web management, and can keep abreast of the developments on a wide front, will find there is a bright future for them.

In the medium to longer term the work is likely to develop beyond the focus on creation and maintenance of websites. Webmasters will be involved in the development of new services for new audiences using new technological platforms. The webmaster will also be involved in the development of online communities and loyal followers of his or her website. In this model the webmaster will create, develop and maintain a thriving online community that will provide mail, instant messaging, chat and other community-building initiatives to visitors in order to help to retain them on the site. The webmaster becomes in effect a commun-ications manager, organizing content and features that will allow site members to communicate with site managers and one another, and in many organizations a facilitator for knowledge management.

Training

Training is an important element of the cost of your website. You will need to make provision for:

- training in coding for the webmaster and supporting editorial staff
- training and coaching users if appropriate
- technical training for the technical support staff who support the server and connections to the internet and your network

- attendance at conferences and meetings and visits to exhibitions and trade shows
- publications.

You need this combination in order to ensure that your site takes advantage of the latest thinking and products in order to keep at the forefront on the web and to ensure that users of your services, certainly those in the organization, are aware of all the features that you have included. Because the internet uses a number of protocols that demand specialized knowledge, your technical staff should be trained and competent to explain their needs to other computer staff. And without attending trade shows and meetings, your staff will fall progressively further behind the market. You will need to complete the picture by ensuring that a range of the best-regarded internet news journals are available; the resource list suggests some of the best titles.[13] One further element that cannot be costed is time: you will need to allow staff time not only to attend conferences and meetings, but also to read, discuss and surf the web. This is not an area where anyone can keep up to date solely from the printed page. You cannot understand the impact of a Shockwave presentation by just reading about it.

Advertising for a webmaster

A number of newspapers and magazines carry advertisements and you can get an idea whether the type of person you are seeking is likely to be reading the publication that you choose. One much-used source is the *Guardian* Media supplement, which appears on Mondays, or the same newspaper's *Online* supplement on Thursdays. Publications such as *New Media Age* and *PR Week* may be suitable places to advertise. Although cheaper than the national daily newspapers, their charges for display advertisements do not come cheap for a small organization. Advertising in the library vacancies supplements[14] is another means of seeking suitable people, but you will of course only reach people who are already associated in some way with libraries through their work. However, if you are seeking a post where library skills are essential or valuable – for example, information architects or navigation designers – then these library journals are an essential advertising medium.

You will need particular skills in copywriting in order to attract suitable people to your post. Although there is a growing awareness of the important role of librarians in website organization and editing, many of the most creative people do not associate information centres and libraries with cutting edge web work. The danger is either that you will not attract interest from a new profession with some very unconventional members or, worse still, that you will attract the second best candidates that other organizations will not employ. So it also follows that you may need to take more advice than usual in setting up your recruitment procedures.

Consider contacting one of the employment agencies that supply staff to libraries; some of them have branches that specialize in computer and new media work and could be valuable sources of staff. You will need to budget for expenses, this time in the form of agency fees.

Summary

Webmasters and other website staff are commodities in what continues to be a seller's market. They can find a variety of work in many types of organization. They command good salaries (which are if anything rising). Staff have given a wide range of reasons for leaving organizations and many are to do with their perceived value and place in the hierarchy, and the esteem or lack of it that they receive. In view of the high cost of training replacements it would be prudent to see whether it is possible to address some of these in your own organization.

References

1   Francis, C. (1997) Web Skills @ a Premium, *Internet Business*, **3**, (April), 63-4.

2   joinwow.org/sandiego/what.html, 'modified 11-8-98'.

3   Kelly, B., What is a Web Editor? Posting to Web site-info-mgt mailing list, www.mailbase.ac.uk/lists/Web site-info-mgt/1998-10/0010.html and subsequent messages in thread.

4   Kelly, B. (1998) Web Focus Corner: the role of a web editor, *Ariadne*, **18**, (December), www.ariadne.ac.uk/issue18/web-focus/.

5   CIO (1999) *What is a Webmaster?* CIO, www.cio.com/research/careers/edit/job.html.

6   Review of Spainhour, S. and Eckstein, R. (2003) *Webmaster in a Nutshell*, 2nd edn, www.amazon.co.uk/exec/obidos/ASIN/0596003579.

7 www.joinwow.org; see also standard text on individual WOW chapter home pages.

8 Part of www.ius.edu/HR/Jobs/webmaster.html (New Albany, Indiana University Southeast, 2002).

9 Griffiths, P. and Picking, D. (2000) *Staffing the Site: your web team*. Presentation to the Professional Web Management Conference, Guy's Hospital, 4 May.

10 Pantry, S. and Griffiths, P. (2003) *Your Essential Guide to Career Success*, 2nd edn, London, Facet Publishing, 126-9.

11 www.iwanet.org.

12 Ragsdale, K. (2001) *Staffing the Library Website*, SPEC Kit 266, Washington DC, Association of Research Libraries. Summary www.arl.org/spec/266sum.html.

13 See the section of the Resource List starting on page 224.

6

Populating and organizing your website

● ●

This chapter examines:

- what makes a good library website?
- setting up site navigation – the value of librarians
- features that will put your users off your site
- the 'top ten' features of library websites.

● ●

What makes a good library website?

The answer to this question must to some extent be subjective, but it pays to examine other library websites to see what kind of features they contain.

Library websites tend to the extremes of design; functional, flamboyant, static or plain. A few are notable because they combine stylish design and top quality content, but a search of the web will show that a lot of library sites could make a far greater impact for a little more effort.

Plain can be stylish. A design that is functional can also be attractive and helpful to the reader. Plain-coloured backgrounds help to establish authority, and consistent use of colour helps the reader to navigate the site.

Surrey County Libraries' home page (Figure 6.1) shows a number of excellent features. Over the years its various versions have always been clear and uncluttered. Colour is used to distinguish it and other related sites under the 'Learning' banner from other areas of the County Council website. The home page has clear links to the Libraries' services, and the

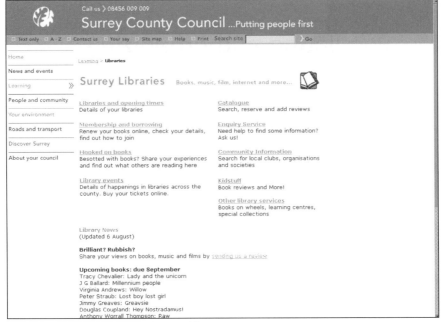

Fig. 6.1 *Surrey County Libraries' home page*

navigation bar at the top provides constant links to the rest of the Council's services on the website. There is news and feedback, and a search box on the top bar, but that bar is more pervasive than in earlier versions, as it now fills the top part of the screen with stronger branding than that of the library service.

Pages lower in the hierarchy show a more basic design and rely on hyperlinks in the text. However, the page remains clear and there is consistent navigation using the colour-coded links at the left-hand side of the page (so they are visible even at the lowest screen resolution). Note the use of a line of text at the top of the page showing the user's position in the navigation tree (sometimes referred to as 'breadcrumb trails'); this reflects a useful feature also used in Yahoo and other major web directories.[1]

Usability issues – screen resolution, streaming, Flash and the PDF dilemma

Some sites seem determined to make it as difficult as possible for their users. Many forget that many users do not alter the screen resolution that

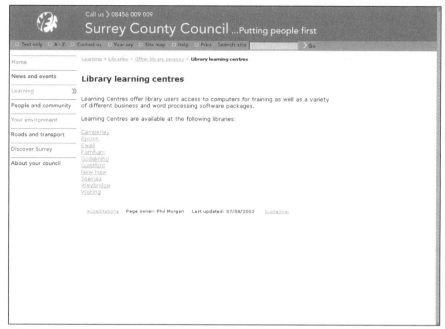

Fig. 6.2 *Surrey County Libraries' website, page for Learning Centres*

was first installed on their computers and see only the top and left-hand areas of the design. One award-winning London borough website was excellent in high resolution, but very hard to use at the basic 640 x 480 screen resolution. Navigation on the right-hand side of the page is invisible to many. And try setting your screen to the lowest resolution to remind yourself just how little space remains for content when the browser buttons and toolbars are all visible at full size.

Few sites now commit howlers like the Canadian site mentioned in the first edition that put its navigation menus below a vast graphic, forcing users to scroll down even to know that navigation was possible on the site (if they had not left again before finding this out). But there are still far too many sites that give you no option but to sit through long animated introductions without offering a way round, and that demand that you download software in order to access the site or parts of its content. The average library may not have much added value to offer that justifies forcing users to download and install the Flash reader.[2] (All they wanted to know was when the library is open.) If you have worthwhile content, users might consider acquiring software to play streaming media (audio or video) – probably Real Player.[3]

The greatest controversy concerns the now widely used and well-established PDF – Portable Document Format – devised by Adobe.[4] While it has the advantage that you can create images of the pages of your printed documents, accurate in layout and locked against malicious or accidental alteration, it also has problems. PDF documents are often laid out in ways that are unsuitable for reading on screen; they can be inaccessible to vision-impaired users and sometimes crash the browser (especially if created in Unix environments, although there is a fix). They are usually large files if the document is more than a few pages long and users have to wait for the reader to open in a separate window. Some usability experts hate them[5] but they have become a de facto standard and are unlikely to fall out of use. It is helpful to give guidelines for the use of PDFs to authors working in and with your website team; those issued by the Office of the e-Envoy in section 4.4 of the *Illustrated Handbook for Website Management Teams*[6] would be a useful starting point, with some of the points made by Jakob Nielsen[5] taken into account.

Usability and vision-impaired users

People with impaired vision have as much right to use the web as other users. web design has tended to run ahead of the ability of screen readers to cope.[7] So while sites designed for early graphic browsers (low numbered versions of Netscape and Internet Explorer) could be handled readily by text-reading software, later browsers were able to handle new features (especially frames) that text readers were unable to deal with. There has been a move away from frames for other reasons, such as the poor ranking that search engines tend to give sites based on frames, and text readers have become better able to cope with recent website layouts and some equilibrium has been restored. Nevertheless many sites offer poor usability to their visually impaired visitors.

Detailed advice on this subject is beyond the scope of this book and warrants a separate volume. Advice is available:

- internationally
  — from the World Wide Web Consortium (W3C) website; the Web Content Accessibility Guidelines[8] are a standard for UK central and local government and many other sites

- in Belgium
  — from Blindenzorg Licht en Liefde[9] ('Blindsurfer')
- in France
  — from Voirplus[10]
- in the Republic of Ireland
  — from the Frontend Usability InfoCentre[11]
- in the UK
  — from the Royal National Institute for the Blind (RNIB) website[12]
  — from the National Library for the Blind website,[13] which includes advice based around the Visionary Design campaign[14]
  — from the Accessible Web Authoring Resources and Education (AWARE) programme of the HTML Writers' Guild[15]
  — from the BBC's BBC Education Text to Speech Internet Enhancer (BETSIE) programme[16]
- in the USA
  — from the Access Board,[17] which is responsible for the implementation of section 508 of the Rehabilitation Act; this leads to a number of 'Section 508' websites of which the most important are the site run by the Center for Information Technology Accommodation (CITA) in the US General Services Administration's Office of Governmentwide Policy[18] and the Access Board's own Section 508 site, which provides links to the official documents.[19]
  — from the Institute on Disabilities at Temple University, Pennsylvania,[20] which has a website checking service called WAVE.[21]

The useful site www.webable.com became unavailable in late 2002 but several versions of its resources are contained in the Wayback Machine www.archive.org. See also 2002's themed issue of *Library Hi Tech News*[22] which focuses on accessibility for people with disabilities, particularly those with visual impairment.

Organizing your website

Alongside the creation of metadata and site indexing, the LIS professional's skill of website organization is the major contribution of the profession to website construction. Sites can readily be created so that they are easy to navigate and that there are logical links between pages, with no 'orphaned' information that is disconnected from the rest of the site. Yet many sites are haphazard, have inconsistent links and make it difficult to know whether the user is looking at a department home page or a personal page in a remote corner of a site. LIS professionals can see immediately that a site organized with no clear navigation or directory structure is vastly inferior to one where files are within directories and sub-directories representing subject areas or other distinct sections of the website.

Time spent on planning the structure of a website is never wasted. An hour spent with presentation software – or even with a sheet of paper and a pencil – will save hours of maintenance later. There should be a flow from the entry point (the home page) either through an organization-based structure – if you must – or through a subject hierarchy to the lower level pages.

Because users can potentially reach any point on your site from a search engine[23] or a reference through a hyperlink from another site ('deep linking'), you should include a link on every page back to your home page and to the top page of any sub-site of which your page may form part. This is also a sound reason for making sure that the identity of your site is clear on every page and that your navigation buttons are available at the top or side (preferably on the left).

Map links between pages on the site to ensure that they are consistent (for example that all links to the home page do in fact go to the same page) and that there are no orphaned pages. If you use a software package to create and maintain your site you can obtain reports to help you to carry out this task and to ensure that the links remain consistent as the site is updated.

How to annoy people with your website

What needs to go on your website? And what drives users mad? You may be a regular reader of internet magazines, in print or on the web. Maybe you make a point of checking the online commentaries of writers such as Jakob Nielsen[24] or the *Free Pint*[25] newsletter. If so you have probably read several articles of the '100 cardinal mistakes in people's websites' variety. The surprising thing is that people go on making those mistakes!

So what are the points to look out for? Some of them are basic and are made in every article. However, the proof is in the pudding, so use these guidelines when considering your own website and use them to check what your design house is offering you. If you are outsourcing your site, as described in Chapter 9, consider incorporating some of these guidelines into an annex to the specification. Refer to the list and insist that the guidelines may only be broken in good and extreme cases. If you get a presentation from the potential suppliers and they break the rules, ask them to justify themselves!

- *Three clicks and you're out* It is widely believed, and probably now true because so many people know, that most users will get fed up with looking for information if it takes them more than three clicks to locate what they are looking for. Then they will go to another site that doesn't hide information or make you work so hard to find it. Navigation is one of the things that people with library skills can greatly improve on a website. More recently this dictum has been proposed as 'You have 12 minutes before the user gives up'.[26]

- *Don't make them wait for it* If your site takes ages to download – and if you fill it with big graphics then it will take ages – your audience will also get tired of waiting and defect. You can use graphics packages to shrink the size of image files to something under 30Kb, ideally to much less still. Try different image formats and see which gives the smallest result. With the poor resolution on most screens nobody will notice that your graphics are only set at 75 dots per inch. Even at high-resolution settings the loss of quality is not that obvious because the images take up less of the screen. Don't make the whole page too big, either. Unless you are offering a document download in one go, cut the file into 50Kb chunks. This works will with graphics – you can see what the picture is more easily if it downloads as nine small squares rather than one big one. If you do offer a large file (such as a report) to download, warn users how big it is. It takes a long time and a lot of pennies to pull down a large file during peak telephone time with a slow modem. The lack of broadband availability in some areas is a bone of contention: don't add insult to injury by designing your site on the assumption that everyone has fast access to large files on the internet.

- *Small is beautiful* Coupled with the problem that big files load slowly is the problem of users who do not know what the scroll bar is. Every survey of web behaviour seems to confirm the same fact, which is that around half the users of web browsers do not realize that web pages do not stop at the bottom of the frame but have to be scrolled downwards (and sometimes sideways). If you cannot get your message into two screen lengths at most, then either shorten your message or divide it into two pages.[27] Try laying your page out so that it is obvious that there is more below the bottom of the first screen. Tackle the sideways scrolling problem by making sure that your page is designed for the lowest resolution browser and not the highest. Set one of your machines to 640 x 480 and check that you can see the right-hand edge of the page. It is a particularly bad idea to put the navigation buttons at the right of a page that is more than 640 pixels wide because they are hidden to users with the basic screen. Never over-estimate the technical equipment or skills of users.

- *Avoid a blinking headache* Never be tempted to use some of the worst excesses of HTML and image-creation software. Fortunately people have largely stopped using the BLINK attribute (a feature handled only by Netscape). And although animated images can be fun in the right places, never fill a page with them and think twice before including any. The first time it's cute, the second time it palls and the third time it's annoying. If you make your user sit through an entire Flash movie or other animation before getting onto the site, they will probably leave before it has finished. This is also the place to mention that white type on a dark background doesn't print out on early browsers (never assume that everyone has the latest) and not every browser handles colours in the same way. And you should also know that using the STATIC attribute in your background can make the user feel very queasy as the text moves and the background doesn't – pretty close to the feeling that brings on seasickness.

- *In the frame* Many sites don't now use frames. Perhaps this is a wishful overstatement, but avoiding them on your site has several advantages for you as a manager. It will allow people to bookmark and link directly to your frame without having to do complex tricks with the right-hand mouse button. It will help the search engines. It will avoid your pages spilling over the right-hand edge of the screen, or alternatively save you from having to write very narrow text columns once the frames are on the left. You can do most of the tricks using tables instead, which is far neater. And discarding frames will save you from the possibility of unconscious copyright infringement when you drop someone else's pages into your frame and make them look as if they were yours all along.

- *Jumping beans* Although active scripting elements can liven up your site, they can also stop your potential users from getting in. Many corporate users configure their networks to be increasingly unfriendly to any potential virus and therefore prohibit the use of JavaScript and ActiveX. Anyway, older browsers do not have any way of dealing with these scripts. If you are sure that the effect you want can only be achieved using active scripting, then provide an alternative site that does not rely on it. It could be usefully combined with a no-graphics, low-tech version of the whole site. Make sure that you include the link on the home page and that it does not rely on any of the banned scripts to take you to the low-impact version of the site. (It has been known . . . .)

- *It was working last week* Websites change frequently – either their entire URL changes, or directory structures or file names. Check that links from your site work properly. Use software that keeps the links within the site working smoothly. If you have contracted the job out, insist that the design house does this check every time it alters the site. If you are doing the work in house, take time to analyse the links, especially if yours is a large site. Check the links to other people's pages especially carefully. If you have not altered your site since last week, it should all still work, but any number of the sites that you link to could have reorganized. Sometimes other webmasters leave an onward link but, if not, you owe it to your users to find the page and update the links. If people have an alternative choice to looking for information that has moved around your site, they will take it. If they have no alternative, you owe it to them to put up some signposts.

- *Don't throw out the old software* Not everyone upgrades every time there is a new release of a browser. A lot of people installed IE5 because it was tied in to a number of special offers around the time of its launch. Fewer people upgraded to version 6 and many more have stayed with early versions of Internet Explorer or Netscape Communicator. Others use lesser-known browsers such as Opera that have other ways of handling advanced features. You can check what happens in older browsers by keeping earlier versions in separate directories on your design computer. Look at the results in IE3 or Netscape Gold before you let your work out onto the web. And make sure you have a Macintosh computer somewhere to check your work. It sometimes happens that something that works well on a PC will cause a Mac to crash.

This is all very well, but what positive features of websites should you look for instead? One way to find out is to go surfing the web to see what you consider is good. Look at sites that are similar in nature to yours. Which are the good ones? Why are they good? Why are some libraries' sites so incredibly dull yet others win awards?

The general computer press often runs articles that recommend the editors' favourite websites of the moment. Useful examples include *PC Magazine*[28] or the online *CIO Magazine*'s Web Central.[29] Take time to look at them. See which of them are doing the kind of things that your website should do and examine the code to see how they achieve it. Don't steal, but adapt useful ideas to your own site.

The top ten features of library websites

Although it is by no means exhaustive, the list below shows ten of the most common features of library websites. Yours can include any, all or none of these. There are problems with some as well as benefits. Decide whether you want to make the commitment to manage these features, as some of them come with a requirement for you to manage them actively if your site is not to fall into chaos or become a target for hackers and miscreants.

1   *Bookmarks* The Library and Information Centre provides its own selection of favourite useful bookmarks to other websites. These links are chosen to be of particular use to the user community that the LIC serves. They need to be edited and kept up to date to ensure that they remain current (no Error 404 messages please!) and that they are still relevant to user needs. Point them to new target pages if the site you link to is reorganized. See also the note on portals under point 9, 'subject folders and subject portals'.

2   *Practical information* Where exactly is the Library and Information Centre? Whether you are catering for an external or an internal audience, a good map and directions will help to add physical visitors to your virtual clients. Maps can be found on a number of external sites such as www.streetmap.co.uk or similar sites in North America and Europe.

3   *Training guides* Perhaps you can provide links to pages that offer advice on training opportunities or use structured training materials that are

designed for delivery over the web. (Take care over copyright issues.) On an intranet you can supply courses designed for your users: on an external-facing site you can provide copies of presentations and other training materials written by authors in your community, or you could develop this concept in conjunction with the training department to offer a kind of 'university of the office'.

4 *Search the site* A search engine is essential for a site of any size beyond a few pages. For smaller sites, a number of the major search engines either allow you to download software to index your site or provide a means of pasting their search panel into your pages. The search engine then processes your visitors' enquiries. But be warned that the downloaded software can be difficult to manage without technical expertise and that the search panels are clearly badged as belonging to the search engine and not to you. Alternatively you can use an application service provider such as Atomz[30] to provide a search facility by spidering your site and returning search results to your visitors.

5 *Online publications* Some sites include electronic journals produced by their organizations as a link from their home page. If you are trying to generate income from the printed version, the electronic journal is likely to be a 'teaser', with one or two full text articles and contents page entries for the rest of the journal. If you are producing a full e-journal, then much more content will be available. In fact the economics of web publishing make it possible for a number of journals that appear in print and electronic versions to have additional articles in the electronic version.

6 *Catalogue* Many library sites have access to their catalogues online – most university libraries do so for example. Many of the popular automation packages for a range of libraries now offer the opportunity to output the catalogue in a web format suitable for searching through a browser, although you may need the supplier's help to set up this feature.

7 *Library Friends* A number of libraries provide a page for their Friends of the Library organization. Users can make direct contact with the Friends, and the library's endorsement is apparent through the link from the web page.

8 *Ask a librarian* In this feature, users are invited to submit enquiries to the library enquiry service online, either in a freeform e-mail, or more likely by completing fields on a form (such as essential contact details,

so that the answer can be returned). The enquirer is then given space to set out the question in as much detail as can be given. There are a few pitfalls in making this work smoothly but this type of service is being well received.[31] Watch out for these points:

- Do not make the space for the question too small – if possible ensure that the box expands if the user continues typing. Otherwise there will be insufficient information to define the query.
- Make it clear what level of service the user can expect – there are expectations of instant answers to e-mail messages, but clearly this is not possible where research from printed sources is called for.
- Your reply may need to make reference to printed books that are only available in the Library. Until licensing of digitization is further advanced, you cannot send a scanned copy of printed materials to the enquirer. Consider asking for a fax number as well as a telephone contact point on your enquiry form.
- Make it clear what kinds of enquiry you will not handle – for example, you probably do not give legal advice even if you are a legal library. Consider including links to services that are intended to provide specialist assistance to the public, for example NHS Direct.

You will need some technical facilities such as scripting on your site in order to provide some of these services. Also look at the next chapter to decide whether you are going to offer these services to anyone, anywhere – even in other time zones, which implies they must be available at all times.

9 *Subject folders and subject portals* A number of libraries make lists of recommended resources available in the format of subject folders. The web gives you the option of providing links to online information and mixing these links with traditional bibliographic references to printed resources. You can make navigation easier for your user if you arrange the links to open a new browser window. This avoids users having to use the back and forward buttons to find the place in your list, as they can simply close the window to return to their current place on the resource list. Information reference links are a feature that is developed by portal sites. These typically consist of a seamless variety of links and embedded information selected by the creators, whether the links are to local resources or to external resources to which the web-

site or library has negotiated access on behalf of the user community. A search engine must be configured to search these sources and some support provided to users, such as document delivery request facilities.[32]

10 *Library publications* Last, but by no means least, many libraries provide links to a catalogue and perhaps an online ordering service or a book-shop operation where their organization's publications can be identified and ordered. The library should of course be the obvious source of reliable information about publications, so providing a link from the library web page is an important service to offer.

References

1 See Street Signs and Breadcrumbs. In Krug, S. (2000) *Don't Make Me Think: a common sense approach to web usability*, Indianapolis, New Riders, 50–89.

2 www.macromedia.com/.

3 www.real.com; note that the free player download button is small and to the right of the screen.

4 www.adobe.com.

5 For example, Nielsen, J. (2003) PDF: unfit for human consumption, *Alertbox*, (14 July); Gateway Pages Prevent PDF Shock, *Alertbox*, 28 July 2003 (offering advice on handling PDFs on websites) and Avoid PDF for On-screen Reading (2001) *Alertbox*, (10 June). All readable from relevant dated links on www.useit.com/alertbox/.

6 United Kingdom, Office of the e-Envoy (2003) *Illustrated Handbook for Website Management Teams*, London, TSO. Also available online in Word, PDF and HTML versions through links from www.e-envoy.gov.uk/Resources/WebHandbookIndex1/fs/en ISBN 0114301794.

7 Of which JAWS (www.freedomscientific.com/fs_products/software_jaws.asp) is the best known; Window-Eyes (www.gwmicro.com) is also widely used. Apple provides a search page providing links to 'assistive technologies' at guide.apple.com/uscategories/assisttech.lasso. Alva Access Group (www.aagi.com) produces OutSpoken software for Mac up to OS 9 but not for OS X; and the World Wide Web Consortium (W3C) has a page of browsing accessibility information at www.w3.org/WAI/References/Browsing.

8   www.w3.org/TR/WAI-WEBCONTENT/.
9   www.blindenzorglichtenliefde.be/.
10 www.voirplus.net.
11 infocentre.frontend.com/servlet/Infocentre.
12 www.rnib.org.uk/xpedio/groups/public/documents/publicwebsite/
    public_webdesign.hcsp.
13 www.nlb-online.org.
14 visdesign.nlbuk.org/mod.php?mod=userpage&menu=
    10&page_id=3.
15 aware.hwg.org.
16 www.bbc.co.uk/education/betsie/inverse/index.html.
17 www.access-board.gov.
18 www.section508.gov.
19 www.access-board.gov/508.htm.
20 www.temple.edu/instituteondisabilities/.
21 www.temple.edu/instituteondisabilities/piat/wave/edit.html.
22 *Library Hi Tech News* (2002) Themed issue, **20** (2).
23 Although you can prevent this happening by using a robots.txt file to
    instruct search engines not to search and index areas of you site: see
    www.robotstxt.org/wc/exclusion.html.
24 www.useit.com/alertbox/; some of the most useful essays are listed in
    the Resource List.
25 *Free Pint*, www.free-pint.co.uk.
26 Proposed in Valdez-Perez, R. (2003) The Value of Organized Infor-
    mation and Technical Challenges. In Delivering It, paper to the
    Eighth Infonortics Search Engine Meeting, Boston, Mass., (April),
    www.infonortics.com/searchengines/sh03/slides/vivisimo.pdf.
27 See also Chapter 9 for thoughts on what this means for the writing
    style you adopt.
28 Willmott, D. (2000) The Top 100 Websites and the Technologies that
    Make them Work, *PC Magazine*, (8 February), 144–59.
29 www.cio.com/WebMaster/unusual.html.
30 www.atomz.com.
31 For further thoughts on this type of service and models elsewhere
    on the web see Kenney, A. et al. (2003) Google meets eBay: what
    academic librarians can learn from alternative information providers,
    D-Lib magazine, **9** (6), (June), www.dlib.org/dlib/june03/kenney/
    06kenney.html.

32 For further information on portals see for example *Vine*, **33** (1) (2003), which is a theme issue containing reports on the UK academic sector and projects taking place there. See also Cox, A. and Yeates, R. (2002) *Library-oriented Portals Solutions*, Bristol, JISC, www.jisc.ac.uk/techwatch/reports/; Dolphin, I., Miller, P. and Sherratt, R. (2002) Portals, PORTALS Everywhere, *Ariadne*, **33** (October), www.ariadne.ac.uk/issue33/portals/intro.html; and Wetzel, K. A. (2002) *Portal Functionality Provided by ARL Libraries: results of an ARL survey*, Washington, ARL, www.arl.org/newsltr/222/portalsurvey. html.

7

Managing technical service provision

●●

This chapter examines:

- whether to publish 24 hours a day, seven days a week
- whether to use an ISP or run your own server
- whether to manage your own site or outsource it
- how to write the specification
- how to choose a contractor
- how to manage a contractor
- service levels and performance measurement
- what happens if only part of the service is contracted out.

●●

You have a number of choices when publishing your site and your future method of operation and some of your costs will depend on the decisions you make. As we shall see in Chapter 9, the answers will also determine whether you publish the results on a server that your library or organization manages itself or pay someone else to do it under contract for you.

The 24-hour web and your library website

When do your customers come to your library? In a corporate library, you might reply that your hours of business are Monday to Friday, from 'quite early in the morning until quite late at night' – shall we say 8.30 a.m. to

6.30 p.m. London time. Public libraries will have a different pattern, and may well be closed on Wednesdays and one other day a week, but could be open on Sunday afternoons. An academic library might say 'we never close' because it has a reading area that is constantly available to students – staffed by volunteers or by the night security service outside the core working day. There is usually no professional service outside the relatively traditional hours kept by business libraries.

All of these are interesting and different patterns but none of them matches the opening hours of the world wide web, which is open for business 24 hours a day, seven days a week, 366 days a year. Of course you will want to ensure that your site is up and running at all times, or you will lose users. So you need to make arrangements that ensure the site is constantly operating and will either warn you about the problem if your site falls over or else will fix it for you. For more ideas on this, see the section on internet service providers (ISPs) below. The more important question is: are you going to provide and maintain topical content at all hours? If your answer is yes, what does this mean in practice?

You might say that there is no need to go to such lengths and that no library service can be required 24/7. But could you provide a news service of any kind, either by issuing press releases or by posting information summaries to the web? Do you intend to make your catalogue available over the web? Or do you want to provide an information service, whether it is an 'Ask the librarian' page that accepts requests by e-mail or scripted form, or whether you have a paid-for information research service through your web page? If you do, consider the annoyance of a user in, say, the USA or Australia, or indeed someone in London on a Sunday afternoon, if your site turns out to have extensive down time that coincides with the times your library is closed. Even if your library does not open its doors to the real public on Wednesdays, it needs to be open to the virtual public that day. It needs to react to events that take place on days and at times that the library is closed. So perhaps the answer is not so simple after all.

It follows that you need to time events such as library catalogue back-up carefully. An analysis of your server logs should show whether most of your hits come from local users or from other parts of the world. By analysing the file it may be possible to determine that demand falls off at a particular time of day, perhaps early in the morning, and to perform your technical routines at that time in order to minimize the disruption to your users. You may of course discover that demand is high during your night because overseas users are coming online to your service during their day-time. Once again, the server logs will also show this. They should also allow you to identify those countries that provide the most demand and consider whether you want to provide additional content for those countries (possibly in another language).

This means that you must roster staff to ensure that your enquiry service can meet its published target times to reply, just as you do for the physical version of the service based in the library. Often an enquiry service will offer a stated turn-round time for enquiries. If you follow this route, remember to take into account that if there is no intervention by your staff before the enquiry is accepted (for example, they do not telephone the enquirer to agree a price and time schedule), then the clock starts to tick as soon as they send the enquiry. Whatever the time of day or night is where you are, it can be 12 hours or more behind the time somewhere else. Many sites that offer guaranteed turn-round times therefore telephone the client to perform a reference interview before setting the clock running. Similarly, if you provide a news service on your site, you should set up a system that will ensure that news information reaches your site quickly at any time when your press communications section issues it.

Whether these additional costs and routines are worthwhile is for you to decide. If you expect a member of staff to be on the premises 24 hours a day so that catalogue back-ups can be performed in the early morning then you will have extra overtime, heating and lighting costs to consider; or, if you automate the process, you may need to pay someone standby fees in case the process stops and needs intervention to restart it. If you are running an enquiry service over the weekend you will also have to pay staff extra to be present on Sundays, as you will if they stay into unsocial hours in the evening.[1]

Using an ISP or doing it yourself

An alternative way of dealing with the technical side of running a website is to use the services of your ISP. You will need an ISP whatever you do, whether that ISP is a part of your academic institution, your local authority computer department or a commercial provider. Many organizations have seen rapid growth in their websites and have chosen to migrate to a remote commercial ISP because of the complexity of maintaining their own on-site servers. Basic web hosting is now available at very low prices and unless your organization has a large and internet-aware IT section, it may not make commercial sense to run your site in-house.

However, ISPs vary greatly in their service levels, and the same company can vary widely from month to month in the quality that it offers to its customers. If you have the freedom to choose a commercial supplier there are league tables that can help you to choose one; an example is the monthly table describing tests carried out by *Internet Magazine*.[2] The magazine also prints a useful list of questions to ask potential hosts about costs, speed, webspace, backups, security, reports, scripting and domain name transfers.

These tables have appeared for a number of years and it is possible to track the performance of an individual supplier by consulting back issues. Does your selected supplier move rapidly up and down the table, suggesting there may be problems with its availability or with its ability to manage large numbers of incoming connections to popular websites that it hosts?

The *Internet Magazine* table (now restricted to the 100 best performers each month) provides a fairly comprehensive list of the most reliable ISPs available in the UK. The ISPs vary from national services to those based in particular areas or towns and it may pay you to choose a local company if your site is likely to be an important customer for their services. By getting to know the company personnel you can ensure that you continue to receive good and personal service even if your ISP subsequently grows large and prospers nationally.

In some institutions such as universities there is almost certainly long experience of providing connections to the internet and of hosting websites. There may even be experience of hosting library sites, for example for the main university library. Discover whether there are existing service level agreements and consider whether these are acceptable for your own site.

To rely on even a good ISP that is some distance away does not make for an easy management task. When problems arise it may require considerable time on long-distance telephone calls to resolve problems satisfactorily. Face-to-face contact is not an easy option because library or computer service staff need to travel considerable distances for a meeting at the ISP's premises.

An alternative used by some websites is to rent rack space in a local ISP in order to keep their own computer on the ISP's premises. This provides direct access to the ISP's high speed telecommunications links but avoids having to rely directly on a service maintenance section that may be less good than that provided by other suppliers. This still requires you to keep staff on call in case there is a problem with the computer that carries your website, but it does mean that your computer is in a secure location that is continuously staffed by the ISP. If your own staff member is unable to attend, the ISP may be able to provide back-up cover at a reduced fee. Otherwise it may be possible to dial in to the computer to restart the server or make other adjustments. Distinguish between a monitored service, where the ISP will inform you of problems but will expect you to fix them, and a managed service, where the supplier also fixes the problem (but of course charges more).

If you go for a rented space, or if you do the whole job yourself, you will need a suitable computer to run the site, together with a telecommunications link. The server software is likely to be cheap or free, although you will need expertise in order to run it. Many university and other computer centres run the Apache server,[3] which now has a stable second edition; if your organization runs Windows NT, the Microsoft Internet Information Server comes bundled with it but requires proper configuration from its out-of-the-box state. Any other functions that you want to include such as e-commerce will of course require further software, and you or your staff will still have to acquire further skills to operate it.

You will need to ensure that the site remains available even if there is a power or communications failure. This is most easily achieved with what is known as a 'mirror' site, that is, one that is an exact image of the original site but held by a separate ISP or at a different computer location. This has advantages beyond ensuring reliability. You can add urgent news to your site by taking down one mirror site some time in advance of the news release, adding the item to the site, and then switching back at the moment of release before updating the original server.

Some organizations use mirror servers on different continents to try to even out the communications delays caused by the varying loads around the world at different times of day. The use of multiple servers increases site security since it leaves the potential hacker with a larger group of targets to be successfully cracked before the target site can be completely sabotaged.

You may decide that the complexity of your site is beyond your capacity to manage. In that case you may want to pass the management of the whole site to your chosen ISP, rather than simply out-house the server.

In-house or outsourced?

An organization that is starting its website faces a number of important decisions about the way that the site is managed. Several of these are choices of whether to manage the site in-house or to contract it out (outsource). For a small site it may be the cheapest option to run the site in-house, but deciding to run any site as a 24-hour, seven-day operation changes the economics and raises many problems that will require staff time and financial resources to solve.

- Do you manage the service yourself?
- Do you use the help of your IT department?
- Do you pass the service to an external supplier?

You can help yourself to decide on the best way of resolving these questions by considering various factors relative to your service.

Should the technical aspects of running the website be managed outside the LIS service?

Consider these practical questions of service supply and management:

- Is the traffic on your site small ? If so, you can probably manage with the existing arrangements, but review them at regular intervals as traffic grows.
- Is it essential to make the service available day and night, seven days a week? If so, you need to answer 'yes' to the next questions or else consider external hosting.
- Do you have a constant presence on-site of staff with enough IT knowledge to deal with server or software problems? Perhaps your library is open 24 hours, or the IT department provides constant cover. If so, can people providing such cover be trained or contracted to fix the library web server if it crashes during the night?
- If you have no continuous presence at the workplace are you sure that the person on call at 3 a.m. on Sunday morning (for that is when these things happen) will turn out at once to fix a fault? Does this apply when that person is you?!

Your answer to these questions will help to lead you towards deciding whether a third party supplier should host your service. You may be able to contract with another part of the organization rather than an external supplier, but whichever sources are available to you it will pay to plan as if you were going to outsource the service completely. If you pass management to another department, the service is likely then to be provided under a service level agreement and the terms of that agreement should resemble as closely as possible those of a contract with an external supplier.

If outsourcing, should you use an in-house supplier or an external web hosting company?

If you have now decided not to run the website on a library computer there is a further choice for many between the in-house supplier and an external web hosting company. To make this choice a further series of questions need to be answered.

- Does the in-house service have a back-up web server configured? External web hosting services make their money from this service so they are used to keeping this kind of facility instantly available. Would the in-house service have to close down another application to start the back-up server and how long would this take? How are priorities allocated in this case – that is, would another service be restarted first in preference to your website, and is that acceptable to you?
- Can the in-house service provide you with a mirror server or servers? This kind of facility is useful when, for example, you wish to launch a page at an exact time (for instance, to coincide with a press release or announcement to the organization). A copy of the website is held, including the pages to be released, and at the set hour the service is switched to the new computer so that the news is instantly released. Hosting services are used to this and will make the switch for you or give you the facilities to upload the files to do so. In-house services may need to be persuaded of the need for this service and for a sophisticated means of operating it. And a mirror server is of course invaluable if there is a breakdown of its parent server. Preferably it will not run from the same power supply . . . and in the best cases it will be in another geographic location entirely.

- Do you already have high bandwidth communications (such as broadband) available to your computer or in your IT section? Costs have fallen considerably but outsourcing the site could still be a cost-effective alternative to installing upgraded communications links.

You are likely to be concerned with questions of trust and reliability with your own computer section, just as with an external supplier. Most organizations now rely so much on the web that your in-house team should be used to the technical issues, but you may still argue that it would be better to trust the web service to an experienced outside supplier rather than wait while your IT section learns more about web servers or supporting your choice of software. But many organizations realize that their websites make an important statement to the world, so they need a constantly available presence to maintain their reputation externally.

The increasing complexity of websites

It is not just technical questions that need to be answered. Websites are becoming increasingly difficult and complex to establish and manage.

Online bookshops continue to provide the kind of service to which many libraries can only aspire. They combine description and bibliographic details of a wide range of publications and multimedia, search facilities, sales or popularity rankings, advance publication details, out of print publication details, secondhand sales information and facilities that remember visitors' purchases, preferences and potential purchase lists. They provide links to advertisers and allow associates to link to their own publications through a link that generates pay-per-click (or per purchase) revenues. All this underlies the actual information content of the site, which is constantly edited and updated! Further functions include the moderation of users' contributions such as commentaries on particular books. It is thus a major task to maintain a website and outsourcing is one way in which many organizations are able to manage them – they engage a contractor to write, maintain or otherwise manage part or all of their website.

To run a service of this type, and to provide others, your server must run suitable software and the associated files. If your IT department cannot provide this, or cannot support it, then you will need to outsource. Your specification must make it clear that these features are necessary.

Going outside your organization

What next if you have decided to go outside your organization for website hosting and management?

The simplest and cheapest option is to take space on someone else's server, such as that of your ISP. This will usually give you an amount of server space for the website and maybe for a few e-mail addresses. What it will usually not do is to give you your own domain name. Although a number of august bodies do not seem to mind their website URL being in the form www.organisation.ISPname.co.uk or www.ISPname.co.uk/~organisation, this format can convey an impression of an organization that has not quite made the big time. (It looks particularly amateurish if you have the name of a free hosting service in your organization's URL, but a number of corporate websites still do this.) It also follows that if you fall out with ISPname.co.uk and move the site to rivalISP.co.uk, you will have to rename the site and do a lot of hard work in order to make the new site known to your users and to the search engines.

It is better to use your own domain name and then to run the site on a remote computer located within your ISP company. It will operate just as if it was in a cupboard in your own office, but of course it is no longer you but the ISP who will be checking it during the small watches. Many ISPs offer the choice between having a share of a computer with a few other users or a dedicated machine at a higher price. For a very large site you can place your own machine within a network centre and receive limited support and back-up as part of a package that gives you direct access to the internet.[4-5]

What will you outsource?

So far we have looked only at the question of outsourcing the hosting and technical operation of the website, which is quite a common area of outsourcing. But there are more aspects of the site that can be outsourced. Some or all of the editorial and design work can also be passed out to third parties, until it become feasible to purchase the entire operation from external suppliers. You can also outsource the publicity for the site. Different considerations apply to each of these options.

Editorial help

Chapter 5 looked at the skills that you should expect to find in a webmaster and other web editorial people. Library staff members are likely to have some but not all of the skills that you require. Chapter 5 also discussed using agencies to obtain staff for web editorial work, but you may decide to outsource the whole job.

A glance at the directory listings that appear in a number of internet magazines will confirm that many companies are in the business of writing websites. How do you know which ones are good and which are worth the sometimes large sums of money they ask?

There is no substitute for examining the work of these companies. Spend some time searching the web and note which sites you like. Choose commercial sites in your own country; ignore the big international internet and computer companies unless you think you can afford international internet company prices. Use the View Source command (Internet Explorer – View Page Source in Netscape Navigator) to read the page code and look for any information about the authors. Many editorial companies insert their name in a note that does not display in the browser, either at the start or sometimes in a copyright or other statement at the end.

Use the directories printed in the internet press to discover which sites the companies listed there have designed. Visit the sites in question and ask yourself whether you (or your managers and colleagues) would want a site like them and if you could argue that it would be money well spent to pay one of these companies to create such a site.

Identify two or three companies that you might be comfortable working with – have they projected the kind of image of the organizations they work that might be right for you? Is their approach in tune with your views? Contact your chosen companies to see if they can give you some indication of price and whether they would be able to provide you with further references. (You are likely to have to specify what you want, at least in outline – see the next section.) Which sites are they particularly proud of? Use your information research skills to discover what has been said about these sites and their authors in the computer press. The main internet magazines review websites in each issue, and often discuss the work of the editorial companies on other sites.[6]

The tender documents

As with any other kind of outsourcing purchase, you will need to specify exactly what it is you wish to purchase. You may need to do this by inviting more than one organization to pitch, or your organization may allow you to make the choice of agency without a formal competition. Whether or not you need to ask agencies to compete, you need to have a firm specification in order to avoid future doubt. However, given the amount of work that goes into a bid, some smaller agencies are likely to refuse to pitch unless a large contract is available to be won. This is especially true if there is strong and well-funded competition. Small agencies are also likely to be wary of potential clients who pick the cheapest bidder to build the site that the most expensive bidder proposed at the presentations to the client.

Your invitation must indicate any restrictions that you need to observe, such as if you cannot include JavaScript or ActiveX. Say too if you want no frames and include details of any corporate designs that need to be incorporated, such as a logo. Err on the side of stating the obvious if it will avoid disputes later about whether the obvious should indeed have been self-evident.

How do you get any idea of costs? Magazine reviews of websites do on occasion quote the prices that the owners paid the designers and editors, and one (*Internet Works*) has a regular feature that shows what agencies propose for a fixed sum of money to be spent on renovating a named website. Be prepared to be shocked: the editorial companies ask the kind of sums that you would expect to pay your senior managers as a year's salary in order to provide you with a medium-sized site. But, as we have seen, the cost of training is also high, and if you insist on training your own staff to do these tasks you will then have to pay them well in order to retain them along with their new and marketable skills.

You may receive offers from individuals at a much lower price than other agencies and designers are prepared to work for. You should know by now that there is no such thing as a free lunch and you can count yourself very lucky if you do get a good website produced for very little money.

Design

Even if you decide to supply your own editorial services, you may want some help with the design elements of the site. The skills needed to design web pages are different from those that produce good library display work, so you may need to consider hiring in a professional web designer or taking the job to one of the many external design agencies.

You should expect a good designer to know how to achieve maximum impact on your web pages while achieving low download times for your visitors. Knowledge of the various software packages on the market is often looked for in recruitment. You could expect a designer to be able to show you page layouts that included graphics (either static using Photoshop or similar image handling software, or animated images created using packages such as Flash) and other multimedia elements such as sound.

But the ability to create attractive and useful pages that suit your requirement is as important as any technical skill. An all-singing, all-dancing animated page with sound is no use if the designer does not know how to give your visitors access to your online catalogue database.

Look again at the copyright and intellectual property issues mentioned in Chapter 9. Make sure that the copyright is assigned to you in any work you commission, or at least that you have the right to make unlimited use of the works and images on electronic form and in print. Be clear that these rights are different and that you need the right to publish in electronic form.

Usability

Before you get too enthusiastic about the design that you now have, ask yourself how your site visitors are going to use the site. The design may look wonderful but if users cannot find information or navigate the site this effort is wasted. Usability testing seeks to identify problems in order to correct them. It consists typically of a session with potential website users (volunteers, specially recruited or invited) during which they are asked to carry out a number of specified searches or tasks on the site. This might be to find a particular page (library service hours or the catalogue), to locate a particular item of information that may involve using the search facility; or to order a document from the Library or to discover a statement of a library policy. The searchers are observed, either directly by a scribe sitting with a facilitator or in some specialist organizations through a two-way mirror that allows observers to take notes on the proceedings and to see a copy of the screen used by the volunteer (who in this way of doing things can retain anonymity). A typical usability testing session for a library website is described by Norlin and Winters (2002).[7]

Reaching an agreement with a supplier

Once you have decided to outsource any or all of your website operations you need to reach an agreement with the supplier. Be suspicious if he or she declines to reach any kind of agreement with you; the larger and reputable companies are used to doing this area of their business in a traditional way, no matter what other reputation they make have for unconventional behaviour. You may still go with your choice, but you will be taking a risk if you come to a loose arrangement rather than a firm agreement. These are the stages to go through. The stages are therefore very much as for other contracting procedures:

- Establish your management structure for the project.
- Specify your requirement and select your potential suppliers.
- Invite the potential suppliers to tender against the requirement.
- Select the best response, taking all factors into consideration.
- Appoint the selected supplier, after negotiating any outstanding issues.
- Manage the project to its conclusion (including paying the supplier when the work is done!).

(*The Complete Guide to Preparing and Implementing Service Level Agreements*,[8] would be useful reading in this context.)

Establish a management structure

This may be determined by the organization where you work, and a formal project management method may be imposed on you. If so, consider keeping your own team reasonably small by combining roles, for three reasons. First, you are likely to be dealing with a comparatively small and inexperienced company; expecting them to deal with the requirements of an entire team from your organization may simply frighten them! Second, it makes for a better working atmosphere in this kind of project if the teams know each other reasonably well, and that kind of atmosphere suits the internet business best. Third, and important for the success of the project, the business and operation of the internet is not particularly well understood, especially by middle and senior managers. Anything you can do to reduce the need for your management to learn about the internet while they are in the middle of a project would go a long way to avoid possible disasters. Use your knowledge of your colleagues' understanding of the web when selecting or proposing your management team and make sure that your managers are well briefed before meetings!

Specify your requirement

This is the task that probably needs most work if you are to have a good result. You know little enough about the company that wants to work for you, but they have only a slight impression of your organization from which to devise a strategy that they hope will persuade you to employ them. Why do you want this website? Are you in the middle of a cultural change that it is going to support? You need to tell the agency what you are about, so that you and they do not waste time on designing and reviewing the wrong thing. You should prepare a comprehensive specification of your requirement. Include:

- a description of the organization – even if you are the local council or college, or the area's largest employer, there is no reason why the agency should know about you in any detail.
- a statement of where you have reached with the web – have you already got a site, have you got a share in one, or is this a completely new venture?
- as much as you can say about your intentions for the site
- as much as you know about your audience, intended and actual; you may be able to provide information from server logs if you have a site at present
- any special requirements (such as including access to your library catalogue, provision of feedback forms or an online forum, and so on)
- time constraints, if there are any.

It would be helpful to state any other factors, such as the fact that you are running the site on a campus IT service that uses Unix, NT or whatever. You are likely to hit problems if some of these other factors are not declared, for example if you are unable to run JavaScript or other features and fail to declare this before the agency designs a state-of-the-art site that uses a forbidden feature.

You may have a sum of money in mind but do not declare it to your potential suppliers, otherwise you may find their bids are uniformly priced at a sum equal to your budget! Remember that if your site is a large one you may need to carry out a tender through the *Official Journal of the European Union* (the EU GATT route) if the total cost is estimated to be above the threshold for these open tenders – around £100,000, depending on exchange rates.

Select your supplier

Your choice is probably going to be based on a number of factors. You might consider rating your bidders against some or all of the following measures:

- How well did they understand what you wanted?
- Do they understand your organization and the way it operates? (Was their suggestion appropriate for you? Are they suggesting that they will do things your organization doesn't need?)
- Do you feel comfortable with the supplier and his or her team? (Could you work with them? Are they asking you to do too much for yourself? Are they asking you to do things you don't understand?)
- Are you confident that the supplier's suggestions will work? How you will manage if they don't?

After that, you can look at issues such as the total cost and the number of days' work that the bidder is offering you for the money. Do you think the time is enough? (Can you afford any more?)

Add to this list using factors that matter to you and your colleagues. If you cannot reach a decision by ranking these issues alone, especially if the result is close, try weighting the different headings. Maybe you think it is very important, for example, that you get on well with the supplier's team. Give that factor a high weighting, maybe counting the marks at double their score, while you only give timing a normal score because it's a less critical factor for you. Again, your situation will be unique, so devising your own headings, weighting and scores will be an important job that only you can do.

Negotiate

If you have any outstanding questions to resolve with your chosen supplier, this is when to do it. Don't allow anyone to sign the agreement until you are sure on every important point. If the price is too high, see if there is any leeway. If you want the project to be timed to allow your best display designer to be available, get it put into the agreement at this stage. And so on. When you're happy, then sign.

Record an agreement

The internet business seems to have grown very fond of service level agreements (SLAs). They have the benefit for the web businesses of setting out standards and terms in a way that provides a statement of the level of service they aim to provide, without forming a cast-iron guarantee over which they can be sued if they fail to deliver. There seems to be a general and widespread use of SLAs that makes it difficult to find any hosting or design service that will give you the kind of contract that you can take to a court of law. However, consider that many of the companies are relatively small, so that a lawsuit would be likely to cause them to cease trading – either because of the cost or because a large proportion of their staff would be spending their time in court. The effect in any of these cases would be to prevent you from recovering any benefit from your legal action. The best course is to look for the most advantageous terms you can find in a service statement and go with that company. If they consistently fail to deliver, you and other customers would no doubt be looking together for another supplier, and would be rather the wiser about the signs to look for in your next supplier.

The document, whether a contract or an SLA, should record a number of points. It should include a clear statement of the term of the agreement and the length of notice that needs to be given by each party and state clearly what is being supplied! The following areas will also need to be addressed.

- The most common operation will be posting updates to the site, rather than the creation of new pages. It needs to be clear how often these can be made: weekly, daily, or several times daily if necessary. Is there a limit on what an update comprises, either in terms of file size or in terms of how many files can be updated at once? Is the limit sufficient for all situations and what happens if it is not?
- At the outset the contractor will probably need to supply page templates. Who owns these? What happens when they need amendment or

when a redesign is needed to refresh the site?

- What constitutes additional work? Does the contract cover, for example, adapting the website to work on web TV or WAP mobile phones?
- Are there security measures in place that satisfy you and your advisers? This applies both to an ISP that hosts your site and to any agency that manages content for you. If any of the information that you publish is sensitive – for example because there is a press embargo on your organization's annual report – then you need to ensure that the agreement contains a clear statement of responsibility for any breach of security.

What guarantees are there about connectivity? What happens when the ISP fails to deliver sufficiently good service? Moving to another ISP is a major operation, but the agreement needs to show how this would be done. In particular, it needs to spell out who owns scripts and other code that has been created for your site. If you need to move it, then it must function exactly as before on its new site. Clearly it cannot do so if the ISP will not release code on the grounds that you do not have the right to it.

One other area of possible disagreement is over the ownership and registration of domain names. As pointed out in the section of Chapter 8 about domain names, you must be sure of the charges associated with the name. Find out the cost of transferring a domain name to another ISP before you sign what appears to be a cheap agreement for obtaining and registering a name on your behalf. If an inefficient supplier can then charge you several hundred pounds to move the registration to another provider it is a poor bargain.

Multiple agencies

Take care if more than one agency is working on your site. You may find yourself in the unwelcome position of spending time editing pages created by different designers and therefore lacking a common 'look and feel'. You may become pig in the middle where two designers disagree about the way of going about a task or where one wants to amend the work of another. It is probably easiest to let each agency handle a complete site or sub-site, rather than having them contracted to design or alter parts of the same site. Make sure that the contracts state clearly what each is to do and in which areas of the site.

Although it may seem to be inviting trouble to engage two or more agencies at once, remember that many of them are small businesses with a limited number of employees, so their resources will be stretched by working on a large site, or by making a large number of amendments. If you have a deadline, you may end up by engaging more than one agency – but be prepared to spend time on project management instead!

Summary

In this chapter we have looked at the issues to consider if you decide to contract out any part of your website operation. Above all, be sure to compile a good specification of what you want – asking for advice or looking at good examples if you are unsure how to describe it – and ensure that you have sound agreements with the supplier. Your ideal is to have a firm hold of the process while ensuring that you do not stifle what is probably a small company. Try to approach the relationship in a spirit of co-operation: your supplier is probably not used to working with libraries, just as you may not be used to working with designers!

References

1   For further discussion see Pantry, S. and Griffiths, P. (2002) *Creating a Successful E-Information Service*, London, Facet Publishing, 32–3; Smith, K. (1999) Delivering Reference Services to Users Outside the Library, paper presented to *1999 and Beyond: partners and paradigms*, Sydney, (September), www.csu.edu.au/special/raiss99/papers/ksmith.html; and Jane, C. and McMillan, D. (2003) Online in Real Time: deciding whether to offer a real-time virtual reference service, *The Electronic Library*, **21** (3), 240–6.
2   www.internet-magazine.com.
3   www.apache.org.
4   Morris, B. (1999) Finding the Ultimate Host for Your Big-time Site, *Internet Works*, **18**, (Spring), 52–5.
5   Is your site in safe hands?, *Internet Magazine*, **54**, May 1999, 30–4.
6   Gassman, N. (1997) Web Design: stepping through the minefield, *Internet Business*, **8**, (September), 86–7.
7   Norlin, E. and Winters, C. M. (2002) Usability Testing Example. In *Usability Testing for Library Web Sites: a hands-on guide*, Washington, American Library Association, 49–64.

8   Pantry, S. and Griffiths, P (2001), *The Complete Guide to Preparing and Implementing Service Level Agreements*, 2nd edn, London, Library Association Publishing.

8

Managing registration, publication, design and accessibility

●●●●●●●●●●●●●●●●●●●●●●●●●●●●●●●●●●●●●●●

This chapter examines:

- how to choose and register domain names
- the authoring tools that are available
- how to publish a site in languages other than English
- how to make your site accessible to all your users
- how to design for the different browsers
- how to get your site known inside and outside the organization.

●●●●●●●●●●●●●●●●●●●●●●●●●●●●●●●●●●●●●●●

Choosing and registering domain names

Domain names are the names that appear in the URL of websites, such as 'ourname' in 'www.ourname.co.uk' or 'www.ourname.com'. They provide a means of converting 'raw' IP (Internet Protocol) addresses such as 98.37.241.30 into more memorable and more easily handled names. There are a number of rules about what can and cannot be registered; these rules have been progressively tightened over time but many names were registered before the more recent changes so there are a number of exceptions to the rules. The choice of a domain name can be complex or straightforward depending on various issues; the problem is that a number of them are not within your direct control.

Domain names contain items of information that are divided by the 'dot' between each item of information. The last item is the top-level domain (TLD), which is often a country code (ccTLD) such as .uk, .de (Germany), .fr (France) and so on. Some countries have found considerable value in their ccTLDs, for example Tuvalu (.tv). Some entrepreneurs have discovered value in other country codes that happen to have meaning in other languages: for example the Austrian ccTLD, .at has become used to create a range of names such as dine.at. (Sub-domains can then be sold such as 'dine.at/joes'.)

Domain names that fall within the '.com' top-level domain were at first mainly North American commercial websites but more recently it has become common for many companies and other bodies to register names in '.com' from countries around the world. There are many examples of British and European companies doing this and it has a number of advantages. The .com domain names:

- prevent North American and other companies from registering names that are used by British companies, especially those trading in North America – although in the case of disputes over a name the naming authorities have taken domain names away from British companies in favour of the American firm of the same name
- allow multinational organizations to register an international site, and then to use country-specific domain names for their national subsidiaries
- are better known than other country specific domain names and are likely to be searched first by people who know the name of the business they are looking for but not in which country its head office is located.

Domains in the UK

A number of domains are available within the UK but they have specific rules of eligibility. These rules are set out on the website of Nominet,[1] which is responsible for administering these domains. The most commonly found is '.co.uk', which is intended for business use, but a wide interpretation is taken of the meaning of 'company' in this context. If you were looking for a domain for personal use you could still choose '.co.uk' for first preference, but new choices such as '.name' have become available.

Non-profit organizations can use the '.org.uk' domain. Societies and associations are found here, as are some charities and other similar bodies. There are similar domains in other countries, including '.org', which is now widely available, and country-specific domains (which are subject to local rules) such as '.asso.fr'.

Local and central government in the UK use the '.gov.uk' domain. There are strict eligibility rules for this domain,[2] and only a limited range of bodies and their related agencies can qualify. There are also strict rules about the way that URLs containing this name should function: in particular the home page must appear for the organization on whose behalf the name is registered when the URL is entered. (This is varied slightly because many government department websites' home pages appear below a news ticker that is delivered by a central server, and which in effect places the departmental home page within a frame.) Similarly, academic institutions use the '.ac.uk' domain: once again eligibility is rigorously controlled.

Companies that are either limited companies or PLCs may use the domains '.ltd.uk' and '.plc.uk', respectively. However, strict conditions apply, matching the regulations for company registration. Probably because of this, and because users tend to search first for the '.co.uk' suffix, there has been little take-up of these new domain name opportunities and most companies tend to register as '.co.uk' where possible.

New domains have progressively been brought into use in recent months. The '.info' suffix seems ideal for many library applications, although the registration process may throw up a challenge to registrations that are not made by the owner of a similarly named trade mark. Other new TLDs include '.biz' for business use, and a TLD for museums (although not for libraries) has recently been introduced. Recently a growing number of ISPs have transferred to the '.net' domain.

There are a few special domains for use by public bodies in the UK. These include '.police.uk' for official websites for police forces, and '.nhs.uk' for use by bodies within the National Health Service. Registration takes place through the IT authority for these bodies and cannot be made by organizations outside the public authorities concerned. There are also rules about the use of some suffixes to indicate some types of public sector organization, notably '-leb' to indicate library and education boards in Northern Ireland. And a few national bodies enjoy domain names of their own, notably the British Library (www.bl.uk). Administration of these domains is something of a grey area: they pre-date the rest of the TLD system in the UK, with the result that the management system lies outside the control system for 'mainstream' domain names.

Suggestions that Scotland and Wales should have their own second-level domains, '.sco.uk' and '.cym.uk', respectively, did not come to fruition.

Registering a domain name

If your organization is not one of those able to use one of the special domains mentioned above, you could carry out the registration procedures for your organization but it is probably easiest to use a commercial service to do this for you. Charges are low and there is competition between registration services. You can carry out the job online. Visit one of the companies that specialize in registering domain names. You can find advertisements in many of the magazines about the internet, frequently setting out indicative costs. Take care to discover how these costs are structured before you sign up: some companies charge only a small amount to register a name but have penalty costs for moving to another company or if you choose not to host your site on their servers. Others have higher costs for registering but do not charge you to hold your site on another server. You may well find you are presented with an invoice for the cost of the domain name registration and another for handling e-mail sent to that domain, typically using an address such as webmaster@yourdomain.com. You will eventually receive a certificate from the registrar showing that you have registered the domain name, but do not get one for the e-mail address.

First, however, you need a name to register. You can use the search engine on many of the websites of the companies that sell registration services in order to discover whether your own name is available within any of a range of domains. For example you may be able to register only as a '.co.uk' or the '.com' version may be available as well. Many of the sites now offer searches on a range of other TLDs. You do not necessarily have to register using the site where you searched for your name.

You may find that your name has already been used; there are only a limited number of domain names available. In addition some names have been the target of speculative purchases – although this cannot happen in some domains such as '.gov.uk' or '.police.uk'. But in other cases names have been purchased by people with no claim or title, with the sole intention of selling the name on to the namesake company or organization at a considerable profit. Although it is more difficult than it used to be to register names to which you have no claim, it is still not impossible.

Recently, the buy-for-profit scam has been overtaken by a rather more aggressive form of cybersquatting. Sharp operators snap up domain names when the owners fail to renew expired registrations, or else pass off fake websites as genuine in order to spread false information about the companies or organizations they are targeting. There is more information and advice about this later in the chapter.

Domain names can contain up to 63 characters. This may be useful if your organization has a long name that it could not previously register, especially if it is not its policy to use acronyms or abbreviated forms. However, take care not to produce something that is difficult to enter.

The website www.llanfairpwllgwyngyllgogerychwyrndrobwllllantysiliogogogoch.com is a site incorporating the name of the village in Ynys Môn (Anglesey), North Wales. A moment's reflection will show that although people may wish to visit the site, they may have difficulty doing so because it includes the name of a place that they might not know how to spell! Few people are therefore likely to enter the correct URL directly into the browser. Careful marketing is needed if you choose a very long name. An earlier version of this site in the '.co.uk' subdomain was linked from a site www.llanfairpwll.co.uk, which at least gave searchers a sporting chance. Consider a link from a simpler URL if you insist on doing something as complicated as this.

You might also want to ensure that your site does not become known for the wrong reasons, by checking that words strung together cannot be read in other ways. The URL of the Turin-based electrical equipment company Powergen Italia clearly does not have the same nuance in Italian as it does in English.

Be the first to register your domain name

Remember that you are not obliged to use a name that you have registered straight away – indeed many people register the names of companies with no intention of setting up the websites to match. One of the groups that register such names is quite open about the lessons to be learnt from this kind of operation, and insist that companies should protect their intellectual property better.[3] Organizations and companies should be alert to the value of their names on the internet and, if they are unconcerned to register those names themselves, they should be prepared to pay others for the eventual value of those names.

You might consider whether it is worth registering any variants of your name that could be used by others. While you cannot register your name in all domains because of the legal constraints, you could register in those domains where your name might be in danger. You cannot for example register in the '.plc.uk' domain unless you can produce the documentation showing that you are registered as such with Companies House – but nor can anyone else who intends to misrepresent themselves as you. The cost may be around a thousand pounds but this sum would easily be used in legal fees to pursue anyone wishing to pass themselves off as you.

A number of organizations have found that their names are not available for registration when they submit a request to the naming authorities. Names have the potential to be big business, and it is easy to lose the use of yours if you do not register it. The cost of registration has fallen dramatically in recent months. This not only has the effect of making it a cheap precaution to register names you are likely to use – it makes it cheaper for people to buy your name along with many others!

There are relatively few safeguards. As mentioned above, UK regulations make it impossible to register company names as '.ltd' or '.plc' domains unless Companies House documentation can be produced showing that the name is being registered to a limited company of the same name (either a plc or company limited as appropriate). The '.gov.uk' domain is strictly controlled through CCTA, the central government IT agency, so there is no opportunity for the speculative registration of a '.gov' domain name; similarly some other special domains such as '.nhs' are controlled centrally. But note that there is nothing to stop anyone registering names that would fall into the controlled domains as '.co.uk', '.org.uk' or even '.net' instead.

What was a marginally amusing aspect of the earlier days of the world wide web has now become a potentially critical issue for many organizations. The skills of reputation management have become important for LIS professionals – and here too is an area where their expertise can make an essential contribution. Perhaps the term 'reputation monitoring' might be more appropriate in the context we are examining.

Some hazards of domain name registration

We saw above some examples of what can happen when you fail to look after your domain names, do not re-register a popular site in time and become the victim of cyber-squatters. Once this happens, not only have you lost the name of the domain and the website that you spent so much time building up, but you have also lost any future control of what the new owners do with your name.

Unfortunately very few people take over domain names in order to put out a better version of your website; generally they do it to market pornography, sell dubious services and goods, or otherwise make use of your previously good name for their own benefit. It takes very few of your former users to click through to the squatter's site and buy something in order for this exercise to be worthwhile from the squatter's financial viewpoint.

What can be done about this? One simple step is to ensure that your intellectual property is adequately managed – and that means not simply the copyright in your pages but also your domain names. Keep careful note of when you acquired the domain, and how; then ensure that registration renewals are completed in good time. Even if your ISP failed to inform you that the registration was about to expire, you will have considerable difficulty and additional cost in establishing that it was the ISP's fault (and even then this will not get you your domain name back if it has been cybersquatted).

The good news for some webmasters and website managers is that the registration system in several countries provides some protection. The rules governing the registration of academic and government sites is generally tightly controlled and official sites of universities, colleges and government departments are not going to be replaced by offensive sites one night. Similarly, rules on the use of registered trade names mean that squatting in domains such as '.ltd.uk' and '.plc.uk' is not possible; and some countries are strict about the need for business registration to be demonstrably in order before they will allow domains to be registered. But other domains such as '.co.uk' and '.com' are largely uncontrolled, and order is maintained only by systems that allow you to take legal action against people trying to squat on your domain name.

So how bad can it get if you lose a domain name? The first problem is that you will need to move your site to a new name, and get your users to find this new name without the benefit of your website to tell them where you have gone. (And, face it, it is very unlikely that the new owners will be providing a link to wherever new you end up.) This involves time, expense and rebuilding your online presence and online business. If this was as bad as it got, then that would be difficult enough.

But suppose that, like the work–life balance organization that fell victim to cybersquatters in early 2003, your site turns into a pornographic network. What damage would that do to your business?

Another possible hazard is that someone might launch an attack on you on the web by setting up a spoof site or a site criticizing your organization using untrue material. How would you find out and what would you do about it?

Website managers should take advantage of LIS professional skills to keep an eye on what is happening. Applying the techniques of what is known as reputation management could be a worthwhile investment of time and energy.

Reputation management

At its simplest, reputation management does what it says on the tin: it's about ensuring that the reputation of your company, organization or community is seen in a positive light and that you maintain control of that reputation. It involves handling any attacks on it by third parties according to a predetermined plan, and ensuring that unjustified attacks are not only rebutted but stopped from recurring by legal or other means if necessary. This is clearly an area where public relations skills can make a big difference to the perception of the organization.

But if library and information professional skills are used alongside public relations skills your organization can do a lot more in the way of effectively managing its reputation. LIS professionals have the depth of understanding and knowledge of the online environment to be able to locate and identify problems before they become crises, and the research skills to ensure that full details of cyber attackers and detractors are tracked down. Their understanding of intellectual property questions means that they are able to offer expert advice on cases of passing off or the unauthorized re-use of an organization's copyright materials. PR people are of course used to using cuttings services to monitor their reputation in printed publications – but are they aware of how web-based editions of many publications differ from the printed versions, and how to search this additional material?

Commercial services such as Cyberalert[4] and Infonic[5] not only monitor the world wide web but extend their searches to internet message boards, discussion forums and chat rooms where corporate reputations may be attacked and rumours started.[6] Library and information professionals can carry out similar work for their organizations by scanning the web for product and service reviews, consumer opinions on product strengths and deficiencies, signs that customers are airing their service problems on the internet or scams involving the use of your organization's name. By searching frequently you should be able to identify issues with the potential to have an adverse effect on the organization's reputation. As shown by cases such as that of the Emulex corporation,[7] whose share price was decimated in a matter of minutes by rumours, this can be a deadly serious problem capable of ruining a business and causing severe operational difficulties for public bodies.[8-9]

Competitive intelligence

Techniques used in competitive intelligence can be helpful. You could gain considerable insights by combining specific details about your organization, its allies or competitors with an overview of information in the public domain that relates to the current market conditions affecting your organization. Using this data you could ensure that your website gave prominence to the way that your organization was reacting to these conditions, or provide additional information to ensure that your website visitors were fully updated from your organization's point of view. There is a strong case for the involvement of LIS professionals or professionals in the field of competitive intelligence to advise in this area.

Other misuses of domain names

We looked above at the ways that reputations can be damaged by inadvertent loss of domain names. However, there is another way that this damage can occur, which is when your organization's name is used in a way intended to make it the target of abuse. One widely used method is for protesters and others with a grudge to register a version of your name ending in the word 'sucks'. The site www.companyethics.com/ contains links to around 30 such sites directed against major international companies: you can judge from the standard of the sites whether this kind of attack is likely to lose you much sleep. You could be a target if any part of your organization carries out controversial research. The standard of protest sites tends to be poor, but they can be difficult to trace. Grudge sites often make unauthorized use of copyright material and case histories show that action for infringement (for example, in the case of a French site encouraging a boycott of Danone products[10]) has been an effective counter-tactic. Nevertheless, one simple lesson that a number of British banks have learned is that it costs very little to buy up 'yournamesucks.com' and 'yournamesucks.co.uk' and then have no website at the relevant URLs.

Think what terms might also be associated with your organization and consider whether you should register these too. As before, it is too late if someone else takes them first, and you will then have to consider whether you want to take legal action either to recover the domain name or to stop someone else making what you consider unreasonable use of it. The appeal route is through the domain name registration bodies – ICANN in most cases, although there are different registrars for the newer top level domains. There have been a number of high profile cases involving domain names, especially those using the names of high profile personalities. The decisions in these cases have not followed a predictable pattern and quite often large sums of money have had to change hands for no suitable result so far as the complainant is concerned. Typically, decisions have been based on evidence of whether either party acted in bad faith and whether passing off took place.

Particularly with '.com' domain names, the whole world can claim to have first call on a domain name. Thus the Armani fashion house failed to remove 'armani.com' from a graphic designer named Anand R. Mani who lives in Canada and has traded under the name of A. R. Mani for the last 20 years. This decision eventually went to the World Intellectual Property Organization (WIPO) for resolution.[11] And, with WIPO in mind and to make the point about impersonation, see how long it takes you to discover which is the real World Trade Organization website, www.gatt.org or www.wto.org.

CASE STUDIES

There have been many examples of the registration of domain names either as a speculative move or as a deliberate move against particular organizations and companies. Strangely a number of the best examples come from the world of railways.

- Great North Eastern Railway eventually took legal action to prevent a lobbying group from voicing its criticisms on a website registered using a name based on GNER's initials, with a different domain suffix.
- Chester-le-Track, based at Chester-le-Street station, makes no secret of its policy of registering names that other transport operators have failed to register. Staff spent one afternoon, for example, registering the names of all the lines of the London Underground as '.co.uk' domain names. Some years after its creation, Chester-le-Track continues to rent out some of the domain names that it owns to the railway companies that failed to register them in time.[12]
- A correspondent to *The Times* noted that his village name had been registered as a domain name on the internet thus preventing the village from using this name for its proposed website. The managing director of the company that had made the registration replied,[13] defending her company as 'pilots, not pirates'. Their intention was to provide a national network of community sites with a local webmaster collecting and placing information on the internet. In order to establish the network, the company had registered 15,000 British village names as domain names when registration fees were reduced in September 1999. The company's intention was to sell on only 1% of these names at a 'cost from £500 upwards' to cover the cost of re-registration every two years. The original correspondent's reaction, describing the company as pirates, shows that there is more than one view of this kind of enterprise, but also that it is quite feasible to register large swathes of names that may be related to you and your community or organization.

Some companies have begun registering variants of their names and linking to their real websites from the incorrect variants. Consider, if you are registering a website for an organization that could in any way be targeted by protesters, whether you should register derogatory variants of your name as well as the mis-spelt ones. As the examples above showed, it may be disgruntled customers who make life difficult for you, not international cyber-carpetbaggers. Check variants on your own name and see if they are registered. If not, it could be worth doing so yourself, and preventing embarrassment if they are used in an unwelcome manner by someone else. While you might not want to be the registered owner of 'any-townonseaisthepits.co.uk', you might decide it would be better than letting a disgruntled resident own it.

Web impostors and rogue information sources

Scams that take over vacant registrations, such as that of the Work–Life Balance Trust mentioned above, in order to mount pornographic websites are at least obvious. That change, or a protest site against a company's products, would have been obvious to any visitor – however much of a shock it was to people expecting to find advice on balancing their working and personal life to discover instead a site selling penis enlargement pills.

Far more difficult to deal with are sites that place plausible information on sites that appear to be genuine, but in fact contain disinformation and lies intended to cause financial or political damage to the target organization. Another scam is the e-mail campaign that asks people likely to have registered at your website to re-register 'as details have been lost in a computer malfunction' or some such excuse. The victims respond and re-submit their registration details and possibly their credit card numbers to a fake site with a similar URL to yours set up by the fraudsters, allowing them to use this information for their own financial gain.

What has this to do with you, the website manager, other than being a nuisance? The answer may be that victims of malpractice based on your site may consider that you are to blame for their loss, because you did not pursue the fake site and force its closure. Your LIS professional skills should be to the fore here. Make frequent use of search engines and read discussion groups to look for evidence of unauthorized use of your identity or brand. Ensure that there are no sites that purport to be yours when they are not. Particularly if your organization is present in a number of countries, check that nothing has been placed on a website abroad (and possibly in a language other than English) that is intended to deceive. Consider setting up an early warning system, either through regular searches or else by using an automated script that will do regular scans of the web to find a string of characters and return details of the websites where they have been found, allowing further checks to be made. (You may not want to make these checks from a terminal that delivers information to the remote server showing that you are visiting from the organization being targeted. The cybercafé has its uses beyond serving coffee and providing tourists with e-mail facilities.)

It may prove difficult to get some sites taken down, particularly if they are based outside your own country. Contacting the ISP that hosts the site will sometimes be successful, particularly where an infringement of intellectual property (breaches of copyright or registered brand names, for example) has taken place. Outright defamation will often persuade many ISPs to remove a site rapidly. Otherwise it may take legal action, or threaten to do so, in order to get the offending site closed down. This may involve taking action in another country, which could be costly but not as costly perhaps as letting the infringement continue.[14]

Authoring tools

There are a number of ways of writing websites. Unlike word processors, there is still no universally accepted software that provides foolproof WYSIWYG authoring, so that there is a wide range of software in use. Indeed, many authors continue to prefer to write simpler pages of HTML code by hand using Notepad rather than using authoring software!

Otherwise a range of software is in use. There are products from a number of major software companies including Microsoft (FrontPage), Allaire (Home Site), Softquad (HoTMetaL, XMetaL) and Adobe (PageMill and GoLive), either as current products or as working superseded editions that are easily downloaded from the web or from magazine cover discs. The simpler editors vary in the way they present the developing website to the author and a WYSIWYG interface (such as a word processor provides) is not always found. For complex websites, more advanced software such as Macromedia's Dreamweaver has become very popular and that package is currently regarded as the market leader. But there are some very good free software packages, notably Evrsoft's 1st Page 2000. Links are on the website that supports this book. Other sites are still constructed in programs such as Netscape Composer, which comes bundled free with Netscape Communicator, and FrontPage Express, which is also free and included with Internet Explorer 5. The complexity of the site is the critical factor; sites that rely on advanced features cannot be constructed without more advanced and possibly expensive software.

Each program, clearly, has an associated level of investment in training and experience in order for your editorial staff to make the best use of them. Constructing static pages using simpler software packages is a relatively straightforward process that can be learnt fairly intuitively to a highly skilled level in a few weeks. On the other hand, many training organizations make a good living from supplying training courses for Dreamweaver and other advanced authoring and site creation software. As a result you can expect to pay more for staff who have skills in using this software.

One other cost that you should take into account in your business case for software is that of technical support. Free software generally does not come with supplier support, and if you decide to save by using freeware or shareware, you may have to balance this against the cost of additional technical support within your organization. For one or two applications – notably server software, where the free Apache is the market leader – you will have to rely on advice within the user community (such as discussion lists) to help. But as this is the basis on which open source software is now distributed and supported, this model too is changing. If you decide to use the Linux operating system and open source software, you may find that the business case becomes more persuasive in a short time from the publication of this book.

HTML output from office automation software

A number of standard office automation products such as Microsoft Office, particularly in recent versions, include options to handle HTML. URLs can be input as file references, and the File menu includes the option to save as HTML.

This makes it possible to:

- create a web page by saving a word processed document as HTML in software such as Word (WordPerfect, WordPro, etc.)
- save spreadsheets and presentations in Excel in a format that can be downloaded from the web (1-2-3, etc.)
- present databases such as telephone directories, publications catalogues

and simpler forms of library catalogue on the world wide web by a simple command in software such as Microsoft Access (Approach, FileMaker Pro, etc.).

However, one unwelcome feature of many such 'automated' HTML writers is that they include unnecessary code in their pages – as much as 30% of what they produce is redundant by some estimates. This is because they will, for example, open and close every cell in a table and give font and colour information even if those cells are empty, whereas only the definition of the cell itself is needed. Many editors prefer to re-edit machine-generated HTML to remove these redundant sections of code, so that the pages load faster on the user's machine.

Dynamic page content from databases

Producing database output from office automation products only provides your users with a snapshot of the database at the time that it was output. To produce truly dynamic content (as opposed to dynamic presentation), additional functions are required on the server. Server side includes (SSI) process macros in order to retrieve information from your database on the fly, and top and tail the information with standard headers and footers. At the simplest level these are the macros that present you with the appropriate greeting for the time of day. In more complex applications, information can be retrieved and presented to users from a database or catalogue in accordance with their requests (or their access rights). Thus, users from a science department on an academic intranet might be presented with new acquisitions in the science collection when accessing the library pages, whereas the business school members would see new titles on commerce and finance.

This process is transparent to the user, who is presented with information by what appears to be standard HTML in the browser. The processing remains on the server, and the output of the scripts that operate on the server are produced in HTML for delivery to the client browser.[15] Production of web pages in this way has rapidly become the norm. Databases that can output to the web can of course be used for other purposes, such as the printing of catalogues or reports.

Mac or PC?

You may find that your choice of software requires you to decide whether to use Macintosh or PC machines for your site designers. Some of these programs work better on the Macintosh platform and you may get better results working on these machines. The best advice is probably to have both available, even if this upsets your computer section: many of the visitors to your site will be using Macs and you should ensure that they are able to view all the facilities and features of your site.

You should check the results of your editorial work on both Mac and PC platforms if possible, as the displayed results can differ considerably. You can control some of the effects by using tags such as the <FONT> control in your HTML code to specify the font to be used, and cascading style sheets may also offer a means of ensuring that the browser display is as close as possible to your intentions.

As with so many areas of the web there is a training overhead in your choice of software: if you decide to use even moderately complex software then your editors will need training that will make them more valuable to other employers.

In fact there is no universal advice to help you to decide what software to use, or whether to contract out the construction of the site to your ISP or a design company. The answer will depend on the complexity of your requirement and whether you can express the purpose of your site in a way that is within the capabilities of your team to construct.

Publishing a site in languages other than English

Your site should cater for users whose preferred language is not English, even though the main content is almost certain to be in English. A number of issues need to be considered.

Which languages do your visitors use? There are likely to be two groups for a UK-based site: Celtic languages and ethnic minority languages. The ethnic minority languages contain two further groups: those that are capable of being reproduced by a PC as text and those that are not.

Celtic languages

You almost certainly have an obligation to provide a website in Welsh if your organization provides any services in Wales. Welsh is straightforward enough in terms of coding, although it has accented letters that are not present in English. There are four characters that do not occur in other European languages: the upper- and lower-case 'w' and 'y' circumflex. These can be rendered in HTML using extended characters,[16] which can be seen by Internet Explorer and Netscape versions 4 and above. Your word processor may be capable of producing these characters; they occur in the symbol character sets and are reproduced correctly when saved as HTML. The remaining accented characters are in the normal set that can be obtained using the Alt key and the number keypad, by inserting symbols or by installing an alternative keyboard configuration on your computer if you constantly use another language. Beyond these considerations, Gaelic and Welsh present no major problems if you have staff who are at home in these languages.

You should consider whether to have a bilingual home page (preferred by the Welsh Language Board) or whether to have a button on your home page that leads to an alternative home page in Welsh or Gaelic. Be sure to provide the same facilities, such as no-frames versions, for the pages in the alternative language.

Ethnic minority languages

For ethnic minority languages such as Greek, which use different alphabets, you will need to ensure that the machines on which you edit the site have set up correctly by installing multilingual extensions. These are available within the installation packs for various versions of Windows and allow Greek, Russian, Arabic, Korean and other characters to be displayed correctly on screen. You can reasonably assume that users of your website who wish to view material in these scripts will have installed the necessary support on their own machines so that they will be able to read the pages correctly.

For many languages such as South Asian languages the usual approach is to create images that contain the text of the site, because many users do not have the required fonts installed on their machines. Downloading pages composed of images can be a long process, and may break the rules on the length of time that it takes for a page to load. But at present this is the primary means by which many websites render these languages.

Using non-roman scripts

A number of sites offer fonts to allow users to render non-roman scripts, for example the Yamada Language Center at the University of Oregon.[17]

The shareware word processor, Parsnegar,[18] which will allow an Urdu speaker to create web pages, handles Persian and Farsi, Arabic, Urdu, Kurdish and Assyrian. Software is becoming available for other South Asian languages but not yet to the same extent.

If you need to include material on your site in a language where fonts are not readily available, it may be worth taking the work to a specialist designer. The result of scanning in hand-written text and rendering it as an image is unlikely to be very impressive.

The resources to display Chinese and some other languages can be obtained on the web and Internet Explorer 5 and above will automatically prompt you to download the required fonts. There are a number of alternative sources of commercial word processing software, and on some of these sites it is possible to obtain trial versions.

As with South Asian languages, you have the option to construct a site entirely with graphics, but as text in Chinese can be indexed by search engines a considerable opportunity is lost if you build entirely in graphics files.

If you have a Chinese speaker who can provide the text of your Chinese web page, you can use one of the companies that specialize in preparing that text for the web. These companies may prove to be the simplest means of ensuring that every aspect of your Chinese web pages functions correctly.[19-20]

The Chinese Library home page of Westminster City Libraries (Figure 8.1) displays correctly when the Chinese Traditional (Big 5) encoding is enabled using the View-Encoding toolbar choice in Internet Explorer (or similar commands in other browsers).

Managing sites that cater for non-English languages

Consider establishing a separate area of your site for pages in languages other than English. Using a separate directory with a URL that identifies the content will help you with the management of the site, as well as guiding users to these areas. URLs such as www.library.council.gov.uk/hindi, www.library.name.org.uk/urdu or www.lyfrgell.cyngor.gov.uk/cymraeg will make it quite clear what is being offered.

Fig. 8.1 *The home page of Westminster City Libraries in Chinese*

If you offer pages in any of these languages you need to consider what facilities you will offer to people who send you e-mails from links on those pages. Users will expect you to respond in the language of their enquiry and for some enquiries in Welsh you may have a legal obligation to do so.

Finally, if you do decide to offer a service in languages other than English, ensure that your URL does not give rise to unintentional offence or humour in any other language.

Making your site accessible to all your users

People with visual handicaps are now able to make considerable use of the internet, with the help of owners of websites. You should ensure that your site helps these users as much as possible.

Many people with visual handicaps use a piece of software that reads the HTML code aloud to them and enables them to make sense of the content of the page. You therefore need to ensure that what is written in the code makes sufficient sense when put into words. Here are some considerations to take into account.[21]

Graphics

Ensure that you use the ALT tag on all graphics and use a meaningful alternative text that explains the content of the graphic. This is good practice regardless of the needs of the visually impaired. You need to take particular care when using Microsoft FrontPage because it defaults to an ALT tag containing the name of the graphic file and the size of the file in bytes. If you insert a meaningful statement and then re-edit the page you may lose the description that you added, so take care to look at every completed page in your browser to ensure that all graphics are represented by text in your published version.

Tables

Earlier screen readers had problems with reading tables, as they read words straight across the page and ignored the divide between columns in a table. New versions do not have this problem, but it is still worth bearing in mind that some older copies of the program may not be able to make sense of text contained solely in tables.

Plug-ins and other enhancements

Make sure that there is an alternative version of pages that depend on software such as Flash or Shockwave, which animate graphics. Ensure that you can reach the page containing this 'quiet' version of the web page in question without the need to use these programs. Make sure there is a link to the text only version of your site from the home page. However, you should ensure that these alternative pages are on your update schedule and are kept as up to date as any other pages on your site. They must be updated in parallel with the enhanced pages when you are updating your site, as otherwise there will be old and new versions of the same information on the site at the same time.

File formats

Using .pdf format files is a very fast way of getting content to the web, and allows you a degree of security because the files cannot be altered unless you have the full Acrobat program. It has recently become possible to convert .pdf files into a format that can be read by screen reading software[22] but this feature is not yet widely used or known. Using a word processor file format is a very effective way of distributing documents if you have no problem with the user's ability to edit the downloaded file. Therefore it will be helpful if you can provide documents in as many formats as possible: .pdf, rich text and HTML or XML should be a minimum set wherever possible. Remember when providing files in proprietary word processor formats that many users do not upgrade their software frequently and may therefore be unable to read the file, and that Macintosh users are dependent on Microsoft and other suppliers to release versions for their machines. The rich text format is a good standard that suits many word processors; it should be adopted in preference to expecting users to update to each new release of Word.

The guiding principle is to make the presentation of your site as clear as possible. If you do this, all users will benefit and will be able to navigate with ease. You can find a complete guide to the features that you should take into consideration on the website of the World Wide Web Consortium (W3C).[23] This area of the W3C site will give you a detailed guide and explanation to all of these points and to other technical matters that belong to a specialized volume on mark-up languages.

Bear in mind that your work to help disadvantaged users will assist you in preparing for new browser technologies such as those for mobile telephone networks. The W3C guidelines address these new technologies and indicate the next areas to be considered in developing your website's user base.

Designing for different browsers

Library-based websites will need to cater for visitors using a range of types of machines and browsers. These could be text-based connections by the Lynx browser running on a large Unix-based machine in a university's computing centre. They might be visits by researchers working from home or a small office, and running the latest version of Netscape or Internet Explorer on a fast PC via a dial-up link or broadband line.

Many websites have been criticized for designing only with the latest versions of the major browsers in mind. When frames were first introduced, a number of sites were branded as arrogant for presenting users of older browsers with a message telling them to get a more modern browser. Not surprisingly, many users simply went to sites that they could still read.

Now the trend has turned against the use of frames but the arrogance has spread to insistence on users obtaining Flash or other software in order to view unnecessary animations and graphics.

Remember that your design is always in the hands of the user, who may have set the browser so that it ignores all your use of fonts and font sizes to achieve a particular effect. Look at your design in a browser that has been set to use only Times New Roman and Courier typefaces, and try increasing and decreasing the font sizes in the browser window to see what happens. If your navigation buttons vanish from the right of the screen (a bad place to put them anyway), or only three lines of text are visible at low resolution, you need to think again about your design.

Obtain copies of several browsers and see what happens to your site in each of them.

Getting your site known inside and outside the organization

None of your efforts will have much value if nobody can find your site again. You need your users to know that you have a website and where to find it. You need to take a number of actions to ensure that your work is used.

Inside the organization

Your colleagues need to know that you have a website and where people can find it. If you have an intranet, things are simpler, but there are a number of steps you can take in any case.

- Place a copy of your internet website on the intranet, so that everyone on the network can view it. Many companies consider this to be one of the principal benefits of their intranet. Do not however assume that everyone knows how to use the site.
- Arrange short demonstration sessions and show people what is there and how to find it. Describe how the search engine works, and the tips and tricks for getting the most accurate results. Show the 'what's new' page and demonstrate how users send e-mails and other messages to the service managers.
- Most important of all, make sure that everyone understands how to give

the URL to telephone callers and visitors. If someone has telephoned to get information, they must be given an accurate reference if they are to be told to look on your website for the answer to their questions.

- Make sure that the telephone operators have the URL pinned up in the call centre.
- If you have a press office, make sure the staff there put the URL on every press release. (Ask them to give you copies of each release, so you know what visitors will be looking for on the site!)

Outside the organization

There are two ways in which you need to get your site better known: in print within your user community and on the web for all potential users.

In print, get as much coverage as you can from newspapers and magazines that are seen by your user community. Ask the staff newspaper to cover the launch of your site, or a major makeover and redesign exercise. If you have a particular success story, send the newspaper an item. Ask the local press to cover a website for your community, or for example if you are building a portal on your intranet that will be available to library users to provide links to useful external sites. Trade magazines may provide coverage of specialist sites for their areas of interest, where web applications aimed at their audience continue to be newsworthy. Apply the publicity effort that you use for your other services to publicizing your website. You may need to explain rather more, or talk to a different contact from your usual press 'stringer'. Finally, do ask to see the story before it goes to press. Quite often, the technical issues that need to be explained can get confused in journalistic style. Be sure that the story will not provoke replies from technical people pointing out the impossibility of what you appear to have said. You need to appear credible as well as innovative in the way the story is presented.

On the web, the way to attract visitors is by getting your site listed on the many search engines that help users find their way around the internet. You can do this by letting the engines find and index your site, by paying a placement expert to do it for you or by using software such as Submit-It! to do this for you automatically.

Finding aids on the world wide web

There are two different types of finding aid on the web; many people refer to both as 'search engines' when in fact they are not.

Different types of finding aid

Search engines are software programs that provide information about the content of websites found by 'spiders' or 'crawlers' – automated systems that constantly follow links and look for websites to include in a list produced by the search engine in response to enquiries. There are many search engines that specialize in particular countries and a number operate in languages other than English. The second type of finding aid is the directory site, which is compiled by an editorial team, often one made up of librarians. It provides a classified listing of sites by topic and sub-topic, allowing the searcher to drill down until a sufficient level of detail is obtained, and then to choose from the websites listed on that page. (A third newer type of finding aid provides 'metasearch'; sites of this type send your query to multiple search engines and aggregate the results.)

A search engine often can be distinguished from a directory by the presentation of the home page. The user is typically presented first with a box or a form, where he or she enters some words to be found in the web pages to be returned. A directory site will appear as a list of topics, usually with four or five sub-topics listed beneath it, all as clickable links that lead to further similar pages. There is a sort of convergence going on, in that many search engines now include a set of directory-style links and many directories allow the user to search for particular words within the whole site or within the category chosen. But the essential distinction is in the level of human intervention; the editorial teams at the directory sites will always have a better understanding of your site than a machine.

Improving your ranking

How do you improve your ranking on these directory and search engine sites? You cannot, unless you are very lucky, expect your site to be at the top of every list. Each search engine has a different way of calculating the rankings and what works to get your site at the top of the first page of one site may well prevent it appearing in the top hundred references on other sites. Some engines have changed their ranking algorithms to prevent them from being rigged once it has been discovered how the ranking is compiled.

There are entire websites devoted to telling you how the various search engines produce their ranked lists. You can also get some clues by reading the help pages on the major search engine sites, although in a number of cases the exact method by which the list is arranged remains a secret. It is worth taking the time to read these sources, as they will give you some ideas about what you need to do for your particular audience.

Consult sites such as Search Engine Watch[24] and particularly Greg Notess' site[25] and his magazine columns in *Online* and *Searcher*. Notess is a librarian and his columns are a valuable source of information. They tell you about changes in the way that search engines work, and about new services, but also keep the user's and library's needs in mind.

Use these sites to see whether there is a specialist search engine in your subject field. It may be worth discovering how to get high priority on a specialist search facility rather than aiming to be in AltaVista's top ten. On the other hand, if your primary audience is the general public, then your concern should be to improve your rating on the most popular public sites.

The clue to improving your rating often lies in honing the metadata elements on your web pages – the hidden information that appears in the headings. For example this is part of the information that appears on a page of the University of Sussex website:

```
<META name="description" content="Official University Units
and subject groups can set up Unit pages on the WWW server
- please contact the USIS team">
                    [information about the content of the site]
<META name="keywords" content="homepage web presence
information provider publishing USIS">              [keywords]
```

The first line of information gives a short message that summarizes the content of the page; the second provides a number of words that users might be searching for, including 'USIS' the acronym of the service. Note that a search for 'Sussex' on the metadata would not have found this page.

If the META content field contains a sufficient number of precise keywords to identify the subject of your site, it should improve its rating. Think about the words that your visitors might use to describe your specialist subjects. Include these rather than technical terms from a thesaurus if that is how your main audience will try to find you. On the other hand, if your target audience is made up of specialists, use their language.

Some search engines limit the number of words that they index to around 25, so you need to be able to express your message in a short space. In fact some engines go on to discard pages that contain very many words, typically 50 or more, because it is likely that the authors are trying to rig an improved rating for the page by repeating a keyword many times. You can improve your chances of a high rating by varying the content of the META content field on related pages. Keep the basic descriptors on each page and add words that are relevant to particular pages. Users are more likely to find one part of your site and link back to your home page if necessary. If every page has identical strings of metadata, your users will have to find the precise match for the string; if you vary the terms on each page, users will be able to find you by entering a wider range of terms.

Look for your own site on the search engines and directories. Use the version for the country or countries where you think people are most likely to look. It is very pleasant to be found by overseas search engines but if you are missing from the one that your main audience uses, you have a problem.

Think about the ways in which people might search for your site and include suitable terms to help those people. If you need help in considering the searching techniques of people outside your usual community, investigate the search engines that have pages that show you current searches by other users.[26] You can learn a great deal by spending half an hour watching how people go about finding information.

Using registered marks or brands

If your organization owns or is known by any registered marks or brands, you should search for these terms at regular intervals to ensure that your name is not being used in ways that you would prefer not to see. Increasing numbers of internet sites are placing unrelated search terms in their metadata strings in order to trap users searching for genuine information on a topic. Often brand or trade names are used, which could include yours. (There is a debate about the ethics of including your competitors' brand names in order that people looking for their product find yours too. Check out your rivals' practice, perhaps in conjunction with the advice on reputation management in this chapter.) Follow the top 20 or 50 links on the major search engines when checking your own ratings. If your competitors are ahead of you, analyse their data and see why they are ahead. (Use the several excellent descriptions of the way search engines work to help you.) If your name is being used to peddle pornography or libel, then contact the host to get it stopped. If that fails, consult your lawyers.

Getting listed on search engines

There are several ways of alerting the search engines to your presence. Many of them have a facility for submitting details of your site to the compilers. In the case of a robot, your message goes into a file of URLs that the search robot will visit in due course. The robot will then compile an entry based on its analysis of your site and that entry will appear in response to searches once it has been added to the list.

You need to know two things about this process. The first is that it takes several weeks in many cases, which means that if you want to publicize something that has a deadline, such as a conference announcement, you need to move as early as possible to submit details. Second, the search robot is unlikely to check that page again. If you change the page by adding new indexing, you need to re-submit it. If you remove the page, visitors will still arrive – or, to be more precise, they will get the infamous '404 – page not found' message unless you leave a page in its place that refers on to the revised page or back to your home page. Potential visitors will stop bothering to follow links to your site if there are too many broken links from search engines.

It is not suitable to give general guidance in a book, because search engines tend to change their search systems at fairly frequent intervals so advice is quickly out of date. The links and references provided in the Resource List and the companion website to this book (accessible at www.facetpublishing.co.uk) will take you to current information about the way that search sites are indexing and what their present criteria are for inclusion or exclusion of your site.

Submitting your site to the directories is perhaps easier. You can submit your site directly to many of the international and national directories using forms or links on the site, although you are dependent on the human indexers for a mention. So long as the subject matter of the site is obvious from the page that you nominate, you should be able to expect a nomination.

You may want to check the category to which you have been allotted to ensure that it is the most appropriate for your organization or community. An information professional should have a good idea of where his or her site should be placed. However, the directory services make increasing use of professional help and may have a better idea of the ways in which their users seek information about websites.

Software packages are available that will submit your website to a range of search engines – check the front cover discs of the internet press for a suitable program. These have the advantage of listing search engines in specialist fields as well as the general ones. Otherwise a number of websites such as Submit-It![27] will do the job; though commentators have little enthusiasm for these services as it is impossible to know whether the search engines chosen are likely to be used by potential customers for your website.

Advertising banners

Some of the search engine sites will allow you to build in links to their search engines as part of your site. This is useful for a small site and provides you with the power of a top quality search engine in exchange for an advertising banner on your site. But this may not be appropriate for you as your organization may have a policy about third party advertisements.

Policy on the acceptance of advertising will vary from organization to organization. For some sites, the income from advertising banners makes the operation viable, while for some organizations it would be inappropriate to accept any form of commercial sponsorship. If your organization manufactures or sells a product or service, the website may be a means of promoting it.

UK government websites are permitted to accept advertising.[28] There are guidelines that draw attention to ensuring that advertisers' branding does not conflict with the site's own brand, that endorsement of the advertiser's product is not implied, and that there is no contradiction between the advertiser's message and those of the department or government.

There are industry standards for banners, with a maximum size of 468 x 60 pixels and file sizes that do not exceed 12 Kb. Bear in mind that any additional files will slow down your page as it loads. Remember too that if your page uses horizontal frames – perhaps in order to include navigation buttons at the top – then the advertisement will take up much of the screen on some computers. Check where you are required to place any advertising banners. Some sites put them at the bottom of the home page, not the top; if your agreement allows you to do this, it may reduce any income from referrals to the advertiser, but it may keep visitors on your site long enough for them to find out about all your services.

Other ways to get your site listed

There are several further ways that may be appropriate in terms of getting your site linked, listed or noted. These include:

- submitting to relevant discussion lists
- contacting magazine editors and news desks on trade and other publications
- joining news groups and alerting the group to relevant changes or new sites
- contacting other webmasters to suggest mutual links between related sites.

Specialist search engines may exist in your subject area. A number of portals and metasearch websites provide links to lists, and claim to contain links to hundreds, sometimes thousands of engines.[29] Searching these sites and submitting to engines and individual websites that you identify could be a cost effective method for you.

What are people looking at?

In order to manage your site effectively you need to know what your visitors are looking at (and what they are not). This is done using statistics supplied by the server, either using widely available software on your own server or by asking your ISP to provide you with a web log analysis.[30] A number of free tools are available to help you[31] in addition to the main paid-for programs WebTrends, OneStat, Clickstream and Hitwise.

The log will give you valuable information about the numbers of visitors who consult each page; you can see where they come from and at what time of day they come. The result can be sorted into order, so that ranking by number of visits will bring the least popular pages together. If they are in a particular area of the site, and especially if other pages in that group remain unvisited, there may be a case for archiving these pages or even removing them from the site. However, if they are particularly important pages in your view or that of the authors, you may want to consider instead whether the indexing and signposts to those pages could be improved.

If you need official audit figures, comparable to circulation figures for printed periodicals, the electronic service of the Audit Bureau of Circulation at www.abce.org.uk can provide you with certified figures.

The use of cookies can help to track visitors to and through your site and can be unobtrusive – although you will lose some visitors who will leave the site rather than allow you to leave a cookie file.[32]

Summary

This chapter has covered a wide range of topics concerned with getting a website launched and has shown that many important steps have to be taken before a corporate website of any kind can be started – far more than for a personal site. As manager, you need to consider how each of these elements is to be managed.

References

1   See www.nic.uk/rules/rup2.html.

2   See www.e-envoy.gov.uk/Resources/WebGuidelinesArticle/fs/
    en?CONTENT_ID=4002794&chk=M66aCp and United King-
    dom, Office of the e-Envoy (2003) *Illustrated Handbook for Web
    Management Teams*, London, TSO, section 1.9,
    www.e-envoy.gov.uk/Resources/WebHandbookIndex1Article/fs/
    en?CONTENT_ID=4000064&chk=fUJBmm.

3   See www.chester-le-track.co.uk/htm/domains.asp.

4   www.cyberalert.com.

5   www.infonic.com.

6   Kassel, A. (2000) The Last Word on Web Monitoring and Clipping
    Services, *Searcher*, **8** (8), (September), 24–35.

7   Ryan, M. and Long, K. (2000) Is it Real or is it Emulex? How the
    media safeguards against bogus releases, *The Scoop*, (October),
    www.web.archive.org/web/20020614222926/wwwpressaccess.com/
    thescoop/0010_emulex.htm.

8   Mintz, A. P. (2002) *Web of Deception: misinformation on the internet*,
    Medford NJ, Cyberage Books.

9   Piper, P. S. (2000) Better Read That Again: web hoaxes and misinformation, *Searcher*, **8** (8), (September), 40–53.

10 Griffiths, P. (2001) All that Glitters: the role of the information professional in handling rogue information on the Internet. In *Online Information 2001*, Proceedings, Oxford, Learned Information, 17–23; Crouzillacq, P. (2001) Danone ne goûte pas au boycott sur Internet, *01.net*, Paris, 01.net; www.01net.com/article/145698.html and illustrations at www.paranos.com/gueule/jeboycottedanone.html; Haig, M. (2003) When Customers Attack, *Internet Works*, **76**, (Autumn), 20–9.

11 arbiter.wipo.int/domains/decisions/html/2001/d2001-0537.html; and see report of the case on Ananova. www.ananova.com/news/story/sm_365617.html.

12 www.chester-le-track.co.uk.

13 Letters to *The Times*, 11 January 2000 and 22 January 2000.

14 See Colombo, J. and Awcock, K. (2003) Impostors, Accidental Tourists and Web Brands, *Information Security Bulletin*, **8** (4), (May), 129–42; Lewis, E. (2001) Combating the Brand Pirates and Logo Thieves, *Guardian*, Media supplement, 3 September, 58–9; Osler, F. and Hollis, P. (2001) *The Activist's Guide to the Internet*, London, Prentice Hall, www.cyveillance.com, www.infoguerre.com, www.c4ifr.com and www.ege.esisca.fr.

15 Williams, H. E. and Lane, D. (2002) *Web Database Applications with PHP and MySQL*, O'Reilly.

16 Ŵ ŵ Ŷ ŷ.

17 babel.uoregon.edu/yamada/guides.html.

18 www.isc.com.au/.

19 Gay, P (1998), China in Your Hands', *Internet Works*, **10**, (September), 92–5; this is a particularly useful and thorough guide, which includes advice on a range of topics from the choice of software to cultural issues (such as favourite colour schemes – use red! – and the need to be even-handed in order to avoid giving offence to either the Taiwanese or the Chinese).

20 Links to Chinese language resources are available from Westminster City Libraries' Chinese Library page at members.aol.com/wlclss/support.html.

21 Further information is under the heading 'Accessibility' in the glossary.

22 See http://access.adobe.com/tools.html for further details and links to the required software.

23 www.w3.org/TR/1999/WAI-WEBCONTENT-19990505/ wai-pageauth.html#tech-identify-changes.

24 www.searchenginewatch.com.

25 www.notess.com.

26 For example, All-the-Web (www.alltheweb.com/recentqueries).

27 www.submit-it.com: a particularly useful page is submitit.bcentral.com/subcats.htm, which lists the geographical and subject search engines to which the service sends notifications. See also www.promotionworld.com and Wilson, J. (2000) *Web Site Promotion: a lot of what you need to know to build site traffic*, Laguna Niguel, California, SunDesk, www.virtualpromote.com/promotea.html.

28 United Kingdom, Office of the e-Envoy (2001) *Case Study of Advertising on a Government Website*, Web Quality Briefings 1, OeE, www.e-envoy.gov.uk/assetRoot/04/00/21/04/04002104.doc.

29 Many of the subject search resources mentioned in the first edition are no longer available. search.com (www.search.com) continues to provide one-stop access to over 1000 search engines (unlisted), while newer metasearch engines such as Ixquick (www.ixquick.com) have become well established. As printed resources such as this go out of date quickly, you should look at online resources such as the columns by Greg Notess in *Online* magazine (notess.com/write/onthenet.shtml), which are available free of charge on the web as well as in print.

30 For a detailed explanation see Nicholas, D. et al. (1999) Cracking the Code: web log analysis, *Online and CD-ROM review*, **23** (5), 263–9; and Wilson, J. (1999) *Understanding Web Site Traffic Analysis*, Laguna Niguel, California, SunDesk, jimworld.com/trafficreports.html.

31 Free Traffic Analysis (2003) *Internet Magazine*, **108** (October), 100–5.

32 Cartwright, D. (2000) Learn More About Who Uses Your Site, *Internet Magazine*, **67**, (June), 145–9.

9

Managing website content

●●

This chapter examines:

- how to set out the content of a website
- the techniques that ensure information is up to date
- how to ensure that your colleagues take responsibility for the information they create
- how to establish an acceptable use policy
- what use a style guide can be, and where to find some useful examples
- issues concerning copyright and intellectual property
- other legal issues
- how to use software to manage site content
- how to archive your site
- how to manage discussion and chat facilities, including site moderation and
- how to add a weblog to your site.

●●

IMPORTANT:

Parts of this chapter discuss legislation, and potential new or changed legislation. As a result there is little or, usually, no case law on which to base definitive advice. You must ensure that you seek competent legal advice if you intend taking any action that could be seen as setting any kind of precedent or could otherwise affect your organization's legal position. In a corporate body, advice should come from its legal advisers. You may need to persuade them of the seriousness of the issues. You may also have to point out to them that if any important part of your target audience lies outside your own country they may themselves need to consult further on international legal aspects of what you intend to do.

Setting out the content

It is important that your users can easily understand and navigate the content of your website. Understanding can be achieved by ensuring that content is written for the web and not simply lifted wholesale from existing material written for print on paper; we shall look at this shortly. The means of achieving sound navigation is to maintain a map of your website to help you to maintain links and to ensure that no pages become detached from the structure. Many sites have a site map that you can look at to help you to devise your own. You can construct the map as a paper document, either by hand or by using a computer program such as Visio that is designed to construct charts showing relationships. Some authoring software (Microsoft FrontPage for example) constructs and maintains a table of links for you, and can represent this as a diagram.

Maintain the map as you add, move and delete pages. Ensure that none is orphaned (left without links) and keep the links up to date so that users are not presented with error messages. It is best practice to include information about the date of creation or last amendment, and the name of the person who supplied the information. See Figure 6.2 (page 77), for an example.

Keeping your website up to date

There is little point in running a website that does not change and is constantly out of date. Users will not trust it to contain current information to suit their needs and will not return to it. Earlier in the book we looked at the ways of ensuring that the validity of the information was demonstrated. Even if information does not change between your validation checks, you should ensure that the date on your page is amended to show the last time the currency was verified.

How else can you do to manage the information content of your website? How can you manage your users?

Method 1: Name and shame

Put the name of the person who is responsible for the content on the page they have contributed! This has two effects.

- On a positive note, it identifies the person in the organization who is responsible for the topic covered by the web page. Your users can get in touch with this person either by e-mail (use an embedded link using the mailto: command) or by telephone or fax if details are given. Responses of this type of query can help page editors to provide information that is pertinent to the users of the website. Identifying writers can give them pride and motivation that will ensure that they keep the details current.
- On the other hand, if there is a name attached to a page that is constantly out of date or appears to have last been revised several months ago, you have the details of the person concerned immediately to hand. You are able to identify at once the person to whom you should talk to get something done. If it turns out that the author responsible has left the organization, you should at least be able to identify where responsibility for the topic lies in your management structure and ask a local manager for a new contribution.

Adding this information should be a standard part of editing a web page. Chapter 6 looked at navigation methods and suggested that pages should contain a 'breadcrumb' trail to guide users through the various layers of information. It is a simple matter to design a web page so that the author's name and contact details appear in a similar way in another part of the page. By creating templates in many of the popular website construction tools, you can provide your authors and editors with a standard format where they can supply the necessary details.

Method 2: Throw out old pages

If identifying purveyors of out-of-date information is not enough to bring them into line, consider removing their work completely from the site.

This policy is often countered by saying that removing the information makes the website less useful because an integral part of the content is now missing, and that users will go elsewhere for information. But which is the more dangerous – a website that includes incorrect information passing itself off as fact, or a website that has an obvious gap in its information? Anyone doing research that involves verifying data from multiple sources will soon discover whether yours is a site that can be trusted – and will no longer visit if it becomes evident that yours cannot.

You could always replace the page with a warning that you are updating the information, although using the 'under construction' logo is considered bad form.

Throwing out poor quality content is likely to be a controversial move the first time you do it. The author will probably complain and may set his or her boss onto you. Explain that inaccurate information is worse than no information at all and that you will replace the page if the content is validated or revised. Show that gaps in the website are no use to you and that what you want is accurate and current content.

Set public standards, perhaps by laying out guidelines on your intranet, showing the maximum permitted time lapse between updates of different types of material. Send reminders if information is out of date. (Some database software will create these for you automatically and send them if your e-mail system is compatible).

Method 3: Write it yourself

Don't do this unless it's essential to maintain the most important topics on your website. But you would clearly be on shaky ground in terms of organizational politics if you were to name and shame your director's office – at least, if you expected some kind of future in your organization. And although you would hope to be warned if the organization was about to change its slogan or mission statement (see on), you might need to replace pages that senior people had forgotten to update. In these cases you will need to write something yourself.

Some kinds of content – such as mission statements – do not change very frequently. Perhaps your organization is one of those that re-brands itself or changes its corporate colours every year or two. Events such as this are usually heralded long in advance and the website will be one of the areas that need to plan a schedule for the makeover. If you are not remembered at these times then you need to market far more to your internal customers! Corporate content such as this can have a far longer duration than, for example, the latest news releases, but you still need to verify the dates.

Draw up a grid showing the expected lifetime of the pages on your website and use it to provide a prompt list for obtaining updates from your contributors. Ensure that the list of authors is checked against the organization's directory at regular intervals. Use library publicity to remind section managers to tell you when an author leaves the organization, or simply changes section.

Method 4: Making authors responsible

All, or nearly all, of the people in your organization will by now be aware of what the web is. Many probably use information from their favourite websites. So it has become easier to describe the problems of out-of-date information and to explain to writers why you need them to be responsible. Do not however assume that the connection between your colleagues' habits as information users and information suppliers is obvious to them.

Education of website contributors can be slow: after all this may be a major cultural change for many of them. They need to understand that it is not just their colleagues or the local users that they are inconveniencing. There could be global interest in some areas of work. Local history is one example of a topic where the sum of worldwide expertise about an area is likely to be concentrated in one library service in a local area. If your contributors fail to update information or to report new discoveries this not only makes for a dull website but it deprives the global audience of information that the organization's money has paid to create.

Presentations can demonstrate the problem in a way that sending out memoranda to offenders can never do. Show how difficult it is to research current concerns using three-month-old newspapers. Demonstrate examples of incorrect information that will cause real problems to your users; these could be anything from giving old information about charges or benefits to giving contact names of people who left the organization a year ago.

Publicly thank people who co-operate with you and hold them up as examples of good practice. It can be a way of shaming others into working with you, and you should not be too proud to use the effects of shame. It can be a useful ally.

Your corporate information management policy should make explicit the responsibility of every member of your organization in this respect. If it does not, can you have the point added? But, above all, you will need to be patient. It all takes time.

Method 5: Make a committee responsible too

Many organizations have an internet editorial committee of some sort. This gives extra power to your decisions, for example, to remove offending pages. If a representative group of authors has set rules that some of them then break, it gives authority to the webmaster if he or she removes pages for these breaches.

Make sure the committee meets frequently and regularly – at least every two to three months – and give them a mixture of policy and practical issues to deal with. Report what the web team has been doing; describe successes and failures, problems and solutions. Let the committee members know about resource issues to do with both staff and budgets. Show them how the site will be developing and how they are expected to contribute, with information, resources or both.

Don't swamp the committee with formal papers but do make sure members know what's going on. Make sure that their decisions are recorded and send the record back to them as a list of action points or decisions. Use the committee to help you to manage the site effectively, and to provide a means of collective decision-making for the tough issues as well as a champion at the highest level through the chairperson.

Acceptable use policies

Does your organization have an acceptable use policy (AUP) for the internet, either for its use as a research tool or for publication there? There may well be one for the use of the web in the organization. Typically, it will specify the kind of material that users can view and will prohibit them from accessing some specific types of material. For example, unless it is done for well-defined official purposes, most policies ban users from accessing race or sexual hatred material, or pornography. This policy may be administered in association with some kind of filtering software that blocks access to known offensive sites, or may even restrict access to a specified list of approved sites.

A similar kind of policy is required for publishing on the web, particularly if you intend to give any kind of editing rights to people outside your LIS. The types of material that will be unacceptable will echo many of the categories that your AUP lists for incoming materials. You will probably prohibit the inclusion of material that constitutes sexual or racial harassment, or that includes any other kind of hate material, depiction of pornographic or violent images or textual content.

Why would you do that? After all, your organization is not (I imagine) in the business of publishing pornography or stirring up hatred against some section of the community. The reason is that you must have a policy that covers the organization against the actions of any of its members of staff who decide to do something like this as an act of spite or revenge on the organization. It is not unknown for employees who are working out their notice, for example, to sabotage the corporate website. They may do it by hacking in, but why go to that bother and commit a crime by doing so? How much easier to plant something unpleasant at a third or fourth level page and wait for the search engines to find it, and then for someone to tell the press what is there. (This emphasizes the importance of keeping a map of the site, preferably software generated, and looking out for any unusual new pages, particularly if they have no links to or from them.) In this situation, a published acceptable use policy gives you some means of defending your organization and of being able to impose stiff penalties on anyone who misuses their ability to edit the website.

Among the activities that you are likely to want to protect yourself from are not only pornographic publication and harassment but also defamation and incitement to crime or fraud. You may be in a position where you need to be concerned that your site does not contain advertising or inadvertently appear to endorse any product.

You also need to ensure that your information editors comply with the law. The most important Acts of Parliament that you need to ensure that your writers comply with are the:

- Computer Misuse Act 1990
- Data Protection Act 1998
- Copyright Designs and Patents Act 1988.

You may also find that you or your colleagues are subject to the Official Secrets Act 1989, whether or not you work for the government. Some provisions of the Charities Act 1993 may also apply to you; for example you need to ensure that your charity registration number appears on every page of your website just as it needs to appear on each separate paper publication. And there are other statutes that are not specifically related to computer and information use that should be complied with, of which the Race Relations Act 1976 and the Race Relations (Amendment) Act 2000 are probably the most obvious examples.

Some other issues

A typical AUP will thus contain clauses that set out clearly what the acceptable standards are. It will state that the organization will not tolerate material that harasses any person inside or outside it, whether that is on sexual, racial, religious or any other grounds. What else might it usefully contain?

Quite often there are guidelines or instructions about the use of names, intellectual property and other elements of the organization's constitution. You might find statements on the following subjects.

- *Name* Does your organization have a formal or long name that has to be used for legal reasons? There may be rules about capitalization of the name – Fares and Charges Office, or Fares and charges office? – or the form of the name: Borsetshire University, or University of Borsetshire? Your organization may be known by a short version of the name that cannot be used in some contexts and guidance should be given on when this is so.
- *Emblem, coat of arms, logo* Are there rules on the way that your logo can be used? It may be that you have to reproduce a registered trade mark in a particular way, or in a number of central and local government cases there will be rules about the way coats of arms can be reproduced. For example, if the royal crest appears anywhere in your logo there are very precise rules about the way it can be shown and no text can appear above it.
- *Intellectual property* You should set out the rules for making documents and other information available if they do not belong to the author, and set out what should happen on these occasions. For example, rights may belong to a college or university under the author's contract of employment, or the item may already have appeared in a publication that has been assigned the copyright. Take additional care when you let

contracts to external authors or consultants to produce documents that you intend to publish on the web. Under UK copyright law, unless the contract states explicitly that the copyright in the document passes to the person or body that commissioned the work, the author retains it. Be sure that your contracts include a right to publish any commissioned documents in electronic form on the web, as otherwise it may be argued that you have copyright only in the printed version. For the same reason, you should ensure that if you obtain illustrations from an external source, you license the use of the image not only on paper but in electronic form. This may involve an additional payment but will save you from one of three unpleasant possibilities: having action taken against you for unlicensed use of the image; having to redesign an entire publication with new images for the web; or having to pay an unexpected and large additional fee for this further use of the image.

- *Use of external ISPs to publish information on behalf of the organization* You may decide to allow contributors to place information about your organization directly onto servers outside it. However, there are possible complications. First, your official webmaster will have no control over the site, which is a situation to be discouraged. Second, the use of a server that inserts banner advertisements into pages as a condition of service could associate your organization with undesirable products – or those of a competitor!

Because of the growth of computer facilities in public libraries, the People's Network is working on AUPs. Its (undated!) pages include a template AUP,[1] and links to those library authority websites that include AUPs.[2]

Note that your ISP may also impose an AUP on you and your contributors. This is likely to cover the more technical aspects of your site as well as reinforce rules on pornography and other breaches where the ISP may have liabilities if an offence is committed. ISPs may impose restrictions on the use of e-mail for marketing purposes, laying down rules on how contact data may be gathered, stored, used and disposed of on its networks. You will have to accept responsibility for these aspects of use of your website on behalf of your organization, and impose these conditions in turn. You may need to set up and administer additional mailboxes to receive reports of e-mail abuse originating from areas of your website. Make it explicit to your organization that you will pass on liability for all costs incurred as a result of anything that your contributors do, if this leads to your ISP imposing penalty charges. If your IT department makes these arrangements with ISPs, record in writing that the information service does not accept liability for penalties imposed as a result of technical infringements on the ISP's servers.

Writing for the web

How many times have you been presented with copy for the website that consists of the unaltered content of a company brochure or a feature extracted from the organization's newspaper? Unfortunately many of your contributors will be unaware of the difference between electronic and printed publications, and the fact that people read them in entirely different ways.

At a trivial level, a surprising number of people do not read below the 'fold' in a web page represented by the bottom of the initial screen.[3] This means you must ensure that pages contain important information, and that information needs to be at the top of the page. Your authors must write in a concise way and use lists and bullets to increase impact. Your navigation, as we have seen elsewhere, needs to fit in to the top of the page if it is not to be lost at lower screen resolutions. So your authors need to be aware of this constraint when setting out their pitch. They should adopt a style based more on tabloid journalism than broadsheet style – short sentences that tell the story in a few words[4] and draw the reader down the page. So simply converting existing documents into brochure-ware will not do.

It is not only possible to write clearly and well for the web, it is possible to get your achievement certified with the Plain English Campaign's special Internet Crystal Mark.[5] At present 25 organizations are members, mainly legal or financial bodies and local or central government organizations.

Provide guidance and perhaps some courses in this essential writing skill. It works in many other business contexts. In the next section we look at style guides, but a number of useful publications deal with the issues of web writing itself[6] and are worth reading.

Style guides

Do you ever look at a website and think what a mess it looks? Perhaps pages are in different styles and type families, or perhaps there are different coloured backgrounds for no apparent reason. Perhaps on some pages the graphics are clickable links to other related topics while on other pages they are – well, just graphics. Or maybe some pages have handy links in them that return you to the top of a long document while others just let you scroll to the top or bottom if you want to find a link to anywhere.

Websites like this are crying out for guidance. Providing your own contributors with a style guide would ensure that they knew what standards they were expected to conform to (and therefore the reasons that you might reject their pages from your site). It would ensure that your site had a consistent appearance and that users could understand their location on the site, and how to navigate in various directions from that point. It would ensure that your site was not one of those that people disliked using because it was a mess.

A style guide would provide a reference source that would answer some of the questions that came up earlier, and others like:

- Which typeface should be used on the site?
- What are the rules for using the organization's logo?
- Are there any words that have to be spelt in a particular way as a matter of policy? How do we capitalize the name of the organization?

If you give your page editors extensive rights then you may extend your style guide to include some technical questions as well: do you permit frames (not so popular as they were, as they affect search engine rankings) and when do you insist that tables are used? Does the site use JavaScript or ActiveX?

Some questions of style

Apart from the reasons we saw above that writing for the web differs from writing for the printed page, it needs a less formal style (unless of course you are reproducing a formal document on the web). You can encapsulate guidance and instructions on this in the style guide that you issue to your contributors; you might put it on the intranet for ease of reference and as an example of good practice. Look for current style guides that universities and other bodies publish on the world wide web, and you can get a lot of ideas for your own guide from these sources. Frequently they will point you to an issue that you had not realized could be a problem for you!

Some style guides have effectively torn up the rule book, but then so has the technology industry. Did you see the word JavaScript above? Does your word processor object when you type it without a capital letter in the middle of the word? And how would people react if you started to put capitals into words that happened to be made up of other words – Pro-Portion, AtTenDance ?

Other questions arise from the style of the web. How do you file names that put dollar, pound or euro signs instead of the letters S, L and E? How do you quote web addresses, with or without 'http://' in front? Is it email, e-mail or E-mail?

Another issue that may bring you difficulties is the international nature of the web. If yours is a multinational organisation, the web style guide is going to have to take account of differences in language between British and North American English (or other national and regional English usage). This extends beyond the use or meaning of words to some points of punctuation and some points of grammar. A guide may need to take account of the location of the author and make allowances accordingly, or else to insist that everybody follow one or other convention. However do not get hung up on these issues: the position of a full stop or comma is not going to affect the value of a website even if it is inconsistent. But they might explain why your team is constantly moving round the punctuation in pages written by your office in New York.

It's also easy to upset people, perhaps unwittingly. You may be reporting a speech by somebody in your organization that includes some kind of expletive – for example in describing a poor idea or unreasonable behaviour by using common words of abuse. You should remember that some 'nanny' software will shut out your page if it discovers this kind of language, and that you will therefore lose part of your audience for the page. Set down the limits in your style guide, although you may also have to train your senior staff to keep their language within limits. And talking of differences between versions of English, don't forget that some terms that are common in one country are considered vulgar or obscene in others.

Part of the problem is not so much writing for the web as writing for a worldwide audience, many of whose members do not speak English as fluently as your authors. The style should be clear without being over-simplified or patronizing, and convey the essential message of the text in a couple of screens of reasonably sized text. Long, complex pages are not wanted. Authors need to learn how to keep the content at a high level while making the language simple. It is a discipline that it would probably do the average executive no harm to learn. Books on newspaper style are worth consulting: both in the level of writing and in the brevity of their text, news reporters are taught to convey the essentials of a story in as few words as possible. Storage is cheap, but people's time still has a price.

Fortunately there are several guides at hand. One of the most widely known internet style guides is the *Yale Web Style Guide*.[7] This grew out of the widely used and highly praised website on site design created by the Center for Advanced Instructional Media at Yale University.[8] In the best traditions of the web, this website has created a book of the site, followed by related sites by each of the authors, and then another book by one of them.

Local instructions

Even when you have identified a style guide that reflects your approach, such as the Yale guide, you will need to set out some local instructions. The rules about using coats of arms were mentioned just above, and many universities and other bodies have strict rules about where their arms may be used.[9] You may decide to provide a download site or a disc containing an approved copy of the logo to potential users with instructions on how it is to be used.

Resource, the Council for Museums, Galleries and Libraries, sets out its rules for the use of its name and logo[10] and is setting out its house style in a related page. Apart from use of your name and logo, you may want to set rules on citation of references, and on naming people (both in terms of identifying individuals, and how you will cite them, with or without post-nominal qualifications). And a list of acronyms peculiar to the organization is a common feature of many websites.

These instructions should extend to providing clear guidance on when sites may include official logos and other items implying that the site has been endorsed by the organization. In many academic and other bodies there is an ill-defined line between personal and corporate information, such as when it is issued by an officer of a society but appear to contain personal opinions.

There are issues to be addressed where an academic server is to be used for hosting sites relating to business activities based at the college or university. In the UK, a JANET proxy connection licence is required; the terms and conditions as well as the relevant application forms can be downloaded from the JANET website.[11]

In many instances such as these you will need to monitor current developments. *It is essential that you develop and amend policy as new issues arise.* (These may be technical such as bug fixes for software, legal such as the implementation of the new data protection legislation, or administrative such as establishing rules for quasi-commercial use of your server.) Your editorial community must be primed to act on any instructions or guidance that you issue: in the worst case, your institution could be exposed to legal challenge if someone fails to implement guidance.

Copyright and intellectual property

Another aspect of the work of editing a website is ensuring that it does not breach any copyrights or use other people's intellectual property without permission. You also need to ensure that others are not using your site's copyright material without your permission.

Copyright

You have copyright in the original content of your website just as you and others have in any original work. However, you need to establish ways of knowing that the materials on the site are original. This will allow you to demonstrate that your material that appears unexpectedly on other sites has been used in breach of copyright, but it will also allow you to be sure that your site is not breaching anyone else's copyright. Illustrations are a particular source of difficulty because their copyright may belong to someone other than the author of the accompanying text. If one of your colleagues offers an illustrated article, it would be as well to include a basic check on the origin of text and graphics.

Your copyright may be breached when others copy your material and add it to their website without permission. You may be able to locate such use by using the many search engines on the web: give your files unusual names and use features that allow you to search for files. Many people do not even go to the bother of changing the names of documents or graphics before using them as if they owned them, so if you find an unusual file name that matches part of your site, it could be a clue to unauthorized use. You do not have a great deal of redress, especially if the offending site is outside your home country, but you could try writing to the webmaster pointing out the problem. It may, after all, be a genuine mistake that he or she would be happy to correct, or to acknowledge the origin. If your organization has a policy of pursuing breaches of its intellectual property rights, it may be a long drawn out process – but it may be possible to extract some kind of penalty payment.

There is a growing body of work on internet copyright; there are e-journals and journal articles that will help you and there are several discussion lists that frequently touch on this area. You may find conflicting opinions expressed in these sources; again the only course of action when in doubt is to seek a view from your corporate advisers on the line that they would be prepared to defend.

Copyright relating to the Transport for London Underground diagram

It is surprisingly easy to infringe copyright with the best of intentions. London Transport has for a long time licensed the copying of the famous Harry Beck Underground diagram that is recognised the world over. In the early days of the web a number of sites scanned in a copy of the map, and were later contacted to ask them to remove it. London Transport itself originally added the map to its website in a number of sections so that it was impossible to download a single file of the diagram. Its attitude has slowly changed as its website has developed and the map can now be downloaded as a single, printable file in a choice of formats. With the integration of the Tube website into the Transport for London site following the transfer of the London Underground to TfL on 15 July 2003, it has finally become possible to download the map without acknowledging a copyright warning message. However, the wording of the message on the download page has become more complex than before:

> The copyright in the material contained within the document you are about to view belongs to Transport for London. All rights reserved.
>
> Except solely for your own personal and non-commercial use, no part of this document may be copied or used without the prior written permission of Transport for London.

By clicking on the link above to view the map, it is understood that you have read this copyright notice and accept these conditions.[12]

Links to other websites

The unique experience of using the world wide web is the ability to link from one page to another, either on the same site or on a different site that carries relevant related information. Unlike the pages of a book that move in sequence, the web allows you to jump between the links in any order that seems relevant to your search and discoveries. The user very soon becomes used to this experience and learns to navigate in search of content; but there are some severe dangers in this very fundamental aspect of the web.

First, there is the danger that by providing effective links on your home page you may lose the very traffic that you have been building up so carefully through your publicity and registration work for your website. But, you may say, we would never divert traffic off our site as soon as it arrives. Yet this is the very effect that occurs on many websites because the most prominent feature of the visible part of the home page (especially on a low resolution screen) is a skilfully designed advertisement!

These advertisements are a real problem for many webmasters. A number of companies offer a small premium for a 'clickthrough', that is, where the user enters a sales site through an onward link from an external site. There is nothing intrinsically wrong with this system: it helps to pay for a number of truly excellent websites (such as the *Alertbox* columns written by Jakob Nielsen[13]). The sums paid for referrals (typically around three US cents) or the small percentage commission on sales help to defray the webmaster's costs, so he or she will be anxious for you to follow the reference. On the other hand, once you have left the referring site you may not go back and your further business there is lost. A sensible approach is that taken by a number of authors who use a link inserted by themselves, rather than a display banner, which takes users to the recommended commerce site. At the same time the authors make it clear that they obtain a small revenue in return for any purchases made through their reference. Some state that if each reader made one or two purchases a year through the link rather than visiting the online bookshop directly then the site's costs would be covered.

You may conclude from this that a scheme like this could help your own site. It works better in a commercial environment and many publicly funded authorities may frown on such ideas. Is it really so different from allowing a bookshop a concession to operate in your library? That is for you and your managers to decide.

You may have little choice over the placing of advertisements on your page if you choose to place your site on one of the many free web services that are now available (such as Yahoo! Geocities). The terms of service of many operators insist that you place an advertisement in a stated position at the top of your page. If you really do not want to include advertisements on your page then your choice of hosts for your website will be limited as a result. But you need to consider the image that is created by your choice of host, and by the fact that your web address will not be 'mylibrary.org', but 'freewebservice.com/mylibrary'.

If it important to you that your identity as 'mylibrary' should be the element that is identified first, then you need to make other arrangements. The same is true if you are unhappy that your domain is '.com' or '.co.uk' rather than '.org' for a not-for-profit enterprise. In this case you will need to register a top level domain of your own, as many ISPs that offer server space as part of your subscription will also provide a subdomain of their own commercial domain name unless you make additional payments. You could investigate the availability of '.info' domain names, and museum sites could qualify for the new domain '.museum'.[14]

The danger of hidden links

When you have resolved the issue of advertising links, you are ready to start considering the wider issue of hyperlinks to other sites. There was an unwritten convention in the early days of the web that you should obtain permission from the site that you intended to link to before making that link live. With over a billion pages on the web that ideal is becoming less workable. And if you seek permission from another site it is now quite likely that your request will be ignored or that you will be seen to have somewhat quaint old-fashioned manners. But just try linking to a major website in the wrong kind of way!

The issue of linking to copyrighted material remains contentious. Cases such as that involving Totalnews, which had compiled its website by linking frames on its pages to news stories on other websites, set more recent practice.

In 1999 London Transport instructed webmasters to link to a page ahead of the Tube map rather than to the map itself. This allowed London Transport the possibility not only of displaying its copyright notice but of inserting any advertising material that it might choose to add in order to offset its costs in making the material available.

This request was widely discussed in newsgroups, but the general conclusion was that the request should be complied with. Some members of the discussion made reference to a case involving the Totalnews service. Their practice had two outcomes: to make it appear that the item in the frame was original content created by Totalnews when in fact it had been written by someone else, and to deprive the original author of any advertising revenue to be gained from banners on his own home page. As the *Shetland News* case described below was settled out of court in Scotland, and there has been no major UK case since, there is little UK case law (under English or Scottish law) to guide you. Reading the articles on these cases will help you to decide whether you should seek advice on your own plans.[15]

Case law continues to be made, and in the USA a San Francisco federal appeals court decided in July 2003 in favour of a search engine that had deep linked to a copyrighted photographic image.[16] The advice here, as elsewhere, is to check with your own advisers if you are in any doubt.

The unforgivable error is to link to another website in such a way that it makes it appear that the linked page is part of your site. This might be done, for example, by placing a link in a list of pages elsewhere on your website so that the visitor would be taken to another site when the link was clicked. Especially if the referring site was put together using frames, it might be impossible to tell that the work was someone else's. There have been a number of court cases in the UK that have arisen from this kind of practice. The Totalnews case mentioned above and a further case involved the *Shetland News* and the *Shetland Times*. This was heard under Scots law and settled out of court so there is still no case law to call on. What seems certain is that it falls outside acceptable practice to link to another site without acknowledgement and where the only clue is for those users who observe the linked URL very carefully. And, as the London Transport example above showed, there may well be conditions that you will have to agree to before getting permission.

Broken links that go nowhere

If you refer to other websites, make sure that you make frequent checks that the links still lead somewhere. Other people have a habit of reorganizing their sites just when you least expect it. One effect of this is that links that worked perfectly suddenly lead nowhere and users receive the 'Error 404' message to the effect that the page is unavailable. The work schedule for your site should include a weekly check on the links to other sites. Use suitable software to follow the links. On most software that allows you to download complete sites, it is possible to specify the number of levels that the software should read, so that you can instruct it to follow all the links that lead to other sites.

Remember that if links are broken it is a reflection on your own site rather than the site you failed to link to.

Who's linking to your site?

What about sites that link to your website? Are any of them sites that you would rather not have dealings with? A number of the major search engines allow you to find out who has references to your site. By prefixing the URL of your site or a particular page with the instruction *link*: in a number of search engines (try all those that support it[17]), you can obtain a listing of those sites that have an onward reference.

There are limits of course, especially if your site is popular, as there are usually limits to, perhaps, the top 200 sites in any search you make. You can find rather more than 200 sites by a number of search strategies. First, carry out the search on several engines at different times of day. Many engines carry out updates by taking part of their database offline in order to add new records, so that the same search will call up a different 'top 200' records at different times of day. Second, use one of the engines that allow you to eliminate duplicates from the same site, so that once you have found a site that links to yours you do not have to use up more of your 200 hits on pages from the same site. Third, try entering your site name rather than using the *link*: command. This time, you will hope that your site does not feature at the top of the list – since you will be looking for references to your site rather than the site itself. Then repeat the search using the URL of any major sub-sites and examine the results.

Clearly there is no point in pursuing most of the sites that refer to yours: without the links you would have few if any visitors, and they may well be links that point you out as an example of good practice. But if there are any unwelcome links, pursue the matter and attempt to persuade the webmaster to drop the link. Legal action is a costly extreme but, as the cases above show, if you have a commercial reputation you may need to take action to safeguard it. In less extreme cases, you may wish to drop a friendly note to a webmaster to point out any errors in links to or descriptions of your site.

'Deep linking' – linking to other websites at a level below the home page – has advantages and disadvantages. The advantage is that you can refer directly to information on another site without making your user navigate or search to find the details that you are linking to – perhaps on a site that has an entirely different concept of navigation to your own. But there are disadvantages too. It can appear that information is in a different place from its true location – the 'hidden links' referred to above. And the user can also be dropped into the middle of a site without any indication of who operates it and how reliable it is.

In order to deal with this problem on your own site, you may want to consider including disclaimers where this is appropriate. If you are a public supplier of information then this should be as reliable as possible and a total disclaimer may not be appropriate, but where for example the information has been supplied by third parties you may need to include a suitable statement. This could be worded in a form that gives a warning not only about liability for the content but also offering to remedy any inadvertent infringement of copyright. *As before, you should be guided by your own legal advisers who will need to ensure that your proposed wording is compatible with your organization's particular circumstances.*

Image thieves

Is one of your images or some other part of your site remarkably popular? When you examine your server logs, you may find that one page or graphic has received an unexpectedly high level of 'hits' by users. This would be particularly interesting if the rest of the page shows no sign of such activity, or if the page on your site that links to it does not enjoy the same level of interest. In the case of a single graphic, the activity is probably because someone else has incorporated your image into their site.

There are two ways of taking someone else's image and using it without their agreement. One is simply to copy it. In that case you may find your original graphics turning up somewhere else, or that onward links are constantly made to your site from unexpected quarters (perhaps from a country that you are not targeting, for example).

The other way of stealing an image is to link directly to it from within a page of code that thereby steals the image and makes it part of someone else's site. In other words, a reference to a graphic in a page of HTML will not be a link to a file on the same server but will be a full URL that calls the image from your site and inserts it into the page displayed on the user's browser.

Fortunately you stand a good chance of detecting these cheats. Many people who copy images then simply add the file to their own page with no further ado. If you use a search engine that allows searches for file names, you can look for sites that include a file with the same name as the file that you suspect has been stolen from you. You may well discover that not only is the name the same, but so is the file size and maybe even the date and time information. This is almost certain proof. You can contact the site owner directly and request that the file is removed (or perhaps that a credit is inserted referring to your site, if you prefer). If all else fails, try contacting the ISP who is hosting the offending site and ask them to take action.

Those search engines that allow you to look for specific images using a command such as *image*:[18] will help you to track down your images on other sites. Give your files unusual or random names, as these will be easier to find. There are thousands of files with titles that are somebody's name with .jpg or .gif extensions. There are fewer called 'fred_01.gif', and fewer still called 'xghfsufd.jpg'! So, a search for your randomly named file should produce very few hits and enable you to identify any unwanted users of your files. (Try a number of search engines, as they all index different areas of the web. Even if they do not offer an *image*: search command, put in the name of the file in the hope that the offending page has been fully indexed.) One other more complex method is to use software that places a watermark in your original graphic, so that it can be readily identified as your own in any dispute. Look for software that retains the watermark even when the image is processed further, for example if its dimensions are altered or if it is changed to a different file format.

You can use a similar approach to find pages that include hidden links to your site. Use the *link*: search command, or else once again enter the file name as a search. And the same courses of action are open to you as before. One other stunningly simple way of foiling the cheats is simply to rename or move the file on your own site and amend your code accordingly! This will leave a broken link on the offending page and stop your intellectual property (and your hard work) from being stolen.

Some other legal considerations

Depending where you work, you will need to take some other legal considerations into account when establishing and managing your website.

Do you want to encourage feedback from your users? One way is to provide a link that opens a mailing form addressed to the webmaster, but you may want to allow more general feedback. This will involve the use of scripts that send a message to the server for collection and analysis. You will have to decide how (and how often) you will collect messages from the server, and you also need to be sure that you protect the information so as to preserve your visitors' rights under data protection and privacy legislation (both where you are and where they are, so you should adopt best practice that is likely to stand up under any legal system). It has been reckoned that about half of the users of the web will not provide their details if they have to register in order to use a site: if you want people to register, perhaps because you are offering reports that have a commercial value, think carefully before you make visitors register to use your site. You may get better results if you only use registration or a password in order to protect high value areas such as reports, rather than the whole site.

In local and central government, you will have to consider what role the website is to play in your organization's approach to open government and freedom of information issues. Schemes under actual and proposed legislation are likely to involve extensive use of official websites in order to make information available by a wide range of public bodies. You will need to monitor a number of government websites[19] in order to keep up to date with developments and with the requirements you need to comply with.

In any organization, you will need to ensure that your site complies with data protection legislation if any kind of information about your users is collected. You have a number of duties in law that are explained on the Information Commissioner's website.[20] The implications for official sites are set out on the Information Age Government Champions' website, where the section on data protection in the corporate IT strategy provides useful guidance for all site managers whether or not they work in government. Keep a watching brief for case law in this field.

If an important part of your target audience lies in other countries, be certain to check what rules apply there.

- The French data protection website includes an extensive form that can be used to ensure that a new site or pages comply with French data protection law.[21]
- Under US law, it is not legal to collect and store personal information from minors under 13 years of age. A number of ISPs have had to change their procedures to ensure, for example, that registration forms and other pages comply with the law.

Using software to manage content

Since the first edition of this book appeared there has been a boom industry in content management (CM) software. (This is frequently referred to as CMS, confusing it with content management systems; this term refers to management methods that may well involve the use of CM software, but could equally consist of a robust management routine for handling issues like page and site updating.)

A number of large sites have used CM software for some years and there is an established market of tried and tested packages, although it remains a viable option for organizations to install bespoke systems.[22]

Systems typically not only provide the means of page creation, but allow you to ensure that editors do not overwrite each other's work, manage colours, manage images (and animation, sound and video files), expire and retire content, and to carry out various housekeeping tasks like adding or deleting pages and sections to the website.[23]

Figure 9.1 shows a composite screen grab from Kitsite, the system used by the BBC and the *Guardian*, showing the site content list and a demonstration screen with content inserted.

A good business case can be made for the use of a content management system on larger or more complex sites. Particularly where organizational changes occur (such as mergers between companies or public bodies – the pharmaceutical industry and UK central and local government are pertinent examples), it is far easier to make changes using a CMS than to unpick websites by hand.[24]

Archiving your site

Websites are frequently updated with new material so there is a choice to be made from the outset of whether you will archive all or part of the sites that you create or are responsible for.[25]

In many public sector organizations you will have a service obligation to make documents available – certainly while they are current and arguably in permanent form. In order to comply with freedom of information legislation, many documents will be published and ideally they should be made available thereafter on a website. (Remember that after an initial decision has been made to release a document under freedom of information legislation that document will be published. Later requests to view the document will be met by a claim for exemption because the document is in the public domain, so that it will make sense to put it in a place – your website – where it can be quickly retrieved in response to future requests.) Even though changes in political direction in central and local government will lead to changes in policy, it is important for historical record and research that documents issued by previous administrations are archived. Where public sector organizations close or merge, thought should be given to ensuring that the documents on the website continue

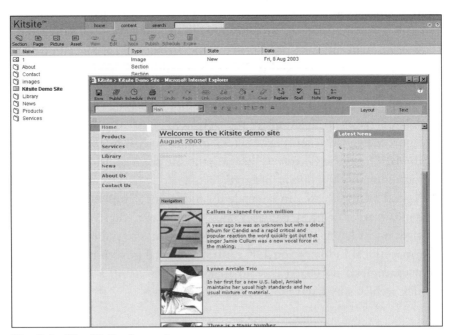

Fig. 9.1 *The Kitsite demo site*

to be available. This may be done by including them in the website of the successor organization, or by transferring the domain to the new organization and providing appropriate links from the old URL. Bearing in mind the number of links there are likely to be on the world wide web, this will be the preferable course of action for many.

There are initiatives that will help the webmaster in this task, but they should not be relied upon to provide a solution. Of particular interest is the Internet Archive or Wayback Machine, www.archive.org.[26] It states: 'The Internet Archive is building a digital library of Internet sites and other cultural artifacts in digital form. Like a paper library, we provide free access to researchers, historians, scholars, and the general public.' Based at the Presidio of San Francisco in the USA, it draws on the Alexa archive (www.alexa.com) and other sources to assemble an archive containing snapshots of websites taken on a range of dates – often the dates on which major changes were made to the sites. The work of the archive is also connected with attempts to solve the problem of broken links. One connection is with the Digital Library Project at University College Berkeley, which proposes the use of 'robust hyperlinks', with codes generated from the unique content of each web page; when entering the URL produces an error message, the code can be submitted to search engines in order to re-locate the missing page.[27]

Library and information professionals should watch for useful development and good practice in the initiatives to preserve web and other electronic resources associated with national libraries, and the work of those national record offices that are considering ways of archiving important government websites.

The existence of independent archives of websites may turn out to be useful in the event of future disputes over site content. Look again at your policy on allowing search engines robots to access and cache your site[27] if you decide to allow a full record to be kept.[28]

WEBSITES AND CURRENT PROJECTS

- Camileon (Leeds) A project to use web technology to re-digitize important resources based on early and now obsolete digital technologies (notably the BBC Domesday Disc)[29]
- Kulturaw3 A project at the Kungliga Biblioteket, the Swedish national library (www.kb.se), to collect,

preserve and make available Swedish web pages;[30] see also the NWA project

- NEDLIB The Networked European Deposit Library www.kb.nl/coop/nedlib/
- Nordic Web Access (NWA) project A project by the five Nordic countries to find principles, methods and tools to access archives of their countries' websites[31]
- Pandora (National Library of Australia) http://pandora.nla.gov.au/index.html (see Figure 9.2).

Fig. 9.2 *The PANDORA home page at the National Library of Australia website*

Discussion groups and chat rooms

If you offer the facility for your visitors to post information and comment through bulletin boards and discussion groups, you will need to take steps to advertise your own role in this process and to ensure that your visitors do not post any information that falls foul of legal requirements or your own acceptable use policy. Users of a number of discussion groups on high profile websites have been found posting obscene or racist comments. You should provide a link to your acceptable use policy in a prominent position on the page that contains the posting form, so that it is crystal clear what you expect of your visitors. You have a number of options for the manner in which visitors post information to the site and may need to change this policy if you encounter problems.

Options include:

- full moderation – users post messages to the moderator, who decides whether or not to accept them, and posts accepted messages only to the web
- registration with minimum moderation – users must be registered to post messages to the site but the moderator takes action only to remove offending messages; offenders are warned or disqualified from the group for repeated offensive postings, so that postings to the site can be monitored at regular but extended intervals, perhaps once or twice a day
- active moderation – any visitor to the site can post a message but offending messages are removed from the site as soon as possible.

The last option demands the highest level of resource to allow active intervention at any time. Remember that offensive behaviour can occur at any time of day or night, and at weekends. It can, as some site managers have found, be very embarrassing for such messages to be discovered first by journalists and others rather than by the moderator because they were posted late on a weekend night.

If you want to offer chat room facilities these questions will be particularly important. You should consider permanent moderation of chat rooms where pre-registration is not needed.

Remember that it is easy to create a string of aliases using portal sites that offer e-mail facilities, so that you may be unable to discover the identity of offensive visitors. Indeed, if you bar one IP (Internet Protocol) address or user from the site, they may well have access to other identities through which to pursue their campaign (see page 111 for an explanation of IPs). The same visitor can have differing IP addresses on each visit to your site if their ISP uses dynamic addressing, so it may be difficult to find a certain way of stopping an abuser from coming to your site. If offending messages come from a major portal such as Yahoo!, it may be possible to have the abusing identity closed down, but for many smaller services it is likely to be difficult to do this. Indeed, it is quite possible for someone to register with a service on the other side of the world to obtain an e-mail address. Your best defence is vigilance. Ask yourself whether, if you are likely to be a target for abuse, the effort of protecting yourself is worth the expected benefit from the chat or discussion facilities.

Weblogs

What if you, as website manager, were to write the entries in a discussion, providing commentary and providing links to other interesting sites and pages? This is in essence what is known as a weblog, or 'blog', and writing them has become an increasingly popular activity. They amount to a kind of diary website, where the author posts comments and links weekly, daily or several times a day, providing a combination of personal opinion and critique mixed with links that allow the reader to see what part of the web has caught the author's attention. In the LIS professional context, there are now a number of library or librarian blogs that provide links to useful resources or information about new publications and websites. See the examples provided in Figures 9.3, 9.4 and 9.5.

Blogs provide librarians with a way of providing lists of constantly updated links to web resources, and of drawing customers' attention to events or other features of library life and activities. They offer a useful way of highlighting news although care is needed where your conditions of employment insist on political neutrality, for instance in the public sector. Official blogs are probably more difficult to pull off successfully: they demand continual attention and updating, but the payoff is immediacy, and a real sense that the community is in touch with events at the library as they happen. Librarians already contribute a number of personal blogs to the web, highlighting their credentials as LIS professionals as well as bloggers. These blogs are simpler to write, but there is a danger that personal comment may be seen as having an unwanted or unpermitted bias. Library authorities should consider whether blogging should be looked at as a separate activity from website construction and provide additional guidance for those staff whose position makes them subject to restrictive rules on political activity and comment. The nature of blogging makes it more likely that rules will be inadvertently be breached through the journalistic events-as-they-happen approach adopted.

Fig. 9.3 *Peter Scott's weblog (blog.xrefer.com)*

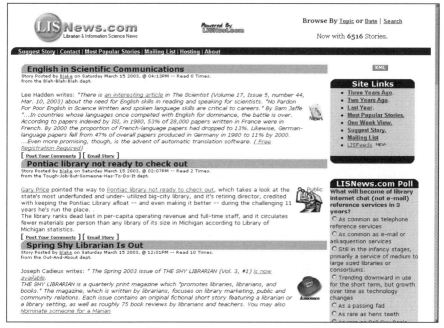

Fig. 9.4 *Librarian and Information Science News (www.lisnews.com)*

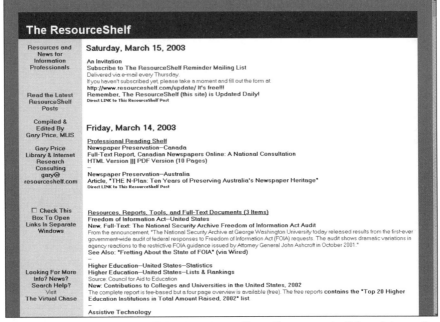

Fig. 9.5 *The ResourceShelf, by Gary Price (http://resourceshelf.freepint.com/)*

Producing blogs

Although blogs can be written simply by editing a file and republishing it for each update, there are two other routes to producing a blog. One is to host it on one of the websites that have sprung up for this purpose, the most obvious one being Blogger (blogger.com) but there are at least five other major sites that host blogs. Entering new material on these is relatively simple. Registered authors simply update their blogs online, with the site publishing it when completed. Websites like this have the advantage that they highlight sites that are frequently or recently updated, or may select an interesting blog to highlight on their own editorial pages. On the downside, the author (or the library) does not manage the server on which the blog is loaded and may be unable to deal quickly with any hack or other interference with the site. The second route, which deals with this problem to some extent, is to use blog authoring software within the organization and then to publish the result through the library's usual hosting and updating arrangements. Examples of software include Radio UserLand, although sites that provide software also like to provide content links to make their wares more sticky to the visitor.

Political blogs

Political blogs are a new phenomenon. Central and local government politicians are beginning to be aware of their potential; if the growth follows the pattern of political websites in general then we may expect a number of elected representatives to be compiling online journals within the next five years, although whether they can do this live from the debating chamber will depend on the country and the chamber in question.[32] From the library webmaster's point of view, care will be needed if the politician wants his or her blog hosted on the organization's server; rules on political neutrality probably extend to this kind of arrangement, and the politician will need to make separate arrangements. Frequent links to the library website could be seen as a good thing, but once again a view needs to be taken of the overall balance of the blog. If there appears to be a danger of readers imputing a political bias to the library's website as a result of a politician's blog, senior management needs to become involved in reaching a solution.

Enhancing the blog

An official site can provide a number of services to enhance the blog. You could, for example, offer subscribers the opportunity to receive an e-mail alert when new content is added, so that they do not miss news or comment from the library. Because the blog is visible to everyone, everywhere, it may be appropriate to add content specifically aimed at local people – perhaps even a separate thread, possibly with a password provided to library patrons.

Mobile blogging

A further development is mobile blogging, or moblogging: this is done, as the name implies, from mobile telephones, particularly 2½G and 3G models that allow photo messaging. Users upload graphics and text messages to websites in real time.[33] This gives the possibility of covering library events in real time and of allowing those using their phones for web access to receive the coverage. Although primarily a Japanese phenomenon, there are a few European moblog sites at the time of writing, and more can be expected once third generation mobile telephones become more widespread.

The use of blogs on intranets

There is little evidence yet of what should be an obvious use of weblogging, which is the use of a blog as part of an intranet to provide commentary on activities within an organization or community. Bausch, Haughey and Hourihan[34] suggest that the chronological nature of the log makes it especially suitable for meeting notes, announcements and team building activities. But it is perhaps too early for many organizations to get to grips with the potential of this technology.

If there is any drawback, it is that experience of all these types of blog suggests that – wherever they are posted – the effort of updating them is considerable, and a blog should not be embarked upon without taking full account of the time it will take.

Indexes to blogs

Indexes and gateway sites to blogs are increasingly found not just on blogging software provider sites and through search engines.[35] General sites such as Blogwise (www.blogwise.com) offer indexes organized by country or topic. These and specialist sites such as www.libdex.com/weblogs.html (which points to library weblogs) are not just a way of supplementing the search engines. They are often the only sensible way of linking to relevant weblogs, given that these are by definition text-rich, frequently metadata-rich and link-rich (as an important feature is linking to other blogs and to websites of interest to the author). The result is that standard search engines results can be flooded by links to blog pages, while adding the term 'weblog' or 'blog' to a search is a good way of achieving instant information overload.

Other novel ways of indexing are being tried out: blogs in some cities are now being indexed using maps of the transport systems, such as for Washington, DC (www.reenhead.com/map/metroblogmap.html) and for London (www.londonbloggers.co.uk) . A word of warning: maps are covered by copyright, whether it is produced by the national mapping agency or by a transport authority, and you need permission to use them as a means of navigating your website. The London Underground map is heavily protected in copyright terms, and getting the required permissions should rank ahead of the effort needed to provide hotspots that link to relevant websites.

Wikis

Blogs are closely related to another longer-standing type of website known as a wiki. These are a collaborative website writing environment where the site software allows users to create hyperlinked pages relating to those on the site, and to build a kind of online encyclopaedia reflecting the collective knowledge of the site users or members. The model could be a useful one in building organizational intranets as well as building a true sense of community on a website. But you will need to think carefully about the issues raised before launching.[36]

A cautionary tale

One activity above all is recommended to website managers: surf your site! Use the site as if you were a member of the user community looking for information. How easy is it to find what you might be looking for? Does the site talk your language or some sort of officialese? Does the search engine find the document you are looking for, or does it produce 50 candidate documents even though it was given a precise title?

Be critical. Look to see what is on the site, especially if you have as suggested given responsibility to content owners. If you have access to the root directory system, examine the time and date signatures on the files. Be suspicious of any files that bear stamps applied during late night sessions at weekends. This story, timed at 12.56 a.m. on Sunday morning, sat for several weeks on the BBC news website before it was spotted:

> Business: UK Business Summary
>
> **Enter the great Jaffa Cake debate**
> If these jam-filled concoctions were cakes they would escape the VAT. Because they are soft and not hard they were deemed to be cakes and therefore VAT free.
> But the 1974 Master of the Universe asked the VAT tribunal to exempt him because he is the Supreme Authority in the Universe and therefore he should not pay it.
> He lost his case.

Summary

This chapter has considered several essential points. You must ensure that your website complies with a number of legal requirements. You should keep your knowledge of those requirements up to date and develop the knack of knowing when to ask your legal advisers for help. You must determine the level of resource that you are prepared to contribute to regulating and moderating the site. Your answer determines how readily you can defend your own intellectual property and prevent others from making misleading links to your site, or from passing parts of it off as their own. Even without such facilities, you need to consider if and how you will preserve your site for the future.

References

1 www.peoplesnetwork.gov.uk/infra/AUPKit.rtf.

2 www.peoplesnetwork.gov.uk/infra/policies.asp.

3 Reported, for example, by Jakob Nielsen (2000) in *Designing Web Usability*, Indianapolis, New Riders, 112, 115.

4 Krug, S. (2000) *Don't Make Me Think: a common sense approach to Web usability*, Indianapolis, New Riders, especially Chapter 5, *Omit needless words*.

5 www.plainenglish.co.uk/internetcrystalmark.html; there is a charge for membership.

6 As well as Steve Krug and Jakob Nielsen, look at Hammerich, I. and Harrison, C. (2002) *Developing Online Content: the principles of writing and editing for the Web*, Chichester, Wiley; and Usborne, N. (2002) *Net Words: creating high impact online copy*, New York, McGraw-Hill. There is a range of free guidance from respected sources in the internet and IT industry, such as Sun Systems at www.sun.com/980713/webwriting/.

7 Lynch, P. J. and Horton, S. (2002) *Web Style Guide: basic design principles for creating web sites*, 2nd edn, USA, Yale.

8 www.webstyleguide.com.

9 See for example the University of Sussex Information Services guide at www.sussex.ac.uk/USIS/.

10 www.resource.gov.uk/home/namelogo.asp.

11 See www.ja.net/connect/apply_licence.html and the pages linked to it.

12 tube.tfl.gov.uk/content/tubemap/.

13 www.useit.com/alertbox.

14 Start from the page index.museum/ to reach country lists of existing registrations and the conditions for registering sites in the .museum domain.

15 www.ariadne.ac.uk/issue6/copyright/intro.html (*Shetland Times* case); Burk, D. L. (1998) Proprietary Rights in Hypertext Linkages, *JILT*, **2**, e-journal at elj.warwick.ac.uk/jilt/.

16 www.ala.org/Template.cfm?Section=Intellectual_Freedom_ Issues&Template=/ContentManagement/ContentDisplay.cfm& ContentID=25306.

17, 18 You can find out the current position from sites dedicated to search engines, for example in the table at www.searchengineshowdown.com/features/.

19 www.lcd.gov.uk/foi/datprot.htm and www.dataprotection.gov.uk. The material on the Lord Chancellor's Department website will move to www.dca.gov.uk in late 2003 or 2004.

20 www.dataprotection.gov.uk.

21 www.cnil.fr/declarer/internet.htm.

22 See for example, Rogers, C. and Kirriemuir, J. (2003) Developing a Content-management System-based Website, *D-Lib*, **9** (5), (May), www.dlib.org/dlib/may03/kirriemuir/05kirriemuir.html.

23 Grant, A. (2000) *Content Management Systems*, UKOLN, www.ukoln.ac.uk/nof/support/help/papers/cms.htm.

24 See Browning, P. and Lowndes, M. (2000) *JISC TechWatch Report: content management systems*, Techwatch report TSW 01-02, London, 2001, www.jisc.ac.uk/uploaded_documents/tsw_01-02.pdf. See also Gersting, A. (2000) Knowledge-driven Content Management, *Virtual Business*, **8**, (October), 10–12; (Andersen Consulting – now Accenture – has developed a best practice toolkit for managing content within a corporate information strategy); Hill, S. (2001) Manage Your Content on the Web, *Webspace*, **5**, (May), 32–3; [Top ten tips] Lelic, S. (2001) Knowledge at your Fingertips: developing an effective content management strategy, *Knowledge Management* (Ark Group), (March), 6–8; Mitcheson, M. (2000) Protecting your Assets: the pitfalls of intranet content management, *Virtual Business*, (October), 14–17; Sanborn, S. (2001) Content Management Moves Ahead, *InfoWorld.com*, 16 February,

www.infoworld.com/articles/hn/xml/01/02/19/010219hncmovrvw.xml.
For a summary of current issues in content management, including
the developing use of XML see Gaspar, S. (2001) Content Management Tools Automate Web Page Production, *Network World*, 19
February; www.itworld.com/App/1041/NWW0219feat2/.

25 For further information see Arms, W. Y. et al. (2001) Collecting and
Preserving the Web: the Minerva prototype, *RLG Diginews*, 15 April,
www.rlg.org/preserv/diginews/diginews5-2.html#feature1; Hakala, J.
(2001) Collecting and Preserving the Web: developing and testing
the NEDLIB harvester, *RLG DigiNews*, **5** (2), (15 April),
www.rlg.org/preserv/diginews/diginews5-2.html#feature2; Hirai, J.
et al. (2000) WebBase: a repository of Web pages. In *Proceedings of the
9th International World Wide Web Conference (WWW9)*, Amsterdam,
The Netherlands, 15–19 May, Elsevier Science,
www9.org/w9cdrom/296/296.html; Masanès, J. (2002) Towards
Continuous Web Archiving: first results and an agenda for the
future, *D-Lib Magazine*, **8** (12), (December),
www.dlib.org/dlib/december02/ masanes/12masanes.html; Rauber, A.
et al. (2002) Uncovering Information Hidden in Web Archives: a
glimpse at web analysis building on data warehouses, *D-Lib Magazine*, **8** (12) (December),
www.dlib.org/dlib/december02/rauber/12rauber.html.

26 Kahle, B. (2002) The Internet Archive: the editors' interview, *RLG
Diginews*, **6** (3) (June), www.rlg.org/preserv/diginews/
diginews6-3.html#interview.

27 news.bbc.co.uk/1/hi/sci/tech/790685.stm,
www.cs.berkeley.edu/~phelps/Robust/index2.html.

28 See www.robotstxt.org/wc/exclusion.html#robotstxt for technical
details.

29 Darlington, J., Finney, A. and Pearce, A. (2003) Domesday Redux:
the rescue of the BBC Domesday Project videodiscs, *Ariadne* , **36**,
(July), www.ariadne.ac.uk/issue36/tna/intro.html.

30 Arvidson, A. (2002) The Collection of Swedish Web Pages at the
Royal Library: the web heritage of Sweden. *IFLA, 68th General Con-
ference and Council, Glasgow, August 2002*, [proceedings], The Hague,
IFLA, www.ifla.org/IV/ifla68/papers/111-163e.pdf.

31 Brygfjeld, S. A. (2002) Access to Web Archives: the Nordic Web
Archive Access Project, *IFLA, 68th General Conference and Council,*

Glasgow, August 2002, [proceedings], The Hague, IFLA, www.ifla.org/IV/ifla68/papers/090-163e.pdf.

32 Whitford, B. (2003) Political Blogs: a brief guide, *Guardian*, 15 July. The article lists current UK political blogs; the online version www.guardian.co.uk/online/webwatch/story/0,12455,858719,00.html has links. For a useful discussion of the issues raised by permitting employees to write weblogs, see: Suitt, H. (2003) A Blogger in their Midst, *Harvard Business Review*, **81** (9), (September), 30–40.

33 Rheingold, H. (2003) Moblogs Seen as a Crystal Ball for a New Era in Online Journalism, *Online Journalism Review*, (9 July), Los Angeles, University of Southern California; Perrone, J. (2002) Weblogs Get Upwardly Mobile, *Guardian* Online supplement, 12 December, www.guardian.co.uk/online/webwatch/story/0,12455,858719,00.html.

34 Bausch, P., Haughey, M. and Hourihan, M. (2002) *We Blog: publishing online with weblogs*, Chichester, Wiley.

35 For a survey see Bradley, P. (2003) Search Engines: weblog search engines, *Ariadne*, **36**, (July), www.ariadne.ac.uk/issue36/search-engines/.

36 Godwin-Jones, B. (2003) Blogs and Wikis: environments for online collaboration, *Language Learning and Technology*, **7** (2) (May), 12–16, www.llt.msu.edu/vol7num2/pdf/emerging.pdf.

10
Your intranet

• •

This chapter examines:

- the uses of intranets in organizations and communities
- the implications of these functions to the LIS professional intranet web manager
- extranets that serve defined communities.

• •

Intranets were initially viewed as 'internal websites' when they first appeared in the mid-1990s. Since then it has become clear that they have distinct qualities that makes them central to many organizations. Intranets demand an entire book to themselves, and sure enough they have generated some, but you will notice that the technical-based literature dates from the mid-1990s while more recent books and articles about intranets focus more on their communications and organizational aspects.

This chapter looks first at the way intranets are used and considers how these affect LIS professionals; it then considers other applications such as extranets, which bring an organization and its major external stakeholders together to do business using web technology.

Why intranets?

Around the time that commercial players began to enter the internet website market, discussion began about a kind of internet website that ran entirely within an organization – the intranet. This allowed companies and other organizations to provide a range of information services to employees and others at their desks, by making use of HTML and other technologies that had recently revolutionized the internet.

The potential of intranets

Intranet models were developed by a number of expert commentators, for example Forrester Research (1996)[1] and Cap Gemini (1999).[2] A feature common to these models is the idea that intranets run in generations. The first generation intranet consists of pages where information is deposited, sometimes in order only to wither, and where users with an information requirement have to search (with or without the aid of a search engine) for any likely pages that will help them. Their search is likely to be guided by their knowledge of the organizational hierarchy, but not much else. Information may still need to be checked for accuracy and currency as it may be out of date.

The second generation intranet develops from the benefits gained through full use of the intranet, and adds additional value through shared work functions. By broadcasting information, using e-mail and push technology, and through the use of discussion groups and bulletin boards, organizations can move to a full service intranet.

In 1996 Forrester identified four elements in this stage of intranet development: e-mail, directories, file management and print management, with a fifth overarching element of network management that supported the first four. He predicted that these elements would be based on open standards by 2000, but proprietary standards remained in more common use than he had expected.

A second generation intranet becomes part of its users' normal business activities. Additional functions are built in to take advantage of this, but then development stops, and ongoing costs are for licences and maintenance rather than for creating new functionality. Many intranets remain in this stage and are now typically full of disorganized and unstructured information. Even the purchase of advanced and expensive search engines does little to deal with the problem. It also needs extensive work to configure the search engine by identifying and recording the terminology within the documents making it clear which items of information relate to one another, so that searches retrieve all relevant items. You will of course recognize this work as something that LIS professionals are excellent at doing.

In the third stage, which Forrester called the 'full service intranet' and Cap Gemini labelled 'Sell It', the intranet becomes a valuable collaborative tool. Documents can be shared and the processes of collaborative authorship streamlined through document workflow software. Papers and reports can be made available at various stages in their life cycle (with suitable caveats about how far they are complete) to reflect the current state of knowledge on a given topic of policy or research. Search engines and other software familiar from the web can be used on internal networks and (unless they are shut out of the files) locate the various versions of a given document.

The intranet can also be used as a means of distributing software and files as well as documents that contain information. Unless you have technical responsibilities that involve some kind of interaction with this software broadcasting, you are unlikely to need any detailed knowledge of the process, but the fact that this happens on your intranet may mean that it has a good capacity for transporting multimedia and other large files.

The uses of intranets
For internal communications

Internal communications departments make good use of intranets as they provide a simple means of broadcasting important messages to members of the organization. But if you are managing an intranet where internal communications messages make up a large part of the content, you should insist that there is a constant flow of material to refresh the site and that agreed standards of quality are adhered to. For example, set the requirements for readability and usability, which have been dealt with elsewhere in this book. Also set standards for information review and retirements as stale or poor quality content will deter users from visiting the rest of the site.

Internal publications are hosted on many intranets (but the contract for illustrations taken from the organization's internal newspaper must allow for their reuse in electronic media). With digital cameras in the intranet team's armoury of hardware, rapid coverage of events is possible.

To increase productivity

IT departments discovered early in the history of intranets that browser technology would allow them to provide links to software applications and workflow tools through icons on the intranet page. Especially where organizations installed multi-function portal sites, users would find the familiar desktop icons for their word processors and other programs embedded as clickable links to the software, rather than having to use a toolbar or the desktop itself.

For collaborative working

Following from the provision of workflow tools or groupware, the intranet can provide a means of displaying collaborative working tools. Typical applications of this type would allow joint authoring of documents, with these being conveniently ready for the intranet is required. Documents can be made available at various stages in their life cycle (with suitable caveats) to reflect the current state of agreement and knowledge on a given topic of policy or research. Intranets also allow collaborative online working, for example using shared whiteboards, videoconferencing, and management round-tables based on discussion group technology. This kind of application is close to Forrester's concept of the full service intranet.

In the personalized office

Browser technology, drawing on the use of cookies, allows a personalized experience. So, for example, forms on the intranet can be partly displayed pre-filled with the user's personal data. These same forms can then be submitted electronically on many intranets. Travel claims processing and stationery orders are among the transactions commonly provided on this kind of intranet. Time is saved, mail costs are reduced, and there is an electronic record from the outset. Authentication can be a problem to be resolved if workstations are used by a number of people.

In each of these four types of intranet, the LIS professional may have to lobby for sufficient room on the front page to provide links to useful services and headline information. For example, if the IT department is the main operator or intranet developer, it may be difficult to convince IT staff to invest sufficiently to provide a good search engine facility rather than a cheap or free program that came out of the box with the rest of the software. Depending on how much is to be searched, you should argue for investment in a robust search engine from the inception of the intranet. This will allow you to be confident in arguing for professional activities such as metadata management and detailed indexing of the intranet pages. With a good search engine in place you will know that items indexed by your team will be properly retrieved and ranked in order of likely significance to the user.

To give access to e-learning facilities

Intranets provide a channel to members of the user community who want access to electronic learning facilities, such as computer-based training (CBT) packages. With appropriate access controls, it is possible to provide access from the desktop to CBT facilities on the network. In this way employees can undertake training at the desk, with support being provided either by interactivity in the program, or through the organizations' internal e-mail facilities.

A number of companies produce training videos in electronic format as CD-ROMs or DVDs. Materials produced specifically for computer-based training can often be networked. Those that provide training divided into short sessions of around ten minutes' duration are good candidates since employees can often fit in a short spell of online training to complete a working morning or day. Particularly useful are those programs that leave some kind of cookie that allows the user to resume at the point where he or she left the program on the previous occasion. Other possibilities include the use of electronic training materials designed with the intranet in mind, such as the Ashridge Virtual Learning Centre, which gives access to a range of learning guides on a range of management skills, competencies and techniques. This can be accessed via the college's extranet, by loading a CD-ROM to the customer's intranet, or by replicating an area of Ashridge's machine to the customer's Lotus Domino intranet server.

Use of training materials such as these examples may dictate the resolution, colour settings and even the browser version on your network. Because the training materials refer to publications that may be in your collection, there is an opportunity for the library to provide links to the catalogue or to other information about the publications cited.

As an interface to HR intranets

In this model, the intranet builds onto where the personalized intranet described above leaves off in order to provide an interface between the organization's human resources function and the employee. In the simple version, the staff manuals are loaded. In the most advanced version, the employee uses a personal password to gain read (and perhaps limited write) access to HR databases such as personal records of office location, home address, educational achievements and so on.

Sharing intranet space with functions like this, and coping with the safeguards necessary to ensure that your services do not compromise the security of confidential information, is likely to be a difficult business. Nonetheless it may be the only way to get the enterprise-wide exposure needed.

Intranets and the library and information service

Then there are the services that the LIS itself can offer. There are a number of obvious advantages for an information and library service that has access to the parent organization's intranet. It can publicize its services to its user community through a variety of pages, some of them generally static (such as opening hours and details of key staff) and some of them refreshed more frequently (such as details of new additions to stock or a journal alert listing service). Other information providers in the community are likely to be doing the same, for example by producing pages to describe the functions of their teams. However, the LIS can release more time for value added work by placing basic information and frequently asked questions on the intranet.

An intranet can assist the information professional to develop document delivery services, although licensing issues must be carefully examined – in the UK recent developments in copyright licences make this easier, although licences are still for document delivery and not document storage as many libraries would prefer. Documents can be delivered to remote printers alongside users' work stations, either as a result of their own searches, or through the action of a researcher or librarian following an electronic search of the digital library and remote databases. Network fax and e-mail offers the possibility for externally sourced copies to be delivered to the network – although care is needed to ensure that the network will accept attachment files from beyond the fire-wall. Selective dissemination of information services can provide abstracts and article summaries by e-mail, or order bulletins to be printed at the user's terminal, and the intranet allows the direct posting of the results of research on electronic databases.

The library can gave access to its catalogues or to other information sources on the intranet. In some cases the catalogue or other bibliographic database will be connected directly to the network and interrogated in real time by the query software; in others, regular output will take place from the database to a file that is available to the intranet, but any changes made since that output will not be picked up.

Of particular value could be a service to provide links to sites that have been evaluated and checked to a stated professional standard, allowing users to be confident in the quality of the information they retrieve. These are often described, not totally precisely, as information portals, whether or not they contain features such as a search engine.

Intranet portals

A growing trend is for the central intranet of large organizations to become a portal site, that is, one that provides a range of links to other sites inside or outside the organization. In some cases there are links to dozens or even hundreds of smaller intranet sites, which are managed and edited at section level within the community.

This is a practical approach. It avoids the need for a single, central team who edit the entire intranet, placing responsibility instead on different sections to create and maintain content, and focusing central effort on providing accurate links in the portal, some central editorial content and liaison with the technical team that make the system work. This approach was taken at General Motors to tackle the complexity of the intranet that would otherwise need to be edited.

Portals can be used to provide a consistent approach to the information content of an intranet and to get users accustomed to following links to the information that they want. Forrester Research advocates a two-stage plan: the organization of information content and then the addition of collaboration tools and other advanced function. In the first phase, navigation is simplified by better organization of content and improved search facilities. A single point of access is created that gives users access to all subject content without repeatedly logging in to other servers. Common standards are created for publishing and content is tailored to users' needs. Much of this work can involve information and library professionals. Their contribution only narrows in the second phase of the project, where network access is given to document workflow and other tools alongside information services on the same portal. They then continue to manage the information content as before, while users can now use that content directly, for example by cutting and pasting details into documents in the workflow area of the intranet.[3]

Bear in mind that on an intranet it is possible to arrange links to sites of commercial interest to your organization without the danger of a competitor becoming aware of either the topic, or the grouping or the selection of sites offered. Information can be provided on an intranet that may be more sensitive in nature than might be released to the internet, subject to protecting information where necessary through the use of passwords or other security measures, and ensuring that legal requirements such as data protection regulations are complied with.

Library and information services staff are often responsible for arranging the supply of external news feeds and other information resources on intranets. If the network includes a search engine it may be possible to configure it to search internal and external sites simultaneously and to return a single ranked list of results.

It is sensible for the library to compile and maintain information databases. Database entry is a familiar task to the cataloguer while, as with internet web pages, the addition of metadata will ensure rapid retrieval of relevant entries in a search. Other kinds of information can be added, for example copies of graphics and other intellectual property in visual form owned by the organization showing the terms for use and the licences that have been granted. Research results can be shared, as can information about particular sites or equipment. Product information can be made available to all community members, or consultancy results and hints can be provided for reference.

The knowledge management intranet

A frequent consequence of introducing an intranet is that users begin to complain or information overload. Whereas they may have been used to receiving a few printed documents from time to time and having a directory that was updated every quarter, they now have access to the entire range of the organization's documentation. Because it is difficult to scan and compare documents on the average office screen, they will consume reams of paper in printing off whole documents where they would previously have been content with photocopies of two or three of the most pertinent pages from the circulating paper copy. Web technologies make it easy to publish, but provoke users into creating massive downloads and printouts, largely on the off-chance that they might be useful. The LIS staff have an important role to play in teaching good information management behaviour, including how to search the intranet effectively, and how to identify materials to benchmark information contained on the intranet to ensure its currency and accuracy. Knowledge management (KM) has become a vast subject that is beyond the scope of this book, but many of the published works on KM identify the important role of intranets in managing an organization or community's fund of knowledge.[4] The combination of search tools already familiar to librarians and information scientists and the skills such as indexing that are part of their professional stock-in-trade will greatly assist the average organization to cope with the volume of information it produces and to manage its knowledge content.

As with internet website pages, there are likely to be questions of document ownership, and of the responsibility for maintaining the accuracy of intranet pages. An editorial team is likely to be faced with constant demands to update information that proves to be out of date, and each out-of-date page reduces the overall credibility and value of the intranet. Library bulletins and other information must be continually updated and, from the site management viewpoint, page owners should be in no doubt that they are responsible for upkeep.

LIS professionals have been increasingly involved in knowledge management intranet development in recent years. The KM intranet provides an amalgam of different types of intranet, for example collaborative working and the information portal. The features that can be incorporated are many, and the number continues to expand as software houses and intranet developers continue to look for 'killer' applications. A KM intranet is likely to include some or all of these features.

Communities of interest

Groups with a common interest can be brought together, for example if they are working on related issues in different offices or sections. The libraries within an organization can provide a single virtual presence even if they are widely spread across a number of campuses, or the offices of a company around the country. Forms and e-mail allow users to route enquiries to the most appropriate expert section, rather than their being restricted to dealing with the site librarian who may need to conduct a reference interview before making contact with a subject expert in another library and passing the information at one remove through a second, and consequently imperfect, interview by telephone. Libraries and information services in multinational companies can establish a 24-hour service by aligning the hours of professional service across the libraries in different countries.

Other similar communities of interest can be provided for researchers, particular groups of specialists (chemists, social workers, engineers or whoever).

Discussion groups

These are frequently found on intranets, where they offer a kind of informal collaborative work area. Ideas can be exchanged on a variety of topics, although some moderation may be required to ensure that postings do not stray too far off topic, and perhaps to ensure that they are about topics related to the organization or community.

Discussion groups are often managed using a list server, operated using the same software that runs many internet mailing lists. A number of freely available software packages are widely used, notably Majordomo (for Unix servers), LISTSERV and Listproc.[5] As an alternative, some web editing and site management software (FrontPage and ColdFusion, for example) include the forms and other routines that add postings to discussion groups and add details to the indexes of the group's documents.

Search facilities

Obvious perhaps, but search engines and other software familiar from the web can be used on internal networks and (again, with the correct permissions) locate the various versions of a given document. There is considerable potential for the library and information service to be involved in developing the use of the engines, as well as supporting the management of the versions, ensuring that the most accurate, authoritative and recent version of a document is located when search terms are entered.

There is a growing body of evidence about the importance of LIS professional skills in this sphere. The technical skills found in converged or hybrid library services (where the IT function and the library come together somewhere around the library computer room to develop a particular combination of library technology activities) are of great value in knowledge management. LIS professionals can use their skills in metadata application to ensure that content is easy to organize and retrieve. They can use their technical skills to create the technical structures, be that hardware, software or XML coding. And, not least, LIS professionals can apply their understanding of knowledge flows and information requirements in the organization to ensuring that the intranet meets those needs through its combination of functionality and content.[6]

Some other intranet facilities
Electronic forms

Forms can be used to query databases, or to provide an interface to search engines that can interrogate news feeds from a number of the familiar database providers or from news organizations. Applications familiar from the internet, such as newsgroups, can be provided for the internal community using the intranet. And forms used to interrogate these. (Note that we also looked above at the use of forms to carry out administrative routines such as ordering of supplies.)

Internal trade

A number of intranets provide facilities to order internal supplies, such as stationery supplies from an online catalogue. In the extranet model, lists of products can be available to customers sharing the supplier's intranet and, if security permits, download ordering guides and interactive online order forms. At a more mundane level, interactive forms can be used to order refreshments.

Acceptable use policies for intranets

Unwanted postings can be as much of a nuisance on internal systems as they are on the web. Going heavy-handed to the employees or community members causing the problem may not succeed, even if the web team has any management authority to discipline them. Cutting off access to an intranet for troublesome community members is a rather counter-productive measure, so other forms of persuasion are needed.[7]

Your acceptable use policies should prevent people from posting commercial material (or at least posting it twice). You may have to be ruthless, and if you are going to allow members of staff to publicize their bring-and-buy sales of handicrafts, you must be very clear whether this also allows people to advertise their relatives' motor repair businesses, or whatever quasi-domestic business they may have. Your best course of action is to suggest that worthy or charitable causes stick to local notice boards, and that you have a simple, understandable policy: no commercial messages. In any case, if your organization is on more than one site, most users will be at best uninterested and at worst annoyed by such messages.

You should be particularly clear that posting chain letters is an unwelcome activity, although many are dressed in clothes that the web user will more readily recognize than many other colleagues. Some are plausible, and even originate in good faith.

In 1999, an e-mail message circulated widely from a North American containing a warning about an allergic medical condition associated with a particular range of healthcare products. Although the message could be authenticated, it alleged in effect that the brand was potentially unsafe. Users passed on the message, as they were encouraged to do by the signatories of the article, but it could well have been the subject of a legal case had the manufacturer or its local subsidiary found the article. Many more messages to bulletin boards are the get-rich-quick variety, which should be barred from your system.

Managing your intranet

As with managing your internet site, you will need to consider what central resources to supply for the management of your intranet. If a central support group is to be provided, decide whether it will be the same group that supports the internet site, or whether it will need different skills such as knowledge of additional software or other technical tools. Will the same guidelines apply as to your internet website, or will you need additional guidance? You may wish, for example, to lay down rules about using the intranet for commercial activities, or to deal differently with harassment or unsuitable content. You might want to set out a policy on dealing with misleading or outdated content; after all, you can put a caveat on your external-facing sites to the effect that your information should be checked before use, but this could be inappropriate for your intranet, which should always be current if it is to become a trusted tool. Do you need a quality assurance section? You certainly need the power to remove poor quality or dangerous information.

The business benefit of having an intranet

Intranets are frequently presented as an instant creator of business savings, because of the economies that can be made by placing directories and procedures manuals on the network. Thus, the first year savings typically show thousands of per cent return on the investment. This is deceptive for two reasons. First, because no other applications can generate such large savings, it is difficult or impossible to grow further savings of this magnitude. While the print and paper savings continue year on year, a static intranet offers no further large-scale savings by converting other applications to HTML. Second, further investment will be needed to realize additional savings, for example through the use of collaborative workgroup software or document management programs. Your vision for the intranet therefore needs to incorporate a path for the development of benefits, and some indication of the difference that it will make in the organization.

Intranets certainly do produce business benefit, but not on the scale suggested by many early writers. A full business case would need to cover the cost of software, network licences and staff resources. The case will project the likely growth of the network, in terms of users, documents, servers and storage. As the network grows, it is likely to need to call material from legacy systems, so a range of IT platforms will be needed and quite probably be the means of translating documents from earlier file formats. For example, there are likely to be large numbers of Wordstar documents in many older systems. If there is to be a link to external systems, a firewall or firewalls will be needed to protect the intranet from incoming degradation and attack. The bandwidth both within the internal network and of the link to the external network must be sufficient for the expected volume and type of traffic (for example will there be heavy use of audio or video multimedia files?). All of these technical issues have costs associated with their solution.

How is business benefit is to be measured? Will it be by a smaller number (or proportion) of incorrect decisions made as a result of using out-of-date information? How will you know? Will there be a financial payback, even if that is only savings in paper? Is the true cost of the webmaster and the web team represented – including the cost of training and any 'golden handcuffs' to make the team members remain in their posts? Some savings will be unquantifiable – it is impossible to set a price on more efficient information seeking behaviour, although the cash value of a saving of just ten minutes a month for every employee is surprisingly large.

Finally, never underestimate the cost of maintenance. The basic cost of the intranet will be added to by the need to maintain and develop the system, pay licence fees and salaries, and to process and add documents. Some estimates reckon that 50% of the original investment will have to be found each year to maintain the intranet.

Application service providers

Leased access to software is now widely purchased through an application service provider. This access can be provided from an intranet, using a secure link to a third party website where authorized users from the organization can have access to specialist software without the need to install it on the intranet itself. Sun provides access to competitive analysis software; however, this system could work for any package where the cost of installation across the network is not justified and where a few users (but not always the same few users) at a time need simultaneous access. The software need not be installed on the intranet but input to it and the results are transmitted through the intranet and internet to the software house.

Clearly this requires firewall settings that allow some transactions to and from the ASP computer. The services may be paid for, but there are also some free services such as the Atomz search engine. Before allowing services such as this to have access to your sites, consider whether the savings are outweighed by the risk, and act accordingly.

Extranets

An extranet is an area of an intranet where trusted third parties, such as customers or agencies, have access to information through a secure link or firewall. This allows these third parties to have access to information targeted, for example, at major users of your service, such as academic and other staff working away from campus, councillors, etc.

Providing an extranet for customers or stakeholders is becoming increasingly common, with perhaps as many as 20% of business organizations providing one. An extranet allows your partners to enjoy secure connection to your information, ordering systems and other features of your intranet – or perhaps to areas specially designed for extranet users rather than giving full access to the employee intranet.

There are likely to be issues of security – to ensure that it is not possible to hack in to your system or gain access to areas not intended for clients to use – and of intellectual property management, to ensure that rights to use images, documents and other material are not exceeded by providing access beyond what has been licensed.

Before deciding whether to take a hand in extranet development, assess what information the library service holds that will be of use to your organization's external stakeholders and would not be available to them on an internet website. There is likely to be only a small amount of material that falls into this category: judge whether the return for your involvement is likely to be worthwhile.

It is more likely that you will reach the decision that you should participate if the extranet is one of the public sector extranets that, confusingly, regards themselves as intranets. The Government Secure Intranet in particular can be regarded not only as government's intranet but also as an extranet for each of the contributing organizations.[8] So too for intranetworks in the health service, criminal justice system, and so forth. In each of these cases, other organizations on the networks can be seen as customers or stakeholders for any given member. Many of the security issues have already been taken care of in technical architecture. Issues of document security have also been dealt with since a conscious decision needs to be taken to publish material to the intranet, so proper publication procedures should ensure that rights in the published material are safeguarded.

Summary

This chapter has seen that while at one level the intranet is a kind of internal website, it has far greater potential as its use develops. Starting with static replication of external-facing web pages, it can develop dynamic, personalized content and evolve into a tool that allows collaborative working as well as instant access to current information. There is an important role for LIS professionals from the early stages onwards. Even when more complex network functions are added, the ready availability of information through the content-based areas of the intranet guarantee that it has a continuing role.

Intranets have reached a kind of stability now that their role is better understood. Read the literature and follow the weblogs and other websites that provide up-to-date information, as these will give you a better grasp on a topic where much of the published literature remains in print several years after publication, and where there is a lot of theory, less business evidence, and little enough in the way of best practice to follow.

References

1   Pincince, T. J. (1996) *The Full Service Intranet*, USA, Forrester Research Inc.

2   Cranfield University, Knowledge Development Centre (1999) *Intranet Benchmarking and Business Value: the Cap Gemini/Cranfield intranet study – summary report*, London, Cap Gemini UK.

3   Walker, J. (1999) *Building an Intranet Portal*, USA, Forrester Research.

4   See for example Chapter 7, Technologies for Knowledge Management. In Davenport, T. and Prusak, L. (1998) *Working Knowledge: how organizations manage what they know*, USA, Harvard Business School Press.

5   Detailed information is in Schwartz, A. (1996) *Managing Mailing Lists: Majordomo, LISTSERV, Listproc and SmartList*, USA, O'Reilly.

6   Stoddart, L. (2001) Managing Intranets to Encourage Knowledge Sharing: opportunities and constraints, *Online Information Review*, **25** (1), 19–29.

7   Schwartz, A. and Garfinkel, S. (1998) *Stopping Spam: stamping out unwanted e-mail and news postings*, USA, O'Reilly.

8   Cumming, M. and Cuthbertson, L. (2001) Wired in Whitehall: a survey of internet and intranet use in government, *Aslib Proceedings: new information perspectives*, **53** (1), 32–8.

11

Developing your website

● ●

This chapter examines:

- how to update websites
- some ways of monitoring the site
- how to get feedback from your users
- how to stay at the leading edge
- when to give your site a makeover or a rebuild.

● ●

Keeping your website up to date

Would you rely on last week's newspapers for your news, or to form your view of the world? Would you be confident that you had not missed anything important? Of course not. Major world events happen in moments, and news reports are close behind.

Your website is no different. If it contains any kind of topical content, it needs to be kept up to date. Websites that LIS professionals are likely to be involved in running may well contain data of this sort. It could be news or it could be product information. News of a library exhibition that you would like your patrons to visit or information about a fines amnesty are both types of information that need to be current and accurate. It will be a considerable disappointment to a web visitor to read details of something interesting, only to find that it has been superseded, or to discover that your offer has expired when he or she arrives with your heavily overdue books.

There are a number of different ways that your website can disappoint in this respect.

- Far too many sites have pages with a 'last revised' date that is months old. Is the information still current, or have you forgotten to remove out-of-date details?

  Remedy: Make sure that every page has a note at the bottom giving the date the text was last revised. Even if information is still current, change the date at least once a month (or at a sensible interval for your business) to assure the visitor that the page has been checked recently. Personal pages can probably be left for longer, but their already lower credibility is further diminished if they appear to be out of date. Set up a routine to scan the site at regular intervals – perhaps monthly – to check that no pages are more than an agreed age. The owners of outdated pages should then be contacted to either update or remove the pages. Challenge owners who revise dates but never content, asking them to show why the page has not changed and justifying the continuing need to publish the page.

- Check that pages do not contain references to past events that make it appear that they are outdated – for example references to things happening 'after Christmas' or 'this summer' when it is nearing winter. Which year would these be? Leaving information on a website that refers to an exhibition that has closed gives the impression that other information around it is also suspect. That is especially true if you choose to put all information on events and promotions onto a single web page.

  Remedy: Keep a record of all the pages that contain time-limited information, so that you make sure to visit them and remove expired details and links. Set up a rolling programme of checks to ensure that you do not inadvertently abandon pages of old announcements. If your editorial software supports this feature, make sure that you have not left orphaned pages lying about your site with old details on them. And consider whether you should set editorial guidelines that advise on using phrases like 'this Christmas', which will avoid the semantic problems described here.

- You may cause confusion if the title field or some of the hidden fields contain date information that does not relate to the document itself. *Remedy*: Be sure that you are not using a template or a copy of another page that creates inaccurate date information in the metadata or elsewhere.

There is a particular problem if your pages are refreshed frequently. A news site may issue three or four different versions of a page each day, and even the details of community events can alter if times, dates, venues or organizers are changed. You will need to make certain that your system issues the right version, and you may need to make archive copies of the different versions.

Database driven web pages

Archiving is more difficult but creating timely content is generally easier if you create this kind of dynamic content from a database. Instead of typing reams of HTML code into your pages, you need only type the text that the viewer will see into the database. The software creates the page 'on the fly', that is, it generates the page image whenever it gets a request from a user. To do this it reads the latest version of the story or other information that you have placed on the database to form the record requested. This information is then pasted into the code that will generate a page image when it reaches the browser.

This database approach to creating web pages is the only way that many sites cope with large volumes of ever changing stories. The person who enters the information onto the database does not need to be an expert in HTML, or indeed to know any, because the system creates the entire page around the plain text that is typed or pasted in.

You can find sample versions of a number of database systems on the cover discs of computing magazines. Complete versions of some older versions are often made available, so that you can try out the technique before committing to a full-scale exercise or employing a specialist contractor to create a database for you.[1]

Ignore updates at your peril

Other parts of this book have stressed the importance of marketing your site. You will have submitted details to various search engines and quite possibly spent both time and money in promoting your site. You can destroy all this effort by failing to update the information. Visitors to your site will discover that the information is old; not only will they stop coming to visit, but they will start to use other sites that they consider more reliable. Any kind of recognition that you have earned for your site will be eroded as word gets around that it has become stale and tired, and this erosion will continue if the virtues of your rival sites are then discussed. Be thorough in your updating and do not leave any pieces of abandoned code around the site, especially if they contain date information!

Check information on each page in a rolling programme and change the date of the page each time you check. If individual items of information on a page contain time sensitive information, put a date against those too. Some information is relatively static (such as details of public transport services) and remains constant between changes on given dates. Links to relatively static and long-term information such as copies of maps or timetables, which normally change only twice or three times a year do not need a visible date on the screen once it is known they are current (although including a date may make things simpler for validating some sorts of information). But details of particular events such as the opening of a new route or fare changes do have dates against them, to give warning to the public.

One last tip – watch copyright dates, which are often tucked away at the bottom of the page. Make sure that they are aligned with changes in the calendar year. If you like to put a range of years at the bottom of a page to show how long it has been there (© 1997–2003), then update your pages at the start of each year. This kind of thing is much better done with templates in your web editing software, or you can set up your database driven pages to show the latest date.

Monitoring your site

How many sites have you visited that include one of those counters that inform you that you are 'visitor number x' to that particular site? Do they make you think how popular the website is, or wonder why anyone would bother to advertise such a small number of visits? And have you ever refreshed the page, to see whether or not the website can detect that the same person has come back?

If you said 'yes' to any of these questions, then you are already likely to be wondering what value such features could possibly have on your site. The answer may be: not much. Knowing the number of visitors to your site is not much use if they can fix the counter to make it over-register. You need a routine that does better than that, probably by placing cookies on your visitors' computers.

But wouldn't it be even better to know where your visitors came from and how long they stayed? Better still, what did they look at? Do visitors stay on one page for a long time? Once you have started to answer these and similar questions, you can start looking for some reasons, and either improve your best practice or else do something to try to put the bad things right. You can find much of this out from the website log, compiled using software such as WebTrends.[2]

Opinions have begun to vary on the value of the level of detail that is available from website logs. Some operators find it useful to know how visitors have moved through the site: the trail could show that there are problems with the navigation, or that most people abandon the site at the same page, suggesting that there is a problem to be overcome (or that this may be the site that contains all the essential information, with the result that people can leave your site fully satisfied!). Others argue that there are so many ways to navigate the average site, especially a large site, that the effort of analysing the logs is wasted since they say nothing useful. For many operators the truth lies somewhere between these two extremes. The level of detail that web analysis software can produce is mind-numbing in its sheer volume; however, judicious use of the high level detail (particularly numbers of unique visitors and the identity of the most visited pages) can provide exactly the sort of evidence that senior stakeholders consider to be the evidence that convinces them of the value of the organization's web presence.

Keeping up with change

The problem in keeping up with change is that there is too much of it and that there is too much advice available to you. But you and your webmaster need to know what is happening in the world of the web in order to decide if you are going to incorporate the latest developments into your site.

The best way of keeping up with the web is by using it. There are many newsletters and other information digests that are made available by companies and individuals who have made their home on the web as media commentators and pundits of the new cyber-frontier. Their newsletters and bulletins are available at a range of frequencies from daily to monthly, either as e-mail bulletins or by regular posting to a website. When issues appear less frequently than this, the web can have moved on considerably and the news content will be out of date – although any commentary may of course still be perfectly valid.

Just like printed news sources, the style varies considerably and the type of content varies depending on the frequency of the bulletin. Expect that a daily bulletin will bring you breaking news stories and discussion of current key issues to do with the internet. There may also be features sections containing further valuable details and guidance, but these are secondary to the daily commentary. Among the best examples are the *Anchordesk* written by David Coursey (and Jesse Berst before him) for ZD-Net and the *Webreference Update Newsletter*. Both now have half a decade of comment and experience behind them. You may well discard much of these bulletins but they repay the few minutes needed to scan the daily issues. They are properly edited e-journals with good journalistic values as well as a balance (different in each case) between the technical and business aspects of working the web. Weekly, fortnightly and monthly bulletins generally have a different style and can be more considered. They tend to behave more like ordinary websites, with extensive links to relevant stories rather than reference to another part of the day's news. Their commentators can often take a longer view of issues and offer advice and good practice guidance as well as news. These sites produce a quality of editorial content that rivals magazines taken from the news-stand. Some of the best of this breed include the long-standing fortnightly *Alertbox* written by Jakob Nielsen of the Nielsen Norman Group, and the CIO series of magazines supported by a range of sub-sites that have specialist content (such as 'web professional', 'extranet' or 'intranet') updated at fortnightly intervals and a general site updated daily. At a different level, considerable value can be had from British resources that are produced on a more modest scale. Among these are the *Internet Resources Newsletter* produced at Heriot-Watt University, the *Free Pint* newsletters and *Ariadne*, which appears four times a year. Ideas on the development of the web can be gleaned from a range of knowledge management publications and newsletters, some of which are listed in the references to this chapter.

You need to stay in touch with the web in order to learn about its progress. All the above newsletters are full of links to other parts of their parent sites, and to the sites that the writers describe in their articles. Unlike a bibliography on a printed article, the references on a web journal are live! When the commentator describes a new website, you can go and take a look. You can follow through comments about, for example, the difference between the Flash and non-Flash versions of a website by simply clicking on the link. You can often find out (from the source code) which software was used to compile the site, and compare the design with your own site. You will never understand the experience of a visitor to your site if you do not constantly visit other people's and note what you like and dislike while you are there.

New web technologies

Your plans need to include a policy on which technologies you are going to include on your site and which you will ignore. The use and take-up of new technologies has been littered with casualties. Web TV has not yet reached the level of market penetration that was forecast; this has implications for social inclusion, since this was predicted to be the way that the excluded social groups would gain access to the world wide web. Portable telephones using Wireless Application Protocol (WAP) have turned out to be an interesting use of technology, but again the limitations of the technology have prevented it from becoming a mass market application in the way that mobile telephone companies had wished. However, as noted in the section on weblogs, there is evidence that third generation mobiles are being successfully used in Japan (and, slowly, elsewhere) to upload pictures to moblogs (mobile weblogs), and there continues to be a limited market for access to simple information using WAP protocols. A range of handheld computer devices under the generic title of PDAs – personal digital assistants – are being used to access a range of specialist services, primarily financial data and related sites. These require you to produce stripped down versions of your web pages that need tailoring specifically to the device that you are addressing. All of these technologies allow you to provide users with a condensed version of your lowest resolution page, but you can imagine that the restrictions imposed by the display capabilities of these devices limit you to a very basic page. It's even possible to use games consoles as a means of accessing information services[3] but this must be seen as a limited application and unlikely to be justifiable in terms of making a business case for investing resources in this platform. But use of cross-platform markup language such as XML may make it cost-effective for you to re-purpose information for these devices; you may have information that lends itself to this kind of treatment.

These systems have yet to achieve critical mass. It remains to be seen whether the advent of third generation mobile telephones can create the conditions where user demand makes these services economically viable. Current content is limited but already includes news services,[4] while the nature of the mobile telephone networks means that services that can make use of information about the user's geographic location will be particularly attractive. The technology makes it possible to offer services giving directions to your nearest service point based on the enquirer's co-ordinates – and that information could well be provided to you automatically by the telephone network rather than the user having to enter this data.

Summary

New formats now allow web pages to be transmitted to a variety of display devices. These services probably continue to fall outside your immediate concerns, but your website management strategy should include a commitment to review the state of new web technologies such as these at regular intervals, and to decide whether to accommodate them in your offerings. The fact that these technologies have proved so slow in taking off does not mean that sites are wedded to HMTL for the rest of time.

You should also consider whether users of your intranet and extranet are likely to access the system using devices other than personal computers. If so you will need to duplicate the information that you supply in these formats on those networks or devise suitable new content.

References

1   For a case study see Gardner, M. and Pinfield, S. (2001) Database Backed Library Websites: a case of the use of PHP and MySQL at the University of Nottingham, *Program*, **35** (1), 33–42.

2   www.netiq.com/webtrends/default.asp: for other possibilities see the list at dir.yahoo.com/Computers_and_Internet/software/internet/

world_wide_web/servers/log_analysis_tools/.

3   Kirriemuir, J. (2001) Accessing Electronic Information Sources Through Computer Games Consoles, *Aslib Proceedings*, **53** (2), 23–31.

4   In March 2000, the *Economist* began an online edition for Palm Pilot and Windows CE handheld computers, see www.economist.com/email/#MobileEdition and AvantGo.com; and IBM launched a new product, WebSphere Transcoding Publisher, to filter existing data for transmission to mobile terminals, see www-3.ibm.com/software/pervasive/products/mobile_sols/ transcoding_publisher.shtml.

12

Golden rules of web page content

These guidelines were welcomed by readers of the first edition, but there are still plenty of examples of commercial sites that do not observe them. They are largely common sense, but can make considerable difference to your readers' experience of your site, and their willingness to visit you again.

The golden rules

Branding

Make it clear on every page who owns the site, include your corporate brand if you have one, and link back to your home page on every page. Sites 'deep link' to any relevant page of a website, not necessarily to the home page. Too many sites still brand the home page; after that you could be anywhere. Make the website consistent. There should be an overall look and feel, even if you need to differentiate pages about different parts of your community – by using different background colours with a common page design for example. Cascading style sheets (CSS) offer a simple way to ensure this consistency for the newer browsers but do not absolve you from designing the site properly for all your visitors!

Content

Who's it for?

Don't fill a page for the general public with things you need a degree in computing to understand. Don't talk down to fellow professionals wanting to consult your catalogue on line. And remember, it's not your bosses who use your website, it's your customers. Design for your customers and use words they understand. Nobody is much interested in your organizational structure – let them find out who to call with their enquiry, not how big a cheese that person is.

Content

Keep it fresh

Keep it fresh and keep them coming back. Make sure your 'What's New' page has things on it that are new now. Make sure every page has two dates on it – the date it was last refreshed and the date it becomes obsolete. Make sure your pages never get to the second date. Say whose page each one is and if appropriate provide a mailto: link so users can get in touch.

Graphics

Make them small and make them count

If you must have big graphics, make a thumbnail version and put that on your page instead with a link to the big, slow-loading image. Only serious web users have broadband, so design for the majority of your customers not the web enthusiasts. If your home page has more than around 20Kb of images on it, people will start getting bored while they load.

Name that picture

Make sure that you put something intelligible in the ALT text field. Never mind the file name: what's in the picture? And shame on you if you leave the ALT text field empty, or allow FrontPage to leave asterisks there – users of screen readers will have no idea why the image is there, or what it does.

Don't be as annoying as everyone else

The 'under construction' image is the most hated item on the web. If you haven't finished it yet, don't make it a page. Leave the link out and tell people you're working on it. It's their telephone calls you are wasting here, and in Europe that means money too.

Be safe with colour

If you are designing a corporate image or other graphic that depends on a particular shade of colour, make sure you choose one of the 'browser safe' colours that will reproduce accurately. Recent computers with 24-bit displays can show over 16 million different colours whereas those earlier machines still in use can only display 256 shades. So unless your colour is one of those 256 colours, the browser cannot display it accurately on any but the most recent machines. In order to handle this, select your colours from one of the many lists on the web. As not even all the 256 shades are available because the designers of Windows reserved some, and the creators of Netscape reserved a few more, there is a limit of 216 shades that are certain to display accurately on all platforms.[1] For more information visit www.webreference.com/dev/graphics/palette.html, or a useful page on the IFLA site, www.ifla.org/I/training/colour/colour.htm.

Links

Check them

You cannot check your links too often. Users dislike getting the '404' message. If your site has too many broken links, people will stop visiting you.

Identify them

Use alternative texts not only to provide floating captions to images, but to indicate where the links go to. This helps users to assess the value of the links quickly and decide whether to follow them.

Page design

Design for the web

Design for the web, not the printed page. Break the document into two screenfuls of information at a time, maximum. Every survey of typical web users shows that half of the sample doesn't know you can scroll down to read what's under the bottom line of the screen. If your page is more than 30Kb including all the graphics, it's probably too big. web pages do not have columns – only printed pages do that. (Do you truly recommend scrolling up and down a page to read the columns?)

Make it easy to navigate

Don't hide the links in the middle of chunks of text – highlight them. Use buttons or a navigation strip. Make sure that people who don't use graphics can navigate, so provide a link to a text-only page or ensure that your script will detect a text browser and display appropriate information.

Schools – an extra golden rule

On a school site (or any sites concerned with young people), protect the identity of students and above all do not publish personal information, names, e-mail addresses or photographs of individual children. If you are collecting information from the USA, this is a legal requirement under the Children's Online Privacy Protection Act of 1998,[2] so companies like AOL ensure they no longer collect information from children under 13 – but do you really need to collect more than very basic data anyway? Look at the current web-based campaigns to improve children's safety on the internet and apply those standards wherever possible, even if they are not legally mandatory among your audience.[3] Figures 12.1 and 12.2 show examples of two of them.

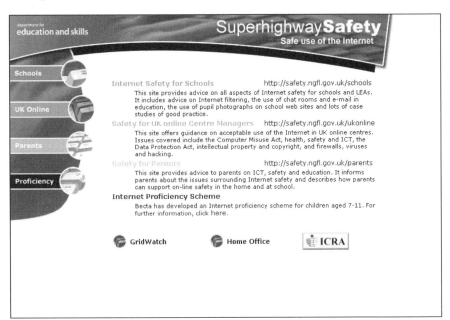

Fig. 12.1 *The UK Government's Superhighway Safety site (safety.ngfl.gov.uk)*

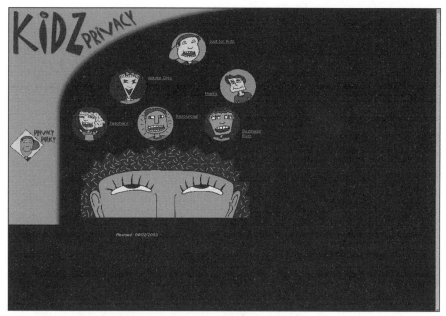

Fig. 12.2 *The US Government's Kidz Privacy site (www.ftc.gov/bcp/conline/edcams/kidzprivacy/index.html), provided by the Federal Trade Commission*

Screen size

Don't design for people with 19-inch high resolution screens. Try out your page on a 14-inch screen fed from a 486-based PC, and then try it with a Mac. If you don't like what you see, nor will your users. If you put pictures on the right hand side, see if they're still there on small screens. If you rely on those pictures to navigate the page, you may be in big trouble. Use the TABLE WIDTH attribute so that it sets tables to percentages of the screen width, not so that it spills off the right hand side of small screens. If you're going to provide content for WAP phones or PDAs (personal digital assistants), get hold of one and look at your site. A browser-based emulator will show you what the site looks like, but you can only simulate navigating the site with tiny buttons by using it for real. The same goes for whether the layout and colour looks right or not.

Standardize – Don't go out on a limb

Use standard software to create your effects. Don't expect users to download vast software files that they will never use again – stick to software that everyone has. Use multimedia files that can be read by Real Player or Media Player. Use XML, HTML or industry standard file formats such as Word to contain long documents (if you can't split them into shorter files in HTML). Stick to conventions – blue underlined text for hyperlinks, purple for followed links – and don't confuse the visitor.

Think about your users

Make the user's visit a productive one. Provide interactive content if possible, rather than just reprinting your brochure in electronic form. Think about what users want to know, not want you want to tell them.

Think global

Remember that a worldwide audience sees your page, not just the people in the neighbourhood. Include content that helps a global audience, and exclude any that will offend people in other cultures.[4] Make the site accessible to everyone by using appropriate technology to help those with physical difficulties. Include links and text in any appropriate languages.

Think low-tech

Not everyone uses recent browsers. Give people a way round frames and JavaScript. Give people a way round images, too. One not very smart way that too many people use is to put a link to the text version in an image map; another one is providing a JavaScript link to the non-JavaScript page, which is as much use as a bucket with a hole in it.

References

1   Wilby, D. (2004) Web-Safe Colours, *Internet Magazine*, **113** (January), 34, contains a colour chart and both hexadecimal codes and RGB proportions.
2   www.ftc.gov/ogc/coppa1.htm (HTML format), www.ftc.gov/ogc/coppa1.htm (PDF format), PL 105-277, sections 1301–8.
3   Kidz Privacy (US government site) at www.ftc.gov/bcp/conline/edcams/kidzprivacy/index.html; Internet

Crime Forum IRC sub-group, *Chat Wise, Street Wise – Children and Internet Chat Services*, ICF, 2001, www.internetcrimeforum.org.uk/chatwise_streetwise.html (HTML format) or www.internetcrimeforum.org.uk/chatwise_streetwise.pdf (PDF format) and an area of the Telson Spur, a Canadian academic resource site, has extensive resources on subjects including internet children's internet safety at www.snark.ca/fam.htm#Family/. The UK Department for Education and Skills has a Superhighway safety site at safety.ngfl.gov.uk/.

3   See for example, Bradley, R., *Considerations for Connecting with a Global Audience*, www2002.org/CDROM/alternate/679/.

Resource list

This chapter is in two parts. The first provides further reading and references. Some of this material information backs up the references in the chapters and some is helpful additional material that adds to the information in the chapters. The second part of the chapter contains short notes on common terms – topics of interest to library webmasters and website managers. However, it is not a technical reference tool, so you will need to refer to books aimed at web developers and technical editors for further details – for example, if you want to know how to use Perl or PHP rather than simply knowing what they are and what they can do.

Further reading and references
General reading

Agarwal, S. (2001) Moving Towards a 'Grown-up' Intranet. In: *Online Information 2001, Proceedings*, Oxford, Learned Information, 55–6.

Ashenfelder, J. P. (1998) *Choosing a Database for your Web Site*, Chichester, Wiley. Supported by www.wiley.com/compbooks/ashenfelder.

Bradley, P. and Smith, A. (1995) *World Wide Web: how to design and construct home pages*, London, Aslib. A basic guide to HTML writing.

Bradley, P. (2002) Writing for People, Writing for Search Engines. In: *Online Information 2002, Proceedings*, Oxford, Learned Information, 15–19.

Burdman, J. R. (1999) *Collaborative Web Development: strategies and best practices for Web teams*, USA, Addison-Wesley. Book and CD-ROM.

Carter, M. (2002) Cyber house rules, *People management*, **6** (13), (22 June), 28–36. Human resources management in the web environment.

Clyde, L. A. (2000) A strategic planning approach to website management, *The Electronic Library*, **18** (2), 97–108. The strategic planning process provides a useful framework through which to view the many tasks associated with website development and maintenance and to conceptualize their relationship to one another. The author is webmaster of the International Association of School Librarianship. – Extract from author's abstract.

Crowe, S. (1999) *Webwise: a simplified management guide for the development of a successful web site*, USA, Group West.

Cunliffe, D. (2000) Developing Usable Websites – a Review and Model, *Internet Research: Electronic Networking Applications and Policy*, **10** (4), 295–307. Model derived from a survey of literature on the creation of websites, particularly small-scale sites. A useful extended bibliography drawn from the more theoretical end of the spectrum.

DeConti, L. (1998) *Planning and Creating a Government Web Site: learning from the experience of US states*, Manchester, Institute of Development Policy and Management, University of Manchester.

Donnelly, V. (2000) *Designing Easy-to-use Websites: a hands-on approach to structuring successful websites*, Boston, MA, Addison-Wesley.

Fleming, J. (1998) *Web Navigation: designing the user experience*, USA, O'Reilly. A book and CD-ROM showing good practice in website navigation facilities and site architecture.

Ford, A. and Dixon, T. (1996) *Spinning the Web: how to provide information on the Internet*, 2nd edn, London, International Thomson Computer Press. Book and CD-ROM based on British and US material, including technical detail of some software installations and configuration.

Ghosh, S. (1998) Making Business Sense of the Internet, *Harvard Business Review*, March–April, 126–35.

Haggard, M. (1998) *Survival Guide to Web Site Development*, Washington, Microsoft Press.

Horton, S. (2001) *Web Teaching Guide: a practical approach to creating course web sites*, USA, London, Yale University Press. 'Designed to answer the questions an educator who lacks extensive technical experience asks about creating a Web site.' Written by one of the authors of the

Yale web style guide.

Junion-Metz, G. and Stephens, B. (1998) *Creating a Power Web Site: HTML, tables, imagemaps, frames and forms*, New York, Neal-Schuman. Intended for libraries, this book and CD-ROM include a large number of ready-made scripts to provide forms and other features for library websites.

Lieb, T. (2001) *Editing for the Web*, 2nd edn, New York, McGraw-Hill. The earlier website supporting this book has now been abandoned in the state it reached before publication of this second edition.

Lymer, A.et al. (1998) *UK Business and the Information Superhighway: the impact of the Internet on SMEs*, Occasional research paper 23, London, Association of Chartered Certified Accountants.

Lynch, P. J. and Horton, S. (2002) *Web Style Guide: basic design principles for creating web sites*, 2nd edn, USA, Yale. Based on the famous Yale style guide.

Mercer, R. (2000) Intranets – Moving the Organisation from a 'Push' to a 'Pull' Mode. In *Online Information 2000, Proceedings*, Oxford, Learned Information, 271–2.

Merrick, N. (2000) Learning Zone, *People Management*, **6** (13), (22 June), 44–8. Learning resources on the Department for Education and Employment intranet.

Miller, R. (2001) The New Name Rush, *e-business*, April, 72–5. Discusses issues around the new top level domains.

Musciano, C, and Kennedy, B. (1998) *HTML: the definitive guide*, 3rd edn, USA, O'Reilly.

National Grid for Learning (2001) *Superhighway Safety: safe use of the Internet*, London, NGfL, http://safety.ngfl.gov.uk.

Niederst, J. (2000) *HTML Pocket Reference*, USA, O'Reilly. A brief pocket guide to HTML coding, providing syntax and sample coding for each HTML tag.

Niederst, J. (2001) *Learning Web Design: a beginner's guide to HTML, graphics and beyond*, USA, O'Reilly.

Niederst, J. (2001) *Web Design in a Nutshell*, 2nd edn, USA, O'Reilly. Includes HTML, multimedia and interactivity. New edition covers DHTML, XHTML, WML, SMIL.

Nielsen. J. (1999) *Designing Web Usability: the practice of simplicity*, Indianapolis, New Riders.

OMB Watch (2001) *Plugged In, Tuning Up: an assessment of state legislative*

websites, Washington DC, OMB Watch,
www.ombwatch.org/npadv/2001/stlg/index.html.

Oppenheim, C. (2000) Does Copyright have any Future on the Internet? *Journal of Documentation*, **56** (3), May, 279–98.

Osler, F. and Hollis, P. (2001) *The Activist's Guide to the Internet*, Prentice Hall. The use of the web, Usenet and other services to pursue political ends.

Perry, M and Bodkin, C. (2000) Content Analysis of Fortune 100 Company Web Sites, *Corporate Communications: an international journal*, **5** (2), 87–96. Reports a survey showing the range of content from simple company brochureware to more complex and interactive promotional sites.

Primich, T and Varnum, K. (1999) A Corporate Library Making the Transition from Traditional to Web Publishing, *Computers in Libraries*, November/December, 59–61.

Recruit Media (1998) *Engage: Editorial Issue*, London, Recruit Media. An edition of this recruitment and design agency's newsletter that deals with writing for the web.

Rosenfeld, L. and Morville, P. (2002) *Information Architecture for the World Wide Web*, 2nd edn, USA, O'Reilly. Rosenfeld and Morville are two librarians who formerly ran Argus Associates, a consulting firm specializing in information design for websites and intranets. Each now works on separate projects.

Rosenfeld, L. (2000) Information Strategy: seven pitfalls to avoid in information architecture, *Internet World*, 15 December, www.internetworld.com/magazine.php?inc=121500/12.15.00 feature3long.html

Shaw, D. (2001) Playing the Links: interactivity in .com and 'not.com' site, *First Monday*, **6** (3), March, http://firstmonday.org/issues/issue6_3/shaw/index.html.

Smith, G. J. H. (1996) Building the Lawyer-proof Web Site, *Aslib Proceedings*, **48** (6 June), 161–8.

Society of Information Technology Management (SOCITM) (2001) *Better Connected 2001? A snapshot of local authority websites*, Northampton, SOCITM. Summary details, www.socitm.gov.uk.

Spainhour, S. and Eckstein, R. (1999) *Webmaster in a Nutshell*, 2nd edn, USA, O'Reilly. A reference title covering HTML 4.0, CSS, XML,

CGI, SSI, JavaScript 1.2, PHP, HTTP 1.1, and administration for the Apache server.

Starling, A. (2000) How to Get Your Site Noticed, *Internet Magazine*, **71** (October), 123–7. Discusses how to submit your site to search engines.

Sweeney, S. (2000) *101 Ways to Promote Your Web Site: filled with proven internet marketing tips, tools, techniques, and resources to increase your web site traffic*, 2nd edn, USA, Maximum Press.

Terrett, A. (2000) *The Internet – Business Strategies for Law Firms*, London, Law Society Publishing.

United Kingdom, National Audit Office (1999) *Government on the Web; a report by the Comptroller and Auditor General*, House of Commons paper 87, session 1999–2000. London, The Stationery Office. Extensive commentary on UK Government departments' websites and use of electronic business tools.

Walker, A. (2000) Hard Copy to Dot com: developing a new marketing information web site, and building a community of interest, *Business Information Review*, **17** (2), June, 72–7. Discusses how a small independent market research company without the resources of a major parent company developed a highly sophisticated website on its own.

White, M. (2000) Matching Intranet Content and Business Culture. In: *Online Information 2000, Proceedings*, Oxford, Learned Information Europe, 265–8.

Yeoman, T. (2001) Will it Pay to Webvertise? *Government Computing*, **15** (3) (March), 30. What should happen to the revenue from advertising on local authority websites?

Young, K. (2001) Domain Name Management, *IT Week*, **4** (10), 12 March, 36. Early investment in a more professional approach to buying and maintaining domain names can save a lot of time and money later.

Legal and regulatory issues

DISC PD 0012-1: 2000 – Guide to the Practical Implementation of the Data Protection Act 1998, rev edn, BSI-DISC, 2000.

DISC PD 0012-2: 2000 – Guide to Developing an E-mail Policy, BSI-DISC, 2000.

DISC PD 0012-3: 2000 – Guide to Developing an E-commerce Policy,

BSI-DISC, September 2000.

DISC PD 0012-1: 2000 – Guide to Managing your Database, BSI-DISC, December 2000.

Charlesworth, A. (1999) *The Data Protection Act 1998*, JISC senior management briefing paper 9, London, JISC.

Temperton. E. (2000) How to Monitor E-communication, *People Management*, **6** (13) (22 June), 54–6. Covers acceptable use policies and includes some advice on the Regulation of Investigatory Powers Act 2000.

Standards

Central and local government websites in the UK are expected to comply with centrally set standards or best practice. These standards may prove useful to other web managers who are not bound by these standards. They are published by APLAWS and the Office of the e-Envoy and listed below.

APLAWS – Accessible and Personalised Local Authority Websites (www.aplaws.org.uk) provides a standardized model for local authority websites in the UK. APLAWS's name reflects the determination to provide sites based on user needs (the citizen focus) rather than the organizational structures of local authorities. The project is in the process of moving to provide national coverage but some useful documentation is already available from the website, notably a metadata framework document (www.aplaws.org.uk/products/ product_metadata.cfm) . APLAWS also publishes a category list and recommendations for local authority website information architecture.

The Office of the e-Envoy publishes a number of standards for government including:

Channels Framework: delivering government services in the new economy, London, OeE, 2002.

e-Government Interoperability Framework, Part one: Framework, Version 4.0, London, OeE, 2002; part two: Technical Policies and Frameworks, Version 5.0, London, OeE, 2003.

e-Government Metadata Standard, Version 2.0, London, OeE, 2003.

Documents are available at www.e-envoy.gov.uk or in the case of standards at www.govtalk.gov.uk

Technical

Ervin, J. R. (2000) Dynamic Delivery of Information via the World Wide Web, *Library Hi Tech News*, **18** (1), 55–60. A case study of converting a Microsoft Access database into a dynamic website using Internet Information Server 2 (IIS 2). Contains useful sample code for various functions including forms.

Ford, A. (2000) *Apache Pocket Reference*, USA, O'Reilly.

Guthrie, P. (2000–1) Dynamic Databases, *Internet Works*, **38** (November 2000)–**40** (January 2001).

Harmsen, B. (2000) Adding Value to Web-OPACs, *The Electronic Library*, **18** (2), 109–13 'Web-OPACs enable librarians to add value to their catalogue data. One feature which has become almost standard for new library software is including links to full text or multimedia documents corresponding to a particular citation. Other features which have not yet become common but will soon do so include: links to publishers, links to corporate sources, and links to journal titles.' – Author's abstract.

Jascó, P. (2000) Developing and Maintaining Your Web Pages, *Computers in Libraries*, **20** (9), October, 58–60. Discusses use of low cost HTML validator packages to allow you to check that your HTML and links are valid.

McGrath, M. (2000) *WAP in Easy Steps*, London, Computer Step.

Mitchell, S. (2000) *Designing Active Server Pages*, USA, O'Reilly.

Roberts, G. (2000) Designing a Database-driven Web Site, or, the Evolution of the InfoIguana, *Computers in Libraries*, **20** (9), October, 26–8, 30, 32. The InfoIguana is an ASP application that provides personalized access templates that allow searching of a Microsoft Access database containing bibliographic information.

Internet resources

Anchordesk. A daily briefing on the computer industry with a strong emphasis on internet and web stories. Available as e-mail by registration at www.zdnet.com/anchordesk/.

Ariadne. A quarterly internet bulletin with a printed equivalent that contains slightly fewer articles, www.ariadne.ac.uk.

Free Pint. A UK-based fortnightly newsletter on internet topics, with issues focusing on subject information and feature articles, www.freepint.co.uk.

Internet Resources Newsletter, Edinburgh, Heriot-Watt University Library, monthly, www.hw.ac.uk/libWWW/irn/irn.html. Warning: this URL is case sensitive.

JILT (Journal of Information, Law and Technology). Published three times a yearby Warwick and Strathclyde Universities, this includes many useful articles on legal aspects of the web. Helpful on issues of copyright, data protection, etc., elj.warwick.ac.uk/jilt/.

Nielsen, J., Alertbox articles at www.useit.com/alertbox/ especially the following:

- Be Succinct! (Writing for the Web) (15 March 1997) www.useit.com/alertbox/9703b.html.
- Content Creation for Average People (1 October 2000) www.useit.com/alertbox/20001001.html.
- Differences Between Print Design and Web Design (24 January 1999). www.useit.com/alertbox/990124.html.
- E-mail Newsletters Pick Up Where Websites Leave Off (30 September 2002) www.useit.com/alertbox/20020930.html.
- The End of Web Design (23 July 2000) www.useit.com/alertbox/20000723.html (including comments on the effect of using ASPs and syndicated content).
- Failure of Corporate Websites (18 October 1998) www.useit.com/alertbox/981018.html.
- Information Foraging: why Google makes people leave your site faster (30 June 2003) www.useit.com/alertbox.20030630.html.
- International Web Usability (August 1996) www.useit.com/alertbox/9608.html.
- Intranet Portals: a tool metaphor for corporate information (31 March 2003). www.useit.com/alertbox/20030331.html.
- Is Navigation Useful? (9 January 2000) www.useit.com/alertbox/20000109.html.
- Tagline Blues: what's the site about? (22 July 2001) www.useit.com/alertbox/20010722.html.
- Ten Best Intranet Designs of 2001 (25 November 2001) www.useit.com/alertbox/20011125.html.
- Ten Good Deeds in Web Design (3 October 1999) www.useit.com/alertbox/991003.html.

- Top Ten Guidelines for Home Page Usability (12 May 2002)
  www.useit.com/alertbox/20020512.html.
- Top Ten Web Design Mistakes of 2002 (23 December 2002).
  www.useit.com/alertbox/20021223.html This article has links to
  earlier top ten mistake lists in the series.
- Usability Metrics (21 January 2001)
  www.useit.com/alertbox/20010121.html.
- Web Pages Must Live Forever (29 November 1998)
  www.useit.com/alertbox/981129.html.
- When Bad Design Elements Become the Standard (14 November
  1999) www.useit.com/alertbox/991114.html.
- Why People Shop on the Web (7 February 1999)
  www.useit.com/alertbox/990207.html.

Papers from the UKOLN workshop *Managing the Virtual Branch: Public
Library Web Managers' Workshop 2000,*
www.ukoln.ac.uk/public/events/managing.

Wired. *Hotwired*. An e-mail newsletter available by registration at
www.hotwired.com.

Mailing lists

A number of mailing lists in the UK provide support to webmasters and
other staff. These are operated by JISCmail and can be accessed through
the site www.jiscmail.ac.uk.

web-support
website-info-mgt; Discusses how to manage an institutional website.
uk-web-focus-w3c; Disseminates information on W3C.
The general library discussions lists lis-link and lis-iis also frequently
    contain relevant items.

Codes of practice and acceptable use policies

BECTA (2000) Checklist of Issues to Consider When Schools Publish
    on the Web. In *Connecting Schools, Networking People 2000: Part 4 –
    Schools On Line*, London, BECTA.
JANET (1995) *JANET Acceptable Use Policy*, Didcot, UKERNA,
    www.ja.net/documents/use.html.

University of Sussex Information Service, *Standards for Publishing on USIS*, University of Sussex, www.sussex.ac.uk/USIS/www/ standards.shtml. This code of practice includes a useful indication of which standards are mandatory.

Keeping up to date

Most of the current information you need to keep abreast of developments will come from the internet itself, and from newspapers and periodicals. Relatively little news will come from books, which you will use more for reference and background material.

You need to spend some time each week surfing these sites for information and making prints of the items you find useful. Many sites do not keep long archives available – although some do, and their value is further enhanced – and the search engines are often poor if you have only a vague recollection of the date or headline of a story.

Magazines

Internet Magazine. Monthly, London, Internet Magazine, www.internet-magazine.com.
Internet Works. Monthly, Bath, Future Publishing, www.iwks.com.
.net. Monthly, www.netmag.co.uk.

e-zines

Ariadne, www.ariadne.ac.uk. Available in printed form with slightly differing content, published by the UK Office for Library and Information Networking (UKOLN), University of Bath.

Newspapers

Newspapers have largely ceased including weekly supplements dealing with internet and related issues but the *Guardian* continues to publish the supplement *Online* on Thursdays, www.newsunlimited.co.uk/online/.

Common terms and additional notes
Accessibility

The availability of your web pages to users with difficulties that make use of the browser a problem. This covers users with visual difficulties; users whose first language is not the language of your web page; users of text-based systems and others not using graphics.

Publications

Oppenheim, C. and Selby, K. (1999) Access to information on the World Wide Web for Blind and Visually Handicapped People, *Aslib Proceedings*, **51** (10), (November/December), 335–45.

Web resources

Bobby (www.cast.org/bobby/) is a tool that offers analysis of web pages submitted to it and reports on their accessibility for people with disabilities. However, it does not cover all possibilities – for instance it does not highlight problems with text in columns, which causes difficulties for all but the most recent speech converters for web pages.

The Royal National Institute for the Blind (RNIB) has a Better Web Design Campaign whose home page (www.rnib.org.uk/digital/) provides links to various useful sites including the W3C (World Wide Web Consortium) Web Content Accessibility Guidelines (www.w3.org/TR/WAI-WEBCONTENT/), which provide detailed guidance and advice.

Adobe provides information about the use of its Portable Document Format (PDF) on a special website (access.adobe.com). Its white paper *Optimising Adobe PDF Files for Accessibility* is available at access.adobe.com/white-paper.html.

A discussion of issues of accessibility with particular reference to government websites is contained in: United Kingdom. Office of the e-Envoy (2003) *Quality Framework for UK Government Website Design: usability issues for government websites*, London, OeE, www.e-envoy.gov.uk/webguidelines.htm. The publication takes an extended look at a range of issues connected with usability (not just for users with visual impairment, for example). The appendices contain a usability toolkit that will help test your site, whether or not it falls within the scope of the e-Envoy's remit within government.

Active server page

A web page generated 'on the fly' by software at the server. ASP is the method used by Microsoft server software; other forms of scripting such as CGI (Common Gateway Interface) will achieve the same end. The code is invisible to the user, so that for example a routine used to generate an ASP page containing a catalogue entry will retrieve a page of HTML that will look to the user as if it had been hard-coded individually by the web author. One difficulty is that because the pages are created only when called for by the user they are not retrieved by search engines and are not found by user searches through these engines. For more information in a library context see: Yerkey, N. (2001) Active Server Pages for Dynamic Database Web Access, *Library Hi Tech News*, **19** (2), 133–42.

Publications

Wessinger, A. K. (2000) *ASP in a Nutshell: desktop quick reference*, 2nd edn, USA, O'Reilly.

Application service provider

A company that provides computing services that allow its customers to purchase particular applications or programs rather than buying, installing and managing those applications themselves. These services are provided to the customer from the ASP's computers via wide-area network or the internet. Done properly, using an ASP can allow the customer to re-allocate its resources to business-critical areas and 'out-task' simpler operations to the ASP. In web services, some out-tasked services are search engine management and content management systems. See www.asp-street.com and www.aspnews.com. In the fields of interest to readers of this book, the epixtech library system (www.dynix.com) and Atomz search engine (www.atomz.com) are examples of ASP products.

Publication

Bisson, S. (2000) ASP Explained, *Internet.Works*, **37**, (Autumn), 79–85.

Blog

See Weblog.

Brochureware

Web pages that are direct copies of existing print documents, usually those that simply publicize the organization.

Browser

The software on a personal computer (PC or Macintosh) or other device that provides the means of locating and retrieving files in a hypertext system from a web server. The most popular graphical interfaces are Microsoft Internet Explorer and Netscape Navigator, but other browsers are widely used including Lynx (a text browser) and the Norwegian browser Opera, which comes in several versions for a range of European languages. Its installation file size remains small and Opera is very supportive of website accessibility. You may also find users with Cello and Mosaic, two earlier browsers. Apple has developed Safari, a new browser for Mac OS X, which will also run Omniweb. Linux and Unix users can run Konqueror.

Publication

Parker, S., Cartwright, D. and Norman, T. (2003) Web Browsers, *Internet Magazine*, **104**, (June), 109–13.

Cascading style sheets

Style sheets are a means of describing style elements on a web page, such as font, type size and colour, and some layout elements, without the need to constantly add new tags to HTML and now to XML. They can control both screen and print layouts. A new format, XSL or eXtensible Style Language, has been developed to work with XML.

Publication

Meyer, E. R. (2000) *Cascading Style Sheets: the definitive guide*, USA, O'Reilly.

Web resource

Nielsen, J. (1997) Effective Use of Style Sheets, *Alertbox*, 1 July, www.useit.com/alertbox/9707a.html.

Common Gateway Interface (CGI)

CGI is widely used to manage interaction between the user and the server when a web page needs to call any program or other function on the server, for example to interrogate a database or make calculations. Although a range of technologies has become available to manage CGI interactions – such as Active Server Pages described above – many web designers prefer to continue using Perl, one of the earliest programming languages in this context. Typically a page containing a CGI script will contain a form or other area where the user can enter personal data or an enquiry; sending the form to the server invokes the script and a page of HTML containing some kind of customized content will be returned. Although this will appear to be a conventional page, it will have been generated on the fly and will not therefore be indexed by search engines.

Christenberry, J. R. and others (2003) *CGI Fast and Easy Web Development*, USA, Prima. This is a basic book intended for newcomers to CGI, whereas the two other titles below are technical reference mainly aimed at programmers.

Cornell, G. and Abdali, K. (2003) *CGI Programming with Java*, New Jersey, Prentice Hall. This book covers Java and servlet technology, which are two alternatives to Perl in managing CGI.

Guelich, S., Gundavaram, S. and Birznieks, G. (2000) *CGI Programming with Perl*, 2nd edn, Sebastopol, CA, O'Reilly. Guelich (the author of the first edition) has provided a page of CGI-related links from an article 'News – Why learn CGI?' to be found at http://web.oreilly.com/news/cgi_0700.html.

Content management systems

Cooper, A. (2000) Evolving Human Networks to Create and Manage Content. In *Online Information 2000, Proceedings*, Oxford, Learned Information, 273–6.

Cox, A. and Yeadon, J. (2001) Practical Content Management on the Web: an overview. In *Online Information 2001, Proceedings*, Oxford, Learned Information, 31–5.

White, M. (2002) Content Management, *Library and Information Update*, **1** (6), (September), 36–7.

Cookies

Short text files that are left in the cache of the user's computer and allow the server to store information that identifies the visitor on a repeat visit. Cookies can be used to personalize the visitor's experience, for example by storing details of pages visited and using this information to tailor the menu offered on a repeat visit. Users can refuse to accept cookies so there must be some alternative content available or they will be forced to leave the site.

Database driven websites

Some uses of database driven websites for library web managers are discussed in Chapter 8. Catalogues are a popular feature of library websites (see Chapter 6), and are of course database driven. The book by Ashenfelder (see 'General reading' above) is a useful resource; see also Thomas, N. R. (2002) *Researching Database-driven Library Websites*, Glen Ellyn, Illinois, College of Du Page, www.cod.edu/library/libweb/thomas/DatabaseReport.htm. See also Roberts, G. (2000) Designing a Database-Driven Web Site, or, The Evolution of the InfoIguana, *Computers in Libraries*, **20** (9), (October), 26.

Directories *see* Search engines

Domain name

Domain names are the alphanumeric names that identify computers – mail or web servers – on the internet. They are unique names and refer forward to the numerical identities – 'IP addresses', see under 'Internet Protocol' below – that attach to each computer on the internet, making them more memorable and allowing users to brand their websites using the domain name they have selected. They are used in URLs and in e-mail addresses.

There are a number of registries that control the registration and use of the names, and rules about what can and cannot be registered. You will need to deal with different registries depending on the type of name that you want – '.com' names are handled in a different place from '.uk' names, for example. The names are unique, so once they have been registered they cannot be used by anyone else unless either you fail to pay the registration maintenance fee and they become available again, or you sell the name (or bequeath it if you are an individual).

The domain name has several parts – at least two – separated by dots. The name becomes more specific working from the right. It will often, but not always, tell you about the registration, so that domain names ending in .uk are registered in the UK, and those ending in .de in Germany. However, many people worldwide use the .com and .org suffixes (or top level domains – TLDs – to give them their technical name), which are non-geographic but administered from the USA. These names are not therefeore necessarily registered by American companies.

Web resources

www.nic.net is the registration authority for .com, .net and .org domain names, whichever country you are in; www.nominet.org.uk is responsible for registration of the .uk TLD. This TLD is divided into a number of second level domains (SLDs). See www.nominet.org.uk/news/guides/reg1.pdf for details of the system.

Hit

See Metrics.

Home page

The introductory page on a website. It sits in the default directory and should provide links to all parts of the site and to contact and other details. The normal convention is for the home page to have the URL of the site with the file name index.htm or default.htm: this allows browsers to find it when the URL alone is entered into the address bar.

Home pages that are constructed to provide a large number of categorized links to other parts of the site, or to other sites, are known as portals. Yahoo is one of the last major portal sites on the web.

Internet Protocol (IP)

IP is the term used to refer to a set of standards describing the way that information is passed between computers on the internet. Typically it is cut up into 'packets' in a set format that each need an address at the top in order to allow the network to direct it to the correct receiving computer. These IP addresses have typically consisted of four groups, for example 62.253.64.5 (which identifies a network centre belonging to one of the UK cable networks), or MSN is 208.68.171.247, with the address format in each case being known as IPv4. These addresses provide direct connections to the computers in question, and when they correspond to websites, the sites respond to the browser's request. When you type in the request as msn.com, the browser connects first with a 'domain name server' or DNS which looks up the IP address that corresponds to the domain name before sending the request to the 'raw' IP address. But with the enormous number of devices now connected to the internet, even the large number of unique addresses offered by this format (between 0.0.0.0 and 255.255.255.255, the highest possible number) is insufficient for future needs. Many users who currently share the same IP address when using dial-up are switching to broadband connections that are always connected, and need to present a constant and unique IP address. A new format known as IPv6 is now being introduced which will help overcome these problems by providing a large block of new IP addresses. See www.ipv6.org for more details.

In Europe, IP numbers are managed by the Regional Internet Registry (or RIR), an organization known as Réseaux IP Européens, or RIPE, at www.ripe.net. The website includes the facility to query the RIPE database so as to identify the identity of any given IP address.

Intranet

Typically described as an internal version of the internet, an intranet provides information to the desktop computers on a network (in a company, a university, a school etc.) using web technology.

Publications

In addition to the references for Chapter 9, the following are useful:

Intranet Communicator, London, Intranet Communicator.
Virtual Business, London, Ark Publishing.

Agarwal, S. (2001) Intranet Usability – Tackling the Management Issues around Implementing Usable Design on an Intranet, *Vine*, **31** (3), 17–19

Ali, Y. (2001) The Intranet and the Management of Making and Using Skills, *Journal of Knowledge Management*, **5** (4), 338–48.

Best Practice Intranet Management (2001) Theme issue of *Strategic Communication Management*, **5** (4) (June/July).

Flood, G. (2002) Is your Intranet Working?, *Information World Review*, **181** (June), 14–15.

Peterson, M. (2001) Intranet-based Service Delivery – Making it Work, *The Electronic Library*, **19** (1), 19–25.

White, M. (2002) Getting the Most from Intranets and Extranets, *MyITadviser*, **14** (May), www.ncc.co.uk/ncc/myITadviser/archive/issue14/business_processes. cfm.

Web resource

Intranet Focus (www.intranetfocus.com) is a site operated by a LIS professional information consultant and contains a number of papers about intranets.

Java

A programming language, originated by Sun, which operates independently of the computer platform (PC, Mac, etc.) and can thus be relied on to run in the same way whatever machine the user is running. Some organizations do not permit Java on their networks.

Link

A hypertext area within a document that, when clicked or otherwise selected, takes the user to another document within the website or on another site.

Metrics

In web use statistics, each occasion on which a file forming an element of a web page on your site is called for by a visitor. Thus one click to read a web page can create many 'hits', for example HTML, graphics and media files could all be 'hit' by a request for a single page. Better statistics are provided by measuring page impressions, user sessions or unique visitors. Unique visitors is probably the most useful measures in collecting web use statistics, especially if it is possible to distinguish unique visits or visitors – that is, visits by different users to the site rather than a figure that includes repeat visits by the same user. In Chapter 8, ABC Electronic was mentioned as a means of obtaining more accurate audit, if required, along the lines of newspaper and journal circulation audit figures.

Publication

Foan, R. (2002) Being Accountable, *Internet Works*, **63** (October), 38.

Portable Document Format (PDF)

A file format devised by Adobe that allows the user to view a document as it is laid out on the original page – in other words, with the effect of a photographic reproduction. Not all search engines can index documents in this format and users must download special free software to allow them to view the documents. The format is widely used and is a de facto web standard.

Web resources

The Adobe site (www.adobe.com) contains links to the reader. Many websites that use it provide a link from their pages but not all organizations consider this appropriate. access.adobe.com contains information about the accessibility issues in using .PDF files.

Splash page

Websites often use an introductory page, usually containing a graphic, and including an instruction via a REFRESH tag to redirect the user to another page after a set time (say, 15 seconds). After the REFRESH has taken place, the user sees the true home page, or possibly a further splash page, which in turn directs the user forward. There are some legitimate uses, such as alerting the user to planned down time, or displaying an animation while larger files are loaded in the background. However, this feature can be very annoying, particularly so where some kind of interaction is expected from the user. Think carefully before including a splash page as part of your basic design. Users' reactions to these pages frequently include closing the connection to your site.

Uniform resource locator (URL)

The address such as www.cilip.org.uk that identifies a website. It is preceded by http:// (meaning hypertext transfer protocol) for a world wide web address, but there are other transfer protocols that will work in many of the popular browsers, notably gopher:, which fetches ('go for') a text file. The transient nature of many websites has led to the development of the concept of a Persistent URL, or PURL, meaning that there will be an ongoing presence at the URL quoted that will refer users forward to any new site. But PURLs have not been widely adopted and the problem remains.

Undernet

The area of an intranet or website that is unconnected to the rest of the site, perhaps through lack of correct links or perhaps deliberately as a test area, and that often is not indexed because of the lack of proper metadata and other indexing links. The problem is probably more familiar than this useful term to describe it.

(Unique) visit

See Metrics (page 233).

Weblog

Weblogs can be briefly described as pages containing several items of information arranged by date, usually in reverse order, and either reflecting an individual person or group's thoughts or centred on a topic of interest. They are covered in detail on page 170–4 of this book. For a history, see Blood, R. (2000) Weblogs: a history and perspective, *Rebecca's Pocket*, www.rebeccablood.net/essays/weblog_history.html.

Publications

In addition to references 32–6 of Chapter 9, see:

Blood, R. (2002) *The Weblog Handbook: practical advice on creating and maintaining your blog*, USA, Perseus Publishing.
Blood, R. (2002) We've Got Blog: how weblogs are changing our culture, USA, Perseus Publishing.
Stauffer, S. (2002) *Blog On: building online communities with weblogs*, USA, McGraw-Hill Osborne.
Stone, B. (2002) *Blogging: genius strategies for instant web content*, Indianapolis, New Riders.

XML

A sub-set of SGML, the Standard Generalised Markup language used for text markup systems, which allows website content to be reused for a variety of platforms, for example to allow you to produce WAP or PDF from the same content as your HTML. The organizations producing the government standards mentioned above are producing XML schemas suitable for use on government websites. The importance of XML will grow as a variety of channels come into use for delivering the content of your web-site.

Publications

Harold, E. R. and Means, W. S. (2002) *XML*, 2nd edn, USA, O'Reilly.
Levell, K. (2002) The XML Factor, *Internet Works*, **63**, (October), 74–7.

Index

Introduction
to Museum Work

G. Ellis Burcaw

The American Association for State and Local History

Nashville

Library of Congress Cataloging in Publication Data

Burcaw, G   Ellis.
  Introduction to museum work.

  Bibliography: p.
  Includes Index.
  1. Museums. 2. Museum techniques.   I. Title.
AM5.B88   069   74–32248

ISBN 0–910050–14–7

Printed in the United States of America
Second Printing 1976
Third Printing 1978
Fourth Printing 1979

Contents

Preface

This is not meant to be a complete textbook for museum workers. It is a supplement to the available publications which deal with museums, museum work, and museum theory,[1] which is based on the lectures given at the University of Idaho in the course Introduction to Museology. The material in this book relieves the student from having to assimilate a great amount of information from many different sources.

Museum training takes several forms: college and university courses for credit; correspondence study; on-the-job practical training; short-term workshops and seminars; professional meetings; scholarships, fellowships, and internships; vocational training; special programs leading to a certificate; and others. The directory of museum training (available from the American Association of Museums [AAM], 2233 Wisconsin Avenue, Northwest, Washington, D.C. 20007) describes formal opportunities in the United States and Canada.

Though the term "museology" is not in common use today, it has a long and legitimate history. Few people, within or without the museum world, have regarded museum work as a profession in its own right. The extreme position of the uninformed layman has been (and all too often still is) that anyone who can spare the time can manage or do the work of the local museum. Not significantly differ-

---

1. Standard works which would be used along with this supplementary text might include: Carl E. Guthe, *So You Want a Good Museum* (Washington, D.C.: American Association of Museums, 1957, 1973): Carl E. Guthe, *The Management of Small History Museums* (Nashville: American Association for State and Local History, 1959, 1964); Raymond O. Harrison, *The Technical Requirements of Small Museums*, rev. ed. (Ottawa: Canadian Museums Association, 1969); *The Organization of Museums: Practical Advice*, Museums and Monuments Series, Vol. IX, (Paris: UNESCO, 1960).

ent is the opinion that is occasionally heard from the large museums, of whatever kind, that museum workers need but to be specialists in a particular kind of job (and need have no theoretical understanding of museums in general). This widespread point of view has led to the tacit conclusion that there is no museum profession, no such thing as museology, and, consequently, no need for general museum training. A generation ago one could count on one hand, even with a finger or two missing, the opportunities that existed for formal museum education. Now such opportunities number in the dozens, and many schools offer or plan to offer master's degrees in museology programs. A few universities are even planning study and work programs that will lead to the doctorate.

Obviously, museum boards and museum directors are raising their standards; and museum jobs, which are steadily increasing in number, will go more and more to those who have not only a sound liberal arts education but also museum training. Learning the principles of museology on the job is just as inefficient and uncertain as learning any other profession on the job.

The museum worker, especially one in a decision-making position, must be or become a professional—a person who has knowledge and standards which the educated layman does not have. If those who oversee a museum do not have professional attitudes toward it, it may not be managed well. If, for example, the museum happens to have a good director or a good department head, it may decline rapidly if an ignorant or careless board of trustees replaces him with someone who is not a professional museologist, however faithful and skillful a taxidermist he may be, or however effective a public relations person he may have been in some other employment.

Training in museology is designed to broaden the outlook of museum workers and to introduce students, who are not yet launched on a career, to museums and museum work. I hope that this supplementary text may be of use to students, whether or not they have access to an introductory classroom course in museology, and to those devoted amateurs who are already working in museums and who recognize the desirability of improving their skills. Its purpose is to help develop professional attitudes and standards.[2]

G. E. B.

2. If no other museum training is available, the student or museum worker of any age might consider a correspondence course. He should inquire at his nearest college or university, or write to the National University Extension Association (NUEA), Suite 360, 1 Du Pont Circle, Washington, D.C. 20036.

Part I

Museums and Collections

1

Museum Defined

Since this book is about museums and museum work, it is necessary to begin with an understanding of what a museum is. Put another way, the most important single accomplishment for the student is to learn to define the word "museum."

A newspaper story a few years ago was headed, "W—— Plans Museum For Celebration." The story said that the owner of a vacant business building had given permission to the local Booster Club to use it "as a museum during the W—— Days celebration July 2. Antiques and artifacts for the museum will be accepted either on a permanent or on a loan basis. These may be brought in as soon as there has been an opportunity to clean the building. Anyone who has items to display for that day only may do so, according to the program chairman."

Another news item described a new library building at a junior college. In addition to mention of classrooms, offices, kitchen facilities, and restrooms, the article said, "the basement contains a museum of Indian artifacts, a storage area, (etc.)." Has the word "museum" been properly used in these news stories?

Before we can answer that question, we need to define some terms, establishing a basic vocabulary.

Definitions

Object
> a material, three-dimensional thing of any kind. "The paper bag contained three objects."

Museum object
> an object in the collections of a museum, collected for its own sake. For example, a cassette tape collected as such and not

3

for whatever sound might have been recorded on it. "The curator brought a museum object with him."

Specimen

usually synonymous with museum object but properly having the connotation of an example or sample; a representative member of a class of objects. "The sedimentary rock exhibit needed a limestone specimen."

Artifact

an object produced or shaped by human workmanship or, possibly, a natural object deliberately selected and used by a human being. (For example, a shiny pebble picked up on the beach and carried as a good luck charm.) A cultural specimen. "The archaeologist examined the tray of rocks to see if it contained any artifacts."

Art object

an artifact of aesthetic interest (though not necessarily intended to be an art object by its creator). "The niche in the gallery wall was meant to hold an art object."

Work of art

something of aesthetic importance created by a human being (note that works of art are not necessarily art objects; for example, a symphony). "Her clay pot was a work of art, but so was her cherry pie or, for that matter, her dancing."

Collections

the collected objects of a museum, acquired and preserved because of their potential value as examples, as reference material, or as objects of aesthetic or educational importance. "The museum collections are housed mainly in the south wing."

Collection

a unit of the collections, consisting of objects having something of importance in common. One may speak of the bird's-egg collection of a natural history museum, or of the J. W. Whiteford collection if Mr. Whiteford has donated a large number of important, similar objects to the museum. "The handgun collection was moved in order to make room for the Johnson and Smith collections when they were acquired."

Accession

> the acquiring of one or more objects at one time from one source, or the objects so acquired. "We made ten accessions last month totaling 218 objects. The Ramsey accession was placed in the top drawer overnight. When he delivered the sofa after lunch he told us that that completed the accession. The sword was the third accession from Miss Baum. A previous accession from her consisted of over a thousand butterflies."

Registration

> assigning a permanent number for identification purposes to an accession and recording this number according to a system. "As soon as the accession was registered, it was turned over to the graduate students for study."

Cataloguing

> assigning an object to one or more categories of an organized classification system (to be described in a later chapter). "The chair was catalogued as a Civil War item, and it was also entered in the catalogue with the furnishings of the former governor's mansion."

Classification of collections

> the establishment of the major categories of the collections on the basis of anticipated use. This is a prior condition, or prerequisite, of good collecting. Art objects are collected primarily for their aesthetic qualities; as unique, artistic creations. History objects are collected primarily with the intent of interpreting (explaining) the past. Science objects are collected primarily to demonstrate and/or interpret natural phenomena and the laws and applications of science. "The art curator saw no value in the old lithograph and called it hideous, but it was just what the history curator had been looking for to complete the decorations of the parlor of the historic house that was being restored as an annex of the museum. The curator of botany was on an expedition collecting specimens for an exhibit of tundra vegetation."

Display

> the showing of objects, depending on the interest of the viewer in the objects themselves. "A shoe store displays shoes in its window."

Exhibit

of more serious, important, and professional connotation than "display." It is the presentation of ideas with the intent of educating the viewer, or, in the case of an art exhibit, a planned presentation of art objects by an informed person to constitute a unit. As such, it might be an identifiable part of an exhibition. "A museum uses objects and labels in preparing an exhibit." "There was an exhibit of engravings in the Victorian Art Exhibition."

Label

written material in an exhibit to identify, to explain, and to inform. Labels may also be called signs, titles, captions, text, etc. Often the labels accomplish more real education in an exhibit than the objects. "The main label was placed at eye level. The only other labels in the case were the captions on the photographs."

Exhibition

an assemblage of objects of artistic, historical, scientific, or technological nature, through which visitors move from unit to unit in a sequence designed to be meaningful instructionally and/or aesthetically. Accompanying labels and/or graphics (drawings, diagrams, etc.) are planned to interpret, explain, and to direct the viewer's attention. Usually, an exhibition covers a goodly amount of floor space, consists of several separate exhibits or large objects, and deals with a broad, rather than a narrow, subject. "The art museum director organized an exhibition of the 19th-century paintings." "We added an exhibit of quartz crystals to the rock and mineral exhibition. We then displayed some crystals in the sales room."

Art show

a temporary display of art objects, commonly the paintings of one or a few contemporary artists; informal connotation.

Art gallery

a commercial establishment for the buying and selling of art objects; or a separate exhibition room devoted to art in a general museum; or an art museum; The word "gallery" places the emphasis on the *displaying* of works of art, regardless of the ownership of the objects. "When the art teacher retired, she opened a gallery on Main Street to handle the work of her former students."

Art museum

a museum devoted to one or more of the art fields (dealing with objects). The emphasis here is on the *ownership and preservation* of important collections. "The finest collection of Oriental ceramics in the Southwest is in that art museum."

General museum

a museum dealing with several or all fields instead of just art, just history, just geology, etc. "The director is an anthropologist and his assistant is a historian; but since theirs is a general museum they need to hire a curator of art."

Encyclopedic museum

a general museum that has practically no limitations as to time, space, and subject placed on its collections, and which seeks broad coverage in all fields. "The coverage of some subjects is rather superficial in that encyclopedic museum, but at least they can claim with some justification that they have something of interest to every visitor."

Historic building or site

a structure or location of significant historic connections, often associated with a famous person or event; may include exhibits of pertinent objects. "The museum took over the administration of two historic houses, and the curator of history immediately began to plan for the authentic refurnishing of some of the ground floor rooms."

Preservation project, old fort, "village," etc.

preservation, restoration, or reconstruction of one or more buildings so as to re-create the environment of a past time and place.

Botanic(al) garden

grounds with or without greenhouses, for the scientific cultivation of plants for study and display.

Arboretum

a botanical garden that specializes in trees.

Herbarium

a systematic collection of preserved plant specimens.

Zoological garden
> a professionally designed and managed compound where live animals are kept for study and display.

Aquarium
> a building equipped with tanks for a collection of animals that live in water.

Children's museum
> a museum intended exclusively for young children, with everything scaled to their physical size and mental capacity, usually managed by elementary school teachers, with hobby classes, story hours, etc.

Planetarium
> a machine which projects tiny spots of light on a domed ceiling to represent the stars and planets, and the building which houses such a projector.

Nature center
> a facility for outdoor learning about nature, including a natural site for field study, with facilities and services for an interpretive program.

Visitor center
> a facility for the interpretation of a historical site or natural region, usually with a small auditorium, exhibits, and an information desk. Established by the National Park Service, forest service, state park departments, and other agencies accommodating tourists.

Science center
> a kind of permanent exhibition (like a miniature world fair) which emphasizes the spectacular aspects of physical science such as space exploration, optical illusions, television, and electronic cooking.

Art center
> an establishment by and for a community where art lessons are taught, the work of local artists is shown, and other art interests of the community are accommodated. The performing arts may be included, but ordinarily there is no permanent collection of objects.

Other definitions will be given throughout the book, but we are now ready to consider definitions of "museum."[1] Note that a "center" is not a museum. A "center" may be, but is not necessarily, a permanent institution, educational, nonprofit, and the owner and preserver of a collection. The essential distinction is this: A center exists to make possible entertaining activity; a museum exists to make important educational or aesthetic use of a permanent collection.

"Museum" Definitions (from several sources, numbered for future reference).

A museum is

1. a building or space within a building significant chiefly for preservation and/or exhibition of collections.
2. a building to house collections of objects for inspection, study, and enjoyment. (Douglas A. Allen)
3. an institution for the safekeeping of objects and for the interpretation of these objects through research and through exhibition. (Edwin H. Colbert)
4. a house of marvels, or a house of keeping (from two terms in the Gaelic language meaning "museum")
5. any permanent institution which conserves and displays for purposes of study, education, and enjoyment collections of objects of cultural or scientific significance. (International Council of Museums)
6. an institution for the preservation of those objects which best illustrate the phenomena of nature and the works of man, and the utilization of these for the increase in knowledge and for the culture and enlightenment of the people. (George Brown Goode, 1895)
7. a permanent establishment, administered in the general interest, for the purpose of preserving, studying, enhancing by various means and, in particular, of exhibiting to the public for its delectation and instruction groups of objects and specimens of cultural value: artistic, historical, scientific and technological collections, botanical and zoological gardens and aquariums, etc. Public libraries and public archival in-

---

1. Perhaps the most useful feature of a definition of "museum" is precisely that it enables one to see weaknesses in a museum or, at least, that it helps one to maintain a proper set of values in the face of adverse pressures.

stitutions maintaining permanent exhibition rooms shall be considered to be museums. (International Council of Museums, 1960)

8. a nonprofit permanent establishment, not existing primarily for the purpose of conducting temporary exhibitions, exempt from federal and state income taxes, open to the public and administered in the public interest, for the purpose of conserving and preserving, studying, interpreting, assembling, and exhibiting to the public for its instruction and enjoyment objects and specimens of educational and cultural value, including artistic, scientific (whether animate or inanimate), historical, and technological material. Museums thus defined shall include botanical gardens, zoological parks, aquaria, planetaria, historical societies, and historic houses and sites which meet the requirements set forth in the preceding sentence. (American Association of Museums, about 1962)[2]

9. a permanent, educational, nonprofit institution with catalogued collections in art, science, or history, with exhibitions open to the public.

10. an organized and permanent nonprofit institution, essentially educational or aesthetic in purpose, with professional staff, which owns and utilizes tangible objects, cares for them, and exhibits them to the public on some regular schedule. (American Association of Museums' definition for the purposes of the accreditation program)

For further clarification, the key words used in the definition are further defined as follows:

a. organized institution: a duly constituted body with expressed responsibilities.

b. permanent: the institution is expected to continue in perpetuity.

c. professional staff: at least one paid employee, who commands an appropriate body of special knowledge and the ability to reach museological decisions consonant with the experience of his peers, and who also has access to and acquaintance with the literature of the field.

d. tangible objects: things animate and inanimate.

2. With minor changes, this has been adopted as the official definition of the Canadian Museums Association.

e. care: the keeping of adequate records pertaining to the provenance, identification, and location of a museum's holdings and the application of current professionally accepted methods to their security and to the minimizing of damage and deterioration.

f. schedule: regular and predictable hours which constitute substantially more than a token opening, so that access is reasonably convenient to the public.[3]

11. a permanent, public, educational institution which cares for collections systematically. (Short definition, used for convenience in this book)

Since this is a condensed definition, some explanation of the terms used may be in order:

a. permanent institution: the museum is an organization that will in theory have perpetual life, and a life of its own apart from other organizations. The existence of the museum is assured regardless of who its employees may be at any given moment, or regardless of temporary economic recessions.

b. public: the museum is not only open to the public, but exists only for the public good.

c. educational: the museum exists for the purpose of providing education, inspiration, and aesthetic enrichment for all the people; development of the individual; and cooperation with other public educational agencies. It does not exist primarily for entertainment, commercial profit, the personal satisfaction of its employees or sponsors, the self-seeking interests of a clique or club, the nostalgia of elder citizens, to serve the private hobby interests of a few, to promote tourism, or any other noneducational end. For the educational use of collections, research is essential and requires such facilities as a reference library and a study room.

d. collections: important objects useful in an educational and/or aesthetic program; significant objects, not curiosities, relics, rarities, or "collectors' items." Two points must be stressed here: 1) The distinction between art museums, which are, strictly speaking, not educa-

3. Marilyn Hicks Fitzgerald, *Museum Accreditation: Professional Standards* (Washington, D.C.: American Association of Museums, 1973), pp. 8–9.

tional, and all other kinds of museums, which are. In the short definition, the word "educational" is used to mean all the proper work of all kinds of museums. That is, not only the imparting of information but cultural enrichment and a broad exposure to the accomplishments of civilization and its gifted individuals. 2) The kinds of objects that belong in the collections of museums are not necessarily the kinds that the general public would recommend. More about this later.

e. systematic care: thorough documentation, good and permanent records (registration and cataloguing), eternal preservation and security, organized filing of objects (storage) that is logical and accessible.

12.   a nonprofit institution, in the service of society, which acquires, conserves, communicates and exhibits, for purposes of study, education and enjoyment, material witnesses of the evolution of nature and man. (International Council of Museums, draft version of new statutes, 1973)

In addition to the above definitions, the following statements are pertinent to an understanding of what a museum is:

"Museums of whatever kind all have the same task—to study, preserve, and exhibit objects of cultural value for the good of the community as a whole." (UNESCO)

"The term 'museum' must today be reserved for official institutions in the public interest." (Germain Bazin)

The Swiss National Museum was appointed, by statute, "to house important national antiquities that are historically and artistically significant and to preserve them in well-ordered arrangement." (1890)

"An efficient educational museum may be described as a collection of instructive labels, each illustrated by a well-selected specimen." (George Brown Goode, Director of the U.S. National Museum 1889)

Finally, two further definitions from the International Council of Museums:

Museology is museum science. It has to do with the study of the history and background of museums, their role in society, specific systems for research, conservation, education and organization, relationship with the physical environment, and the classification of different kinds of museums. In brief, museology is the branch of knowledge concerned with the study of the purposes and organization of museums.

Museography is the body of techniques related to museology. It covers methods and practices in the operation of museums, in all their various aspects.

EXERCISES—CHAPTER 1

The logical starting point in museum training is a clear understanding of what the museum profession regards as being a "real" museum. Anyone has the freedom to call anything by any name. Not everything called a "museum" would be so called by museum professionals. The student must come to appreciate the differences between the kind of institution that can qualify for accreditation by the American Association of Museums and the kinds that cannot. As you write your responses to the following, show that you have assimilated the definitions and that you know what a museum is.

1. The epilogue of *So You Want a Good Museum* by Carl E. Guthe contains the essence of good museum practice in the form of four obligations the museum assumes. If you have access to this publication, state the four obligations in one word each in order of importance (starting with the most important and ending with the least important). This will require some thought.
2. *On the basis of the previous question*, would you say that museums exist for the sake of exhibits? Why? What would you say about an institution that has an excellent Sunday afternoon lecture series but no catalogue of the collections?
3. From the definitions of "museum" what would you say is the whole purpose of a museum, or why do museums exist? (Briefly.)
4. What would be your reaction if someone pointed out an old building to you in your home town (such as the post office or the high school), and said, "That building would make a good museum"? On the basis of this lesson, criticize the statement. Do not get into architectural technicalities; that will be our concern in a future chapter.
5. Compare museum definitions 6 and 9. Which seems more descriptive of a good, true museum, and why?
6. For the purposes of this book we shall use definition No. 11. Visit a museum in your vicinity and examine its operation sufficiently to apply this definition to it. Is it a true museum? If not, how does it fall short? If it can be considered a museum, what is the greatest weakness in its operation on the basis of the definition?

7. Is a library a museum? Why?
8. Is a planetarium a museum? An arboretum? A zoo? An art center? A historical society? (Explain your answer in each case, that is, say "why," and base your answers on definition 11.)
9. Refer to the two news items cited at the beginning of Chapter 1. Was the word "museum" properly used in these news stories? Why?

2
History of Museums

In the first chapter we were concerned with what a museum of today is. We must now consider museums of yesterday. We must not assume that museums suddenly sprang into being, like an invention. Museums have a long history and have changed in nature, as have other institutions.

Two related natural tendencies or "instincts" of people seem to be universal and timeless. These are the desire to accumulate objects and the desire to show them to other people. We should recognize, however, that "human nature"—whatever that is—is molded in large measure by culture. People in other parts of the world may hold material objects in less esteem than we do.

In our culture, almost every person collects something, or at least has a few objects of which he is especially fond and which he is happy to have other people admire. Almost every community has one person (or several people) noted for a collection on display in his home. Such collections may be of rocks, house plants, arrowheads, souvenir cups and saucers, Navajo rugs, guns, butterflies—the list is endless. Many people who have used their leisure hours in accumulating objects decide on retirement to "open a museum." Often a local museum gets its start when one or more local collectors lend or donate collections for this purpose.

Hand-in-hand with this natural tendency to collect things (obviously, more developed in some people than in others) is the desire to show them to others; to seek approval and admiration, to gain prestige by the respect and envy engendered by the ownership of interesting, beautiful, unusual, and commercially valuable objects. (This is not to say that this is the sole or even the main motivation for collecting. Once a collection exists, however, the common tendency of

15

the owner is to have other people see it and admire it, and there will always be people happy to oblige.) This, then, creates museums.

Almost every community of any size in the United States has its "museum," which is visited and enjoyed. (Whether it actually accomplishes a significant amount of public education is another matter.) Collections have existed from the earliest times, though notable collections in the past have belonged to individuals of power and wealth, not to the general public. For example, archaeologists have reported finding objects of an earlier time together in a palace of a later time; obviously, the king's personal collection of antiquities. Wealthy individuals in ancient Rome had enormous collections of paintings, statues, gold and silver vessels, tapestries, and other works of art. This kind of "hoard" is known throughout history.

Of course, collections are (and have been) made with different motivations and serve different purposes. Dr. Alma Wittlin lists six different kinds of collections based on different motivations on the part of those who have assembled them: Economic hoard collections (a pirate's treasure); social prestige collections (the art collection of a newly rich family; conspicuous consumption); magic collections (the bones of saints in churches); collections as expressions of group loyalty (football trophies in the high school lobby, or a museum on an Indian reservation containing objects formerly made and used by that tribe); collections as means of emotional experience (those that result from an overwhelming passion and drive to collect, whether they be of paintings, sea shells, stamps, or whatever); collections as means of stimulating curiosity and inquiry (for example, the clothing and tools of primitive tribes assembled from afar for a world fair).[1] Dr. Wittlin points out that though some motivations which were at work in the past are not now considered appropriate for building the collections of a public museum, they may still be powerful driving forces in the minds of museum trustees and others who have connections with our museums. In other words, regardless of the lip service paid to "public education," "modern museum methods," and the like, you may wonder why your museum is not more in tune with the times, why its new building will look like a Greek temple on the outside and have an inefficient interior arrangement, and why it is not more responsive to the needs of your community. If you do wonder, look more closely to

1. Alma S. Wittlin, *Museums: In Search of a Usable Future* (Cambridge, Massachusetts: M.I.T. Press, 1970). This book is recommended for reading on the history of museums, as is Germain Bazin, *The Museum Age* (New York: Universe Books, 1967).

see what medieval notions are moving the people who move your museum.

This is not meant to imply that people capable of creating real museums exist only in the present. The Museum of Alexandria in Egypt was essentially like those of today. A little history may provide orientation.

On the death of Philip of Macedon, ruler of Greece, his son Alexander III ("The Great") set out to conquer Persia and build an empire. On his death at the age of 33 in 323 B.C., his generals divided his empire. His half-brother, Ptolemaeus (Ptolemy I), chose Egypt and adjoining parts of North Africa and Arabia for his share. His capital was Alexandria on the Mediterranean Sea (founded by Alexander for the administration of Egypt). Alexandria was a Greek city, and for hundreds of years an important center of western civilization. Ptolemy's descendants, also called Ptolemy, continued to rule until Egypt became a Roman territory. The last of the dynasty was Ptolemy XIV, son of Cleopatra and Julius Caesar, murdered by Augustus in 30 B.C.

About 290 B.C., Ptolemy I established a center of learning dedicated to the muses (hence "museum," house of the muses, "mouseion" in Greek). It consisted of a lecture hall, a mess hall, a court, a cloister, a garden, an astronomical observatory, living quarters, the library, and collections of biological and cultural objects. In fact, the collections probably embraced all the museum fields. The head, or director, of the museum was technically a priest. There were four groups of scholars: astronomers, writers, mathematicians, and physicians. All were Greeks, and all received salaries from the royal treasury. Research was their function and purpose. In later decades, as students multiplied about the museum, its members undertook to give lectures; but it remained to the end an institute for advanced studies. The Mouseion was the first establishment ever set up by a state for the promotion of literature and science. It was at the same time the first museum, research center, liberal arts college, and advanced study institute—the distinctive contribution of the Ptolemies to the development of civilization.

Ptolemy died at age 84 in about 283 B.C. It is interesting that he founded the Mouseion when he was 77 years of age. His descendants strove to improve it, especially the library; it was the greatest achievement of his dynasty.

The museum library was housed partly at the museum itself and partly at the Temple of Zeus (Jupiter Serapis). At its height it consisted of about 400,000 volumes, or as many as 700,000 different scrolls. The most famous library of all time, it came to overshadow the collections of objects. Some authors have, therefore, regarded the museum or collections, as being located in the library, rather than the library as being located in the museum. Civil commotions damaged the library at various times, and the collections and library housed in the museum proper were largely destroyed during an uprising or riot in the reign of Aurelian (A.D. 270–275). The part of the library located in the Temple of Zeus was destroyed under Theodosius the Great in the name of Christianity when he destroyed all the heathen temples (about 380-390). The destruction is erroneously attributed to the Arabs under Omar when they conquered Egypt in 642.

We must not assume that Ptolemy I created the concept of the museum. That distinction goes to Demetrius of Phalerum (the original port of Athens) who moved to Alexandria on his expulsion from Athens in 307 B.C. He, of course, was influenced by the schools of Athens which used natural objects as teaching aids. They in turn were to some degree a legacy of Aristotle, who had a school in Athens (the Lyceum) from 335–323 B.C. Aristotle taught that knowledge must be based on the direct observation of nature, that scientific theory must follow fact, and that knowledge can be categorized along logical principles. Ptolemy likely held Aristotle, who was identified with Macedon and had been Alexander's tutor at the Macedonian court for seven years, in great esteem. Aristotle's philosophy and methods, as expounded to Ptolemy by Demetrius, if need be, would have had a friendly reception.

The reason for this lengthy description of the Mouseion is to make the point that the museum as an educational institution—as a center for research with material objects and for the dissemination of knowledge—is not just a theoretical ideal. There has been a long gap, but during the last hundred years, modern man has been catching up with the ancient Greeks. What the human brain and an enlightened government accomplished two thousand years ago can be accomplished—and is being accomplished—in our time.

After the Greeks, museums as such disappeared for hundreds of years, though we read of the collections of Roman temples. During the Middle Ages, the great churches and abbeys accumulated natural curiosities and religious relics. Private collections of curiosities of art and nature became widespread in Europe in the 17th and 18th centuries. Called "cabinets" or "Wunderkammers," they were a hobby of the wealthy. An example is the collection of Albrecht, Duke of Bavaria, who competed with other European royalty to amass art and oddities. His collection included some 800 paintings, an egg which an abbot had found within another egg, manna which fell from heaven during a famine, a stuffed elephant, and a basilisk.

This emphasis on the entertainment value of an object—because of its strangeness or rarity, or because it gives the viewer a thrill—is the basis of the carnival side show, the wax museum, the "snake farm," and a multitude of miscellaneous collections called museums which reach out for the tourist seeking light entertainment. Some museologists would say that art museums are, though a step up, still on the same ladder. That is, that the guiding principle of the art museum is the collecting and exhibiting of unique and wonderful objects to create an emotional response in the viewer. We shall have more to say in later chapters about the philosophy of the art museum. At this point, however, we should emphasize that the nobility not only collected two-headed animals and other curiosities, they also developed a passion for accumulating real works of art. The collections of paintings and sculpture of most royal families grew to the point that they overflowed the palaces and had to be housed in buildings erected for the purpose. (Most of the important art museums in Europe began as royal collections.) A logical development of the Renaissance was the gradual opening of such royal "art museums" to the public.

Though we take for granted the idea that a museum should be open to the public, such was not always the case. One of the earliest known examples of public admission to a museum is that of Abbot Boisot of the Abbey of Saint Vincent in Besançon, France. On his death in 1694 he left his personal collections to the abbey, with the provision that the public be admitted regularly to see them. The British Museum was founded in 1753 and was said to be open to the public, but it received only 30 visitors daily. These had to apply for admission well in advance. The 15 people allowed in to view the museum at one time were required to stay in a body and were limited to two hours. As late as 1800, persons desiring to visit the British Museum had to present their credentials to the office; if acceptable, they had to wait two weeks for an admission ticket.

The royal French government in 1750 began to open the picture gallery of the Palais de Luxembourg regularly to the public. (Though who were the "public" who were actually admitted? Surely not the dirty and ragged poor.) Plans to make the royal collection in the

Louvre accessible to the public at stated times existed toward the end of the 18th century, but it was the French Revolution that actually created the first public museum by opening the Louvre.

Natural science was not popular in the early 1800's. There were neither collections nor books in this field. For example, it has been reported that there was not a single book on mineralogy for sale in the United States. Not until after 1850 did coherent display of scientific collections for educational purposes begin.

The beginnings of anthropology and the systematic treatment of art date as well from the second half of the 19th century. Paintings were shown chronologically by school at the art museum in Vienna in 1781, but this approach was a rare occurrence until the 1880's, when the Cluny Museum in Paris handled its collections systematically. In 1888, the museum in Nürnberg, Germany, opened to the public six rooms arranged by period. Although we expect any good museum today to have its exhibits arranged according to a logical plan, not all museums show good museological practice. One may still observe paintings hung with no grouping by country, school, time period, or even by artist. In a large and well-known museum in Europe, I have seen paintings arranged on gallery walls by size, with examples by the same artist found in different rooms.

The concepts of the public, educational museum, the systematic treatment of art, and the strong interest in anthropology, science, and technology date from after the middle of the last century. Even though the word "museum" has been in use in the English language for nearly three hundred years,[2] the museum as we know it today—the museum as defined in Chapter 1—is of recent origin.

World Fairs[3]

It has been said that the museum is a development of the last century, stimulated by the great world fairs. Since the 1870's, practically every large fair has created museums. The Centennial Exposition

2. The Ashmolean Museum of Oxford University, the first university museum of modern times, was founded in 1683. It was the first institution in western Europe to call itself a museum.

3. Kenneth W. Luckhurst, *The Story of Exhibitions* (London and New York: The Studio Publications, 1951), was used as a source for much of the information on world fairs given in this chapter. This book provides an interesting history of the great international exhibitions with excellent illustrations.

in Philadelphia in 1876, for example, spurred the building of the American Museum of Natural History, the Metropolitan Museum of Art, the Boston Museum of Fine Arts, the National Museum (of the Smithsonian Institution), and several museums in Philadelphia. Douglas Allan says, "A museum was thus, in the initial stages, a response to the need to house collections brought into being by the enthusiasm of collectors."[4] Put another way, once a government has spent a great deal of money assembling objects to be shown at a world fair, it can hardly throw these objects away when the fair closes. They are ordinarily turned over to museums for preservation and use, and often in the past museums were created because the collections existed and needed to be housed. The public interest in science and art and in visiting exhibitions, stimulated by great world fairs, has also led to public support for the establishment of museums, apart from considerations of caring for collections that already were in existence.

How do world fairs relate to museums? They have certain characteristics in common:

1. Both assemble objects and put them on exhibit.
2. Both use labels and explanatory devices to make the exhibits meaningful to the general public.
3. Both receive and provide for large numbers of visitors; directing them and providing for their comfort and safety.
4. Both provide for the housing and security of exhibits and of the objects within the exhibits.

On the other hand, there are essential differences:

1. World fairs are not permanent institutions.
2. Their main purpose is not education, in the strict sense, but rather entertainment and propaganda.
3. World fairs are based on exhibits, not collections.
4. They combine all kinds of activities, sponsors, and exhibits at one time and place.

An inquiry into the nature and history of world fairs will be helpful at this point, because not only have they been responsible for the creation of museums, but they are also a continuing source of ideas and inspiration for museum exhibition techniques. Indeed, some of the newer institutions, especially in the field of science and industry, appear to blend world fair and museum (the science center).

4. Douglas A. Allan, "The Museum and Its Functions," *The Organization of Museums: Practical Advice*, Museums and Monuments Series, No. IX (Paris: UNESCO, 1960), p. 15.

Two terms need to be defined: 1) A fair is a gathering of buyers and sellers to transact business. 2) An exhibition (in the nonmuseum sense) is a public showing of objects. Synonyms are "show," as in "auto show," "flower show," etc., and "exposition," as in "Century of Progress Exposition" (the Chicago World Fair of 1933 and 1934).

A farmer's market, a flea market, and a sidewalk art sale are fairs. A "county fair" is not a fair but an agricultural exhibition. A trade show is primarily a fair (where manufacturers and wholesale dealers show products to retailers to stimulate marketing). There is, of course, overlapping of function between the two, but the essential thing about a fair is that it exists mainly for selling. The essential thing about an exhibition is that it exists mainly for showing. The term "world fair" is itself incorrect in that it is in reality a gigantic exhibition, not a fair in the strict sense. The point of making this distinction here is so that the student will not be confused when reading the writings of Europeans, who are less likely than Americans to blur the meanings of these terms.

Let us consider the motives that are involved in a large nonmuseum-based exhibition. The exhibitor's motives are: 1) To draw attention to himself or his organization. 2) To advance his material interests or to promote a cause. 3) To entertain for public relations purposes (good will). 4) To compare his product with that of his competitors. The visitor's motives are: 1) To be entertained (recreation). 2) In the case of art exhibitions, exhibits, buildings, flower gardens, etc., to receive the higher form of amusement which might be called "cultural pleasure," "aesthetic appreciation," "emotional involvement," etc. 3) To learn. 4) To transact business or to gain information that may lead to the transaction of business (looking over new refrigerators).

Obviously, these lists do not coincide. Museum curators as well as trade show exhibitors must keep in mind that the viewer of their exhibits must enjoy himself and feel that he is receiving something of value. Only then will the exhibitor achieve his own goals.

The greatest of the exhibitions are the world fairs, sometimes called expositions, or international exhibitions. Some of their characteristics are that they are international, involving governments and large organizations (such as General Motors and the Catholic Church); they are impressive spectacles, immensely appealing to the public and highly entertaining; they have large assemblages of exhibits created by professional, commercial designers (world fairs present examples of the highest development of the art of exhibition); they are showplaces and proving grounds for innovations in the arts and sciences; and in spite of good organization, international exhibitions are so very expensive that they often go bankrupt.

World fairs are a natural development from the industrial, national, and art exhibitions which were held in the early part of the 19th century. The first world fair, or international exhibition, was the Great Exhibition of Industry of All Nations held in London in 1851. It was highly successful, immediately imitated by other countries, and exerted an influence on all world fairs for the remainder of the century.

The original idea of an international exhibition is credited to Prince Albert of Saxe-Coburg-Gotha, the German cousin and husband of Queen Victoria. He was acquainted with the large exhibitions and fairs held in Germany which attracted visitors from many countries. The London exhibition was housed in a single building called the Crystal Palace. Largely prefabricated and made of mass-produced components, the building was erected in only 17 weeks, though it covered an expanse of 18 acres (about the equivalent of 12 football fields).

The excuse to organize a great exhibition is often the celebration of a historical event. Examples are the Centennial Exposition in Philadelphia in 1876, the World's Columbian Exposition in Chicago in 1893 (one year late), the Louisiana Purchase Exposition in St. Louis in 1903, and the Century of Progress Exposition in Chicago in 1933. Great expositions were held in Montreal in 1967 and in Japan in 1970.

Paris has probably been the greatest single center for world fairs, but they have been held in many different countries. During the last century they were housed in single large buildings, one of which eventually reached a size of 53 acres (Paris, 1878). In this century many separate buildings have been used in each of the great "fairs." In the Louisiana Purchase Exposition in St. Louis in 1903 1,576 separate buildings roofed an area of more than 300 acres. The exposition area had 45 miles of roads, 13 miles of exhibition railway, and to see all the exhibits in just one of the buildings—the agriculture building—required a walk of nine miles. The exhibition went bankrupt.

International expositions are of considerable interest to the museum worker because in large measure they have the kind of success he is seeking. Every museum director would like the great publicity, large crowds of visitors, expensive and impressive installations, electronic teaching devices, and artistic and educational exhibits of world fairs. Studying the exhibit techniques of the expositions can help the museum worker to improve the exhibits in his own museum. The principles of good exhibit practice are the same wherever the exhibit is found. They are:

1. The exhibit must first attract the visitor's interest.
2. It must inspire his confidence in the exhibitor and in what he has to say or offer.
3. Having gained the visitor's confidence, the exhibit must reward him by showing him something seriously worth seeing and by enabling him to understand what he sees.
4. It must do this in a pleasing way and in good taste.

EXERCISES—CHAPTER 2

Collections, and what are called museums, may be founded and maintained for different reasons. People who create and promote museums have different motives and different philosophies. Confusion and conflict in museum operation sometimes occur because of a simple lack of agreement as to what a museum ought to be. It is, therefore, essential to the good health of a museum—especially a small regional museum managed by nonprofessionals—that the purpose of the museum be spelled out in detail in writing.

The acceptable museum of today is one that would want to and would qualify for accreditation by the American Association of Museums. In general, "museums" of the past were not truly museums in today's sense. Many so-called "museums" of today more closely resemble those of the past than they do true, twentieth-century museums.

For this assignment, visit and consider one or more museums in your vicinity; or answer the questions on the basis of your remembrance of one or more museums which you have visited in the past; or, if necessary, imagine a museum existing today that you could describe in detail.

1. How does a particular museum (or how do several museums) with which you are familiar resemble:
   A. a Wunderkammer
   B. a private collection
   C. a reference collection for scholars or experts
   D. a place of entertainment?
   (Try to find an example of each.)
2. What antiquated or short-sighted notions that are contrary to the concept of the public educational museum have you observed in operation in any museum? (This may relate, for example, to Dr. Wittlin's list.)
3. Reviewing in your mind the development of the museum of today, what trend do you see for the future? In other words, what do you imagine tomorrow's

museum will be like (philosophically or conceptually, not in terms of technical facilities)?

4. What can you say about the kinds of museums you would expect to find
    A. in one of the new African nations
    B. in a city in the United States
    C. in a European capital
    D. in a rural location in Europe
    based on the history and development of museums? Think in terms of politics, especially.

5. From your experience, what can you say about the attitudes toward collecting and exhibiting on the part of artists or art curators as compared with that of curators in the sciences? (If you have no actual experience in this regard, state what you would imagine the differences to be on the basis of the nature of the material and the histories of art and science museums.)

6. From your familiarity with county and/or state fairs
    A. what aspects justify the term "fair"?
    B. what aspects justify the term "exhibition"?

7. What is the role of amusements (roller-coasters, sideshows, gambling games) at a county fair? What can the museum learn from this, or what application might there be to the program (operation) of a museum?

8. At a world fair, a trade show, the exhibits at a convention, or elsewhere, you have probably observed the work of professional exhibit designers. Compare this with museum exhibits with which you are familiar and comment on the differences and similarities.

9. Describe your own collecting experience. What do you collect? Why do you do it? In what way and under what circumstances do you show your collection to others? What is your motivation for exhibiting? (Do not be superficial. If you give this question serious thought and attempt to answer it fully and without reserve, you will gain in understanding of how museums are created and managed. People are much the same. Museum trustees, directors, curators, and technicians are like you. To understand them, try to understand yourself.)

10. Describe the principal private collection in your locality. (If you have not yet seen it, contact the owner, explain your interest, and try to see it and interview the owner.) What does the collector say his reasons are for collecting? What is his attitude toward placing the collection in a public museum? Which of Dr. Wittlin's list of motivations do you feel are at work?

3

Museums Today

As may be expected, museums are enjoying a phenomenal growth in the United States and Canada. Reports indicate that the Canadian province of Alberta had 18 museums in 1952, 39 in 1964, and 86 in 1971. Reports also indicate that, currently, four to six new museums are formed each week in the United States. A few years ago an estimate counted a new museum in this country every three days.

Some 200 museums existed in the United States in 1876; 600 in 1919; 2,500 in 1940; 5,000 in 1965; and perhaps as many as 7,000 in 1974. This approximates a tripling every thirty years. If the rate continues, we may expect 21,000 museums in the year A.D. 2000.

The American Association of Museums is the professional organization of museums and museum employees.[1] Its *Official Museum Directory*, revised periodically, is the only complete source of information on the museums of the United States and Canada. A glance through the directory makes obvious at once the fact that museums are not evenly distributed either geographically or by population. While densely populated states in the East have approximately one museum per 15 square miles or 15,000 people, some of the western states have only one per 5,000 square miles and 50,000 people. The comparison does not end here, of course, because the size and quality of the museums must be taken into account. How many relic-filled settler's cabins in western towns would it take to equal in educational and aesthetic value only one museum in New York City, the Metropolitan Museum of Art, which is said to have more professional employees than all the art museums of Italy? Parenthetically, the Met also forms

1. For information about publications and benefits of membership, write to 2233 Wisconsin Avenue, N.W., Washington, D.C. 20007.

an interesting contrast with another great art museum, the Prado in Madrid. The Met has more than 840 employees, the Prado 10. The Met's director is paid annually about $50,000; the director of the Prado about $4,000.

One can say, in general, that while good museums can be found in all regions, they tend to be concentrated in large cities in the East, in the Middle West, and on the Pacific Coast. In other words, museums are where the people are and where the wealth is.

It has been estimated that there are 12 to 14 thousand museums in the world, of which half are in the United States;[2] half of these have been created since World War II. Half of the American museums are small, regional history museums. Obviously, a problem exists regarding the quality and value of the collections and the program of the small museum which is founded and operated by uninformed and untrained amateurs. Accreditation of museums, the certification of trainees, and, above all, the recognition on the part of trustees of the importance of securing professional staff to manage museums will help to raise the standards of the local museum.

A pamphlet given to American students en route to Europe states, "In a European museum you will never have that feeling of looking at a vast pile of objects brought together by an amateur with more money than taste." That this is generally true is at least in part a consequence of the governmental supervision of museums in most countries of the world. Most of the museums of France are supervised by the great art history museum in Paris, the Louvre. The Belgian government does not permit the local amateur establishment of museums and is reluctant to establish museums even under its own direction without strong justification. Much the same can be said for other countries. The new governments in Africa deliberately establish museums for their propaganda value. Museums are used as a medium for conveying information and establishing desirable public attitudes. With expert direction and supervision of museums by the national government, professional standards can be maintained. (One is reminded of the generally high quality of National Park Service visitor

2. ICOM reported in 1973 that there may be as many as 20,000 museums in the world, employing about 100,000 people. If this is true, the United States may have less than one third of the world's museums. Of course, the difficulty of dealing with figures of this kind is that there is no common agreement as to what a museum is, or how rigidly to apply the professional definitions of a museum given in chapter one. No one could say, for example, how many museums there are in any one of our states.

centers in this country.) At the same time, democratic countries value the rights of individuals for self-expression and for pursuing vocations and avocations of their choice. Furthermore, supervision of many museums from one office may incline to monotony in presentation, bias, conservatism (in hewing to the line of the political philosophy in power), and discouragement of innovation, fresh approaches, and subjects of purely local interest. This is a philosophical issue which need not concern us further at this point, but let us recognize the familiar source of conflict involving central planning and direction—which may be efficient but may also be narrowly orthodox—versus local planning and direction—which may be inefficient but may also be nearer to the hearts of the local inhabitants.

As the educational level of the average person rises and his leisure time increases, museums are playing an ever-increasing role in the lives of ordinary people. "Our age has the mission to initiate into the cultural life segments of society which have hardly been prepared for it by their day-to-day family surroundings, and for whom the increase in leisure time offers more and more opportunity to visit museums."[3] Families that can travel, and they are in the majority, can experience a great variety of museums. In the New Orleans Jazz Museum the visitor can pick up a telephone, dial a number, and hear a musical selection of his choice. The Pacific Science Center in Seattle (a holdover of the 1962 world fair) teaches mathematics by means of devices that are fun to watch and to operate. In Bath, Maine, the Marine Museum teaches about America's sailing ships of the last century. The Kiwanis Club of Lewiston, Idaho, is restoring two trolley cars that were in use from 1905 to 1925. Mohave and Chemehuevi Indians in Arizona have mortgaged tribal lands in order to buy at auction objects made by their ancestors and placed them in their tribal museum.

Somewhat more frivolous collecting interests many people. The jersey of George Blanda of the Oakland Raiders was placed in the Pro Football Hall of Fame (Canton, Ohio) in 1970. Some communities try to capitalize on a historic event in order to build local solidarity and to attract tourist dollars. Not all such efforts are successful. The Associate Press reported that Reynoldsburg, Ohio, was trying to drum up enthusiasm for a tomato festival on the justification that the basic strain of tomatoes had been developed there by a botanist years ago. Reynoldsburg, however, "never has been a tomato town," and

3. Pierre Gilbert (Director of the Royal Museums of Art and History, Brussels), "The Museum and the Art of Teaching", *Museum*, XX, No. 4 (1967), p. 291.

"frankly, some people couldn't care less whether this is the birthplace of the tomato," said Councilman Gilbert Whalen.

Whatever it is, a museum is probably dedicated to it somewhere. There is a spaghetti museum at Pontedassio, Italy. Germany has a brewing museum in Munich, a wine museum in Speyer, a doll museum in Nürnberg and a bread museum in Ulm. A museum in Wuppertal is devoted to clocks and one in Schorndorf to thimbles. Paris has museums of money, medals, carpets, and music. In this country there is a trend toward ethnic museums in cities. A successful early example is the Anacostia Neighborhood Museum in southeastern Washington, D.C. A "branch museum" of the Smithsonian Institution, its exhibits are not limited to Negro history and culture but include a small zoo, arts and crafts, and a walkthrough general store of around 1890.

Some of the world's greatest museums serve as models for the profession and are worth mentioning here. Their names are well known to museologists. The Smithsonian is not a single museum but, actually, the world's greatest museum complex. It includes the National Museum (Natural History), the National Gallery of Art, the Museum of History and Technology, the Rock Creek Park Zoo, and other branches.

Also previously mentioned was the Metropolitan Museum of Art in New York City. Just across Central Park is one of the greatest of the natural history museums, the American Museum of Natural History. A worthy rival for top honor is the Field Museum of Natural History in Chicago, whose collections date from the World's Columbian Exposition of 1893 in Chicago. The Museum of Science and Industry in that city is housed in one of the buildings of the 1893 world fair and got its start as a result of the Century of Progress Exposition in 1933 and 1934.

The first and greatest of the museums of technology is the Deutsches Museum in Munich, a city which is noted for its great museums. Perhaps the most famous, and some would say the greatest, museum in the world is the Louvre in Paris, housed in what was formerly a palace. Its collections include antiquities from the near East as well as a great number of paintings, some of them gigantic in size. The British Museum in London is likewise noted for antiquities, such as the Elgin Marbles, the statuary removed from the pediments of the Parthenon. The largest museum dedicated to the decorative arts, the Victoria and Albert Museum, is also in London.

Scandinavia has dozens of "folk museums." Many of these are "open-air" collections of actual buildings moved from afar and assembled on one site. Sometimes they are furnished and adjacent exhibit buildings show costumes, agricultural implements, and other objects illustrating rural life in the past. The best-known of these is Skansen in Stockholm, Sweden. A somewhat similar establishment in the United States is Greenfield Village in Dearborn, Michigan. Here Henry Ford gathered on a large tract of land more than 100 buildings of all kinds, ranging from homes to factories. At one side is the Henry Ford Museum, one of the largest history museums in the world, with interiors of rooms and stores, collections illustrating the development of technology, and an enormous transportation section. Colonial Williamsburg in Williamsburg, Virginia, is the world's largest and most expensive historic restoration project. Actual buildings remaining from the 1700's as well as reconstructed buildings appear in their original locations.

The International Council of Museums (ICOM),[4] an independent organization of museums and museum workers, sponsored by UNESCO, maintains a documentation center in Paris from which one may obtain information concerning museums in all parts of the world.

EXERCISES—CHAPTER 3

The purpose of this assignment is to familiarize you with the state of museums in your own locality. It will be necessary for you to learn at least:
A. when they were founded and by whom (i.e., how did they come to be created?);
B. how active they are today as compared with other local museums and as compared with themselves in the past;
C. what sentiment exists for the creation of new museums and where new museums are likely to come from, in your judgment.

1. How many museums are there today in your locality (city, county, twenty-mile radius of your home, or whatever is convenient—but try to include at least four museums, preferably ten or twelve)? How does this compare with 1960, 1950, 1940, before 1940?
2. What plans exist for creating museums in your locality? What organizations and what kinds of individuals are behind any actual movement in this direction?
3. What trends do you see? (In other words, what is the future for museums in your locality? Be able to justify your opinion.)

4. For information regarding joining, and the benefits of membership, address the ICOM office at the American Association of Museums, 2233 Wisconsin Avenue, N.W., Washington, D.C. 20007.

4

Museums and Museum Fields

A museum is characterized mainly by the kinds of objects it collects. That is, the subject field or discipline with which the museum is mainly concerned determines its kind. Confusion as to the proper role of a museum is sometimes the result of a lack of understanding as to the precise nature of the various subject fields. At this point, therefore, we should review them.

The main division in the museum world is between art museums and all other kinds. This is a result of a basic philosophical difference. Art is concerned with unique, highly unusual productions of gifted human beings. These productions, called "works of art", are valued for their own sake. If the creation by the artist results in a durable, material object, it becomes the concern of the art museum. All other kinds of museums are concerned with typical, common, quantity-produced, and natural objects that are valued not in themselves but as examples of the natural world and of human cultures. (This will be further explained in later chapters dealing with the theory of collecting.) In this latter group of museums an additional division exists between the collecting of artifacts as examples of human history and the collecting of natural specimens as examples of the world of nature. The threefold classification of museums is *art, history,* and *science.*

Art Museums

Artists do not agree on a definition of art, and we shall not attempt one at this time. However, we can say that art plays on the senses by the selection, ordering, and arrangement of that which will produce sensation. Art may be created by making things to look at or sounds to listen to, tastes and smells to experience, or even ideas to titillate the mind. Art is infinite. No one can draw up a list of all the arts.

31

For museum purposes, we recognize, at least, that there are the kinds of art activity or creation which result in an object or an arrangement of objects (a material production); and there are the kinds which result in an event or sequence of events, or sequence or arrangement of sounds, movement, or sensations. We may call the latter kinds the *performing arts*. These are nonmaterial, existing as fleeting productions through time; they can never be repeated exactly. Even a novel never produces the same effect on a second reading. (The novel, of course, belongs to the literary or language arts, which are even more removed from the museum's prime concerns than are the performing arts.) Since the performing arts do not create objects which can be collected and used by museums, there are no performing art museums. A so-called "museum of the dance" or "museum of the theater" is either a museum of the *history* of the dance or the theater, or it is not really a museum.

The arts that produce material objects may be divided into two main categories: the Fine Arts and the Applied or Useful Arts. The distinction is whether an object exists solely as an art object—a thing of beauty—("art for art's sake") or whether it is primarily functional—a rug, a chair, or a bridge—and secondarily good to look at. In the museum context the Useful Arts are the *Decorative Arts*, a term applied to objects in interior decoration (furniture, silverware, draperies, etc.). Closely related are dress designing, jewelry making, flower arranging, and others.

The *Fine Arts* embrace two-dimensional pictures produced by painting, drawing, or one of the printing processes (etching, engraving, woodcuts, etc.); or three-dimensional material objects produced as sculpture or as ceramics (baked, molded clay). The fine arts sometimes include architecture (though it is allied with engineering and is certainly a "useful" art) and sometimes landscape gardening.

The third major subdivision of art as regards museums is *Folk Art*, sometimes further broken down into primitive or tribal art, peasant art, "ethnic art," and pioneer arts and crafts. This kind of art is of the people, not created by professional artists as art. The distinction is largely between popular art and elite art which will be discussed later. The materials of folk art include such diverse items as Navajo Indian blankets, Ukrainian painted Easter eggs, and cornhusk dolls from the Appalachians.

In brief, art museums collect the elite artistic productions of civilized societies—paintings, drawings, photographs, statues, furniture, jewelry, textiles, metalware, and some of the crafts of precivilized and pre-urban peoples as well. Major art museums collect and exhibit objects from the ancient civilizations of the Mediterranean and the Near East—Egypt, Babylonia, Greece, etc. These include statuary, jewelry, and other objects of art but also such objects as mummies, tomb inscriptions, metal tools and weapons, and common vessels which have more significance in ancient history and in anthropology than they do in art. Ancient history and classical archaeology have traditionally been included in art museums, however.

History Museums

History museums in the United States and Canada, in the main, are concerned with local history, that is, the history of the region in which the museum is located. All objects made or used by human beings are of potential interest to the history museum. Obviously, selectivity is essential. History museums specialize in a certain time period, a certain limited geographical region, or a particular field. Historical fields include transportation, industry and technology, arms and armor, horology (clocks), numismatics (coins), philately (stamps), costumes, home furnishings, and many more. The essential requirement in a good history museum is that objects must be collected to serve the purpose of public education. For the most part, they must be typical, at one time commonplace, items that can be used to illustrate the facts of history.

Science Museums

There are two major kinds of science museums—technology, or science and industry museums; and natural history museums.

Science and Industry Museums

A museum concerned with teaching the principles of physics, chemistry, and mathematics utilizes models, pictures, and other audiovisual aids. They show and explain commercial products such as automobiles and telephones. For the purposes of "public relations"—advertising, sales promotion, creating good will—industrial and governmental organizations and agencies install impressive exhibits at great expense in technology museums and science centers in major cities. Since no actual museum objects exist apart from the fields of art, history, and natural history, so-called museums of science and industry occupy a special niche in the museum world and perhaps should not be considered real museums.[1]

Natural History Museums

This field, which includes the world of nature and noncivilized man as a part of that world, has four subfields: *Zoology, Botany, Geology,* and *Anthropology.* Zoology, the study of animals, and botany, the study of plants, together make up biology, the science of life. Traditionally, in natural history museums zoology and botany have been separate departments, each with subfields such as herpetology, ichthyology, mammalogy, and others, depending, of course, on the size and completeness of the collections. The botany department will include a *herbarium* or "archives" of plant specimens, mostly dried and mounted on standard sheets of paper together with pertinent information.

Geology is the study of the earth, dealing chiefly—in a museum at least—with rocks and minerals. Mineralogy is one of the important subfields. Another is paleontology, the study of past life, especially extinct forms of plants and animals known only through fossils. Logically, paleontology might be included under biology, but since its objects are rocks, it is more at home with geology in the museum setting.

Anthropology, the science of man, has a major division between *physical anthropology,* the study of man as an animal, and *cultural anthropology,* the study of man through his learned behavior or culture. Usually cultural anthropology, especially in the United States, is thought of as having the divisions of *linguistics,* the scientific study of language; *social anthropology,* the systematic comparative study of social forms and institutions; *ethnology,* the study at first hand of primitive or tribal peoples;[2] and *archaeology,* the study of past human life on the basis of material remains excavated from the earth. The natural history museum (or the anthropology department of a general museum) show its concern with *physical anthropology* by collecting

---

1. Of course, if a science and industry museum goes beyond the presentation of contemporary industrial techniques and commercial products it may, like the Deutsches Museum in Munich, have recorded, permanent collections and educational exhibits on past developments in technology. To a degree, then, it would be a *history* museum.

2. The term "ethnography" is also used. It means the description of cultures, while "ethnology" means the analysis of cultures.

human bones, *ethnology* by collecting the clothing and implements of primitive peoples, and *archaeology* by collecting the durable cultural remains excavated by archaeologists. (Such an academic field as linguistics is, of course, not a museum field because it does not have objects.)

Anthropological archaeology is prehistoric; that is, it is concerned with nonliterate cultures, such as those of the American Indian prior to the arrival of Europeans. Nonanthropological archaeology is oriented toward history and art history. Of this type, *classical archaeology* is concerned with ancient Rome and Greece (and in a broader sense of the term with ancient Egypt, Mesopotamia, Persia, and Asia Minor as well). Similar archaeology is also pursued in the areas of the high civilizations of India and eastern Asia. In Europe a distinction has been made between medieval and post-medieval archaeology. In the United States and Canada in recent years historical archaeology, which is the application of archaeological techniques to the study of history, has increased rapidly. Largely developed by anthropologists trained in prehistoric archaeology, it has a strong interest in the period of early contact between the native Americans and Europeans, and in such anthropological concerns as community structure, social interaction, and cultural change. Even so, historical archaeology is more at home in a history than in a natural history museum.

All museum objects can be thought of as *inorganic*—belonging to geology; *organic*—belonging to biology; or *superorganic* (cultural)—belonging to archaeology, ethnology, history, and art. These last four subjects are related and can be thought of as one, because all deal with the works of man. To summarize: Museums collect and are concerned with animate and inanimate natural objects, and objects made by man.

Figure 4.1 illustrates the relationships among the different types of museums. The purpose of this kind of chart in museology is to show that all fields are interrelated and that any museum object can be used in more than one way.[3] Without this kind of perspective a museum

---

3. Subfields along the lines connecting the major fields indicate areas of collecting and exhibiting as related to other subjects. The circles are but two examples of types of museums or museum departments related to more than one of the standard museum fields. Thus, ancient history and classical archaeology, an important and popular category, is related to history, the arts, and anthropology. Likewise, health museums are based on physical anthropology, biology, technology, etc.

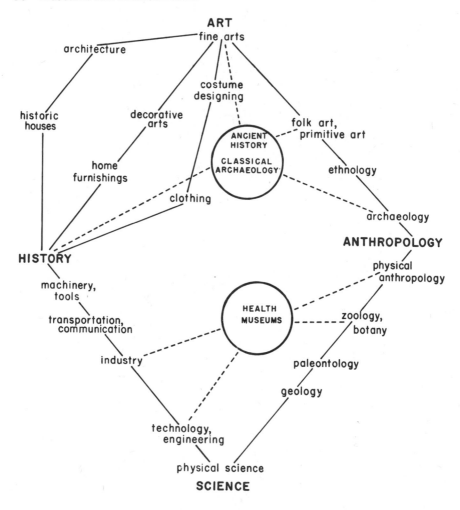

FIGURE 4.1

curator will be narrow in his approach to his collections and will fail to give full interpretation of his exhibits. A common example of this kind of failure is the treatment of ethnological materials, such as the dance masks of African tribes, in some art museums. The masks are shown only as interesting and aesthetic objects, and the cultural context in which they originally functioned is ignored, certainly to the intellectual loss of the museum visitor, and, I suspect, to the detriment of full aesthetic appreciation as well. It works both ways, of course; museum ethnologists may ignore the artistic aspects of their collections and thereby deprive visitors of opportunities for aesthetic enjoyment.

A word of caution: No object entering the collections of a museum has only one potential use and categorical place. Placing it in one department or another is done on a traditional basis for the sake of orderliness and convenience (a painting by Renoir would normally be assigned to the fine arts), but the object might serve in several different ways at different times (the painting might decorate a wall in a historical room exhibit; it might be used to illustrate a step in the development of painting technique; it might be used as an example of easily transferred wealth in an exhibit of economics; it might be used for its illustration of agricultural practices at a particular time and place; and so on).

A final note: A museum need not be limited to one or two fields. There are museums that concentrate on one particular thing, such as clocks; but there are also museums of art and history, of anthropology and history, of art and science, of any other combination. Many museums embrace a number of fields and therefore are called "general" or "encyclopedic" museums. Many general museums have no limitations on their collecting, but this is usually a mistake.

EXERCISES—CHAPTER 4

1. Make an outline of all museum fields you know of or can discover. Use correct outline form; indent for subfields and indent further for sub-subfields. Try to include some areas which can be repeated in more than one kind of museum. For example, "transportation" could be a department of a history museum and also of a science and industry museum. Do not carry this too far, however. For example, art is not properly a branch of history or anthropology as museums are customarily organized.

2. An eccentric multimillionaire named Head has established a museum and named it for himself. The Head Museum collects only heads; either representations or actual heads or parts of heads. However, there is no limitation as to the subject fields by which the collections are catalogued. There are departments of different arts, history, botany, the subfields of anthropology, and so on. As a new assistant registrar in this museum, your job is to

receive incoming additions to the collections and assign each object to its proper and best department. How would you assign the following?[4]
Example: A model of a head of cabbage   botany
(Note: Do not use anthropology, biology, natural history, art, or science as complete answers; use their subfields or major breakdowns. If you do not feel a particular answer is obvious, make a choice and explain why you have made it.)

A. A ceramic head in the form of a wall plaque
B. The head of a bird pickled by an Englishman in the last century
C. A piece of quartz resembling a head, donated by an Indian
D. The head of an Indian carved out of quartz by Auguste Rodin
E. The baked clay head of an animal from an Indian burial mound
F. The skull of a white girl found near the burial mound
G. The head of a Christian saint carved by a Mexican Indian
H. The skull of a dinosaur
I. A shrunken head from South America
J. A model of the human head, used in a medical school

4. This question is not as frivolous as it may sound. It illustrates the assignment of objects, collected by a museum, to specific departments on the basis of the anticipated use of the objects.

5

Organization and Support

Regardless of who owns the museum (city, state, private foundation, university, or whatever), it should have a board of trustees to whom the director reports. The director is the chief administrative officer of a museum; it is he who hires and fires and is in direct charge of the operation. The trustees' responsibility should be largely limited to matters of broad policy and of ensuring the adequate financing of the museum. It is not the proper role of the director to have to raise the money to pay his own salary. Unfortunately, however, circumstances sometimes force him to be a fundraiser, and he cannot devote his time and energies entirely to the management of the museum.

The distinction between the term "director" and the term "curator" is that the former means the administrative head of an organization, and the latter refers to a person who is in charge of a museum collection. The British term "keeper" is perhaps more illustrative of the curator's main purpose. The person in charge of a small museum with simple administrative duties should be called curator rather than director. A larger museum will have a curator for each of the major divisions, such as a curator of history, a curator of art, and so on. Since the curators are department heads, it has seemed convenient to give the same title to other department heads. Thus, we have curators of exhibits, curators of education, curators of television, etc. If a department head has an assistant, the assistant may be called assistant curator of the specific discipline.

In the large museums, subject fields are divided into as many subfields as is useful. In a large natural history museum, for example, the Chief Curator of Zoology may have under him a Curator of Mammals, a Curator of Birds, (etc.), and any number of assistants. There are just as many jobs in a small museum as in a large one, but there are fewer people to do them. The generalist, or person who likes many different subjects and who enjoys variety in his work, may be happier in a small museum. The specialist, on the other hand, would fit into a large institution where the total work is divided into narrow segments. Museum people sometimes create problems for themselves by failing to recognize the difference between museums with few people and museums with many. As a museum grows, its staff must increase with it. The curator of art may then get an assistant to take over some of his responsibility, thus narrowing his job.

In a small operation, after the first person (the director or curator) is hired, the next to be added are a secretary, a janitor, and an all-around assistant. Curators are hired in the second stage; in the third, as many service personnel as the museum can afford. Service personnel are such people as receptionists and clerks, handymen and guards, registrars and librarians, exhibits technicians, and teachers (curators of education and their staffs). No rules govern this, other than the practical ones of the best management and utilization of the collections.

Museum directors should avoid the practice of hiring part-time experts to fill gaps in their staff patterns. When the funds are not sufficient to hire a full-time curator, the temptation exists to find someone who can take the responsibility on a half-time or third-time basis. At best, this is only a temporary expedient. A part-time person in a professional position, one with responsibilities and creative opportunities, will have divided loyalties. He or she may be concerned, while working for the museum, with duties and plans for the rest of the day outside the museum. There is less likelihood that this person would be involved in evening and weekend activities of the museum, and he or she can never feel (or be felt by the rest of the staff to be) completely a member of the staff. A museum staff is a team of individuals conferring, planning, and working together to make their museum successful and respected. Someone who is present only certain hours of the day or certain days of the week cannot be a full member of the team, and this diminishes his or her effectiveness. It is better to treat the part-time employment of experts like the acceptance of loans: It may be done for compelling reasons under certain circumstances for a specific, short-term purpose, which is apart from the day-to-day operation of the museum.

Most museums use volunteer help to fill the gaps in their ideal staff patterns. Sometimes a particular kind of service is left entirely to volunteers, such as classes for visiting school children, the sales department, or the registration and cataloguing of the collections. Volunteer services (which, of course, are free) are so important at many museums that without them the museums would have to curtail their programs seriously or even close their doors. Volunteers are of two main types: Those who work as individuals, directly for and under the supervision of a member of the museum staff; and those who must first belong to an officially sanctioned volunteer organization. This organization may exist solely as a volunteer arm of the museum (often called "Museum Volunteers"), or it may be an organization with a broader purpose but which includes museum volunteer work as one of its functions. An example of the latter kind of group is the Junior League, which in some cities elects to assist one or more museums for a period of time, in addition to other community service projects.

Organized volunteer efforts normally consist of guiding groups through the museum's exhibition areas and teaching visiting school classes. A person so engaged is called a docent. The training of docents should be, and usually is, a thorough preparation for all aspects of their duties. It is administered either by the museum staff or by the volunteer organization itself, or (commonly) by a cooperative effort of both. The docent receives instruction in all subject matter fields in which he or she will have to be informed, becomes completely familiar with the museum, including not only its exhibits but also its operation and philosophy, and is trained in the techniques of managing groups and of teaching children in the museum context. As such training may take months, it requires a sincere commitment on the part of the volunteer-trainee as well as conviction on the part of the museum that trained docents are an invaluable addition to the staff. Once trained, docents may donate much of their spare time for years to the educational work of the museum. Developing a training program is not a step to be taken lightly, however. The most important rule in using volunteers is that their training and supervision must not take more of the time of the professional staff than would the work that the volunteers perform.

The matter of financial income for the museum is, of course, vital. Most museums seem to be poverty-stricken most of the time. This is probably because the public expects more—and their professional staffs desire to give more to the public—than their operating budgets will buy. Although some museums feel compelled to charge for admission or to ask for donations, it is an unusual museum that can support itself in this way. If we divide the number of visitors into the number of dollars in the museum's budget, we get the cost per visitor.

This may range from fifty cents to three dollars, but for most museums the cost will probably average more than a dollar. An admission charge of 50 cents per person would then yield no more than half the funds needed, even if it did not significantly diminish the number of visitors. A large percentage of the attendance at museums is made up of visiting school classes, normally admitted free. Some museums give free admission to retired people, military personnel, members, and others. A visiting family will expect to pay a substantially lower admission charge for young children than for adults. Therefore, a museum that charges an adult one dollar for admission may receive from this source less than one-fourth of the funds that it needs for its operation.[1] A charge large enough to meet operating costs might so diminish attendance that the charge would be self-defeating.

The Museum of Modern Art, in New York City, recently raised its admission charge from 25 cents to two dollars.[2] Studies have shown that the imposition of an admission charge does not significantly change the pattern of attendance; that is, substantially the same people or same kinds of people visit museums whether or not there is a charge.[3] However, it is always regrettable when members of its public cannot use a tax-supported institution. There will be, inevitably, some people who cannot afford to pay an admission charge, or who object to having to pay to enter a museum which they already support through their taxes. A good solution to this problem has been used for many years by the Field Museum of Chicago (and others). On certain days of the week, admission is free and school classes and other groups are received. On other days of the week an admission is charged, and the building is quieter and less crowded. Some museums use the system of a strongly recommended donation. That is, a visitor is not forced to pay an admission charge, but most people

1. To put this into concrete terms, imagine a museum with an annual budget of $50,000 which receives 50,000 visitors each year. (Rather, 50,000 visits, since some individuals will visit a museum many times during a year and be counted each time.) The cost per visitor (or visit) is one dollar. If 40,000 of the visits are by young children and others admitted free, the remaining 10,000 visits would have to be priced at 5 dollars each for the museum to support itself through admissions alone.

2. This is the highest charge among the major museums at the time of this writing. The trend seems to be for admission charges to rise, and for more and more urban museums to initiate a charge.

3. For example: Hiroshi Daifuku, "The Museum and the Visitor," *The Organization of Museums: Practical Advice*, Museums and Monuments Series, No. IX (Paris: UNESCO, 1970), p. 77.

feel obliged to leave a donation. In 1970, the average donation at the Cloisters (the medieval art branch of the Metropolitan Museum of Art) was 58 cents.

Ordinarily, the most productive source of income for the museum is public taxes, budgeted for the museum's operation by the governmental body in charge: city council, state legislature, and others. Museums augment these funds by membership fees, donations, sales desk profits, rentals, annual money-raising events, and, of course, admission fees. As stated earlier, when the level of the museum's accustomed operation is far beyond what would be supported by the annual public appropriation, the museum director may find that much of his time is required, continually, to raise money. It even happens with some museums that their major effort is simply to keep alive.

A rule-of-thumb in a healthier situation is that two thirds of the annual operating budget should be devoted to salaries. Even 75 per cent may not be excessive under some circumstances. Salaries of the professional staff should be comparable to those of libraries and schools in the area. The director of the museum should be paid at least as much as the director of the city library, the principal of an elementary school, or an assistant or associate professor at the local junior college, depending on many factors. The museum, like a library or a school, is an educational institution of great value to the community. Its staff must be as well-prepared and as well-paid as those of other educational institutions of comparable size and responsibility.[4] The museum staff needs not only to be paid adequately, but supported adequately as regards the operating budget. A good museum, like a good school, a good hospital, or a good sewer system, cannot be established and operated at low cost. A community cannot expect to have much of a museum on an annual operating budget of less than $50,000.[5]

4. For a detailed report on current museum salaries, see Kyran M. McGrath, *1973 Museum Salary and Financial Survey* (Washington, D.C.: The American Association of Museums, 1973).

5. Assuming $35,000 for salaries, this would allow a director, a secretary-registrar, a janitor-handyman, a curator of exhibits-assistant director, and some part-time student help (for example, for a weekend receptionist). The remaining $15,000 would have to cover insurance, utilities, shipping, postage, building maintenance and repairs, travel, purchase of objects for the collections, books and subscriptions, memberships in professional organizations, employee insurance and retirement, publicity and promotion, rental of temporary exhibitions, supplies and equipment of all kinds, etc.

Some typical staff patterns are:

A municipal contemporary art and history museum in a large city

Director
  Secretary
  Bookkeeper
Assistant Director
  Curatorial Assistant
  Guards
  Maintenance Persons
  Handymen
Curator of Collections
  Clerk-Registrar
  General Assistant
Curator of Education
  Teacher
  Audio-Visual Technician
  General Assistant
Curator of Exhibits
  Draftsman-Artist
  Preparator
  Cabinet Makers

plus occasional use of tradesmen (plumbers, electricians, etc.), volunteers, and student help as needed, as well as access to city services for publicity, publications, library, photography, etc.

A museum of art and history in a small city

Director (and Curator of Art)
Secretary-Bookkeeper
Curator of Collections (and History)
Curator of Education (and Public Relations)
Librarian (and Archivist)
Janitor-Handyman
  Assistant Janitor-Guard

plus volunteer management of the sales-reception counter, and assistance on a regular basis to the curator and the librarian.

A general museum in a small city

Director
Secretary-Registrar
Curator of Art
Curator of Exhibits
Janitor-Handyman

plus part-time help for weekend duty

The museum of a state historical society

Curator
Secretary
Registrar
Curator of Education
   Assistant Curator of Education
Exhibits Technician
   Carpenter
   General Assistant
with cleaning, maintenance, bookkeeping, guarding, library, etc., pro-
vided within the overall administration of the historical society and
volunteers used at the sales-reception counter and to assist the registrar
with the collections

A children's nature museum in a rural location

Director
Secretary-Registrar
Curator of Education
Librarian
Curator of Animals (or Zoo Keeper)
   General Assistant
Janitor-Guard
   Assistant Janitor-Groundsman
plus an active volunteer organization assisting the Curator of Education

In all cases, the various professional members of a museum staff
should have competence in different disciplines. For example, if the
director of a small general museum is a historian, the curator of
exhibits or the assistant director might be a scientist; and the curator
of education might be an artist. Even in a museum devoted to one
field, such as art, it is good to have other fields represented on the
staff. One of the most widely applicable fields is anthropology. Anthropologists are found in museums of all kinds. Every museum staff
should include an artist, regardless of his primary responsibility.

EXERCISES—CHAPTER 5

Imagine yourself to be the administrator (whether your title be director or
curator) of a museum, and solve the following problems:

1. Your annual budget is $125,000 in a museum of art and history in a community of 40,000 people. You have a small building that is about to be enlarged, and for some reason it has no staff at all. (Let us say the previous staff were all relatives of the ex-director who quit in a huff when he was fired.) The superintendent of schools wants close cooperation between the museum and the public schools. You also have several clubs interested in cooperation. How much money would you devote to salaries? List the staff positions you would create, with salaries, including your own.

2. You have the offer of volunteer help. How might you use them?

3. Your board of trustees recommends hiring part-time professionals. What is your position on this?

4. Your museum gets a lump sum cash gift of $500,000, and the board immediately starts wrangling about what to do with the money. Sensibly, they ask you for advice. What do you propose?

5. Your income consists of admission fees and an annual appropriation by the city government. Because of increased expenses you may have to fire a member of your staff unless you can raise more money. What are the possibilities? Does it matter who the museum visitors are? Does it matter whether many or few school classes use the museum? Give reasons for your answers.

6. You fall on hard times and your budget is cut to $85,000. What do you do, while trying to maintain standards and service to the public?

7. For several reasons, your income is raised by $100,000 (to $225,000), and the new addition to the museum is ready for use. What would your new salary budget be? (Assume that the new wing is adequately furnished and equipped.)

8. Suppose you, the director of the museum, are not a museologist. However, a member of the board of trustees used to be curator in a museum. What, if any, changes in the lines and areas of authority should be worked out?

6
Collecting Theory:
General and Science Museums

Museums are sometimes so busy preparing exhibits, expanding into new geographical areas and subject fields, getting publicity, and raising funds that their most fundamental job or obligation gets pushed into the background. Indeed, in some museums most members of the staff seem to ignore it. I am referring to collecting.

Museums are concerned with objects. Objects are the starting point of a museum, of a museum field, and, properly, of any activity of the museum. Objects justify museums. One determines the kind of museum he has by the kinds of objects in the collections and the uses to which the objects are put. Of all the kinds of educational, public service, and cultural institutions that exist, only the museum is founded on the principle that selecting and preserving objects is of importance to people today and in the future.

The assumption is that all objects can be fitted into some kind of museum or into a department of a museum or can be used in a special exhibition. One should categorize objects by their potential use. A collection of furniture might belong in a history museum, in an art museum, in a botanical museum (thinking of the materials of which the furniture is made), or in a museum of technology (science and industry). The value of the objects depends on how well they serve in accomplishing the goals of the museum. In an art museum the objects must give aesthetic pleasure, convey emotion, stimulate the imagination, and inspire. In another kind of museum the objects must contribute to education and intellectual stimulation.

In both cases, objects also serve these ends indirectly by attracting visitors. An Egyptian mummy may accomplish more in attracting people, who then see other exhibits, than it does simply as an exhibit. Objects may also serve in less obvious ways, such as for research, reference, prestige, and entertainment.

Museums are firmly grounded in man's "instinct" to collect. Whatever the motivation of individuals, museums collect to preserve objects of apparent or possible value that otherwise might be lost to the future, and to bring objects together for use. These are really the same justification (public education, broadly speaking). The difference is only that a museum curator does not always have a specific use in mind for an object when he decides to preserve it.

What do individuals collect? Objects that are impressive and attractive because they are old, expensive, associated with a famous person or place, bizarre, from a remote corner of the earth (today, from the moon; someday, from another planet), the result of adventure or much labor or patience. Objects may also be collected because they are nostalgic or sentimental. What may have great value to the collector may have little or none to a museum (an arrowhead of unknown origin, a button collection sewn on pieces of cardboard, a lock of President Harding's hair, a ship model built in a bottle, a rock from Mt. Everest, a collection of matchfolders). On the other hand, a collection of ore specimens from local mines, a scrapbook made by President Harding, an authentic model of Magellan's ship that circumnavigated the globe, or a Persian rug would be of use to an appropriate museum.

The student may be surprised to learn that there is such a thing as a theory of collecting. Yet it should be obvious that: 1) Museums cannot collect *all* objects that exist; 2) collecting has to be selective; 3) it is an abstraction from the real world.

If collecting is selective (that is, if only a very few objects are selected for preservation out of untold billions or trillions of things), then the question is, "Who does the selecting?" In a way, *chance* selects what is to remain from the past. Artifacts have short lives; accidents cause objects to change or disappear. Another selector is the *donor* who selects from among the objects he owns those which he thinks belong in a museum. Other selectors, such as money, are influential, but perhaps the most important factor in selection is *popular culture*—the stereotypes of the bulk of the population (including the average museum curator) as to what is appropriate to a museum and what is not. Museum curators, as well as donors, have chosen to collect fifty-year-old wedding dresses but not overalls. (I know a museum dedicated to preserving and telling the entire history of a whole state. The museum owns 100 wedding dresses but not a single pair of overalls. Can the history of a state be illustrated by the marriages of women but not the labor of men?)

If a museum is to have a serious purpose and be managed efficiently, thought must go into what makes the museum. The museum cannot accomplish much public education without good collections. Good collections result only from thoughtful collecting. Good collecting requires logical, intelligent planning. What a museum collects matters. The main selector of the objects should be the informed curator, who is guided by a sound collecting plan.

Museum directors and curators must know what to collect, but the general scope of the collection is not properly their decision. If they had to decide to accept or reject objects on the basis of their personal feelings at the moment, much of the time they would be wrong. The founding body, in establishing the museum, should decide on its scope. That is, it should set limitations on the collections and, therefore, on the field of interest and activity of the museum. Guthe says that this is the most important decision the board of trustees will ever make.[1]

The first limitation is one of *geography*. With what physical area will the museum be concerned? The country? The state? The original 13 colonies? The entire world? The second limitation is one of *subject*. Is the museum to be concerned only with art? Art and history? Natural history? History and anthropology? I would say that, logically, the third limitation should be that of *time*. Is your museum to limit itself to the last century? The period from 1870 to 1920? The Middle Ages? Guthe also says to consider *use*.[2] The museum should not collect an object which it cannot imagine putting to a good use. That is, if its potential educational value in the frame of your museum operation seems small at best, that object should not be acquired.

It is the responsibility of the director, and whichever members of his staff are allowed to collect, to see to it that the museum permanently acquires only objects which fit within its limitations. (For a temporary exhibition any kind of object can be borrowed for a limited time; or an object can be acquired with the understanding that it will be sold or sent to another museum.)

1. Carl E. Guthe, *The Management of Small History Museums*, 2d ed. (Nashville: American Association for State and Local History, 1959, 1964), p. 24.

2. *Ibid.*, p. 31.

What to Collect (And What Not to Collect)

It is important that the museum have an *active*, not a *passive*, collecting program. *Active* collecting is determining what the collection ought to contain, in order to do the best possible job of presenting the complete story, and then making a strong and continued effort to locate and acquire those materials. *Passive* collecting is sitting back and accepting or rejecting what is offered. This leads to collections which are largely a reflection of what the general public thinks ought to be in a museum. The potential donor's notions on this score are likely to be wide of the mark, if not downright ridiculous, in view of the museum's scope and its educational aim.

Museum collections grow through donations, purchases, expeditions and other field collecting, informal collecting by the staff (such as at secondhand stores), and by transfer, exchange, gift, and permanent loan from other institutions. (A permanent loan, contracted between two museums of professional standards, amounts to an outright gift in all but legal title. The lender has the legal right to recall the loan, but has no intention of doing so. It is a useful device for a museum which has difficulty, under the law, in disposing of surplus objects in its collections.) Two principal dangers must be avoided:

1. *Do not accept conditional gifts.* A donor may request that his gift of a number of objects be placed on exhibit, be exhibited intact —without separating the objects—and that his name be prominently displayed with the objects. Even though he does not request this, he may, because of his past associations with "museums," assume that this will be done. Only in very rare circumstances, if ever, should a museum agree to these conditions. It is best to have the donor sign a standard accession form which states something like, "I give these objects unconditionally." If you do not use such a form, you might at least explain to the donor how the collections are organized, that not everything is exhibited, and that the donor's name will be forever preserved in the records, though not in the exhibit.

2. *Do not accept loans* for an indefinite period of time or for any purpose other than temporary use. Many small museums cause their future employees much grief, wasted time, and bad public relations when they make it legally possible for lenders or their heirs to recover objects after many years have passed. Build your collections only with objects to which your museum has clear title. Often a person will want to lend something (like an antique

piano) in order to get it out of his house without giving up his ownership of it. This person is seeking to use limited space belonging to the general public as a free warehouse. Do no accommodate him.

If you are now working in a museum which has in its possession loaned or conditionally given objects, first get the approval of the board of trustees; then immediately begin correcting the situation. Separate these objects from the rest of your collections; then write to the donor or lender explaining and justifying your policy (actually, the policy of the museum) and either return objects you do not want, getting written receipts for them, or seek to have objects you do want made unconditional gifts. Once the trustees are involved, any criticism or objection can then be directed, not at a museum employee, but only at the institution itself, or, rather, its policies.

Scientific Collecting

What should a museum of science collect? (Or what should a curator of science in a general museum collect?) The goal of the science museum is to increase knowledge about our physical environment and to disseminate such knowledge to the public. Stated more simply, the museum's job is education in science. But we are speaking of education based on the study and use of tangible, three-dimensional objects. The objects that should be collected are, quite simply, those objects that can be used by that museum in an educational program. They must be in keeping with the scope of the museum, that is, within its set limitations. They must also be collectible. Microbes and volcanoes are of considerable interest to science, but they cannot be museum objects.

Collecting in science is probably easier than collecting in art or history. Text and reference books in any scientific field outline the main laws, facts, and processes that would be interpreted through exhibits for the benefit of the general public. The objects needed are those that can be used in illustration. The small, regional scientific museum will want to deal with its natural environment. The geology of the county, birds and animals of the state, flora of the region, local archaeology—all are suitable fields if they fit the museum's scope. The aim in the collecting should be first of all *accuracy* (be absolutely certain of your identifications of the specimens you collect and catalogue), and second, *completeness*. If you are exhibiting the native trees of your county, be sure you include them all, unless you can justify a sampling; for example, to show trees of local economic importance, or to illustrate differences among large categories of trees where one representative of a category would be sufficient. Do not exhibit some trees and some animals and then imply that you are showing the total natural environment. The honesty and meticulousness of science must carry all the way through to your use of the collections. The main point is that collecting and exhibiting in the scientific fields, as in the others, should be to some larger purpose. Objects and exhibits are not ends in themselves.

Natural history museums occupy an honored position in our profession. Museums in a sense created natural history. In the latter half of the nineteenth century, collecting by these institutions and the study of the collections gave great impetus to the advance of scientific knowledge. The natural history museum deserved its great social prestige. (Today, the art museum has the most social prestige, but this was not always the case.) However, research is the activity that has shown the least progress in the last thirty or forty years. The relative importance of museums in the *advancement* of knowledge has declined (although the importance of museums in the *dissemination* of knowledge has increased). Museum research has declined in importance because it must deal chiefly with the static description and classification of things. That work is now largely done (except for dotting "i's" and crossing "t's"). Zoological research now, for example, is more concerned with natural dynamics; with observation of the relationships among living things, their adaptations to their environments, the growth and decline of populations, the utilization of "niches" in the environment, etc.

Natural history museums have been called "on the defensive" and "static, peacefully sleeping." However, with the necessity for the public to be aware of our abuses of the environment, and the dangers of pollution and overpopulation, natural history museums have as important a role to play in our culture as they have ever had. They can accomplish much good if they will rise to the task.

EXERCISES—CHAPTER 6

1. Describe the museums in your vicinity as to their scope, that is, the limitations placed on their collections. Are these limitations stated in writing? What guidance exists as to what you, as a potential donor, might reasonably offer

these museums? Are there obvious discrepancies between the publicly announced scope and the actual scope as revealed in the collections and the exhibits? Try to find out if employees are guided by a written policy in their dealings with potential donors.

2. List the different ways of acquiring scientific specimens.
3. List the ways objects may be lost to the collections (called "alienation").
4. When a curator accepts a donation, what information should he ask for?
5. What is the most important decision a board of trustees will ever make?
6. What should be the loan policy of a museum?
7. Define passive and active collecting. Use illustrations from a scientific field.
8. If a donor comes to your museum and complains that his donation is exhibited in a dark corner without his name on it and without some of the original objects, what do you say to him?
9. In general, what should a museum collect?
10. Describe an exhibit you have seen, preferably one which can be visited locally, which illustrates that the donor's idea of what a museum should contain has prevailed rather than the opinion of a scholar as to what information should be presented to the public. In other words, give an actual example of an object or a group of objects which does not contribute measurably to the official purpose of the museum.

7
Collecting Theory:
History Museums

"History" is sometimes taken to mean all past events, as in "the history of the world" or "the history of man." To some people, "history" means the written record, as "It is a matter of history that Stonewall Jackson was killed by his own men." This definition allows the term "prehistoric" to be used, referring to time and events that preceded the written record. The broad and hazy separation between history and prehistory is the period of the introduction of written records of behavior. It should be obvious that the boundary between historic and prehistoric occurred at different times in different places. American Indians in the West were still prehistoric after the East was well settled by European immigrants. In remote parts of the world today some primitive tribes may properly be described as prehistoric, and even paleolithic. Museums should shy away from referring to "prehistoric animals." If the term "prehistoric times" is used, the user should be sure it refers to a period before people wrote their own records or before their literate contemporaries provided adequate written documentation.

It has been said that all museums are history museums in the sense that all preserve objects pertaining to past events and situations. This is certainly obvious when we think of collections in history, art, anthropology, and technology. It is less obvious when we think of biology. But even with this subject, the specimens *were* collected, they *did* live, the exhibits show living environments of the past (though recent). Nature changes so slowly that we cannot in our short lifetimes see most of the changes occur; museums, however, deal with these changes—mountain formation, the weathering of rocks, the evolution of plants, for example.

Let us reserve the term "history" for museum activity related to discovering, preserving, and interpreting important knowledge about past human behavior. What, then, should a history museum collect? Suppose that you are in charge of a small history museum, and a prospective donor comes in to give you something. His gift will have no strings attached, and you are free to accept or reject the offer. Would you accept or reject: 1) the wedding suit of your town's first mayor? 2) the wedding suit of your current mayor? 3) the wedding suit of an ordinary citizen of your county of a) one hundred years ago? b) twenty five years ago? c) last week? 4) one left shoe of the present day? 5) a pair of shoes with both heels missing? 6) a well-catalogued collection of birds' eggs? 7) a valuable, antique chair used in another part of the country and brought to your town by newcomers last year? 8) a painting by a great artist which has no connection with your locality? 9) a painting of poor quality of a local scene? 10) a suit of Spanish armor? 11) a magnificent, mounted moosehead? 12) an old piano used for many years by a local piano teacher? 13) a badly rusted shovel with a broken handle picked up at the entrance to an abandoned mine? 14) a miscellaneous collection made over the years by a prominent citizen of your community from his travels in different parts of the world? 15) old bottles? 16) a number of arrowheads arranged in a design on purple velvet in an oak frame? (The donor said that he had collected them from "around here" forty or fifty years ago.) 17) a family Bible? 18) the donor's great-grandmother's wedding dress? 20) a piece of cloth with President Lincoln's blood on it?

Workers in small museums have to make decisions like these almost every day. If you had trouble making up your mind, it is because you did not have a scope in mind. Now set limitations for your museum, and you will find the decisions easier to make. Not to have a clear, written policy regarding what the collections are to contain is a serious mistake. Every museum employee should know the policy. Any staff member charged with the responsibility of acquiring objects for the collections, either by purchase or by accepting gifts, must have not only a very clear knowledge of what ought to be collected, but also the assurance that his superiors on the staff and the board of trustees will support his decision.

To return to the list of offered objects, if yours is a museum of local history, and if history according to your museum continues to the present, your answer to the donor probably should be as follows: "Yes" for numbers 1, 2, 3, and 4; "No" for 5, 9, 12, and 20. Numbers 6, 7, 8, 10, and 11 might be accepted with the understanding that you would sell or trade them. The shovel would be acceptable if you can assume that it was used in the mining operations and, of course, if the mine is located in the geographical area of concern to your museum. The traveller's collection would be acceptable only with the donor's agreement that you were at complete liberty to dispose of the objects separately as you saw fit. The collection might contain some items that you could send to other museums; other items might be sold at your sales counter; and still others might be useful in decorating staff offices. Probably none of the items would be suitable for your collections. The bottles, like the shovel, would have to be tied importantly to the life of your locality to be acceptable, unless you simply accepted them in order to sell them. The arrowhead collection has very little value without dependable documentation as to the original location of each arrowhead. If the prehistory of your region lies within your museum's scope, you might accept the arrowheads for the collections, although their usefulness will be limited. If the donor can remember very clearly the specific locations where he found certain of the arrowheads, these should be singled out immediately and properly identified. They will be of more value than the others. The Bible should be accepted only if typical of your locality, and then only if you have no more than two already in the collections. The wedding dress may be accepted if used in your locality, if in good condition, and if you have no more than two like it from the same time period. You should also ask the donor what else he may be willing to part with. The objects he has offered you may not be nearly as important to your museum as other things he has that he has not guessed that you could use (such as old wallpaper samples, for example).

At the end of Chapter 1, I referred to the Swiss National Museum in Zurich. Before it was created, the National Legislature passed a law in 1890 setting its scope and its purpose. The museum was "appointed to house important national antiquities that are historically and artistically significant and to preserve them in well-ordered arrangement." The law further declared that the museum was to be characteristic and have the greatest possible cultural and artistic value as a "testimony of our past." A few years ago the guidebooks stated that the exhibits ranged in time from "primitive times to 1920." The scope of this museum is clear. The scope of every museum should be as clear.

Another aspect of the Swiss statute is worth considering: It refers to *important, significant* objects. A good discussion of the historically significant object appears in Guthe's *The Management of Small History Museums*. This is one of the most important concepts for any student of museology to master. For an object to belong in the collections of a museum it must signify, or say, something of importance. To what end? The museum's stated purpose. What is a historically significant object? One that can be used *educationally*. The object must be usable in teaching the visitor about life in the past. Will it help you teach the history you need to teach? Accept it. Is the object unsuitable as an illustration of your story? Reject it!

But what is the history that you ought to teach? Books will give the historical outline of your region. In most localities someone will have written a local history. But if no one has written the history of your local area, you will have to do it yourself, at least in outline form.[1] You will have to consult libraries, files of old newspapers, and other sources of information about the geographical area of your museum's interest. After you know the main facts of the history of your region, your job is still not done.

You must be prepared to present to the museum visitor the history of first exploration, early settlement, growth of industries, trade and communication, and the modern commercial situation. You will need to deal with minority and ethnic groups. But you must be prepared to go even further. H. Stuart Hughes, writing in *Current Anthropology*, said that the best definition of history is "retrospective cultural anthropology."[2] Let that be your guide. History and history museums are more and more being concerned with the lives of *all* the people, not only the rich, the powerful, and the famous. Hence, you should include the overalls of the poor laborer as well as the white tie and tails worn by the Governor at his inaugural ball; the mass-produced lithograph that decorated the two-room shack as well as the imported oil painting from the rich man's home; the toys of the Indian child as well as the ceremonial sword of the famous general. As an educator, you are concerned with truth and completeness. Leave the aesthetics to the art museum and curiosities to the circus and remind yourself, every day, that a public institution is for *all* the people, all the time. It is not easy. Historical collecting is the hardest of all. Is it not especially unfortunate that we do not yet have enough trained people for all the history museums?

1. Write to the American Association for State and Local History, 1315 Eighth Avenue, South, Nashville, Tennessee 37203, and inquire about publications that would help you. (Incidentally, AASLH Technical Leaflets, which members receive with *History News* and which can be bought separately, give much valuable information on a wide range of topics.)

2. Vol. 4, No. 2 (April 1963), p. 141.

An Associated Press wire service news item of December 1967 illustrates the way many community history museums get started:

Haconda, Georgia—Because he has always been interested in history, Tatum Bedsole has been collecting articles representative of early American life for more than 30 years. An old log cabin, which he moved piece by piece from his family's farm to his own yard, houses hundreds of items such as Indian relics, arrowheads estimated to be 5,000 years old, a cane mill, churns made of gourds and a hand-made rope bed. Bedsole, a rural mail carrier for the past 47 years, said, "Steadfast courage, determination and hard work built our country and we should always remember it. That's what the things in this museum say to me—and that's what I hope they say to the people who come here to visit."

This beginning could serve as the nucleus of a public museum of local history.

Newspapers outside the large cities often print feature articles on local collectors and the collections they have built up over the years. Sometimes the collection is specialized, such as one of antique bottles. Collections are displayed in homes and places of business, and the newspaper stories refer to the 20 to 40 years spent in accumulating them. Some antique collections are thrown open to the public as "museums." Through incorporation as public institutions and subsequent professional management, some of these may one day be able to dispense with the quotation marks.

Of course, not all worthwhile collections fall into public hands. The syndicated column "Dear Abby" published a few years ago a letter from a woman whose grandmother had left her "her most prized possession"—a valuable collection of 338 antique clocks. The woman signed herself "Prefers Cash" and indicated her desire to sell them; Abby supported her. The clocks are now, no doubt, scattered once again and private hands. The grandmother's many years of work in bringing the collection together, and her special knowledge, were lost. It is possible that she would have preferred to donate the collection to a museum had she known that her granddaughter would not keep it.

On the other hand, not all collecting engaged in by amateurs is of interest to history museums. I shall give several examples to illustrate this point, because amateur collectors assume that they are in competition with museums. Museums sometimes help to foster this point of view by showing collections as collections and not in historical context. (For instance, a display of all the pressed glass goblets the museum owns.) The market price of some objects is a deterrent. In the fall of 1972, a 17th-century flintlock was sold at auction for $300,000. No gun could ever be worth that much to a history museum.[3]

Another kind of object that is collected is the rare stamp or coin that results from a manufacturing mistake. In 1847 on the Indian Ocean island of Mauritius, the British colonial administration issued a one-penny stamp which bore the words "post office" instead of "post paid." Only 14 examples of this engraving error are known to exist. Two of these stamps were bought in 1897 for 50 pounds sterling. Their value in 1954 was estimated to be $75,000. They were sold at auction for $380,000 in 1968. In 1971 a sheet of 100 U.S. eight-cent stamps of the Flag and White House issue was discovered to have no perforations. A philatelic auctioneer said the eight-dollar sheet might be worth $50,000. Later in the year, another purchaser discovered that a sheet of eight-cent stamps showing the exploration of the moon had the horizontal perforations running above the words at the bottom of the stamps rather than below the words. A well-known collector expressed the opinion that this eight-dollar sheet might be worth $100,000. Clearly, such oddities are of no interest to museums as collectors' items, even if the museums could afford to compete at auctions for them.

Sometimes the "rarity" of an object is due to where it has been, rather than what it is. In 1965 an old coin, a 1793 large cent, was secreted aboard a Gemini 7 spacecraft which made a 14-day orbit of the earth. Removed by the flight surgeon who had placed it aboard, the coin was sold for $15,000 and now, according to a coin dealer, might be worth as much as $100,000.

Amateur collecting may have emotional or psychological value instead of financial. The Beer Can Collectors of America hold an annual "canvention" (sic) at which more than 100,000 empty beer cans are on display and offered for exchange. A private hobby might be of more general interest and still not be of much significance in a museum.

For example, a western couple whose hobby is leather tooling had spent more than three years in fitting out the interior of the cab of their pickup truck, including the dashboard, with hand-tooled leather and figured that the cost in time and materials was more than $10,000,

3. This was a French fowling piece made for Louis XIII and sold by the American collector William Renwick at Sotheby's auction house in London to London dealer Frank Partridge, November 20, 1972.

according to a newspaper article. They were quoted as saying that when the truck was at the end of its life span of usefulness, it would be given to a museum with all leather intact. Such a curiosity would be of limited interest to a real history museum.

A popular movement of more concern to museums is the public's greatly revived interest in recent years in the odds and ends of yesteryear. Interest in quality furniture, glassware, silver, spinning wheels, and such materials useful in interior decoration has always existed. Now, however, cast-iron toys, advertising posters, beartraps, tobacco tins, and almost any relic of the past is in demand. "Old fashioned" restaurants and bars use sewing machine cabinets as tables and decorate their walls with what would have been carted to the dump not very long ago. An article in *Time* showed a woman ladling soup from a chamber pot at the dinner table and quoted an antique dealer as saying, "It has some age to it, maybe 15 or 20 years."[4]

What is it all about? Nostalgia. A kind of homesickness for an imagined past as a retreat from the frightening and puzzling world of today. In the May 3, 1971, issue of *Time*, Gerald Clarke's essay "The Meaning of Nostaliga," refers to the popular clichés which constitute the average person's understanding of history. "At a certain distance," he says, "vision fades and imagination takes over. Try as they might, imitators never succeed in exactly reproducing the past. The eye of memory takes in 1936 and the elegance of an Astaire dance or the froth of a Lubitsch comedy; it is blind to Depression breadlines. It catches the shapely legs of Rita Hayworth in 1944's hot pants but neglects the 500,000 U.S. war casualties of that year. It is amused by the crew cuts and slang of 1953 but forgets the anti-Communist hysteria and the fear that followed the detonation of Russia's first hydrogen bomb."

The history museum must not be an institutionalized representation of fads, hobbies, and myths. What concerns the private collector and the entertainment-seeking public should not necessarily occupy the attention of the historian, except as he observes and records the passing scene. The museum must be devoted to the serious occupation of discovering, preserving, and interpreting the forces that created human behavior and the concrete results of that behavior. It must tell *all* the story and do it in proportion; that is, each part of the story must be told in relation to the other parts. To exhibit wedding dresses but no overalls is to lie about history (unless the limitations of

4. "Antiques: Return of Yesterday's Artifacts," May 2, 1969.

your museum require that you collect only female ceremonial attire, which should then be officially stated and publicized).

A history museum can err not only in regard to its view of history, but also as to the temporal limitation placed on its operation. A museum may be so naively founded and administered that the board, the staff, and the general public have no common understanding about its scope. When a closing date or upper limit is set for a small museum of local history, it is usually 50 years or more before the present. Such a museum may be accepting objects of the World War I era but refusing donations of the 1920's. In the 1980's they may accept objects of the 1920's and 1930's. In the year 2020 they will begin to accept the objects with which we are familiar today. But why should a museum give its collecting program a 50-year handicap? The curator, in effect, says "Yes, 50 years from now the clothing we are wearing, our furniture, our pots and pans will be of great value to the historical museum. However, we shall allow most of these things to disappear through accidents of time, and then 50 years from now our successors will search attics and secondhand stores to see what they can find that is still usable." Museums, in theory, go on forever. Just as we are interested in objects of the past, museum curators of the future will be interested in what we have today. Might we not consider collecting objects of today that will be historically significant tomorrow?[5]

In general, objects of the past are harder to come by if they are very old, were made of perishable material, were never very plentiful, were not highly valued in the past, or are highly valued today (by private collectors). The history curator needs to be skilled in locating such objects and in getting donations of them. Might not he save the curators who succeed him unnecessary trouble by collecting objects now while they are plentiful, reasonably priced, and in good-to-perfect condition? The important objects in a history museum are the commonplace, typical, popular, and once-plentiful artifacts of every-day living, but it is precisely this kind of material that is least likely to be stored away in a trunk in the attic eventually to be offered to the local museum.

Progressive history museums today accept two somewhat radical ideas: 1) the best history includes a strong measure of anthropology, and 2) collecting from today's world for tomorrow's makes sense.

5. I developed this idea more completely in my article "Active Collecting in History Museums," *Museum News*, 45, No. 7 (March 1967).

The Oregon Historical Society has established eighty or more location points for continuing, periodical documentation photography. Photographs are taken several times a year from the same viewpoint, making a record of the changing scene. Local historical societies choose the points and make the photographs. The state society stores the negatives and supplies prints. The University of Alaska Museum reported on its Modern Alaskan Native Material Culture Project in the *Western Museums Quarterly.*[6] L. J. Rowinski, Director, described in detail the program for photographic documentation and for collecting objects from Eskimos and Indians in the present day. L. Thomas Frye, Curator of History at the Oakland (California) Museum has interested young people in his city in collecting and donating everyday objects from their environments pertaining to "work, family, and play." The collection is for the year 2069, 100 years after the project was begun. One further example: the Smithsonian Institution stirred up the press a few years ago with an announcement of plans to reconstruct a slum dwelling, a simulated tenement, and more recently got newspaper notice when it added miniskirts to the costume collection.

Collecting only impressive objects of the past without a serious intent to be engaged in social science is antiquarianism. Collections must be useful in an active program of public education. Deadwood must be cleared out. No museum has so much space that it can afford to store objects that are not historically significant. Collections are sometimes improved not only by accessioning but by deaccessioning. Indeed, this "deliberate alienation" (see Chapter 6, Exercise 3) may be temporarily more important to a museum than collecting.

Items to be eliminated from the collections are those that: 1) lie outside the defined scope of the museum; 2) are not significant and which cannot be used for research, exhibition, or loan; 3) are so badly damaged or deteriorated that they are of little or no use; 4) would accomplish more good in another museum; 5) are duplicated many times.

Items may be returned to the donor, destroyed, sold, or transferred to another museum. "Legal considerations and public relations will determine the method of disposition. Disposition should be decided by the board."[7]

6. This is the journal of the Western Regional Conference of the American Association of Museums, VIII, No. 1 (December 1971).

7. Eugene F. Kramer, "Guideposts for Collecting," AASLH Technical Leaflet No. 6 (Nashville: American Association for State and Local History, 1970).

EXERCISES—CHAPTER 7

One of the most important concepts in museology, one that tends to separate the real museums from the curiosity collections, is that of the historically significant object. It can be applied to other fields, of course. One might also speak of the "geologically significant object," the "ethnologically significant object," or even "the artistically significant object." The purpose of this assignment is for the student to grasp the theory of historical collecting, or, to put it simply, to understand what he should add to the collections of a history museum if he were given this responsibility.

1. Define the following terms: souvenir; antique; relic; heirloom; collector's item; nostalgia; sentiment; hobby.
2. What does age have to do with historical collections? What is the relationship of age to worth? Are old things of more importance to a museum than new things? (You may answer this as a single paragraph which includes the points raised in these questions or answer the questions individually).
3. Discuss the importance of the commonplace. What about the unique, one-of-a-kind object?
4. What are the categories of objects in a historical collection? (In regard to condition, documentation, and the like.)
5. What is a history museum?
6. Look about you. List 10 to 20 objects that you can see in the room from where you sit. Now think of preserving these objects for use in an appropriate museum 100 or more years from now.

    Categorize the objects on the basis of historical significance. Which of the objects you listed would you consider to be the best illustrations of life today? Which of lesser value? Which would be of doubtful use or of least value?
7. This one will require a good relationship with several other people or sneakiness on your part. Look into and make inventories of the contents of four or five refrigerators in as many different homes. Safely back at your desk, compare these lists to arrive at similarities and differences. Make up a composite list of average items that would be found in a typical refrigerator in your neighborhood at this time. Leave out unusual items, and do not add anything which you think should have been present, though it was not.

    This list of items would be of great value to a curator of history a hundred years from now. Add any instructions he would need on how to place the objects within the refrigerator.

8

Collecting Theory: Art Museums

In the first chapter, we defined "art object" and "art museum";
now we must define "art." First let us consider what artists do.

All humanity has a drive for beauty. Even the most primitive
peoples decorate their simple possessions and their own bodies. They
also make representations of real and imagined elements of their
environments, such as carvings of animals, or masks portraying
supernatural beings. In the Mediterranean civilizations, statues representing gods and people were often painted in bright colors. Pictures were painted on walls and boards and woven in cloth. Representation of what is real to the artist continues to our day. The fine artist's
creation that results in a material object is called *sculpture*, whether
carved wood, chiseled marble, modeled clay, or whatever. The creation that results in a flat, two-dimensional picture or design may be

Author's Note: A word of explanation may be in order regarding the nature and
length of this chapter. My purpose has not been to write a treatise on aesthetics, or about
art in general, but rather to provide for the majority of persons using this book an
introduction to the kinds of objects collected by art museums—and the kinds which are
rejected—and the traditional attitudes of art museums toward these materials. Most of
the museums of the United States and Canada include objects in one or more of the art
fields but without having anyone on their staffs who is familiar with these fields. Most
beginners are not prepared to cope with the confusion that often exists between a
historical and an artistic attitude toward things of the past. Furthermore, it is basic to an
understanding of museology to grasp the philosophical difference between art
museums and other kinds of museums. It is the aim of this chapter, therefore, to place
art collecting in a larger perspective.

Persons who have had training in the fine arts may find some of the explanations
elementary and some of the illustrations repetitious. They may also regard my interpretation of the complex world of art as biased. Be that as it may, I ask all readers, whatever
their prior acquaintance with the arts, to think seriously about the issues raised in this
chapter.

called *graphic art*. This includes drawings, prints, paintings, and photography.[1]

The liquid in paint is called the vehicle, since it carries the pigment until it is applied to the surface being painted. When the vehicle has evaporated, we say the paint is dry. The vehicle determines the name of the medium: oil for oil paints, water for watercolors. The term "acrylic" is used to refer to a painting made with acrylic resin-based paints. Paint can be applied to a variety of surfaces, so that a "painting" may be a wall, an eggshell, a board, a sheet of masonite, a sheet of plastic, or a piece of canvas stretched over a wooden frame (called a "stretcher"). A print is a picture, design, or image made by a printing process, much as a book is printed. There are four main printing methods, which can be used separately or combined:

1. *Relief Printing*. This is the oldest method for making prints. It is based on cutting away part of a flat surface so that the image required is left to act as a printing block. Examples are *woodcuts* and *"lino cuts"* (linoleum block prints). If raised surfaces are created on the printing plate, the result is an *embossed print*.

2. *Lithography*. This is based on the fact that oil and water will not mix. On a flat stone (or zinc plate) a drawing is made with a greasy crayon. The plate is moistened; water will not adhere to the design. Ink is rolled onto the plate; it adheres to the design but not to the wet stone. Paper pressed onto the stone picks up only the image.

3. *Intaglio Printing*. The image is cut into the printing surface and filled with a greasy printer's ink. The surface is wiped clean, leaving ink only in the grooves of the design. Dampened paper is pressed onto the plate, picking up the ink in the grooves to print the design. The oldest intaglio process is *engraving*, in which the design is scratched into a metal plate with a sharp tool. In *dry point* a furrow with raised edges is made, and the raised edges catch the ink to make the print. In *etching* the plate is covered with an acid-resistant substance, which is scratched away to make the design. The plate is dipped into acid, which eats into the metal plate where the

1. Of course, the decorative arts such as silversmithing and weaving result in objects of beautiful form or beautiful surface design. The main distinction is that the fine arts tend further toward the ideal of "art for art's sake," while the primary purpose of the decorative arts is utility; art, if it exists at all, is a secondary characteristic.

protective coating has been removed. The plate is then cleaned and used for printing, as in engravings. The *aquatint* process is the reverse of etching; the acid is used to remove areas instead of lines.

4. *Serigraphy. Silk screen printing* is the common form of this process. A piece of silk held in a frame is prepared by blocking out all the surface that is not to be used for printing. The resulting stencil is placed over paper, and ink is squeezed through the areas of the silk left open. For color printing, each color is printed by a separate screen.[2]

Obviously, a number of prints can be made from the printing plate or plates prepared by the artist. Because of the progressive deterioration of successive prints through the wear of the plates, artists usually destroy the plates after a certain number of prints are made. (Of course, the economics of scarcity also come into play.) The prints are often numbered (for example, No. 32 of 200). The lower the number, the better the print, generally speaking. A work of graphic art can be reproduced by photography and a printing process, as illustrations in art books are made. When produced individually for framing or matting, these reproductions may also be called prints. To avoid confusion and to establish a standard, the Print Council of America has defined the term *original print* as follows: 1. The image must be created by the artist himself on the plate, stone, woodblock, or other material from which the image will be printed. 2. The prints must be pulled by the artist or under his supervision. 3. The finished prints must be approved by the artist.

Most artists cannot or will not define "art" in words. For museum purposes, definitions are useful, however; therefore I shall attempt one. We might say, briefly, that *art is the deliberate creation of aesthetic sensations*. Art is a work of a human being, not of nature. It is not accidental. It produces something that is perceived through the senses and results in a personal emotional experience. This experience was commonly understood in the past to be a recognition and appreciation of beauty. In recent years, some artists have deliberately created ugliness with the avowed aim of shocking the viewer rather than of giving him pleasure. Artists and art museum people are not in full agreement on whether these creations are art, or whether a new

2. Condensed from Luis Edwards, "Prints: A Glossary," *The Art Gallery* (November 1966).

definition of art is needed. How to deal with much of contemporary art is a problem that we shall put aside for the moment.

A longer definition of art is that it is the conscious, deliberate production of an event or object of beauty (or emotional import) by a human being, employing not only the skill of the craftsman, but, in addition, an element of creativity—original, inventive, instinctive genius. An art object is an aesthetic artifact, deliberately created. The key idea is that of creativity. Art actually lies in the act of creation, not in its result. Therefore, the expert copier of another person's painting may be just as good a technician, and the painting copied may be a work of art. However, the copy is not a work of art (but a copy of a work of art), and if the copier never created a painting of his own he could not be called an artist. A skilled pianist may or may not be an artist. It depends on whether he or she merely reproduces the composer's creation or, in playing, creates something new; a personal interpretation. A cook may be an artist (in his cooking). A painter, in his painting, may not be. A sunset may be beautiful, but it is not a work of art. A photograph of the sunset, even though less beautiful, may be a work of art.

Every museum must be involved in art, even if it is only to recognize that art objects in its collections must be protected from deterioration and that exhibits of all kinds must be artistically prepared. Even science museum curators need to have an understanding of art as it relates to museums. All museum professionals must understand why a museum of science (or natural history) will commonly have a hall of African or Oceanic Art, yet to find a hall of African or Oceanic science and technology in an art museum would be rare indeed.

Let us consider the basis of art. A few years ago the Detroit Zoo auctioned off paintings by chimpanzees. Paintings by monkeys and apes have been sold and even entered in art exhibits, sometimes reportedly winning prizes. This delights the average person because he is convinced that there is nothing of value in modern abstract paintings by humans. Desmond Morris became interested in paintings by apes and decided, after a study involving both human children and monkeys and apes, that only six principles apply to picture making as a whole, covering everything and everyone from Leonardo da Vinci to Congo (a gorilla). They are: 1) *Self-rewarding Activation*. The production of a picture must be pleasurable and satisfying. 2) *Compositional Control*. Steadiness, symmetry, repetition, rhythm, a positive reaction to order rather than chaos. 3) *Calligraphic*

Differentiation. A slow process of pictorial growth, covering the development of marks and lines into distinct shapes. 4) *Thematic Variation*. A pattern selected from erratic exploration chosen as a theme and repeated with variations. The simple replacing the complex as a reaction. A familiar, repeated theme replaced by another and then returned to. 5) *Optimum Heterogeneity*. The point at which the picture is finished. One mark less and it would be unfinished, one more and it would be overworked. 6) *Universal Imagery*. Picture-making by children and by uninhibited, untrained adults is similar regardless of culture. This depends on: a) The muscular factor; certain movements of the hand and arm are more pleasing than others. b) The optical factor; certain visual arrangements are more acceptable to the optical apparatus than others. This is related to the spacing of the eyes, the fact that it is more comfortable to look from side to side than up and down, and other factors. The ratio of height to width that is most pleasing to most people is 1:1.618. It is called the *Golden Number*, and can be represented by a rectangle of these dimensions. It can also be expressed by the proportion, width is to length as length is to length plus width. c) The psychological factor; strong undercurrents at work concerning relationships of elements in the picture.[3]

Morris says that any rules that are basic enough to be applied to several related species rather than one species or (as is more often the case in art history) to one epoch of one species, must indeed be fundamental to the activity concerned.

If art has a biological basis, we would assume that all people, at all times and places, share in this drive for expression. Anthropologists agree that art is a universal aspect of culture. It is the aesthetic component of objects and acts in which the art museum is interested. A canoe paddle to the ethnologist is a tool with a significance for mobility, that is, for the extension of the sphere of activity of the people concerned. If the paddle is decorated, or has a pleasing shape, it may be collected by an art museum and exhibited as an aesthetic object. Why is it that some primitive peoples are more noted for their (folk) art than others? All cultural manifestations, including art, can be understood as satisfying the needs of the society, such as relieving tension. A. W. Wolfe, making a study of this question, concluded "that art develops in those societies where the men of a local community are divided by impor-

3. Desmond Morris, *The Biology of Art* (New York: Alfred A. Knopf, 1962).

tant social cleavages."[4] In other words, art serves ascertainable practical needs.

The contribution that art study can make to history is probably too obvious to mention, but other fields may profit as well. For example, Mr. Xavier de Salas, Assistant Director of the Prado Museum in Madrid, has pointed out that the works of minor artists can be revealing for sociological study. While the great masters were usually highly innovative (even radical and individualistic), the artists of lesser stature were more subject to the influence of their situation, and, therefore, produced work more truly reflective of their times.

Is education, then, the proper role of the art museum? It probably is, especially if the museum belongs to an educational institution. The campus art museum or gallery shares the educational aim of the college or university of which it is a part. Its curators should not be content to engage in repetitious exhibition of the same kind of art but should show art in all possible forms and expressions from all countries and all times. The aim should be a broad education in art history and art appreciation for all of the students. The gallery should introduce students to modern fine arts and strive to engender standards of taste and beauty. The average student may not come to enjoy nonobjective (abstract) painting, but at least he will have seen it; and any assistance in eliminating billboards, utility poles, and automobile graveyards by making future adult citizens aware of the ugliness around us is surely a good thing.

This is not to say that the viewing of art, in itself, will accomplish much. Art museum people are forced to recognize that mere exposure to good art is not enough to teach good taste or an appreciation of art. Docents (guides and lecturers), trustees, volunteers—educated people voluntarily associating with and identifying with an art museum and *exposed constantly to good art*—often do not become literate in art. Gallery guards may be exposed to great art eight hours a day for years, yet still retain the tastes of their social class and educational level. Therefore, because exposure to art is not educational or molding in itself, the art museum that desires to educate or raise standards must embark on a deliberate educational effort.

Art museums in general spare themselves the pain and frustration of such missionary travail and are content to serve only the aesthetic needs of their visitors. Indeed, many art curators and direc-

4. Alvin W. Wolfe, "Social Structural Bases of Art," *Current Anthropology*, Vol. 10, No. 1 (February 1969).

tors will flatly deny any obligation to educate in the usual sense and will maintain that art museums, unlike other museums, are not educational institutions. Philip Johnson, an architect of high and well-deserved reputation who knows a great deal about the functioning of art museums, answered Francine du Plessix' question "Do you regard the museum's role in our society as mostly education?" by saying "Horrors no! I do not believe in education. I hate the thought of all those tots being dragged around in museums, being shoved all that information they can't begin to assimilate. I only believe in *self* education, in the individual going *to* art if he needs it. The function of the museum is to satisfy a deep natural want, as deep and natural as sex or sleeping, for looking at pictures."[5]

You have realized by now that we have been talking about three kinds of "art": 1. The traditional fine art hanging on the art gallery walls (and the decorative arts of high quality), called "art"; 2. Popular or mass art hanging on the walls of the gallery guard's home, called "Kitsch"; 3. Primitive or tribal art as represented by the carved canoe paddle, usually lumped together with traditional rural (peasant and pioneer) crafts under the name "folk art."

All art originated with primitive or tribal art, in the sense that all mankind was in a precivilized state during most of his existence. As culture develops to more complex forms, elite art emerges. This depends on the creation of an artist class which exists to symbolize the high status of priests and rulers. The artist class forms a court or patrician style of art that differs from the tribal or plebeian style. "Domination of the culture by any particular class will always be reflected by art."[6] A few years ago in Europe the bulk of the population consisted of peasants, producing food on the land and supporting a parasitic elite segment of society. The elite were the nobility, the churchmen, and, later, the middle class. Art was then divided into fine art—the art of the aristocrats—and folk art—the art of the common people. With the growth of towns and especially after the Industrial Revolution, an urban lower class developed. Its culture can be called "mass culture." This mass culture of the towns is the ancestor of the popular culture of today, just as true art or fine art is the descendant of

5. *Art in America* (July–August 1966). Note that people involved in the arts and in art museums frequently refer to art museums simply as "museums," as though other kinds of museums do not exist.

6. Herta Haselberger, "Methods of Studying Ethnological Art," *Current Anthropology*, Vol. 2, No. 4 (October 1961), 351.

the art of the nobility. Such folk art as exists in the present goes back to peasant origins.

Figure 8.1 may make relationships clearer, though it must be understood to be hypothetical and only suggestive as to scale and relative proportions of areas. The key to understanding the difference between true fine art and the other kinds of art is the expression "art for art's sake." It refers to an act or an object that has been created solely, or at least primarily, as art. This is characteristic of art in recent times (in the last few hundred years) and appears to be more and more true as time goes on. That is, an example of modern abstract art that does not depict anything real is more truly art for art's sake than is, for example, a portrait by Gainsborough, which is not only a work of art but also a kind of historical document showing how a certain real person looked and dressed. Without meaning to quarrel with those who say that the work of the giants of art history, such as El Greco and Michelangelo, can communicate with all ages, since great works of art have universal and timeless appeal, remember the continuum from the utilitarian object of the tribesman to the work of pure art. Fine art developed out of tribal art as a representation of something that was

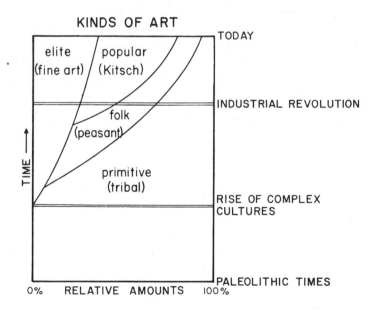

FIGURE 8.1.

real to the culture (like ancestor spirits, not necessarily real to you and me). Art in the Middle Ages served religion and the nobility; a painting was primarily an object useful in religious instruction or as a focus for veneration. Later, landscapes and pictures of people and animals were items to amuse and were appreciated for their subject matter. The radical French Impressionists departed from a realistic technique, and the abstract painters who followed them went even further. Good modern art is less utilitarian (serving a practical, nonart purpose) than was the good art produced in the past, and therefore, many would argue, more truly art.

If this seems hard to swallow, ask a good artist why he does not paint or sculpt in the style of Michelangelo. If he is honest, he will tell you that his style of art is better; or he will say that he does not want to use Michelangelo's style or that he can achieve more satisfaction working in the modern way—which is pretty much the same thing.

Some scholars object to the statement that primitives do not have true art (art for art's sake). Haselberger[7] points out that Himmelheber reported finding in a village on the Ivory Coast nonfunctional items enjoyed as art objects by the natives on festival days. Examples were sword grips without openings for inserting the blades, salve containers that could not be opened, and signal horns that lacked mouthpieces. Thus Haselberger concludes that tribal peoples occasionally do create art for art's sake. However, she seems undisturbed by the fact that the objects started out to be or were made in imitation of real, functional objects. The situation cited is perhaps a transitional one. We may have here an instance of a tribal people taking a step in the direction of art; yet our thesis, I feel, is still valid. Generally speaking, art as art is characteristic only of civilized society. The term "folk art" as applied to ethnological specimens collected and shown by some art museums can be misleading.

Another distinction between primitive or tribal art and true or fine art is this: the former expresses group sentiments, and the latter expresses individual (that is, the artist's personal) sentiments. Returning to our definition of art as an individual creation of genius, primitive art that so rigidly adheres to traditional forms that all the people of a village decorate objects in pretty much the same way hardly qualifies. Anthropologists tell us that individual differences are not ordinarily encouraged among primitive or folk societies. In such an envi-

---

7. *Op. cit.*, p. 345, citing Hans Himmelheber, *Negerkunstler*, (Stuttgart: Stecker & Schroeder, 1935) p. 49.

ronment the so-called "folk artist" may produce objects of beauty and emotional impact without being an artist. He may lack the conscious intent to produce art (as art), or he may be merely a skillful renderer of traditional forms, rather than an innovator who adds his personal creativity to his work.

In an interesting article that appeard in *Life* magazine during the summer of 1969, Robert Phelps dealt with Governor Nelson Rockefeller's collection of objects from New Guinea and elsewhere, which was then on display at the Metropolitan Museum of Art in New York City. Mr. Phelps pointed out that we ordinarily equate "primitive" with "crude," "unschooled," "unintelligent," and the like, but that the objects in this collection of primitive art show great beauty and power. "All the same it is *art*"; he says, "that is, in every piece there is human feeling as well as human craft." He admits, however, that while "The artists were acknowledged by communities, it was as *makers*, not inventors of original feelings. The emotions expressed are family and tribal." One may conclude that although primitive art may have the outward characteristics of art, it is art of another dimension, much as a folksong may be beautiful and well constructed, though molded by the many over the years—not a one-time creation by one person. Rather, the culture has created the art; and the artisan who makes the object that is involved is not the artist but the expert copier of a creation not his own.

The beginning museologist need not be quite so philosophical about the Indian baskets which he has to exhibit. Perhaps more to the point is the distinction made at Cooperstown[8] between the formal and the folk arts; that is, between fine arts and history. Museums use objects according to how they can best serve. Folk arts and tribal arts may be more useful for history and anthropology. If, however, an art museum wishes to call our attention to the aesthetic properties of an object which had a practical function, this is by no means an improper use of the object.

Let us now consider popular art. Confusion arises out of the failure to recognize that two separate kinds of art exist side by side today. One is traditional fine art: the other is popular art or Kitsch. The practical aspect of the problem for the museum worker has to do with the difference of opinion between the museum and the man on the street as to what kind of picture is worth looking at. Mail-order houses

8. New York; the excellent museum-training program of the New York State Historical Association.

and furniture stores stock and sell paintings and prints that are popular with the masses. A reputable art museum would not hang one of these. Why not? Is not the art museum an institution existing to serve the aesthetic needs of the public? Is not the successful furniture store a reliable guide to popular taste? I am not suggesting that an art museum collect and display the kinds of pictures that the public, which it serves, would most want to see. I do hope, however, to throw some light, for the beginner, onto the nature of the conflict.

Fine art directs our attention to its own character or existence; Kitsch directs our attention to pictured concepts, events, and objects. We respond to the *subject* of an example of Kitsch, not to the painting as an object of value in its own right. Fine art is created as an end in itself: the painter wishes the viewer to be aware of the painted surface as a painted surface and to respond to the style, form, and color employed. Kitsch is designed to entertain, to divert, to persuade, or to propagandize; the painter wants the viewer to look through the painting "as if it were a window into nature" and respond to the subject matter.

Norman Rockwell's paintings provide an excellent example of Kitsch. An advertising leaflet for a book about him and his work refers to him as a chronicler of nostalgia who spent half a century finding humor and pathos in the daily trivia of American life.[9] Rockwell would have us join the family gathered around the Thanksgiving table. The true artist, dealing with a similar subject, would hold us back so that we would appreciate the two-dimensional object that he had created, rather than become vicariously involved in the scene depicted. The kind of popular art created by Rockwell has been said to represent a visual counterpart of the anti-intellectualism which characterizes other facets of American culture. When the viewer cannot immerse himself in the subject matter of the painting, he is brought up short. He is forced to see an abstract by Picasso as a painting, not as a device to allow him to daydream about a baseball game, a "date," or a Thanksgiving dinner, and he becomes puzzled about contemporary art.

Kitsch, like everything else, changes. It feeds on fine art; and as fine art develops new styles, popular art picks up the old ones. This phenomenon is observable in other kinds of human behavior. When the stylemakers who glory in setting themselves apart from the masses

9. Thomas S. Buechner, *Norman Rockwell: Artist and Illustrator* (New York: Harry N. Abrams, 1970).

discover that the general public is imitating or taking over their distinctive symbols—whether clothing, furniture, or seaside resorts—they abandon the old symbols and take up new badges of their superiority. The elite classes passed sumptuary laws a few hundred years ago to prevent the peasants from imitating them. The common man, however, lags behind. It takes him a while to become accustomed and to risk braving the scorn of his peers before he adopts a new hairstyle or a new manner of dress. Maintaining status and self-esteem is a continual struggle for most people: they want to avoid the appearance and label of being old-fashioned or a "hick" but not to forge so far ahead as to be called a "kook" or a "weirdo." "The public, thinking it is going along with the modern movement by accepting Picasso, Miro, or Chagall, merely indicates that it has caught up with these art forms that have been with us for a half-century," said Alvin C. Eurich.[10] Eurich pointed out that the artists of any period are inventing new forms of expression, and a great artist may not be completely or enthusiastically received in his own time. "A highly regarded music critic, a contemporary of Beethoven's, wrote 'poor Beethoven, he is so deaf he does not hear the discords he writes.' A patron of Mozart, hearing some new tonalities developed by Mozart, became so furious that he rushed to the music stand and tore the music to shreds. A group of established artists in France ran a now historically famous ad in a newspaper publicly denouncing the French Impressionists as a group of idiots who had banded together to show their art. An established art magazine of the time carried an article stating that Cézanne did not know how to draw straight lines. All of these examples lead to a conclusion that is abundantly clear: any new development in any art form will probably be denounced by the established artists in that form. This is understandable, because a new direction is an indirect attack on the validity of what they are doing."[11]

Conservatism exists, even among artists. A museum curator must not be misled if an established artist of good reputation speaks out against the kinds of art being produced today. These radical forms are not necessarily bad. The art museum might well consider adding contemporary pieces to its collection, but problems may arise immediately. Leaving aside monstrosities like a half-mile of ocean cliff

10. President of the Aspen Institute for Humanistic Studies, speaking at the Governor's Conference on the Arts and Humanities, Boise, Idaho, November 15, 1966.
11. *Ibid.*

wrapped in canvas, many modern pieces are so large that they cannot be moved through the art gallery's doors; or they may be meant to take up a great amount of floor space. A 1970 exhibition by Joel Shapiro at the Paula Cooper Gallery in New York City included a work entitled "38 1/2 lbs. 1970." It consisted of 38 1/2–pound beams of aluminum, steel, and mahogany aligned parallel across the floor. The wood stretched out to a length of about fourteen feet.

The old categories of art are no longer exclusive. Today, paint and materials are combined in three-dimensional forms which are not exactly paintings and not exactly sculpture. Perhaps they might best be called "constructions." Other works of contemporary art are transitory in nature—not intended for long existence. I have seen a plastic sheet blowing in the breeze of an electric fan, several bucketfuls of sand spread around on the floor, and crumpled colored paper thrown against a wall. Similarly, some public performances, called "happenings," are transitory. One might argue that all such examples demonstrate creativity in the performing arts, rather than the fine arts—that they are theatrical events or stunts.

The first problem that the collector of contemporary art faces is what can be collected? The second is what should be collected? In Rebels of Art, George Slocombe says that at any given moment between 1870 and 1900 approximately 40,000 professional easel painters were working in Paris. Allowing for a turnover of most of this number every few years, the total number must have been at least a quarter of a million. If only 20 Impressionists are significant (worth collecting today), we must conclude that, conservatively, only one in 10,000 makes the grade. Using this ratio, we may assume that of the 25,000 art majors in California colleges and universities at this time, only two or three may be expected to achieve lasting, international reputation. Douglas M. Davis predicts an even smaller number. He says that the vast majority of the art objects currently being produced are "surely trash and will never be heard from again. We shall be fortunate if from this decade, so fertile and exciting in its productivity, one or two genuine artists emerge."[12] At the same time, he pointed out, "It is grossly unfair to compare the collective work of the new painters with selected giants from the past, as is frequently done—with Michelangelo or Rubens or Cézanne. We forget that what we know of the art of the past is highly filtered. Thousands upon thousands of bad landscapes, bad portraits,

12. *National Observer*, January 9, 1967.

bad Impressionists, bad Cubists have been winnowed out by museums and textbooks, giving us a considerably warped view of the past as a collective whole."[13] Art museums are faced with a two-horned dilemma. The old, established art is so expensive that most of them cannot afford it, and who knows what to buy of relatively inexpensive contemporary art? What to do? The art institution can avoid collecting problems by not being a museum. The so-called Museum of Contemporary Art in Chicago, established in 1967, intends to avoid collections. The Museum of Modern Art in New York for years maintained a policy against permanent acquisitions. A Middle Western art museum recently sold its collections in order to have money to support an activities program. But remember that institutions without collections are not museums. They are art centers, theaters, libraries, research institutions, or something else. Art museums, except for the wealthy ones that can hold their own at auctions, must depend on the generosity of donors for the works of established artists of the past (what might be called "historic" art) and buy contemporary art carefully.

Buying contemporary art which has not yet become established in our culture (that is, buying kinds of art which are not widely collected for decorative use, or buying the works of an "unknown" artist) presents a philosophical problem for the art museum of serious purpose. The inclusion of a work of art in the collections of an art museum and the exhibiting of the item is tantamount to a statement by the museum's professional staff that it is more than an aesthetic object—that it was of importance in the lives of people, or is representative of a kind of art that had such importance; that, in other words, the object had relevance to the cultural milieu in which it was produced. Therefore an art museum must be cautious in acquiring brand new art, as from the artist's commercial outlet (the gallery which sells his work for him). A more extreme example is the purchase of a work of art created by an artist *for* a museum, to be transferred directly from the artist's studio to the museum's exhibition halls. The painting or sculpture should first have had some use. It should have been accepted and successfully employed as an art object; in other words, it should have played a role in our culture. Then, as a cultural object, it would be eligible for preservation by a museum, *whose reason for existence is the preservation and use of significant cultural and natural specimens.* One can, of course, imagine an exception: Similar to the

13. *Ibid.*

undocumented object in the history museum which has significance because it is typical and representative of a class of objects of documented importance, a museum may consider collectible a painting by a contemporary artist of established reputation, even without an intermediate owner. That is, if the paintings of this artist have won recognition, if they are the product of significant forces in our culture, are illustrative of our times and so on, the museum may buy a painting from him while it is still wet on his easel and transfer it to an exhibition gallery.

In this view, art provides not only high-level entertainment (aesthetic experience) but illustrates cultural history as well. An art museum staff which is so set against the use of their collections for public education (which is the prime necessity for all other kinds of museums) that they flee in the opposite direction and ignore the cultural connections of the objects of art cannot be defended. Not only do they decrease the potential use of their collections (and therefore decrease their collections' worth), they run the risk of having their works of art but a step removed from any accumulation of curiosities, and their museums but a step from any enterprise that merely panders to the superficial and momentary pleasure-seeking of a mentally lazy public.

In collecting the art of today, the art museum curator must try to recognize examples of creative genius. He should also try to select objects that are representative samples of our time and culture, not idiosyncratic oddities. In collecting the art of the past, the chief problem is cost.

Lately, the demand for art has reached enormous proportions, and the number of available art objects is decreasing. As time goes on, of course, objects of the past become scarcer. Fire, war, and natural disasters take great toll of historic art. The floods in Italy in the fall of 1966 were the worst in hundreds of years: more than 8,000 paintings in the Uffizi Gallery in Florence were under water, to cite but a single example. Another cause of scarcity is the museum itself. When a museum acquires a piece of sculpture, it is permanently removed from private hands. Each year, fewer great works of art are available for purchase by individuals. There is more affluence today, however, and art is a socially acceptable form for excess wealth, perhaps more so than private railway cars and ocean-going yachts. It all adds up to high prices paid to dealers and at public auction for works of art.

The prices of items at auction suggest that the value of an object is not the cost of producing it or what the owner paid for it but what it will bring at auction. Market price is tied less to beauty or appearance than to the name of the creator. One of the largest and most respected of the auction houses, Christie's of London, put a price of $280 on a painting, *The Judgment of Paris*, when they thought Lankrink had painted it. When they decided that it had been painted by Rubens, they announced its value as more than $225,000. Why is it that the same painting is worth 1,000 times as much if painted by one man than if painted by another? It can only be that the dollar value of an object is determined by what someone is willing to pay for it. Most museums cannot compete with the people who are willing to pay astronomical sums. With notable exceptions, great art that hits the market today is more likely to wind up in private than in public hands.

Art museums, however, continue to do the best they can. They maintain contacts throughout the world so they can keep abreast of what is becoming available on the world art market. The director often travels to inspect a work of art and decide whether it meets the standards of his museum and will be an important addition to the collections. For example, will it fill a gap? The actual purchase may be handled through an intermediary so that competing bidders cannot judge their competition.

Market prices have expanded even beyond the expectations of the experts. A porcelain teapot worth $3,200 in 1961 sold for $10,640 five years later. A set of seven Chippendale chairs sold for $2,987 in the spring of 1966. Six months later they brought $4,480. Mischa Elman sold in 1972, for $34,800, a Stradivarius violin he had bought in 1907 for $1,200. Old Master original prints multiplied in value 37 times from 1950 to 1970. *Seated Odalisque* by Henri Matisse sold for $350 in 1960 and $4,000 in 1970. Picasso prints increased in value 120 per cent in 1968–69. One of his linoleum cuts, *After Cranach*, worth $600 in the early 1960's, went for $35,000 in 1970.

The "big money" is reserved for oil paintings. To date, the most paid for a painting was the $5,544,000, which won *Juan de Pareja* by Velasquez for the Metropolitan in 1970. This painting, done in 1649 just for practice, is not regarded as Velasquez' best and would probably win no popularity contests for beauty. The highest amount previously paid for a painting at auction, also by the Metropolitan Museum of Art, was $3,285,000 in 1961 for *Aristotle Contemplating the Bust of Homer* by Rembrandt. The highest price ever paid for a painting in a private sale was more than $5,000,000 paid to the Prince of Liechtenstein in 1967 for *Ginevra dei Benci* by Leonardo da Vinci. The painting went to the National Gallery of Art in Washington, D.C.

French Impressionism and paintings of related styles are enjoying a vogue now. They are said to have increased in value one
thousandfold from 1893 to 1970. A few examples: In 1867 Claude
Monet painted *La Terrasse à Sainte Adresse* and sold it not long after for
$80. In 1926, Theodore Pitcairn of Bryn Athyn, Pennsylvania, bought
it for $11,000. In 1967, Pitcairn sold it to the New York Metropolitan
Museum of Art at an auction in London for $1,411,200. Renoir sold his
Pont des Artes for $77. In this century it was once sold for $40,000. In
1968 it brought $1,500,000 at auction. A small (only 15″ X 19″) painting
by Georges Seurat, *Les Poseuses*, was sold in 1970 for $1,033,000. In the
early 1900's, when Modigliani could not pay his room rent, he settled
the small bill with a painting of his landlady's daughter. That same
painting was sold in 1968 for $300,000.

Figures like the foregoing seem unreal to most of us in museum
work. The director of a small art museum or the curator of art in a
general museum will be concerned about the few thousand dollars
needed to keep his work going for the coming year. Not every art
museum or department has a sizable amount to spend on acquisitions. But any amount used to purchase permanent additions to the
collection must be spent with great care. Uppermost in the mind must
be the purpose and scope of the museum. Precisely what is its area of
interest and activity? What do you hope to accomplish by the use of
your collections? How can the collections be improved so that you can
accomplish more?

If spending millions of dollars on a painting strikes you as im-
moral, you are not alone. Is it not legitimate to inquire how much
public good is accomplished by one more painting hanging with
endless rows of other paintings on an art museum's walls? Might not
even the smaller amounts spent by less pretentious institutions be
questioned? They have been and are being questioned. The art
museum itself, as an institution, is under attack.

The common man has held the art museum in awe but felt it was
not for him. Members of disadvantaged segments of society, disil-
lusioned youth, and many artists are more blunt. They see the art
museum as a flagrant example of the Establishment's disregard for the
needs of society. The typical art museum is not relevant to our times,
they would say. Barbara Gold, a columnist for the *Baltimore Sun*, has
criticized the museums of her city. She says that they seem committed
to a suburban elite even though located in the middle of one of our
major cities, and that the three major museums of Baltimore seem to
feel little responsibility toward the city, even though they are city-

supported. This is far from being a unique situation. Even the small museums in small communities must be aware of the current reaction to the traditional role of the art museum. It must, more than ever, be responsible to the needs of its community.

Robert Hughes, for one, is offended by the participation of large public museums in the art market. He asks what the function of past art ought to be in present culture, and refers to the rapacity that impelled the Met's director to spend more than $5½-million on the Velasquez.

The American museum still tends to be an institutional parody of the robber baron's castle, staking its prestige more on acquisitions than functions. The Metropolitan speaks with politic sincerity of "bringing art to the people"—though this did not deter it last October from slapping what amounts to a tax on art education by reinstituting an admission fee for the first time in 30 years. But these declarations are apt to be gutted by the display of a now old multimillion-dollar painting. For what will *Juan de Pareja* on its draped wall in the Metropolitan mean to an intelligent 18-year-old from Spanish Harlem when he sees it and remembers the price? (As well he may, since the Met is not inclined to disguise the market value of its major acquisitions.) His probable reaction will be fury at the wrong priorities that spending $5,000,000 on a painting involves. Who can say that the boy would not be right? In a city that has a Harlem and a Bedford-Stuyvesant, and is already stuffed to superfluity with exceptional works of art, pride in acquiring yet another multimillion-dollar painting is merely an index of fetishism and decayed conscience. [14]

EXERCISES—CHAPTER 8

1. Read and report on two articles from periodicals dealing with art collecting. Pay special attention to references to the art market, what art museums are trying to acquire, and the kinds of objects receiving publicity.
2. Discuss what kinds of museums and kinds of museum activity are most relevant to our times. Should a natural history museum have exhibits on the preservation of the natural environment? A health museum exhibits of birth control, the population explosion, drugs, etc.? A history museum on the contributions of minority groups to the building of America? What is the role of the art museum in American culture today? Are Guthe's four obligations of a museum still valid? (Treat these not as individual questions to be answered

14. "Who Needs Masterpieces at Those Prices?" *Time*, July 19, 1971. Reprinted by permission from *Time*, The Weekly Newsmagazine; copyright Time, Inc., 1971.

but as suggestions for material to be covered in a short essay—at least 300 words.)

3. You are the director of an art museum and have $100,000 per year to spend on building the collections. Would you spend it all each year on a famous name—even if it means a drawing instead of an oil painting? Would you save it from year to year—and every four or five years buy one famous painting at auction? Would you buy several paintings each year by relatively unknown, lesser artists? What effect on your answers would the existing collections of your museum have?

4. Michael Levey, Keeper of the National Gallery, London, said, "One master-piece is worth more in aesthetic significance than twenty minor pictures, all with some historical interest." Comment, assuming "historical" to mean "art historical," and then comment further, assuming "historical" to mean simply "historical" (nonart).

5. Your art museum has a department of decorative arts and no limitation as to time period. What might you collect from today? (Be specific and justify your choices.) Would you collect objects typical of the lower classes? Why? This question is not as simple as it might first appear. You must keep in mind the nature of the typical, traditional art museum.

6. Let us say your art museum has established a new department of popular art. How would you go about collecting?

7. Look at the pictures on the walls of your own home and describe them. Are there prints? What kinds (techniques)? Are there reproductions and origi-nals? Are they of popular art? Fine art? Folk art? Primitive art? How is each enjoyed? (That is, analyze your enjoyment or nonenjoyment.) The purpose of this assignment is for you to describe a collection of art with which you are familiar according to manufacture, style, function, etc. You may limit yourself to one room, and, of course, the collection does not need to belong to you or to your family. You should be familiar with it, however.

8. Assuming that your museum has within its scope the collecting of contem-porary art, how will you deal with the following? (That is, would you accept it in the first place, and, if so, how would you store and exhibit the piece?) In each case explain your decision or how you would cope with any problems you might anticipate.
   A. A fragile construction of thin tree branches, dried grasses, and birds' nests?
   B. A 15′ x 15′ x 15′ inflatable plastic animal?
   C. A very heavy construction of metal plates twelve feet square and eight feet high?
   D. A pornographic painting?
   E. A painting of revolting subject matter, worse than spilled garbage?
   F. A painting advocating the revolutionary overthrow of our government?
   G. A construction of partially burned wagon wheels with an arrow sticking in one of them, lying in a tray of loose dirt about six feet square, with plants, small animal bones, and a buffalo chip or two?

H. A pottery vessel by a college art student?
I. The blue ribbon winners from the fine arts division of your local county fair? (Produced by largely untaught or self-taught "artists".)
J. A painted copy of a painting?
K. A piece of sculpture of high quality lying outside the scope of your museum?

9

Registration and Cataloguing

Even though he understands the nature of museums, the purpose of his own museum, and what the collections of his museum should include, the museum curator is not ready to collect until he knows how to make the records that preserve information about the museum objects under his care. To this point we have discussed the first of Guthe's four obligations of a museum, the obligation to build and maintain good collections.[1] The second obligation is that of records, without which the collections are worth little.

Records enable the museum worker to identify and locate all the objects in the collections. As an object is added to the collections, therefore, complete information about it must be obtained from the supplier and previous owners. The best time to identify the object is when it is being registered and catalogued. It is important to have a good reference library dealing with the subjects that fall within the museum's scope.

Registration is the assignment of a permanent number to an accession.[2] *Cataloguing* is the classification of each object in the accession by subject. Just as a library may catalogue a book according to title, author, and any number of subjects dealt with in the book, a museum may make any number of reference cards to refer to the subjects or areas of interest that a given specimen may illustrate. The numbering system used can be any one that seems efficient for your particular museum operation. A museum which has had its collec-

---

1. Carl E. Guthe, "Epilogue," *So You Want a Good Museum* (Washington, D.C.: American Association of Museums, 1957, 1973).

2. Remember that an accession is the acquisition of one or more objects from one source at one time. It is one transaction between source and museum, or the objects acquired in the transaction.

tions recorded and numbered for many years may still be using one of the older systems. A typical one would use only large, bound books and have one series of numbers for accessions and other series for objects by category, designated by a prefixed letter. Thus A2172 would indicate the two thousand one hundred and seventy second object catalogued in the A category (art, anthropology, archaeology, animals, or whatever that particular museum has chosen A to mean). The full number would include the accession number, ordinarily given first, and the object number by category. 14/H212 would mean the two hundred and twelfth object in the history (let us say) category, which is part of the museum's fourteenth accession.

Many museums today favor the system recommended by the AAM and explained by Guthe and others. It is simply to assign a number for the year, a number for the accession within the year, and a number for the object within the accession. 50.12.3 means the third object of the twelfth accession of 1950. The museum that wishes to avoid confusion among 1850, 1950, and 2050 will place an 8, a 9, or a 0 before the five. If an object has two parts, such as a bayonet and scabbard, the more important, if there is a choice, is called "a" and the other "b." The scabbard, therefore, would be 50.12.3b. (Or 50/12/3b, 50-12-3b., etc.) Each object of the collection will have a number written on it or attached to it, if possible, and for each object there will be one or more written records bearing this number.

The various techniques for attaching or applying numbers to objects have been described many times in the literature (for example, in the books by Carl E. Guthe recommended in the bibliography). In general, the numbering must be permanent without damaging the object, inconspicuous but logically placed and easy to find, small but legible, and protected from wear. A typical example of numbering involves, first, brushing a small amount of white paint onto the object; second, using a small straight pen to write numbers onto the dry paint with permanent drafting ink; and third, coating the numbers with clear lacquer (like clear nail polish). Other methods are used for objects which should not be painted or written on. To number a shirt, for example, print the number on a short strip of cloth tape and sew the tape to the inside of the garment near an edge—either inside the neck band or on the tail at the front.

There will be several kinds of records or files. Commonly, a museum will have an *accession file*, which may be in the form of a bound book or of cards (preferably locked in the drawer with a rod through holes in the cards, as with library cards). This record is arranged numerically. A museum should also have a *donor* (or *source*) file, arranged alphabetically by name of the source. This might also include donors of funds, or even members of the museum's association. Such a file might be kept by a membership secretary or public relations officer, though it must be easily available to the entire professional staff. Another indispensable file is for *accession documents*. Ordinarily, it consists of large envelopes or folders in letter- or legal-size file drawers. The document file includes supporting records such as news clippings, letters, previous owner's written records, publications or references to publications, photographs, research reports, etc., which pertain to individual accessions. Not every accession will have an entry in the document file, and it is not necessary to number a folder for an accession until there is something to put in it. An object may appear in a newspaper photograph with an accompanying story years after it has been accessioned. If no folder exists for its accession, the accession number should be written on a folder, the object number should be written on the newspaper clipping, the clipping placed in the folder, and the folder inserted in the file at the proper numerical location.

The donor file, mentioned above, is normally on cards, as is the *catalogue* or *object file*. This file is arranged alphabetically by name of the object or other name, such as material of which it is made, its historical period, famous person with whom it is associated, Indian tribe which produced it, geographical provenance, or whatever.

Not every object needs a number. For example, if archaeological excavations yield thousands of pieces of broken pottery, scraps of bone, and flint chips, the time and money spent in writing numbers on each piece and filling out thousands of catalogue cards would not be productive in most cases. In such an instance a decision will have to be made as to how to maintain the identity of the objects without unnecessary labor and cost. One accession number might be assigned to all the objects from one season's field work at a site. Individual numbers could be assigned to the most significant objects, including all those described and shown in publications. The remaining items could be assigned numbers by lot. That is, all the potsherds from a particular part of the excavation (a dump, a level, a house floor, a storage pit) could be given a number and stored in a box or drawer bearing that number.[3] Another example can be taken from biology. It

3. The museum point of view; the archaeologist in charge may want additional numbering refinements. Whatever cataloguing, numbering, cross-referencing, etc., are

would be folly to attempt to catalogue individual insects in a collection of several hundred thousand, or the thousands of sheets of plant specimens in a herbarium. Since such collections are filed systematically, it is a simple matter to find any wanted specimen, and a catalogue is unnecessary. It might even be said that the collections and the catalogue coincide in such an instance, adequate identification being on tags, sheets, or containers with which or in which the specimens are filed.

The *accession file* entry, of course, describes the accession as a whole and answers the questions: What was obtained? When? From whom? How? etc. The *donor file* gives the name and address of the source and lists the accessions by number from that source. The *catalogue* describes the individual objects rather completely. A catalogue card will include the number of the object, its source, its name and description, its location in the museum,[4] photographs taken of the object, value, date catalogued, etc. Sometimes a sketch of the object directly on the card will aid in the description. Some museums attach small photographs to the catalogue cards, and others print photographs on heavy paper the same size as the catalogue card, on the back of which the form has been printed. The reverse side of the catalogue card itself is thus a photograph of the object. Photographs should be taken of the most important objects in the collections and the negatives filed numerically, either using the catalogue number or a separate numbering system. Prints can be filed separately or placed in the document file.

"Value" on the catalogue card is sometimes confusing. Even though the real value of a museum object lies in its educational potential, the word in the catalogue refers to money and has to do with insurance. There are three ways of arriving at a dollar value for an object: 1) the purchase price; 2) replacement cost on the market; 3) a consolation figure. A date should be given for the second, since market values change with time. The last kind of valuation is applied in the case of an object that is unique, irreplaceable, literally "price-

called for by the archaeological reference and research requirements can be incorporated into the museum's record system. The same can be said for any of the scientific research areas.

4. This may be written in pencil so that it can be erased when the location is changed, or it may be entered on the back of the card so that changes in location can be added without removing previous entries. This has the advantage of giving the complete history of the use of the object.

less." If your museum should lose such an item, how much money would it take to console you for the loss? We shall discuss insurance in a later chapter.

The description should include the measurements of most objects. It might be well to do these in the metric system in order to avoid conversion of the figures later when the English system is abandoned.

Examples of record cards will be useful at this point. The forms shown here are in use at the University of Idaho Museum. They are not necessarily better than hundreds of other forms used elsewhere, but they will serve to illustrate the characteristics of good collections records.

Any number of cards in the catalogue may be used for a single object. Each card is filed alphabetically, under a category which is considered to be important in the organization of the collections. Cards may be added at any time, and categories may be changed as the collections grow.

The records must be kept safe. They should be locked up, kept in as fireproof a location as possible, and made available only to au-

---

UNIVERSITY OF IDAHO MUSEUM, Moscow, Idaho
registration card

Acc. no. 74-12   Source Troy Trading Post
How acquired purchase   When April 12, 1974

Description of accession broadaxe (head only, no
handle), forged iron, 15 cm x 20 cm

Cost, origin, details, remarks $5.00, made and used
in Northern Idaho, badly pitted

this record made by Arthur White   date April 20, 1974

THE REGISTRATION CARD OR ACCESSION CARD (the file of these cards is the *register* or *accession file*) Filed numerically.

```
UNIVERSITY OF IDAHO MUSEUM, Moscow. Idaho
source card

source  Troy Trading Post_____
address_____812 Spruce Street_____
                   Troy, Idaho   83871_____
              (formerly Jim's Junk)_____
_____

accessions from this source:
number       description                date rec'd
 71-14       Women's clothing, framed   Aug. 12, 1971
             pictures, churn_____
 73-28       blacksmith's tools         Nov. 5, 1973
 74-12       broadaxe                   Apr. 12, 1974
_____
_____
_____
_____

if continued on another card, check here_____
```

THE SOURCE CARD (since most objects in most museums are acquired by donation, the file of these cards is commonly called the *donor file*) Filed alphabetically.

thorized persons. All records should not be kept in one location. Ideally, a duplicate set should be in another building. At least try to keep the accession file and the catalogue in different locations so that a disaster that ruins part of your building will not ruin all your records of the collections.

No entirely satisfactory system has yet been devised for the classification of all historical objects. Several systems for certain kinds of materials are included in the bibliography at the end of this book. The time is not far off when numerical coding for museum objects will open up the use of computers in the recording, storing, searching for, and exchanging of information about museum collections. Eventually, we may hope for central information banks on the holdings of all recognized museums. Any museum can then learn in a few seconds where museum objects of a particular kind may be found, anywhere in the United States and Canada—or even the entire world.[5]

5. Those interested in this matter are referred to *Computers and Their Potential Applications in Museums* (New York: Arno Press, 1968) and Robert G. Chenhall, *Museum Cataloging in the Computer Age* (Nashville: American Association for State and Local History, 1975).

UNIVERSITY OF IDAHO MUSEUM, Moscow, Idaho
catalogue card

name of
category__ Hunter, John M._____ source Troy Trading Post

object no. _71-14-5_____ date rec'd Aug. 12, 1971

other no(s)._432 (previous collector's number)__

description of object apron, muslin, 105 cm x 55 cm,
waist ties, dyed blue, pocket on right side
(drawing on back or card). Made and used in
Troy, Idaho about 1910. Handkerchief no.
71-14-6 found in pocket at time of purchase.

value $8.00 (1971) condition good   photo(s) 513, 514
remarks belonged to Catherine Thomas, wife of
John M. Hunter. She was born in England.
this record made by Alice Johns   date May 23, 1972

PUT LOCATION OF OBJECT ON OTHER SIDE OF CARD

UNIVERSITY OF IDAHO MUSEUM, Moscow, Idaho
catalogue card

name of
category_ clothing, women's   source Troy Trading Post

object no. _71-14-5_____ date rec'd Aug. 12, 1971

other no(s)._432 (previous collector's number)__

description of object apron, muslin, 105 cm x 55 cm,
waist ties, dyed blue, pocket on right side
(drawing on back of card). Made and used in
Troy, Idaho about 1910. Handkerchief no.
71-14-6 found in pocket at time of purchase.

value $8.00 (1971) condition good   photo(s) 513, 514
remarks_ belonged to Catherine Thomas (Mrs. John
M. Hunter) who was born in England
this record made by_ Mary Wittin   date Sept. 18, 1971

PUT LOCATION OF OBJECT ON OTHER SIDE OF CARD

THE CATALOGUE CARD (together, these cards make up the *catalogue* or
object file) Filed alphabetically.

For the time being, most museums will continue to maintain their records according to systems they have adopted. The most we can hope for is that each museum will have, and use, a copy of the principal reference book on the work of the registrar, *Museum Registration Methods* by Dorothy H. Dudley and Irma Bezold Wilkinson.[6] If you do not feel qualified to describe and classify some categories of museum objects, call on experts in those categories to assist you. You may be able to get the short-term services of a volunteer who has special knowledge of guns, sea shells, prints, weaving, or some other subject and will catalogue all the objects in your collections that lie within his area of special competence. He will enjoy the opportunity to put his knowledge to public use and to study your collections.

A final note: Temporary inventories of shipments to and from your museum are also very important. This applies to accessions, temporary art exhibitions, loans to schools, and any other movement of objects to or from your museum. Packing and unpacking must be done under the direct supervisions of an authorized person who is responsible for the inventories. The safeguarding of objects is the museum's prime function.

EXERCISES—CHAPTER 9

1. Let us assume you have found the following written on an object in a museum storeroom: 875–1–2a 2/G691. What can you tell about the museum and the object from the number alone? (Also, what would you speculate?)
2. How should the number be physically applied or attached to the object: a. if G stands for geology? b. if G stands for garment? c. if G stands for gun? d. if G stands for Georgia history?
3. Choose a category (art, history, or whatever) to describe the museum you are working at or the kind of museum you would like to be associated with. List at least six, and preferably more, books you should have for reference in order to catalogue the collections. If you were able to expand this reference "shelf" into a reference "library," what kinds of books would you buy? (If you do not feel competent to do this part of the assignment, get help from your local librarian. The purpose is to get you to understand the kinds of references that would assist you in identifying and classifying objects in your chosen field.)

6. Rev. ed., Washington, D.C.: American Association of Museums, 1968.

4. Look around you, wherever you are, and choose four different and dissimilar objects. Make out records for them, preferably on 4 x 6 cards, inventing details when needed to complete the cards. Be sure to include complete descriptions, so that someone else could distinguish each object from others that are similar. Your cards should have all the information that you would expect to find on such cards in a museum.

5. Assuming that you have access to at least two museums, describe their record systems. Try to get sample forms, fill them out enough to show you understand how they are used. What files do the museums have? What kinds of files (pertaining to the collections) do they lack? Who does the accessioning, the cataloguing, etc? Evaluate the systems.

10
Care of Collections

Caring for collections is part of the definition of a real museum. Since the collections make the museum and the museum is supposed to last indefinitely, the collections should be given meticulous care. "Collections-filing rooms" or storerooms must be provided, and the collections must be organized and accessible. Collecting wisely and preparing good records would hardly make sense if the collections were then allowed to deteriorate or disappear. The first obligation, the adequate management of the collections, involves preservation, the subject of this chapter, and security, the subject of the next.

Any good museum will have more museum objects than it exhibits at one time. The objects on public view may actually constitute less than half of the total collections.[1] The museum has the responsibility to care for and to use all of its objects, whether being exhibited or not. This means that it should provide good and adequate space "behind the scenes" for the organized storage of the collections. As a rule of thumb, the museum should have at least as much space for the collections as for the exhibits. The well-known proportion, 40-40-20, means that of the total amount of space in the museum, 40 percent should be for collections, 40 percent for exhibits, and the remaining 20 percent for everything else (offices, rest rooms, hallways, janitor's closets, lobbies, auditoriums, lunchrooms, workrooms, receiving rooms, carpenter shops, elevators, etc.). Obviously 20 percent may not be enough for all of this. A more reasonable proportion might be 30-30-40. The main point is that at least as much space should be

1. The Field Museum of Natural History, in Chicago, exhibits less than one percent of its total collections at any one time.

devoted to the collections that are not on exhibit as is in the public area where the exhibits are located.

The word "storage," as applied to the collections, must be used with care since it has the bad connotation of things not in use. Guthe prefers "filing" and speaks of the "filed collections," comparing them to the stacks in a closed-stacks library. Daifuku distinguishes between "live" and "dead" storage.[2] Each object should be easy to find and to remove. A one-word characterization of proper storage is "accessible."

Three related faults are typical of nonprofessional museum management. Because of an overemphasis on exhibits, the amateur will put all or nearly all of the collection on display. This results in poor exhibits, too little space for the storage of collections as they grow, and poor management of the stored collections. That storage will be "dead" to some degree. At the worst extreme the objects will be piled in attics and corners of the basement and tied up in unmarked boxes and stacked in out of the way places—essentially lost to the museum operation. Even in apparently good museums, objects may be stored beneath exhibit cases behind panels screwed in place, and the catalogue cards may not show the locations of the objects.

Let us follow the progress of an object as it enters the collections. A donor brings it to the museum and to the director's or a curator's office. Or the donor may have invited the director to send a member of his staff to the donor's home to get the object. The staff member, while talking to the donor, should get as much information as possible about the object. Many museums have accession worksheets which the staff member fills out at that time. He gets names and addresses and the answers to such questions as "What is it? How was it used? Where was it used? Who used it? Where was it made? How much did you pay for it? Did other people in the same locality use the same kind of thing?" and so on. The object is examined and its condition noted, with remarks that might be useful later in handling and cataloguing the object. Once in the museum, the object is assigned a number (registered) and placed in a secure location awaiting cataloguing, cleaned and repaired, and possibly photographed. When catalogued, which should be within a few weeks,[3] the object is placed with other

2. Hiroshi Daifuku, "Collections: Their Care and Storage," *The Organization of Museums: Practical Advice*, Museums and Monuments Series, No. IX (Paris: UNESCO, 1960), p. 124.

3. Some museums set aside a certain day each month, usually the last or the first, for cataloguing all accessions of the previous month.

objects of a similar nature where it can be well cared for and will be easily accessible for future reference and use.

All materials deteriorate; and since the museum is devoted to permanent preservation of its collections, it must maintain the best possible conditions for the longest possible life of each object. Before discussing preservation conditions, however, let us return to the matter of cleaning.

To clean or not to clean is not always a simple question. There are many reasons why we clean an object:

1. *Practical* reasons: removing dirt, foreign matter, material that obscures the surface and form of the object; to prevent deterioration of the object (rust and corrosion must be arrested; fly specks, acidic or alkaline substances on the surface, or substances that absorb water from the atmosphere may cause steady damage). Since the primary requirement in the care of an object by a museum is its preservation, this must be the first consideration in cleaning.

2. *Aesthetic* reasons: to give the object a more pleasing appearance or for psychological effect.

3. *Educational* reasons: to reveal more about the object to the person studying it for research (e.g., the curator) or to the person viewing the object as exhibited (e.g., the visitor).

A decision whether to clean, how to clean, and how much to clean must be based on the use determined for the object. (An object has real value only in terms of its use by and for human beings; that is, in terms of its contribution to human life.) Recognize that one use may preclude another; conflict exists especially between the aesthetic and the educational—or between art and science. The aesthetic approach may sometimes be that of the professional collector, whose attitude toward objects may not be the same as that of the museum curator. For example, a coin collector may value the patina which a coin has acquired over the centuries and feel that the commercial value of the coin would be diminished by cleaning. The curator might feel that more detail of the coin's design would show if the overlying patina were removed and that, therefore, cleaning would enhance the coin's educational value. He should keep in mind, however, that cleaning should not be undertaken if more might be lost than gained. He must be careful not to remove identifying marks or features; to abrade soft metals, such as pewter, or otherwise to destroy evidence concerning the history of the object. In seeking the "original" appearance of an object, we must be clear in our minds as to what that is. Do we want to portray an unused tool fresh from the hardware store? A farming machine, clean and brightly painted? A child's toy not yet played with?

Philosophically, we might think of such items as unborn artifacts. Does the cultural object take on significance when new and perfect or when adopted and used? It is the commonplace, everyday importance of objects which earns them a place in the collections of a history museum. It is their relevance to the life of the people at large. Therefore, it is an object that has been used and is typical that is important. To erase all clues of such use is in a way to create an artificiality and to make the object something of an abstraction. A brand new saw is the *idea of a saw*. It becomes a real saw after a man has sawn boards with it to build a house. The signs of wear, the rusty spots, the patina of age, the chipped corners are evidence that this was a real object in a real world. What you would remove by cleaning is an important part of the real object. To put it another way, the real object is not a saw but a saw that was used by human beings living real lives.

This question of cleaning down to the bare metal or bare wood and then refinishing or repainting relates to the restoration of historical objects. Should a historical museum replace missing parts? Reupholster the sofa? Rebuild a missing building? Make a new handle for the tea cup? We have to refer to the earlier statement that the use to which the object is to be put must determine our answer.

If the use is *aesthetic* (related to art and beauty)—if the object is to be enjoyed for its appearance—then the art, the artist's original creation, must be allowed to come through unimpeded and unimpaired. Keep in mind that art is the creation, the intention of the artist rather than the art object itself. Realize, too, that weathering and oxidation may be part of the art, part of the artist's or maker's intention for the object. If the use is *entertainment*, to create nostalgia or a feeling of awe, the appearance of age may be desired. (Examples are distressed wood furniture, artificial worm holes, beating with chains, "antiquing" furniture, wearing old silver plate down to the copper base.) If the use is to be primarily *educational*, as in a good history museum, but with some attention paid to aesthetic values, a patina acquired through time may be desirable. The ravages of time may lend authenticity to the object, attesting to its history.

How do we know whether to clean, how to clean, and how much to clean? No answer will apply in every case. Judgment must be based on reason, and the answer will depend on the use to which the object may be put. In general, be conservative. Clean too little rather than too much.

While cleaning is a deliberate effort to change an object or at least its appearance, preservation is, in a way, the reverse. It is defensive rather than active, the aim being to prevent changes from occurring. There are several causes of change: 1) *Human loss*—theft, vandalism, careless usage, accidents; 2) *environmental damage*—fire, leaking roof, leaking pipes, dirt, fumes; 3) *climatic damage*—extremes of temperature and humidity, and rapid changes in temperature and humidity; 4) *radiant energy*—chiefly ultraviolet light; 5) *biological damage* —insects, rodents, fungus; 6) *faulty procedures*; 7) *disasters*.

Preservation consists of techniques to prevent undesirable changes from occurring. Storage rooms should preferably be air conditioned and temperature controlled. Some kinds of materials require a higher relative humidity than others. Some kinds of materials are more susceptible to damage from changes in humidity than others. Each kind of material—leather, wood, paper, metal, glass, etc.— should be kept under the conditions that are best for it.

The beginner may, logically, be confused as to how much technique he needs to master at the beginning of his museum training. If he is actually working in a museum, he is naturally expected to master his job, whatever is involved, as quickly as he can. The student or the administrator, on the other hand, without such urgency, is advised to master theory first and then such techniques as he may need for specific jobs. A common mistake of the amateur and the beginner is the assumption that preparation for work in a museum is merely the learning of a certain number of techniques in order to perform museum functions. My attitude is quite the opposite. I feel that an introductory museology course, that is to say, basic orientation for all kinds of museum work and for a broad understanding of museums, must deal with such matters as purpose and organization. Technical matters need to be introduced, but not explored in detail.

All persons who will be handling the collections must practice a few basic principles of conservation: Do not use rubber bands, paper clips, unpadded wire hangers, adhesive tapes, paper of high acidic content, and do not fold textiles or store them tightly crammed together. Avoid extremes of temperature and humidity and rapid changes of these. This usually means not using attics and basements for museum storage. Never allow sunlight to fall on museum objects subject to fading. It is best to keep the light level at a minimum, to omit windows or skylights in storage rooms or exhibit halls, to avoid placing lamps close to objects, and to interpose glass, at least,[4] between fluorescent lights and museum objects. Specifically, do not use unshielded fluorescent lights inside exhibit cases and do use low wattage incandescent lamps (bulbs) in storerooms. Such rooms should be kept dark, of course, except for short periods when someone needs to work there.

A common mistake made by amateurs in museum work is to view potential damage to museum materials as they would view potential damage to clothing, furnishings, butterfly collections, and paintings in their own homes. They forget that while they may expect an article of clothing to last two years, a rug five, a butterfly collection ten, museum collections are theoretically meant to last forever. The light, the fumes, the humidity, the wire hanger, the creases in the table cloth, which cause no observable damage in a short time, will destroy the material in fifty years (or less).

In extreme cases, lack of proper care may become obvious to the public. For a donor to feel that your museum is not adequately preserving the treasured objects which he gave you is a source of bad publicity at the very least. Early in 1967, an Associated Press dispatch reported that Avery Brundage had "threatened to take back the $30 million collection of Oriental Art he donated to San Francisco." Though it was housed in the principal art museum in a special wing built at a cost of two and three quarters million dollars, Brundage's statement that he was unhappy at the *care* given the collection received national publicity.

EXERCISES—CHAPTER 10

1. What are the issues (what problems or controversial matters) are involved in cleaning: old coins, badly rusted gun parts, delicate textiles, oil paintings, animal hides? (This question does not ask for recommendations as to techniques. It is a philosophical question; that is, it is more a museological than a museographical question.)
2. Name various categories of museum objects on the basis of the nature of the materials of which they are composed, and the different kinds of care which these categories must have.

4. Better is a plastic material commercially available which filters out most of the harmful radiation. This is made into sleeves which fit over the fluorescent tubes.

3. Discuss metal shelving in relation to the storing of tea cups and paper.
4. How would you store oil paintings? (See Daifuku, note 2.)
5. Give examples of the effect of humidity on materials.
6. What is fumigation?
7. What examples of deterioration (and/or fading) resulting from light have you observed, perhaps in your own home or in a museum with which you are familiar?
8. Estimate the amount of space devoted to exhibits, to collections storage and to all other purposes in a museum that you would judge to be well run and in one that you would judge to be the opposite. How do the proportions compare? If you cannot compare one museum with another, at least compare the exhibit space and the collection storage space in one museum. How far from being equal are they?
9. If you can get into the collections-filing rooms (storage) of a museum, criticize the organization of the collections and their care.
10. How does the care of the collections (including organization, cleanliness, amount of space, and preservation techniques) relate to the worth of a museum?

11

Security

Security is the most important consideration in the administration of *any* museum. (Next is cleanliness).[1] Security embraces the protection of the museum buildings, its contents, its staff, and its visitors. It includes the care of the collections, insurance against severe financial loss, and physical security (protection against theft, fire, and vandalism).

Museums, by their very nature, must be security conscious. Insurance is a poor substitute for preventive measures because the value of museum collections cannot really be expressed in financial terms. In guarding against theft, carelessness, and vandalism, the museum is placed in an awkward position because good public relations are so important to it. The museum wants to welcome all kinds of people in great numbers and to make them feel "at home." While being friendly and hospitable, the museum must also prevent any damage and disturbance the visitor might cause.

Some museums feel unjustifiably safe from potential dangers. This is partly because not all losses to museums are publicized, certainly not nationally. Yet Joseph Chapman pointed out that in 1964 there were "daily between four and six thefts of art items valued at $5,000 or more."[2] As art values rise, thefts will probably continue to increase. Newspapers frequently carry stories of thefts of art from private collectors and from museums. Almost every issue of a museum periodical carries notices of thefts. Directors of small museums in remote locations cannot reassure themselves that such thievery occurs

1. Douglas A. Allan, "The Staff," *The Organization of Museums: Practical Advice*, Museums and Monuments Series, No. IX (Paris: UNESCO, 1960), p. 63.
2. Caroline E. Keck *et al.*, *A Primer on Museum Security* (Cooperstown: New York State Historical Association, 1966), p. 1.

only in cities. It is worldwide and becoming steadily more serious. Museum thefts have nearly doubled in recent years.

Thieves are removing ancient statues and paintings from the temples and museums of India. A story in the *Los Angeles Times* in the spring of 1969 stated that foreign collectors and tourists are removing stolen goods from the country. Police arrested an American professor and his wife as they were taking aboard ship 37 rare miniature paintings stolen a few months earlier from a $2 million collection in the museum of the Maharajah of Jaipur. The professor said that he had purchased the items in good faith at the residence of the curator of a museum. One hundred sixteen pieces of ancient jewlery were taken from the National Museum in New Delhi, according to the story, and statues of gods as tall as 30 feet were sawed out of their niches.

According to the Ecclesiastical Insurance Office, a church in England is robbed or desecrated every day. Authorities believe that organized crime syndicates are shipping silver, armor, and other kinds of antiques to the United States, where they bring high prices. Organized thievery is rampant in Italy, where churches are being robbed almost daily of art treasures. In the first three months of 1972, 1,598 art objects were stolen from churches and museums, and each year an estimated $10 million worth of archaeological objects are removed from the country. Vandals have raided the Villa Doria Park in Rome, hacking off the heads of ancient Roman statues and removing Etruscan tomb carvings and the artworks of the Caesars. One European travel poster said "Visit Italy Now, Before the Italians Destroy It." In November 1969, a New York art dealer who had taken great precautions to protect his gallery suffered a half-million -dollar loss while he was attending a meeting of the Art Dealers Association of America. The topic discussed at the meeting was current art thievery in New York City.

Germain Bazin[3] said that from 1957 to 1964 fifty museums and seventy churches suffered severe losses from robbery, and that some 900 important pieces of art had disappeared from documented collections. There is hardly a museum of any size anywhere that has not suffered losses. If a museum staff does not take preventive steps, the question is not *"Will* they get by with it?" but *"How long* will they get by with it?" Embarrassing as it is to the profession, internal theft also occurs. A museum must protect itself against its own employees as well as outside agents. All who are connected with a museum share in

3. *The Museum Age* (New York: Universe Books, Inc., 1967), p. 8.

the grave responsibility of security. The problem will not go away; it cannot be ignored.

Vandalism is also a serious problem. The Statue of Liberty became so marked by lipstick in recent years that it had to be coated with a special lipstick-resistant paint. A telephone company in the United States announced recently that vandals put some 11,000 pay phones out of commission every day. According to an official report, an average of 90 public telephone booths is destroyed *every day* in the Irish Republic, which, in proportion to the population, is about twice as bad as the same problem in this country. Signs and markers will probably be eliminated from the Boise National Forest in Idaho because the cost of replacing those destroyed by vandalism has become prohibitive. Museums are not immune. Vandalism heads the list of dangers within museum buildings, says Richard Foster Howard, Director of the Birmingham (Alabama) Museum of Art.[4] We have long had the problem of the individual vandal who slashes a painting or sets fire to a trashcan, but many museum administrators have become concerned with vandalism en masse. Because of changes in their cities, some museums now find themselves in or near slum areas. Participants in race riots and other civil disturbances in the neighborhood of a museum may find it a relatively defenseless symbol of the "Establishment."

William A. Bostick, Administrator and Secretary of the Detroit Institute of Arts, discussed riot security in an article outlining a recent survey.[5] Stanley D. Sohl, Museum Director of the Kansas State Historical Society, spoke on security at the national convention of the American Association of Museums in New Orleans in May 1968. He covered such matters as placing fire extinguishers near windows where Molotov cocktails might be thrown in, outdoor floodlighting of the building and grounds, bars on ground-floor windows and doors, and drawing the blinds over windows at night so that snipers cannot kill the staff. This is not to suggest that the public is the museum's enemy. Up to a point, visitors in the museum prevent theft and vandalism.

A common mistake is to equate security with law enforcement and museum guards with policemen. There is a basic difference:

4. *Museum Security* (Washington, D.C.: American Association of Museums, 1958), p. 2.

5. "What is the State of Museum Security?" *Museum News*, Vol. 46, No. 5 (January 1968), 13-19.

security is prevention; law enforcement is reaction. Museum security measures should be directed toward preventing loss of any kind from any source. Howard speaks mainly of dealing with people.[6] However, measures of different kinds can supplement the guard force. Smoke-sensitive and heat-sensitive devices can set off fire alarms. Acoustical devices can detect movement in a gallery after the building is closed. Burglar alarms protect windows, doors, and skylights. Closed circuit television will allow the supervision of a number of separate areas from one guard post. Delicate electronic devices will sound an alarm if a painting is moved or a floor stepped on. Watchdogs may patrol buildings and grounds at night.

Smaller museums, at the very least, need fire extinguishers of more than one kind. The alkaline-acid type that sprays water is not suitable for electrical fires. The dry powder kind that smothers a fire by excluding oxygen is useful, but the carbon dioxide extinguisher may be the best for most situations that can be handled by the museum staff. It has the obvious advantage that it does not give rise to poisonous fumes and does not leave water or chemical powder on museum objects.

Since museums differ so greatly in their collections and their physical plants, no specific security plan would apply to all of them. I recommend, therefore, that the staff of your museum confer with the fire department, the police, and any other security agencies (do not forget your insurance company) regarding your own situation. The fire department, especially, will be glad to inspect your premises, make recommendations regarding fire extinguishers, and instruct your staff in their use. Remember that the excitement of an emergency is not conducive to reading printed instructions. The person on the spot must know immediately what to do.

One rule of thumb might be in order. Do not have fire hoses or sprinkler systems in exhibit areas and collection storage areas, because the water damage might be greater than damage by a fire that can be extinguished by other means. You should also alert your local fire chief to the damage that his hoses might create in your museum. He should be prepared in advance to treat a fire there with special care. Naturally, museum collections should be in fireproof surroundings, as much as possible. If your museum must be a frame building, try to store the unexhibited collections and the records in a separate fireproof building.

6. *Op. cit.*

The museum guard or night watchman is the most valuable security device the museum can have. There is no substitute for a human being who is alert to possible dangers and prepared to act. Protective precautions must take into account human vulnerability, however. In December 1973 an armed gang overpowered the night watchman at the Fogg Museum of Harvard and made off with $6 million worth of Greek and Roman coins. Howard's contention that the guard force should be organized on military lines and should be in uniform was formerly universally accepted, and this advice may still be correct for most museums. The presence of uniformed guards, however, may aggravate the recent antimilitary sentiment of young people, especially if some of the guards give the impression of being hostile. Conventional street attire with an identifying mark, such as a badge or an armband, may be better for your museum.

Cleanliness cannot be overemphasized as a deterrent to theft and vandalism. Good housekeeping shows that someone cares very much about the museum and that any disturbance will be quickly noticed and resented. Should vandalism occur, repair the damage immediately. One destructive act breeds another. The noncreative mind can be led into repeating what someone else has done. A museum had a statue of a person with hands outspread and fingers separated. The statue was allowed to remain where it was, and one after another, the fingers were broken off.

Insurance is part of the security picture, since a relatively small annual cost will prevent a financial disaster. The museum must protect itself from being wiped out at a single blow. In general, the museum will have a blanket "fine arts" policy which will cover damage and loss to the collections from any cause. This can be in any amount; that is, the museum can buy protection from any degree of loss. The individual objects need not be itemized, but very important objects should be singled out for special mention in the policy. Remember that specific dollar values for the most important items as well as the total amount of coverage should be reviewed regularly. Replacement costs for most categories of expensive objects are increasing. You may also need public liability insurance (who pays the bill if a visitor trips over a potted palm in your lobby and breaks a leg?), and employee-fidelity coverage, too (what if the secretary runs off with not only the bookkeeper, but her typewriter, the cashbox, and the painting in the director's office?).

Two particular points might be mentioned because they are traps for the uninitiated. One is that *when payment for total loss is accepted, title passes out of the museum's hands.* If you feel that the object is a total loss and put in a claim for full value, the insurance company may pay you, take the object, repair it, and sell it. Or if you accept reimbursement for a stolen object which is later recovered, it belongs to the insurance company, which might then sell it for much more than they gave you for it. The answer to this problem is to have your policy so written and the values so listed that you get full, current market value in the event of total loss, with the right to buy a recovered object back from the insurance company for what they paid you for it.

The second point has to do with subrogation, the legal substitution of one creditor for another. In a museum situation it would work like this: Your museum borrows something from another museum, and it is destroyed while it is in your possession. You notify the lender with regrets, he assures you that it was insured, and proceeds to collect from his insurance company. You breathe easier, but the blow falls when the insurance company sues you to recover the amount paid to the lender. It does this on the grounds that your museum is responsible for the financial loss the insurance company has suffered. The way to protect yourself from this pitfall is to obtain written proof, when you borrow an insured item, that the insurance company has waived the rights of subrogation or that your museum is named as an additional insured party with the lender.

As with other aspects of security, the insurance needs of each institution will differ from those of other institutions. The museum director should select a good insurance broker and discuss with him the total requirements of his institution.

EXERCISES—CHAPTER 11

1. If faced with the choice between giving the collection the best possible protection and catering to the wishes of a visitor, what must be your choice and why? Suppose the actions and requests of the director or board of trustees seem to constitute a security danger. As a member of the staff what is your responsibility? For example, you are the curator of collections and the wife of the president of the museum wants to borrow a costume from the collection for a party. The mayor wants the museum's stagecoach pulled in a parade down Main Street. The curator of education wants to lend some Indian headdresses to an elementary school. The curator of exhibits wants to place some objects in the open, not inside cases. The ladies' volunteer

society wants to light your historic house with candles for their annual evening party. What do you do in each of these cases?[7]

2. Why is sharing a building with the municipal library preferable to sharing it with the city government?

3. Name three different kinds of museums that may have three different security risks. (The purpose is to get you to think of problems in relation to the museum's own special situation—location, kinds of visitors, kind of staff, kind of collections, etc.)

4. If you are in a museum, review your insurance coverage with your agent. What potential losses or damage suits are you protected against? In what areas are you vulnerable? If you are not a museum employee, try to discuss insurance with the director of a museum near you, or with an insurance agent. Specifically, inquire about the coverage of collections and all its ramifications. Make a short report on your findings.

5. Discuss photography as a security measure.

6. How does the museum guard against the loss of equipment and supplies which are not part of the collections?

7. Describe what a small museum with a small staff and a small budget can do to make its collections secure.

8. Look at the museum from the standpoint of the visitor. Where may he go and what may he do in the museum, and what may he not do and where may he not go?

9. A historic house museum is entered by a woman wearing spike heels, sun glasses, and a bulky coat, carrying an umbrella and a large handbag, smoking, and leading a large dog and a small child eating an ice cream bar. As an attendant at the entrance, what do you do? ("Have a cardiac arrest," while reasonable, cannot be accepted as an answer. Think first of all of the potential security and safety problems created and try to deal with them.)

7. In May 1973, the wife of the Governor of Idaho was injured when a runaway stagecoach tipped over at the conclusion of a parade. The coach was also damaged.

Part II

Interpretation in the Museum

12
Use of Collections

Now that our hypothetical museum is well organized and has good, documented, well-cared-for collections, we must face the problem of how to use the collections to accomplish the museum's purpose. Other institutions teach, entertain, dispense information, provide hospitality to visitors, and so on. Only the museum is dedicated to the use of the real object for the public good. How, then, can the collections be used?

If everything the museum owned were on exhibit, except for a few inferior items piled somewhere out of the way and ignored, the phrase "uses of the collections" would be meaningless. To the amateur only one use exists—exhibits. A prospective donor may offer something to a museum with the words, "Do you want to put this on exhibit?" If you accept the item, it is with the understanding that you will put it out as quickly as you can; the donor may drop around the following week to see where you are showing "his" item.

The real museum has a very different attitude. Objects are collected because of their educational potential as specimens. The museum worker must force himself to think of the worth of the collections apart from their exhibit value, even though exhibition may be the chief use to which the collections are put. The distinction is basic, and as much as anything separates the good museums (and the good museologists) from the bad.

Since its creation in the last century, the educational, public museum has been devoted to research. The world's largest museum complex, the Smithsonian Institution, was founded by the will of an Englishman, James Smithson, who upon his death in 1829 left money to establish a museum for the "increase and diffusion of knowledge among men." James Brown Goode reiterated in 1895 that museums

109

exist for "the increase in knowledge." Thus the museum's mission is the study of its collections for the edification of mankind.

Guthe explains that the records constitute a research facility.[1] The researcher goes from the records to the collections and works with both. Daifuku speaks of research as pursued in the different kinds of museums.[2] The museum's input is research based on the objects that it has acquired; its output is public education. If museums are to claim the prestigious title of "educational institutions," they must study their collections in depth and interpret them, not merely show what they have collected. *All* museums must do research, for each musum has things that no other museum has; and each museum is unique, also, being concerned with a region, subject matter, or public with which no other museum is concerned in just the same way.

The study of the collections may yield practical results other than the advancement of knowledge. Mummies in the Cairo Museum, X-rayed in December 1970, revealed gold arm bands and jewelry still in place beneath the undisturbed wrappings. Dr. James Harris of the University of Michigan, head of the scientific team that did the work, said, "This is the first discovery of royal Egyptian artifacts since the discovery in 1922 of the tomb of King Tutankhamen."[3] Microscopic examination and technical tests sometimes reveal that museum objects are not what they have been assumed to be. This, of course, requires a thorough mastery of original techniques and materials.

Coupled with the large trade in antiquities, mostly illegal, is a thriving forgery business. *Interamerican*, a newsletter distributed by the Instituto Interamericano, alleged that Professor Spyridon Marinatos, Inspector General of Greek Archaeological Services, believed the gold treasure on exhibit at the Boston Museum of Fine Arts to consist of modern fakes; and on July 30, 1971, *The Times* (London) carried a story by Norman Hammond headlined "Tests show forged Turkish prehistoric pottery in many world museums." According to the article, the British Museum, the Metropolitan Museum of Art in New York, and the Ashmolean Museum at Oxford, among others, have purchased fakes in the last ten years. Technical methods developed in museum research have led to this discovery.

1. Carl E. Guthe, *So You Want a Good Museum* (Washington, D.C.: American Association of Museums, 1957, 1973), p. 4.
2. Hiroshi Daifuku, "Museums and Research," *The Organization of Museums: Practical Advice*, Museums and Monuments Series, No. IX (Paris: UNESCO, 1960).
3. Associated Press dispatch, Lewiston (Idaho) *Tribune*, January 14, 1971.

Even small museums should be concerned with research. Advanced degrees, large budgets, impressive collections, and luxurious surroundings are not required. But some small museums are not so engaged. Why? The word "research" may frighten the staff, who may not feel capable of research. Surely the curator must be capable, or he should not be a curator, in name or in fact. There may not be time for research. The lone curator or the small staff with large ambitions may be devoting all available time to other activity, such as publicity and peripheral programs. The staff may even be overbalanced with clerks, guards, receptionists, teachers, librarians, registrars, guides, public relations people, and so on, to the exclusion of real scholar-curators. Robert Shalkop, Director of the Anchorage Historical and Fine Arts Museum, notes that "careful scrutiny of the staff lists of many museums reveals an astonishingly small number of professionals," relatively few people who are "generating the program, as distinct from those who disseminate or publicize it."[4] He reminds us of the common observation that in our national economy advertising is often more important than the quality of the product.

Perhaps saddest of all is the case of the institution which could engage in research (and which may have done so in the past) but whose director is not a professional museum worker. Such a person may actually be hostile to serious museum work and may downgrade, if not actually eliminate, research. Shalkop puts it this way: "If a director is hired specifically for his public relations skills, he may have even less sympathy for the research program and de-emphasize it for ideological as well as budgetary reasons. Thus the museum finds itself directing an increasing proportion of its efforts toward selling its educational product, and a decreasing amount to creating it."[5]

Research creates knowledge, and museum curators must become authorities on the kinds of materials collected by their museums. Assisting the general public to identify objects is one of the museum's public services. Research done over the years should make this relatively easy, and usually enjoyable, for the curator. He will have to refuse, tactfully, the common request for the "worth" of an object. Most people brought up in our culture regard price as an attribute of all things and will regard any description of an object as incomplete without a pricetag. Since museums deal in objects, people automatically assume that any curator worth his salt will be able to say how

4. "Research and the Museum," *Museum News*, 50, No. 8 (April 1972), 11.
5. *Ibid*.

much an old family Bible is "worth," for example. Even though no one ever offered to buy the Bible from the family that owned it, to them it would still be "worth" a certain amount of money. This unrealistic attitude appears when a visitor asks a museum employee how much an object on exhibit is "worth," and when he brings in something of his own to show the director or a curator. Often he expects a dollar offer and to haggle over the price, then to sell the object. The museum curator can usually sidestep this problem by explaining that museums ordinarily receive their accessions through donation, that museums have no knowledge of market values since they only rarely buy and sell things, that he already has similar objects in his collections, and that he has no money (or very little money) to spend on purchases. Of course, if he wants to buy the object he may do so, but he might still look into the possibility of getting such an object donated. He should at least check with a reputable dealer to find out the going price.

If the visitor to the curator's office is requesting corroboration that he has an object of great value, the curator must, again with great tact and genuine concern, do what he can to help. A member of the public that employs him is requesting his expert knowledge, and the curator must not give in to boredom or annoyance. Good public relations is the museum's lifeblood. Fortunately, skill in dealing with these matters comes quickly. For instance, no Stradivarius violins are lying around in attics waiting to be discovered by eager heirs. "Strads" have been copied through the years, even to the maker's label inside the sound box. (I once got one free with a set of violin lessons.) Nevertheless, it is always possible that a visitor will bring in something of importance, and you do not want a disdainful reception to cost your museum a valuable accession, or, perhaps, a valuable friend.

A relatively new use of the collection has come about with the advent of television. I once put on weekly programs dealing with museum objects and exhibits through a local television station. It was a reciprocal arrangement. I would occasionally lend the station objects to use on other programs and commercials (usually with credit given to the museum, which created publicity and good will) and the station co-operated admirably with me in putting on the museum program. Preparing and presenting this program every week required a considerable amout of time and work, but my staff and I became convinced that it was worth it when we compared program viewers with museum visitors. More people saw *one* half-hour television presentation than had visited the museum in ten years. If you measure your success, not by the banging of the turnstile at your front door, but by the amount of contact you are making with human minds, you must be impressed by the potential application of television to museum work.

Objects may be lent to schools, other museums, and stores. Displays in downtown department store windows have the same justification as television programs. The timeworn expression is "bringing the museum to the people." Hundreds or thousands of people who have never been in your museum will walk down Main Street and see your objects. Your spinning wheel and antique clothing will enhance the store's display, but a sign will give credit to the museum. Such incidents may not accomplish much solid education, but they do create good—and free—advertisement. Incidentally, an anniversary celebration of a store or other business is an opportunity for the local history museum to get in on the act. If they do not think of you first, call them. However, do not ever forget what is more important than great publicity: the safety of the objects.

Objects from your collections may often illustrate the presentations of reputable public lecturers, and you may find such loans worthwhile. In addition, special public demonstrations, such as an antique car in a garage, or an ancient musical instrument used in a concert, may use your objects.

Reference is an important use for any collection. Ned Burns recommended thinking of the museum collections as two series, one for exhibition, the other for study.[6] The first series requires attractive specimens in good condition; irreplaceable items are kept in the second. According to Burns, the value of the collection is not in its size but in its utility.

Biological collections illustrate the usefulness of the collection for reference—for comparison and identification. For example, in the identification of animals, insects, or plants the scientist refers to standard descriptions and to the range of actual specimens on file. When a new species is first described, the "type specimen" is safely deposited in a museum (or museum-like facility) if possible, where it can be consulted for comparison with other related examples under study. The analogy with the iridium meter bar at the National Bureau of Standards is inescapable.[7] When a farmer brings in a creature that is

6. Ned J. Burns, *Field Manual for Museums* (Washington, D.C.: National Park Service, 1940).
7. Since 1960 the meter has been defined in terms of radiation wave lengths of the element krypton.

eating him out of the south forty, the expert can tell him exactly what it is by consulting the reference collections. The farmer is hardly different from the antique collector who wonders about the origin of his tole coffee pot.

We have seen that the collections may be used for reference, for store displays, as visual aids in public lectures and in schools, and for television programs. A principal use is research—the study of the objects in their contexts by the staff and by outsiders. Such research leads to new knowledge, new sources of materials, the avoidance of fakes, and the greater skill and knowledge of the staff. Another obvious use of collections is in exhibits, both permanent and temporary, which will be discussed in the next two chapters.

EXERCISES—CHAPTER 12

1. Explain:
   a. "the two faces of a single coin," preservation and interpretation,
   b. importance of a museum library,
   c. dichotomy between research curators and interpretive curators, (if a curator must interpret, should he give up research? Should a curator engaged in research be divorced from interpretation?)
   d. museum conferences as research.
2. If you are keeping a scrapbook of clippings about museums, is there a story in it related to forgery or museum research? If so, give a short review of it. If not, what do you recall reading recently in this regard?
3. What kind of museum spends the most money on research? Why?
4. Discuss museum television programs pro and con. Should museums concentrate on this use of their collections? Should a museum become a "prop room" for a television station?
5. List four to six different kinds of businesses, professions, or other occupants having sidewalk windows in downtown areas of heavy pedestrian traffic. Imagine and describe window displays based on objects borrowed from a museum. Be as specific as you can, and if you are familiar with a museum, use that museum's collections in your imagination. Relate kinds of displays to kinds of businesses.
6. This assignment deals with research by the small museum. Discuss the possibilities for research in a small musuem with which you are acquainted. What kinds of research projects can you imagine? How would the community benefit directly? How would the exhibits be improved by research? If possible, discuss this with a member of the staff of a museum.

13

Permanent Exhibits

A distinction was made in the first chapter between a display and an exhibit. To put it in other words, an exhibit is a display plus interpretation; or, a display is showing, an exhibit is showing and telling. Therefore, an exhibit should not be thought of as a single object, like a piano in a historic house, but rather as a deliberate interpretation of a subject or a grouping according to a theme—the entire, furnished parlor or the whole historic house is the exhibit. The term "exhibit" carries the connotation that something has been added to the object or objects shown (interpretation) in order to accomplish something of importance (education, in the broad sense). The techniques of exhibit planning and construction assume their proper perspective only with this end result in mind.

While exhibits are the obvious, public aspect of museum work, and while visitors judge the worth of the museum on the basis of its exhibits, much needs to be done well, "behind the scenes," before the exhibit program can be of high quality. The museum worker needs to be aware of the basic techniques of good exhibit production, but he also needs to understand the needs and behavior of the museum visitor—the customer who comes into the museum to get its product. (Or what the visitor regards as its product. Remember that what he wants to get and what museum professionals most want to give him are not necessarily the same.) The museum worker, in other words, must see exhibits from both sides.

Probably the greatest museum of science and industry (technology) in the world is the Deutsches Museum in Munich. Although one thinks of the variety and quality of its exhibits rather than of their sheer mass, their total size will help to make a point. The Deutsches Museum has more than twelve miles of exhibits. A visitor moving at the rate of 20 feet per minute, which is not extremely slow, would take 53 hours, or 21 visits of two and a half hours each, to see all the exhibits. Visiting once a month for two hours and 15 minutes, which is about the limit for a visit (not only do the feet get tired, so does the mind), moving at the ideal rate of speed—the one exhibit designers hope the visitor will use—*a person would need two years to see the exhibits in this one museum*. (Munich, incidentally, is a "museum city." It has many museums worth careful and leisurely visiting.) We have all heard someone say "You can't see everything in that museum in an afternoon. I could spend two or three days there." Actually, two or three weeks would be more accurate, if one is speaking of one of the larger museums.

What does this mean for the exhibit designer? In practical terms it means that he does not have an easy job. He cannot expect every visitor to appreciate fully every exhibit. Designers in large museums must recognize that each visitor will see only a fraction of the exhibits. Curators and exhibit designers should post signs where they will see them every day. The signs should read:

> *A visitor is a pedestrian whose feet hurt, who is tired and preoccupied, and who is on his way to somewhere. An exhibit must stop this person, hold him, and improve him while making him feel good.*

An exhibit that does not do this does not justify the salaries of the people who made it.

Kinds of Exhibits

According to purpose or intent, exhibits may be classed as aesthetic or entertaining—to show objects that people enjoy looking at; factual—to convey information; or conceptual—to present ideas. They may be classed according to the organization of the material as systematic—organized according to similarity of the objects and their "genetic" relationship to each other; or ecological—organized according to area, "habitat," or living relationship to each other.

In Figure 13.1 the examples from history and science, equating the period room and the habitat group, are clear enough. Obviously, the period room is also an important kind of exhibit in art museums, where the fine arts and the decorative arts are combined in rooms representative of the life of wealthy people (whose furnishings and

	SYSTEMATIC	ECOLOGICAL
Art	French Impressionist paintings exhibited together in the same gallery.	Paintings, drawings, sculpture produced in the same social milieu, representing the response in different media to the same forces.
History	The evolution of home lighting with candles, oil lamps, incandescent lamps.	A period room with clothing, furniture, reading matter, etc., representing a real room typical of a specific time, place, and economic level.
Science	Birds of the same and related species arranged according to a closeness or relationship.	Birds, animals, plants shown in a natural setting illustrating the sharing of an ecological niche, a diorama.

FIGURE 13. 1

interior decoration were created by artists). The examples given for art, while not as simple as the example of the period room versus a single kind of art, are meant to suggest that even within the fine arts the exhibitions may be organized in quite different ways.

Characteristics of a Good Exhibit

A good exhibit, regardless of what kind it is, will have certain characteristics:

1. *It must be safe and secure.* It must provide for the protection of its objects, the museum, the staff, and visitors. (An exhibit of nitroglycerine would be questionable, as would be an exhibit of silverware on an unprotected table.)
2. *It must be visible.* The exhibit must be lighted, unobstructed, and shown with a minimum of inconvenience and distraction. Those who have visited regional museums and had to lean over a hay rake to see what was behind it and decided to bring flashlights on their next visit will understand this. (Exhibits near unblocked windows usually suffer because of the glare in visitors' eyes.)

3. *It must catch the eye.* An exhibit that visitors pass by is a failure.
4. *It must look good.* A dirty, crudely made, tasteless exhibit will repel the visitor.
5. *It must hold attention.* An exhibit must educate, stimulate, produce emotion, entertain, or whatever. To accomplish its purpose requires time—long enough to get its message across (naturally, some exhibits require more time than others). Usually, this means the exhibit must stop the visitor for a few seconds to a few minutes.
6. *It must be worthwhile.* When the visitor stops and gives the exhibit his attention, he has entered into a contract with the museum. The museum must not betray his trust. It must give the visitor something of value in exchange and justify his faith that the exhibit is worth stopping for.
7. *It must be in good taste.* Taste must be defined for each museum and each kind of visitor, but the designer must endeavor not to offend. He must respect public mores, accepted standards of decency, the sensitivity of minorities and ethnic groups, religious beliefs, and similar areas of concern to museum visitors. This does not mean that nude statues must be draped, that science exhibits must omit references to human evolution, or that Leif Ericson cannot be mentioned if the museum is in an Italian neighborhood. Shock, used judiciously, may even have value. One cannot accurately describe life without including some unpleasant topics, but like a dash of hot sauce in the beans, a little goes a long way. The museum administrator, his staff, and the board of trustees must be in tune with the times and their community. Their job is to elevate the public, but with the public's consent. Museum work is as much an art as a science.

To summarize, the good exhibit uses significant objects, has an important purpose, and is well planned.

Good planning involves certain fundamentals. Ordinarily an exhibit, whatever its type or size, should have: 1) Good labels, including an easily visible and legible short title, a more detailed subtitle, one or more additional labels giving necessary information, and captions on objects where needed (like a newspaper story). 2) Harmony between objects and labels—they should appear to belong together, both contributing to the same goal. 3) Good design, including layout or arrangement, good use of color, typography, lighting, etc.

Properly done, the planning adds up to a good result, giving the visitor education, information, inspiration pleasantly and in good taste.

What is a good result? A museum is like a business—it invests and expends capital to produce something. Our capital is money; it is also space and the energy and enthusiasm of the staff. Museum workers are paid to spend this capital efficiently. *Efficiency* is the key word. An army that is not efficient loses battles. An inefficient body is ill and may die. An inefficient business goes bankrupt.

Before the efficiency of a museum, or of an exhibit, can be determined, the desired end result must be known and measured against the cost (in money, time, energy, space—whatever the capital expended). We know how much money we spend and how many hours our people work, but we do not know what we are accomplishing. This is the big problem, yet we museum people tend to ignore it while concentrating our attention on the little things. In other words, we may expend much time and effort toward discovering exactly the right kind of adhesive for attaching labels, but we do not concern ourselves with whether or not visitors are actually learning anything from the exhibits.

An exhibit should be designed so as to produce a particular result. To decide *what* to exhibit, *how*, and *where*, without first deciding *why*, is questionable procedure. Just as a museum should have a purpose, an exhibit should have a purpose.

Often the actual reasons or the motivations behind exhibits may be to fill an empty case; to occupy an empty location; to avoid storing something attractive; to please an individual, such as a member of the board of trustees or an egocentric donor; to pursue the hobby of a staff member; or simply to add another exhibit. The only worthwhile justification, however, is to contribute to the education of the visitor—to teach something. But teach something *to whom*? People vary in many ways—in age, sex, size, social class, religion, education, experience, nationality, intelligence, temperament, talents, interests, values. They vary in environment—whether they live in the country or in the city, whether they were brought up in one region or another—in attitudes—whether they are conservative or liberal, old-fashioned or modern, mentally healthy or not, whether they are "folk" in the anthropological sense or whether they participate deeply in international culture, whether they are rich or poor, secure or insecure. Some people are color blind, others do not hear well, some are illiterate or not accustomed to reading. Thinking of museum visitors as "the general public" and assuming that they are all pretty much alike is an ignorant or a lazy escape from thinking of visitors as representing many "publics" or as being individuals. Museum visitors are—to a greater or lesser degree, depending on the museum and its location—heterogeneous rather than homogeneous.

The next question is "Teach *what*?" (in the few seconds that you have the visitor's attention). A paragraph of technical information? An obscure fact unrelated to the preceding exhibit or the next? The exhibit planner should decide what is to be accomplished; plan the exhibit so as to achieve this goal; then evaluate the results to learn how well the exhibit is fulfilling his intention. Only in this way can he achieve efficiency.

The end is not the collections, the museum, the exhibits, or even the viewing of exhibits by visitors. These are all means. The end is the change brought about in the minds of people. This is what museums exist for, and the measure of the success of a museum is how well the aggregate of these mental alterations serve the goals and purposes of the museum. Just as the efficiency of a machine is determined by measuring the amount of work done for a given expenditure of the energy required to operate it, the efficiency of a museum is arrived at by comparing what it accomplishes with what it spends. Unfortunately, though we know what we spend, we do not know what we accomplish.

Studies have attempted to discover what particular exhibits in a particular museum are looked at most and longest, and some museums have even distributed self-testing questionnaires to measure how much information a visitor has acquired in a particular room or exhibition area. These, however, are but the beginnings of the recognition by serious museologists that an exhibit (or a museum) is not necessarily an effective educational instrument simply because it is there. If museums are to justify the spending of public tax moneys, they must give serious thought to what they are actually giving the public in return.

Watching visitors in their museums should be required of all professional employees. Not only will they learn where visitors appear to be disoriented and, therefore, need direction in the form of signs and arrows, but they will find out what attracts visitors and holds their interest. They will discover that certain exhibits are more successful in holding attention, and they should then undertake to learn why. Perhaps the appeal of one exhibit can be re-created in others. The exhibit designer should create exhibits and arrange them in a logical—and educational—progression. The designer is a storyteller. He must be concerned with structure, drama, suspense, climax, relief, humor, and whatever else a good storyteller employs. He must help the visitor to avoid viewing exhibits out of sequence, skipping essential labels, and otherwise failing to get the most out of his museum visit.

How does the designer go about planning an exhibit? There are several approaches to the problem:

The "Open Storage" Approach

As objects are acquired, they are put on exhibit immediately: 1) with no organization at all; 2) together with similar objects; 3) with other objects from the same donor, locality, or time period; 4) in some combination of the foregoing.

In this approach, labeling is either absent or spotty, giving unnecessary information, such as "oil lamp" or "donated by Mrs. Elmer Judd." A "museum" with such exhibits will commonly have a guest register, a conspicuous donation box, and perhaps an attendant who is not well informed. The name "open storage" implies that objects have not been selected from the collections for display as much as that the exhibits are the collections and vice versa. It is a serious criticism of a museum to say that its exhibits have the appearance of "open storage." The object approach is a step up the ladder.

The Object Approach

The exhibit is planned, and the objects are taken from the collections. The intent is to produce an educational exhibit. The objects are 1) selected; 2) arranged in a case; 3) researched; 4) labeled; and 5) lighted. The object approach may be the result of an unintellectual idea or a scarcity of ideas; in the extreme, it may result in a display of objects with little informational content.

Thirty or 40 years ago an advance in exhibit theory called the "Idea Exhibit" was born. It emphasized concepts rather than objects.

The Idea Approach

Concentrating intently on the educational mission of his museum, the curator 1) decides what story or idea should be presented; 2) decides how the story can best be put across; 3) selects needed objects from the collections, acquires them for the exhibit, or uses photographs, drawings, or models; 4) plans the exhibit so as to teach, emphasizing the concepts or ideas with various techniques; and 5) installs the exhibit as a unit. The idea approach may, in the extreme, result in a textbook-type presentation with many words, some pictures, and no objects. It may be the result of a scarcity of objects.

Both extremes are bad.

The philosophical questions are, on the one hand, whether the displaying of objects in itself is justifiable, and, on the other, whether museums should be so compelled to impart information that they do so in such abstract fields as mathematics and psychiatry.

The best solution, as a general rule, is the combined approach.

The Combined Approach

The curator selects both objects and ideas at the same time —based on 1) the significant objects in the collections (what is worth showing), and 2) the purposes of your museum (what stories or ideas that should be put across).

To repeat what was said earlier, an important consideration is that exhibits should be grouped in some reasonable order. Just as an exhibit should not contain a hodgepodge of objects, a gallery should not contain a hodgepodge of exhibits. At the same time, avoid monotony—row on row of the same size case, the same artistic techniques and styles, the same methods of organization. The result of these faults is Victorian classification, merely raised from the level of the object to that of the exhibit.

There are so many different kinds of objects to be shown and ideas to be imparted that it may not be possible in a few words to explain how to create a good museum exhibit. Perhaps most museologists would agree, however, that an exhibit represents an important part of the "story" the museum has to tell. It is a measurable aspect of the museum's scope. Most exhibits, then, are a grouping of objects, labels, and pictorial and electronic aids which together are meant to accomplish something. The typical exhibit will have a large sign saying what it is about (the main label). One or more additional labels will convey essential information. The exhibit will contain carefully selected objects, each with an identifying caption, and a longer, detailed label will be available for the viewer who has the time and interest to read it. Photographs, maps, and diagrams, if these will help to explain the subject matter, may be included. In an art exhibit, large letters on the wall of the room may say "France, 17th Century." This is the main label. Individual paintings will be identified as to title, artist, and the years of the artist's life. Somewhere in the room one or more labels may help to explain the style or styles represented, the development of technique, and even something of the social context of the art works. In some art museums the labeling is largely in the form of a guidebook which the viewer carries with him, or plastic-protected labels mounted on wooden paddles. The visitor uses one of these while he is viewing the exhibit and returns it to a holder as he leaves. In European museums these are commonly available in several languages.

EXERCISES—CHAPTER 13

Every now and then a review is beneficial. What is a museum? A permanent, public, educational institution that cares for collections systematically. What is its basic ingredient? Collections. What is its purpose? Education. How is education accomplished? Through the use of the collections. What does good use require? Records, preservation, live storage. What is a major use of the collections? Exhibits.

This assignment is in two parts: answers to questions about exhibit matters, and the actual study and observation of exhibits and of the public in relation to them. It will be assumed that you have access to a museum where you can spend several hours as a student and as an observer. If you are located too far from the kind of museum where this kind of work would be possible, you may substitute a store. It should be one that has a sizable number of customers and good window displays such as a department store in a town or small city. You will have to get the manager's permission to "loiter" and observe the behavior of customers. You will have to be discreet and as inconspicuous as possible. Offer to give the manager a report of your observations. He will probably appreciate learning what product displays seem to be most attractive to customers.

Part One
1. Define diorama and describe one.
2. An important rule in exhibit making is "art should conceal art." It means that the exhibit designer should be clever enough to keep his cleverness from being obtrusive; that is, that the techniques used in the installation of an exhibit should not distract the viewer from the purpose of the exhibit. Describe an art exhibit, a history exhibit, and a science exhibit in each of which

the advice "art should conceal art" was ignored to some degree. (These can be hypothetical, rather than actual exhibits.)

3. Write label copy for a sample of surface material brought back to Earth from Mars. In the exhibit you will have one or more scale models and photographs. Inlcude all the labels you would use in your imagined exhibit, and also a simple sketch if this would be helpful.

4. Discuss in general terms exhibit cases in relation to exhibits. Why have them? What do they do? How should they be designed? What is bad about them?

5. It has been suggested that art museums should not ignore the historic, human, and social aspects of art, and that other kinds of museums should not ignore the aesthetic qualities of their objects. Discuss.

6. Make an estimate as to the relative efficiency of two museums of your acquaintance and explain how you arrived at your conclusion.

Part Two

In a museum (or store, but explain why you had to select a store):

7. Observe visitors for two hours where there is a fairly steady stream of traffic; entering the building, an exhibit hall, or at some other busy place where the visitor must make decisions. Record and report on his movements, what appeared to attract him and hold his interest, etc. (Relate this to exhibits, not rest rooms, etc.)

8. (This is to be a more specific evaluation of visitor reaction to exhibits than the previous assignment.) Station yourself inconspicuously where you can observe about twenty-five visitors in relation to one or two reasonably good exhibits. Report on how long they spent, what they looked at most, what they looked at least, what they seem to have got from the exhibit on the basis of their remarks and other clues, etc. Try to decide how successful the exhibit is and how it may compare in this regard with other similar exhibits.

9. Choose an exhibit and evaluate it on the basis of the characteristics of a good exhibit.

10. Find an example of each of the following kinds of exhibits, and describe them briefly:
    a. aesthetic (entertaining)
    b. factual (informational)
    c. conceptual (idea-presenting)
    d. systematic
    e. ecological

A human "habitat group" helps to explain the early contact between the Indians and white traders of the upper Great Lakes region.
Courtesy, Milwaukee Public Museum

American colonial domestic life is the subject of the lesson taught in this special "classroom" for visiting school children.
Courtesy, Milwaukee Public Museum

Spanish colonial art in South America shown in a simulated room setting.
Courtesy, Milwaukee Public Museum

An exhibition, like an individual exhibit, should have organization and interpretation. Here, the entrance to a major portion of the museum's exhibit area bears a main label, "Africa," photographs, a map, secondary labels, and three-dimensional objects to prepare the visitor for the exhibits he is about to see.
Courtesy, Milwaukee Public Museum

An exhibit on a single topic, the craft of quillwork among the Plains Indians. The main label, or title, is "Quillwork," and the exhibition of which this exhibit is a part, "Plains Indian Art," is named as well. A porcupine is shown in a suggestion of a natural setting, and individual objects decorated with quills are identified. A long label explains the subject, and an additional label on the right discusses Cree Indian quillwork in particular.

This simple format can be used effectively, even by small museums with limited budgets.

Courtesy, Milwaukee Public Museum

The federal government supplied an exhibit on medical quackery.
Courtesy, University of Idaho Museum

14
Temporary Exhibits

Much of the material covered in the previous chapter applies to this chapter as well. Exhibits are exhibits whether they are expected to last for three weeks or ten years. Some museums today object to the term "permanent" as applied to exhibits, because it conjures up ugly pictures of installations in static museums that have obviously not been changed in many years. Such exhibits are often dirty, faded, and show signs of neglect, to say nothing of revealing outmoded information. Some museums prefer to consider all exhibits temporary and expect to renew them in the course of, say, five years. Not all museums, however, have the staff and money to effect such a rapid turnover, desirable though it may be.

The temporary exhibit, or exhibition, differs from the permanent exhibit in a number of ways in addition to the matter of time. For one thing, it ordinarily employs a greater measure of what I shall call "show business."

Show business is entertainment with a flair; organized, "slick" gratification of the senses. It is drama and opera—and going over Niagara Falls in a barrel. It is conspicuous, noisy, sometimes gaudy and superficial, but universally appealing. Show business may employ the fine arts, but its aim is at mass audience. It uses sound, color, movement, excitement, animals, sex, suspense, and strange and skillful behavior to entertain and to produce a favorable response in its audience. It may be used to promote sales, win votes for a political candidate, to propagandize or to sell entertainment: for example, Smokey the Bear, Macy's Christmas Parade; a rodeo; the "Magic Kingdom of Walt Disney World."

Showmanship in a butcher shop is dressing all the butchers and clerks in flat straw sailor hats and sleeve garters. Meat markets in

129

Germany often provide bread and mustard and sell small amounts of sausage to people who want to make sandwiches and eat them on the spot. There it is business. The same thing in the United States would be *show* business, because of the entertainment factor, the publicity, the novelty. A pizza restaurant is using showmanship when it places its kitchen up front where the work can be observed from the sidewalk through the large window.

"Show business," as related to museums, is the use of techniques to attract and hold attention, stimulate interest, provide entertainment, and create a favorable image. It is not "showing," *i.e..* not *exhibits*, but "showmanship"—the use of color, lights, artwork, motion, and entertainment *in* exhibits. Showmanship appears in other contacts between the museum and the public. It is the totem pole on the museum lawn, a distinctive letterhead, floats in parades, exhibits at the county fair, Christmas parties for children, and continuous short motion pictures in rest areas. "Show business" is fountains with colored lights shining on them; piped-in music; landscaped grounds; a striking building, illuminated at night; billboard advertising; free balloons stamped with the museum's name; an attractive sales desk with an attractive receptionist; distinctive uniforms for the guards; unusual dishes in the lunchroom; interesting newspaper stories. All of these are not educational in themselves, but they serve to attract people, to get them to take advantage of the museum's services, and to do so in a receptive frame of mind.

The big problem the museum faces, in designing good exhibits, is in reconciling the statements *"If you're not in show business, you're not in business,"* and *"The business of a museum is education, not entertainment."* Both statements are valid, and museum people should accept them. The problem is to achieve a proper balance between the two in the activities (including the exhibits) of the museum. The visitor comes to the museum primarily to be entertained, yet the museum exists primarily to inform. The museum must attract visitors and give them a pleasant experience while educating them. The entertainment aspect must be neither too much nor too little. It must be appropriate to the kind of museum, the kind of visitors, the kind of subject matter.

It is possible to entertain and educate at the same time, or to do neither. At one extreme the result will be a midway or carnival, at the other a mausoleum. A good museum combines education and entertainment.

"Show business" may play a larger role in temporary exhibits than in the permanent installations because of the first characteristic of temporary exhibits—the rules are suspended. A temporary exhibit offers much more freedom than a permanent exhibit. The latter must be part of the overall plan; restricted to your fields and purposes; carefully researched, prepared, and installed. It must be economical of space yet justify your investment of time and money. It must be important; it must present a big idea. The short-term exhibition, on the other hand, can be experimental, not limited as to subject matter, quickly and inexpensively installed, and not so serious or important. *It affords the opportunity for going beyond the ordinary scope of your museum and doing so without investing much time, energy, and capital.* A temporary exhibit provides a rare opportunity for visitors and staff to see and to study material which is ordinarily not available. The common example is that of privately owned works of art, ordinarily seen by only a few people, put on temporary public view at the museum.

A temporary exhibit is often rented or borrowed. Called circulating shows, traveling exhibitions, etc., temporary exhibits are available in a variety of fields from a dozen or more sources. They consist of photographs, copies or original art, museum objects, working demonstration machines, etc. Sometimes the cost is only for shipping, usually one way, so that the expense to the museum may range from a few dollars to several thousand dollars. The sources are too numerous to list here, but the Traveling Exhibition Service of the Smithsonian Institution (Washington, D.C. 20560) offers a wide range of subject matter. As one might expect, most traveling exhibitions display contemporary art; however, a few exhibitions in history, anthropology, natural science, and other fields are available.

A temporary exhibit may be borrowed from another museum, a commercial organization, or from a local individual. Single items or entire collections may be borrowed; but the borrowing must be only for temporary use, not on an indefinite basis. A local hobby club or craft group, such as a weaver's guild, a rockhound club, or a garden club, may supply an exhibit. The temporary exhibit provides the opportunity for local group participation; it enables individuals and groups to do something in and for your museum. Becoming involved in your operation makes them more interested and makes them feel more responsible. It is good for the people in your community to say *"our museum."* A variety of locally produced exhibits will attract a varied attendance, perhaps some persons heretofore unreached.

The museum may prepare a temporary showing from its own collections. This may include photographs, documents, and objects which for one reason or another are not part of the permanent exhibits. For example, a science museum may own some art objects. A history museum may have an extensive collection of cuckoo clocks, of which only a few representative specimens are permanently exhibited. An art museum may own the private papers of an important collector and donor.

The cost of a temporary show might be borne by a local industry or business. This might take the form of an annual Christmas gift to the community.

The temporary exhibit usually has a definite opening and closing, with dates that can be announced in advance for publicity. It is sometimes tied to an event that everyone knows about, such as an anniversary celebration, a presidential election, the inauguration of an irrigation project, a popular motion picture, or the arrival of a foreign exchange student. The temporary show can demonstrate a timeliness that will increase community interest and result in much more publicity. A special ceremony, a party, or private preview might be held at the beginning.

The temporary exhibit is often light and entertaining. It might be aimed specifically at children, or it can be simply amusing, with no great educational content. Suppose, for instance, you collected examples of doodling done by the prominent and best-known men and women in the community, mounted and matted them, and hung them as works of art. This would be a trivial thing, but it might result in much friendly feeling toward your museum or society. Naturally, anything like this would have to be handled with good taste and extreme care not to offend anyone. Your local psychiatrist should be asked not to comment publicly.

The temporary exhibit might use a large amount of space, even to the point of seeming wasteful, in order to help establish the mood. An example of this approach would be a photographic exhibit of life on the plains; a large photograph of a farmstead surrounded by miles of flat emptiness might be suspended on wires from the ceiling in front of, but not touching, a completely empty wall with nothing on either side of the photograph for ten feet or so. You would then be surrounding it with empty space as a kind of frame—or rather the absence of a frame—to help create the impression of vast distances.

Special kinds of temporary exhibits need not be confined to the museum building. They may be installed at a county fair, in a store window, a hotel lobby, in a school, or at the airport. By spreading its location the museum reaches out for a larger audience. Like the museum-produced television show, the exhibit is taking the museum out to the people and, thereby, becoming an even more important part of the community life.

Almost all museums need publicity. We need greater attendance and greater public support. Today museums have to compete with television, the automobile, and the many other demands on the individual's leisure time. We want—and desperately need—stories, notices, and photographs in newspapers, announcements and programs on radio and television, and all the other devices for getting the public to be aware of us and interested in visiting our museums. *One of the best means for achieving repeated public announcements of a kind to arouse interest throughout the community is the temporary exhibit.* Since it is temporary and tied to a particular time span, it is news. It is an event, not a permanent community asset. It has human interest appeal, variety, associations with people in the community, the element of civic pride, and a certain urgency. A temporary exhibit program over the months and years can probably be justified in terms of its promotional value alone, though its educational value as an extension of the permanent exhibits will be very great indeed.

Museums of all kinds are increasingly using temporary exhibits as they seek more publicity and as they attempt to reach out to a wider audience. Any subject field will lend itself to this treatment; however, a general rule should be kept in mind. The temporary exhibit is at its best when it presents a simple idea or a unity of objects. Objects that require lengthy explanatory labels, technical matters above average understanding, and anything too complex and obscure to be grasped quickly by a walking visitor should be avoided.

EXERCISES—CHAPTER 14

The distinction between the temporary exhibition announced in the newspaper and on a billboard in front of the museum and the scholarly and expensive permanent installation is a real one for many reasons. This assignment is intended to help the student to appreciate those distinctions.

1. Imagine and list different kinds of temporary exhibits for different kinds of museums.
2. What would you assume to be ten or twelve different sources for temporary exhibits in your community? List sources and describe the exhibits.

3. Give examples of "show business:
   a. as seen in local stores;
   b. as seen in local museums, or museums you have visited.
4. Describe two or three temporary exhibits you have seen in your local museum or in the community outside museums (banks, store fronts, schools). How did these examples illustrate the characteristics of temporary exhibits as set forth in Chapter 14?
5. Two related concepts were introduced in Chapter 14. They are the balance between show business and serious education in the museum, and the greater freedom in temporary exhibit work as compared with permanent exhibits. Discuss these in the context of a specific museum; either the one you are now associated with or another museum with which you are familiar.

15

Visitors and Interpretation

Museums collect, record, and preserve in order to interpret, or increase understanding. Some of the interpretation, as the result of research, reaches the public indirectly in the form of publications. Other interpretation is direct—through exhibits, through guides, through lectures, and otherwise. Interpretation is basic to the concept of the educational museum. The objects alone—without explanation, organization, selection—would not support the educational aim of the modern museum.

Interpretation does not exist in a vacuum. It is communication between the museum staff (as students and teachers) and the public (as consumers of the museum's product). Just as a wise merchant comes to know his potential customers, the museum must know its visitors. Carrying the analogy further, the museum must attract and please its visitors, and leave them satisfied. "Ask the man who owns one" used to sell cars. The museum should so deal with its customers that they will become its public relations ambassadors and recommend its product to others.

The most striking thing about visitors is that there are so many of them. No longer are museums catering to a select few. Coping with throngs of tourists more accurately describes what many museums do today. Not only in our own country are people on the move. Tourism is becoming more and more popular; and money, time, and a breakdown in provincialism are making travel more possible throughout Western civilization.

In 1965, 115 million tourists traveled outside their own countries, throughout the world, and the rate of increase at that time was 12 per cent per year. Scotland receives as many tourists each year as it has permanent residents (more than five million). Foreign visitors to the

135

United States are increasing. A few years ago the number was reported as a million, double that of only three years before. One airline flying in and out of Denver reported that during August 1964 two-thirds of its customers were foreigners.

Tourism is the largest industry of some of our states and ranks very high in many others. The state of Virginia spends more than a million dollars a year to promote travel. Even so, the economic impact of tourism is difficult to conceive. In 1968 campers spent more than $50 million for sleeping bags alone. Camping trucks and travel trailers cost more than $700 million; the ski business accounted for $1 billion, and the total leisure market was estimated at $150 billion in one year's time.

In 1970 the National Park System had 172 million visits, including more than 24 million to the Blue Ridge Parkway and the Natchez Trace Parkway. In 1969, 200 million persons visited the National Forests, and on one day, July 4, 1969, 160,000 persons visited the 19 National Forest visitor centers. It would be natural to expect large numbers of visitors to museums, and such is indeed the case.

The Metropolitan Museum of Art reports more than six million visitors per year. During the school year, one thousand school children come each weekday by appointment. Attendance at the Smithsonian museums in Washington, D.C., was given as 10 million in 1966, and estimates for museum attendance each year in the United States range as high as 600 million and even higher. It is interesting that in spite of this astronomical figure—three times as many museum visits as there are people in the United States—museum visiting is still not regarded as important by the common man, or as reflected in our mass culture. The news media are much more preoccupied with attendance at sports events, and sports occupy a much more prominent place in conversation in a wide range of social gatherings than do museums.[1]

Museum attendance has increased because of increased population; higher educational attainment; increased sophistication in museum fields on the part of visitors; increased use of museums by

1. On the other hand, the Stanford Research Institute reported in the early 1960's that theatergoers outnumber boaters, skiers, golfers, and skindivers combined. Twice as many people attend concerts as see major league baseball and football games. There are more piano players than fishermen; as many painters as hunters. The growth in spending for "culture" was twice as fast as that for sports recreation and more than six times as fast as the growth of spending on spectator sports.

public school classes; increased leisure time; increased mobility; increased desire to travel—curiosity about the world outside one's home environment; increased popularization of approach by museums (for example, simpler and more attractive exhibits). Whether or not greatly increased attendance is a good thing is another matter. While almost everyone would agree that large segments of our society would profit by more exposure to museums (a recent survey showed that 43 per cent of Americans had never visited an art museum), many people would prefer to see less of some visitors. In August 1965 the Providence (Rhode Island) Redevelopment Agency took a public stand "against having a museum in the proposed Roger Williams National Memorial because of the traffic it would draw. Agency members say they would rather forego a possible $693,000 in Federal money for the memorial if the National Park Service insists on a museum."[2] In an Associated Press wire service story that appeared in Montana papers in the fall of 1969, William A. Worf, chief of the recreation and lands division of the Northern Region of the National Forests, reported that vandalism was increasing. "In developed recreation sites," he said, "the vandalism rate was double the national average." In regard to overuse of nature trails, a museum man seriously proposed keeping their location secret from the general public, so that only a few persons would find them and use them. His hope was that these few would be the ones who could benefit most by the experience—whose interest was sufficient to cause them to seek out such park and forest offerings. On the other hand, others might argue that the throngs of city dwellers who know the least about preserving our natural environment are the people who most need what the nature trail has to offer.

Visitors who are principally seeking recreation still demand interpretation; they want informed people to explain things. Many visitors to museums with quite adequate labels still prefer guided tours. They prefer being told to discovering on their own. As Guthe says, preservation of the collections and interpretation of them to the public go hand in hand.[3]

Part of the museum curator's job is to abstract, simplify, and make interesting the important information about the objects he shows. He does not attempt to tell all; he should not dwell on unimportant details. He should render into simple, standard English what should

2. *Rocky Mountain News* (Associated Press), August 29, 1965.
3. Carl E. Guthe, *The Management of Small History Museums* (Nashville: American Association for State and Local History, 1959, 1964), p. 51.

be said. Labels, electronic devices (tape players, radio guide systems, etc.), publications, or human docents can convey the message. This is the most obvious kind of interpretation, though the selection of objects, the layout of exhibits, and other kinds of museum work are also part of interpretation.

Museums are becoming increasingly active in the out-of-doors. For example, a children's museum, a science museum, or a general museum might install a nature trail. A nature trail—a marked path through a natural area, with identified plants, geological outcroppings, animal burrows, and viewpoints—is a self-guided sampling of the natural environment. Outdoor interpretive trails need not be limited to natural science. A historical society might mark a route through and near the community, singling out places of historic interest. An art museum might do the same for buildings of architectural interest. The visitor may receive interpretive leaflets, or cassette tapes, which are played either on the visitor's own portable or automobile machine or on a unit rented from the museum. Such electronic devices are coming into increasing use.

The quality of the interpretation is an important matter. An Associated Press news item of July 1971 said that Lester B. Dill, Director of Meramec Caverns, a commercially operated cave near Stanton, Missouri, had ruled out the possibility of hiring geology students as guides. "They are too technical when they conduct tours," he said. "Tourists would prefer to hear about how Jesse James used the cave to elude the law." But the serious visitor should not be denied the opportunity to learn. Some years ago I visited Mammoth Cave National Park in Kentucky and participated in the guided underground tour. My guide was an unlettered local man who knew or cared very little about geology or geological explanations. His interpretation of one of the world's great natural marvels consisted of giving cute names to formations ("slab of bacon," "setting hen") and telling Methodist-Baptist theological jokes. The issue here is again the question of entertainment versus education. The *museum* does not exist to provide light entertainment for an uneducated clientele. It must balance show-business techniques with education.

We have discussed the visitor in regard to what we hope he will not to do us (security) and what we hope to do for him (education). Now let us think how we can make his visit smooth and pleasant.

In the first place, the museum must be accessible. You can have the best museum of its kind in the world, but if potential visitors do not know about it, do not know when it is open, do not know how to get to it, are afraid to come to its neighborhood, cannot afford your admission charge, or are not well received, yours is not a successful public museum. The visitor must be able to reach it by public transportation, by walking from a downtown location, or by private automobile. If he drives, he must find a convenient and safe parking lot near the entrance.

The entrance should be impressive, easy to find, and to get to. The visitor should not have to walk around the block trying locked doors. If you have an admission charge, post it conspicuously at the parking area and outside the front door. If your building has doors that are not open to the public, have plenty of signs directing the visitor to the proper entrance. That door should say "Welcome," which should be echoed by the friendly tones, smiles, and helpful attitudes of the members of the staff the visitor sees upon entering. A surly guard at the front door can quickly counteract all that the director does to be pleasant.

The lobby is a reception area for visitors. It should be large enough for the marshaling of school groups but pleasant and comfortable enough for friends to meet. The lobby is also a distribution point. From here visitors are sent directly to wherever they most want to go at that moment: restrooms, which should be modern and immaculate; lunchroom; lounge area; offices; sales rooms; auditorium; etc. Signs, directional arrows, directory boards, "you are here" orientation diagrams, announcement boards, and a drinking fountain should be in the lobby.

Immediately adjacent, if not actually in the entrance lobby, should be a reception desk for information and the receiving of groups. Here, too, should be a checkroom for umbrellas, coats, parcels, and briefcases. Hooks on the wall and a sign saying "The museum is not responsible for stolen articles" are not enough.

Places to sit down should appear throughout the public areas of the museum. Seats should be comfortable, with a view not facing a blank wall or the restroom door. The building should have elevators, escalators, gentle (not steep and narrow) stairways, and ramps where needed. It should not be necessary to negotiate a wheel chair or child's stroller up and down steps anywhere between the parking lot and any part of your building.

Rest areas, such as lounges, lunchrooms, and the lobby, should have windows where the visitor can lose the shut-in feeling he may get from windowless exhibition halls.

Museum personnel should be prepared to give the tourist any kind of information he is likely to need: maps of the city and region, names and locations of other nearby museums, restaurants, motels, service stations. Your sales counter should have publications related to the exhibits: not only guidebooks, suggested short tours through your museum and the like, but good quality books on the subjects dealt with by the museum, hobby kits for children, reproductions of your art works, postcards, and in some locations such travelers' needs as photographic film.

A lunchroom is an important feature for almost any museum, especially for a museum not located near good restaurants. Amenities of many European museums are a bar and a dining room where one may get wine or beer with his meal. It would be rare, indeed, were this to occur in the United States because of our attitude that alcohol is sinful and teaching is holy. Rarely do the two get together, except as a special privilege for members. One might argue that even this does not reconcile the two, since the uplifting of the masses is not the primary purpose of a champagne preview.

EXERCISES—CHAPTER 15

In previous chapters we have looked at museums from the inside. In this chapter let us look from the outside, from the point of view of the person who is visiting the museum.

1. The description of facilities for visitors given in this chapter was not complete. Such facilities as were listed apply to a wide range of visitors. Put yourself in the shoes of each of the major categories of museum visitors, adding any additional kinds that the readings left out, and describe what you, as a museum visitor, would want in the way of services and conveniences. What would make your visit more enjoyable and more profitable? Are there some special kinds of museums that should be mentioned?
2. Discuss the matter of charging for admission: 1. to the museum, and 2. to a special exhibition, wing, or performance within the museum. Include in your discussion the possibility that a charge is discriminatory.
3. "Applied museography" is the term given to the deliberate use of museums and their activities in order to effect specific changes in attitudes in the public; that is, propaganda. Does it occur in American museums? Give illustrations of how it might be used in different kinds of museums. How does it relate to such political issues as nationalism, totalitarianism, consumerism, etc.?

4. Discuss the role of the museum in broadening the horizons, uplifting the public, and the like. Is there a connection with different roles for different categories of museums (small local, larger regional, and national)?
5. Discuss traffic patterns in exhibit areas and the design of exhibit installations in reference to visitors' behavior. (Such matters as the location of an exit influencing whether visitors pass up certain exhibits in a room, for example). The aim here is to think of where the museum staff wants the visitor to go, in relation to where the visitor might want to go or might accidentally go.

16
Education and Activities

The reader may well wonder why I have taken so long to get to specific mention of education, when that is the whole purpose of all museum activity. The fact is that we have been discussing education all along. The word as used in this chapter has a special meaning. Museum people speak of their "education staff," "education department," and "curator of education." What they refer to is their work with visiting school classes, loan exhibits to schools, and related activities, which sometimes include guided tours. What makes it so easy for many museum people to use the word "education" in this restricted way is the old view that education is what is accomplished by someone standing in front of a blackboard with a piece of chalk in his hand.

I once lived in a large city where I served on a committee to coordinate public educational opportunities. The committee first compiled a list of all sources of education in the community, other than schools, and included public service agencies, the Anti-Defamation League, and dozens of others. When I suggested listing television stations and newspapers, blank stares told me that my definition of education did not coincide with that of the majority of the committee. Some museums prefer to use the term "school services" for the department, even though its head is called the curator of education. The point of this discussion is that the beginner should be aware that, even in a good museum, the term "education" is often used in its limited sense.

We have previously discussed Guthe's first three obligations. The fourth is activities. Since many activities are for children and are managed by the education staff, the two areas of interest are often grouped together. A related topic is children's museums.

The children's museum is an example of categorizing by type of visitor rather than by subject matter. Physical equipment and installations, as well as exhibits and activities, are scaled down to the size and mental capacity of elementary school children. Often, these museums are operated by the public school district and staffed with certified teachers. The parallel with the children's library is obvious, and such museums usually do not lack public support and volunteer help.

Special techniques have been developed to reach and stimulate the immature mind of the child visitor. Exhibits relate to his own world of experience, and interpretation is more provocation than instruction. An interesting example is found at one of our city zoos where two identical monkey islands were built. Each had the complete complement of climbing and swinging installations that monkeys use in a zoo. Monkeys were placed on one of the islands, and the other was turned over to the children. As a reverse of "monkey see, monkey do" the children imitated the monkeys in climbing, swinging by their arms, and jumping, if not in other activities, and thereby, one would imagine, gained a small measure of humility.

Ordinarily, regular adult museums do not construct special exhibits for children. An interesting exception is the Civic Center Museum of Philadelphia (formerly the Commercial Museum). Here a large portion of one floor is devoted to two classrooms, the education office, an auditorium, the storage room for teaching aids, and a half dozen or more open lesson areas with chairs facing an elaborate "exhibit" on which the lesson is based. Actually, each area is more like a theater with three-dimensional objects. Visiting school classes are also taken to the public areas of the museum where examination of the general exhibits supplements lessons. The public school system provides two teachers; the museum, one.

The key word in the previous paragraph is "lesson." The up-to-date museum prefers to make the visit of the school group a truly educational experience, not merely a holiday from classroom routine. Organized lessons on single topics deal with important aspects of the museum. Museum teachers (either professionals or volunteers) show and explain exhibits, and the children handle real objects. The visit is ordinarily limited to an hour, and several lesson visits are necessary for a child to see the entire museum. The Colorado State Museum in Denver, devoted to Colorado history, offers "Fur Trade," "Cattle, Land, and Water," "Indians of Colorado," etc. The teacher of the visiting school group must make reservations in advance, and he is encouraged to prepare his class ahead of time in the subject matter and to recapitulate the salient facts of the lesson after the museum visit. The teacher who calls a museum and inquires about a "tour" may not be aware that good museums today offer much more.

There are opposing points of view regarding who should conduct the museum lesson—the school class's own teacher or a member of the museum staff (or docent). The principal arguments are that the teacher knows his or her children; the museum person knows the subject. Controversial, too, is the question as to where to conduct the lesson —in the exhibit areas where the presentation may be over the children's heads (in both senses) and where the lesson may be a nuisance to other visitors, or in a special classroom where the experience for the children may not be much different from remaining at school. Even the children's museum has been criticized for segregating its curators and its visitors from the greater collections, exhibits, and expertise of the adult museum. Beginning museologists can profitably discuss all three of these issues. As with many controversies, the best solutions appear to be combinations and compromises.

I might mention in passing that some museums use their education departments as a crutch. Since teachers and docents interpret exhibits orally, curators and exhibits designers sometimes take the easy road and allow their exhibits to rely on the oral interpretation. In other words, they may not interpret the subject matter fully by good exhibit techniques—such as adequate labels. For some purposes, of course, there is no substitute for the live, sensitive, and informed guide, interacting with an audience.

Activities include all offerings and services to the public beyond the maintenance of collections and exhibits. Some of the most common are publications, guided tours, field trips, lectures, art classes, hobby clubs, concerts, motion pictures, other special events, and membership services. These activities stem from the museum's desire to give its community as much as it can, consistent with the limitations of its staff, facilities, and scope. A danger lies in over-emphasizing activities to the point where the museum's more basic obligations—collections and records—suffer.

EXERCISES—CHAPTER 16[1]

Again, it will be helpful if you can relate your reading to real museum operations. Of the museums you can visit, or with which you are familiar (a specific visit to examine "education" services will be of most value to you), choose the one that has the most active education department.

1. Interview the director or curator of education (or both) and make a report as to that museum's school services and other activities for children. Include brochures and other published information.
2. Observe a school class visit and evaluate it in detail as an educational experience for the children. Criticize constructively the adults involved. Include your own recommendations for improvement of the program.
3. Interview a grade school principal and a middle grade teacher as to the school's attitude toward their local museums as community resources and specifically toward "your" museum's offerings. Interpret what you find out.
4. Referring to your reading, as well as to whatever firsthand experience you may have had, discuss the following, pro and con: (that is, give all the arguments for and against, regardless of what you, personally, may favor).
   a. Having the lesson in the museum conducted by the class's own teacher, as opposed to a member of the museum staff.
   b. Teaching the lesson to the visiting school class in a special classroom rather than in the public exhibition areas.
   c. The concept of the children's museum.
5. Discuss group visits to the museum, including main purpose, size, frequency, organization, etc.
6. List all the "activities" of three or four museums of your acquaintance.
7. Decide whether activities occupy too much or too little staff time and resources in a museum with which you are acquainted. Discuss.
8. Discuss the contribution of museums in general to solving present day educational and social problems.

1. Molly Harrison, "Education in Museums," *The Organization of Museums: Practical Advice*, Museums and Monuments Series, No. IX (Paris: UNESCO, 1960) is especially pertinent to some of these exercises.

17

Architecture

To this point we have discussed the nature of the museum and its operation. Only now can we take up the matter of proper housing for the museum. The architectural maxim that "form must follow function" is the paramount consideration in planning a museum building. The building must be created for or adapted to the needs of the museum operation. Too often the converse is the case; the functioning of the museum often must be adapted to fit the building. Remember that a museum is not a building (except for convenience in colloquial usage). It is a dynamic, organized operation involving specialized needs and activities. The building that houses the museum is just a vehicle or tool to facilitate the museum's operation.

A person who says "The old courthouse (post office, city hall, high school) will be vacant next year. Wouldn't it make a good museum?" is showing his ignorance of what a real museum is. The building that has been outgrown or become outmoded for some other specialized use would be no more satisfactory as a museum building (without extensive alterations, at least) than it would be for a restaurant, a department store, a hotel, or any other use for which it was not originally designed. The problem is that the layman does not understand museums. The fact that he *thinks* he understands them changes nothing.

Museum professionals and enlightened laymen who are involved in the planning of museum buildings have to battle those who hold the purse strings. They may also have difficulty with architects, because, even today, the architect who can design a good museum building is a rarity. This is very likely true because the architect, as an ordinary citizen, shares the general ignorance of good museum practice. In other words, he does not know enough to know that he does not know enough about museums. Some architects of high reputation are incapable of designing good museum buildings, and are in demand even though they have demonstrated their ineptness again and again. There are notable exceptions. The museum profession much admires the building of the Museum of the Great Plains in Lawton, Oklahoma, because its architect had the good sense to visit museums, to take the advice of museum professionals, and to develop in his mind a good picture of the functioning of this particular museum before he put pencil to paper. Another good museum architect is Raymond O. Harrison, author of *The Technical Requirements of Small Museums*. He is a museum director as well as an architect, and this rare combination shows in his plans.

If the most important guidepost in museum architecture is that form must follow function, probably the second is the necessity to strike a balance between the building as an attractive object in its own right and its use as a neutral setting for the exhibits. The building should be in harmony with the museum, and there is no question that an impressive building will attract the visitor and help to put him into a receptive frame of mind. A museum of classical archaeology might well be housed in a modified representation of a Greek or Roman temple. The same building would not be a good choice for a museum of modern science and industry. Similarly, a building of modern design suggesting wealth and refinement would hardly be an appropriate setting for a museum of rugged life on the Great Plains.

We must also consider the interior decoration. Just as we might question unfinished concrete and exposed steel beams as the background for historic paintings, we also should feel uncomfortable to see natural history exhibits in a setting of Victorian ornateness. The collections must be paramount. As the frame enhances the picture and does not overwhelm it or distract attention from it, the museum building must provide a suitable but not prepossessing frame for what exists inside.

Security is the most fundamental requirement of the building, and the architect must keep this need paramount. David Vance has used a schematic diagrm to explain the concept of the "zone of safety."[1] Every legitimate location in the building for the collections—receiving room, photography studio, workrooms, exhibition

1. David Vance, "Planning Ahead—The Registrar's Role in a Building Program," in Dorothy H. Dudley and Irma Bezold Wilkinson, *Museum Registration Methods*, rev. ed. (Washington, D.C.: American Association of Museums, 1968).

halls, etc.—is provided with security, and barriers are set up, in effect, between the collections and unauthorized people. What this means for the museum worker, whether in small museum or large, is that the building (including its interior arrangement, equipment, and so on) must be so designed and used as to provide continuous maximum security for museum objects, the primary function of the museum building.

Awareness of building function should extend to decoration of exhibition halls. For example, ample space should be provided before key exhibits used in the education program for every child in an entire school class to be able to see the exhibit. It may be necessary to raise and tilt the exhibit or to provide one or two risers (platforms) on the floor so that children in the rear can see over the heads of children in front. Do not rely on always having short children in front and tall children in the rear. Herding a group in unfamiliar surroundings is difficult enough. Do not multiply your difficulties unnecessarily.[2]

Museum architecture is not a simple topic. Many considerations enter into the fitting together of the museum's operation and its building. Following is a list, in no particular order, of some of the things involved:

Site—accessibility, parking, room for expansion, attractive set-
ting, freedom from fire risk, noise, impure air.
Building style—suitability for location and for subject matter of
museum.
Social considerations—community cultural center, multiplicity of
uses.
Exhibit rooms—proper setting for exhibits, style, color, arrangement of rooms, monotony.
Lighting—natural versus artificial, sky, side, windows.
Flexibility of space—movable partitions.
Services—meeting rooms, library, mechanical matters, separation of public from private areas, ease of communication
between areas, ease of access of public to appropriate service
area (such as the restaurant).
Proportions—room size, ceiling height in reference to materials to
be exhibited.

2. A useful device is colored plastic tape placed on the floor where you want the front row of the class to stand. Getting the children to face exactly as you want them to is as simple as saying, "Put your toes on the yellow line." When you refer to a second exhibit, "Now put your toes on the blue line." This effectively, and in a spirit of fun—very important—swings the group around to face in a different direction.

Use of outdoor areas—gardens, terraces, lawn, grounds.

Storage—location, security, size, accessibility, ease of use by staff, by scholars, climate control, several rooms for varied control.

Traffic control—visitor routes through the exhibition halls, lobbies, other public areas, entrances and exits for exhibition areas, elevators, stairways, closing off part of the building at times.

Entrances—services in lobby, ease of access to entrance, attractiveness, turnstiles, number of outside doors.

Visitor conveniences—restrooms, cloakrooms, lunchrooms, seats, orientation, direction, public telephones, sales counter, clocks, mail box.

Technical considerations—fireproof, dampproof, vibrationproof, noiseproof, floors strong for heavy loads, insulated against changes in temperature and humidity.

Doorways—large enough, where needed, not where not needed.

Staircases—fire escapes, supplemental to elevators, improve communication and movement of staff and visitors between floors.

Roof—accessible, usable for social and other purposes.

Shipping-receiving—access, loading dock, service parking, freight elevator, crate storage, secure unpacking and packing.

Temporary exhibits—special requirements.

School classes—schoolbus loading and unloading, parking, lunchroom, cloakroom, restrooms, etc.

Auditorium—projection, chair storage, restroom for speaker, outside access for deliveries.

Meeting rooms—hospitality arrangements.

Workrooms—shop, conservation, exhibit preparation, photography, research with collections, laboratories, dark room, drying room, office and record room, poison room.

Maintenance—guard room, janitors' closets, supply room.

Mechanical—heating, ventilation, air conditioning, exhaust fumes.

Exhibition space—percentage of total.

Facilities for accessioning—reception of objects, accessioning, cataloguing, preparation, study, storage, routes followed through the building as this work is undertaken.

Greenhouse—for plants used in exhibition areas and elsewhere.

EXERCISES—CHAPTER 17[3]

Every museologist need not also be a museum architect, but every museum worker or student needs to be able:

to evaluate the suitability of a museum building and the organization of functions within it;

to advise his superiors in a museum situation regarding improved security, communication, visitor accommodations, and other aspects of space arrangement;

to use "input" from museum professionals whenever a museum building is being planned or an older building is being considered for museum purposes;

to understand the relationship of the physical plant (facilities) to proper museum functioning.

1. What are the essential activities of the museum operation (as distinct from "activities" in Guthe's fourth obligation)?
2. Discuss windows, doors, basements, and floor coverings in relation to museum requirements.
3. What are the arguments for and against natural lighting and artificial lighting?
4. Imagine that you are the director of a small museum and you have been given the necessary money and authority to make radical changes in the museum housing. You have three options: You may make improvements in your present building, you may acquire an old building previously used for another purpose and adapt it, or you may build a new museum building.
   a. Take a museum with which you are familiar, draw its floor plans, and draw other plans to show the changes you would make. Briefly justify the changes (explain why you would make them). By use of different colors you may be able to show both plans together.
   b. Visit and study an old building in your community, whether or not it is or might become vacant, and draw its floor plans. With additional plans show how it could be altered so that it would serve well as a museum building. Do not neglect any important museum function or service, but if the building is large you need not deal with all of it. That is, you might assume that the museum would not occupy the upper floors or one wing. Choose a building that could, conceivably, be offered to a museum. Such would be school buildings, churches, private homes, post offices, courthouses, city halls, railroad stations, and others. Do not choose a vacant store or a minor part of a building mainly used for some other purpose. Your problem is not only to suggest the removal of walls, adding of doorways, and

3. For these exercises, Raymond O. Harrison, *The Technical Requirements of Small Museums*, rev. ed. (Ottawa: Canadian Museums Association, 1969), will be helpful.

the like, but to show how existing spaces could be used for your museum purposes.

c. Describe your museum operation (real or imagined) in the way that Harrison begins, that is, by a function-space chart and then by a space organization diagram. From this, develop a set of floor plans for a new building that would serve your operation well.

d. As a continuation of the option for a new building, where would you locate it? In a park, downtown, on a main highway on the edge of town, in a residential neighborhood, in a slum area, in an industrial area? Choose one or two possible locations in your own region and justify them.

Part III

Museums and Society

18

Historic Preservation

Of a thousand or so known forts and sites of forts in the United States and Canada, at least 80 are maintained as museums. The remarkable thing is not that so few are maintained, but rather that so many are. Our interest in preserving structures of the past goes beyond any practical ends that might be served. Why do we preserve? Any attempt at explanation cannot ignore the myth that age lends importance. "Many a man that couldn't direct you to the drugstore on the corner when he was 30 will get a respectful hearing when age has further impaired his mind," said Finley Peter Dunne.

Of course, if age alone were a criterion of value, a lump of coal or a rock would be worth much more than any artifact. Nostalgia for the "good old days" plays a large part. How good were those days, however? Now that Sears Roebuck and Montgomery Ward catalogues of past years have been republished, one can compare yesterday's prices with today's. How amusing it is to read that in 1897 coffee was 20 cents a pound and a man's all-wool suit cost $10. We must bear in mind, however, that the average worker made 20 cents an hour and worked 60 hours a week.

For the average person today, history has entertainment value, as witness Walt Disney World's "Magic Kingdom," and the pseudo-Victorian decor of a multitude of restaurants, bars, and clothing stores across the country. There is no doubt that entertainment, nostalgia, emotional identification with ancestors, and similar sentiments motivate much of the preservation of old buildings. Many entrepreneurs and entire communities see the tourist's enjoyment of the historical as a handle on his pocketbook. A few years ago, a national news story described the efforts of Eureka Springs, Arkansas, to get a $730,000

155

Federal urban renewal grant to make itself look older. The downtown section was to be refurbished in 1890's style to attract tourists and declared a historical area. All new buildings would have to follow architectural patterns of the 1890's and such turn-of-the-century trappings as a trolley car were planned.

Another Arkansas attraction, the Ozark Mountain Park, was to include a stagecoach, log cabins, and other typical nostalgic items. Its special drawing power, however, would be the Dogpatch world of Li'l Abner, created by cartoonist Al Capp. Sights, sounds, foods, and—of course—Sadie Hawkins Day would conduct the visitor into a make-believe world of past simplicity and innocence. The replica town was also to have a statue of Dogpatch's most famous military hero, Jubilation T. Cornpone.

Not to be outdone, the Ohio Natural Resources Department decided in 1966 to span the Mohican River to Mohican State Park, near Loudonville, with an imitation covered bridge. A steel bridge with a concrete deck was to be encased in wood so that it would resemble a covered bridge. Thus nostalgia would be served, but not at the price of practicality.

One of the most extreme examples of catering to the tourist's desire to be entertained by history is the transfer of London Bridge to the Arizona desert. The McCulloch Oil Corporation of California purchased the bridge, which had become too small for traffic demands and was gradually sinking into the Thames, as a tourist attraction to promote their newly built resort and retirement town. The 1,005-foot, 130,000-ton granite structure was re-erected at Lake Havasu City and adorned with eight impressive, though unrelated, stone heads, which the owners had purchased from a demolished building in London. In March 1972 the project had cost $7 million.

Is this what historic preservation is all about? Commercialism? Escape for the vacationing worker? Let us look at it from the standpoint of the museum. A *museum object* is a tangible, material, three-dimensional thing that should be preserved, and can be preserved, for educational or aesthetic purposes. An entire building, or even a town, may, therefore, be considered a museum object. A historic house, authentically preserved, restored, and furnished, is really one object. If it were not so large, it would be carted off to a museum building. Indeed, open-air museums do collect buildings and assemble them as exhibits and as research collections. A historic house that remains in place and is administered for museum purposes is sometimes called a museum, a house museum, a historic house, a historic preservation, or something similar. Some of them could be considered as one-specimen museums.

What is the purpose of historic preservation? The same as for museums—public education. The same definitions and tests that apply to other kinds of museums apply to historic buildings.

Newspapers reveal a worldwide concern by educated people for the preservation of antiquities. It is heartening, for example, to read that in 1971 a new superhighway in England was not allowed to obliterate a recently discovered Roman bathhouse lying in its path. Instead the roads were carried on a concrete vault under which the Roman construction is preserved and exhibited. Similarly, when workers encountered a pre-Columbian (Aztec) temple during the building of present-day Mexico City's subway system, the tracks were diverted around the temple, and the Aztec building became part of a station. Not all antiquities fare so well. Other newspaper accounts tell of the erection of plush residential buildings on the 17th-century rampart wall of Old Delhi (India), and that caustic fumes from nearby factories are destroying the 919-year-old bell of Byodoin Temple in Japan. It will ring no longer but be placed in indoor storage.

Historic preservation becomes controversial when it conflicts with making money or the harsh realities of city management. Buildings ranging from cottages to the Pennsylvania Railroad Terminal in New York City have been smashed and trucked to the dump when the land they stood on became more valuable to someone or some corporation for another purpose. The public loses but can do little when the structures are privately owned. One newspaper editor has put the problem this way, "You can't park cars in a lovely old tree-shaded home or a historic old courthouse, but you seldom take groups of school children to see a parking lot."[1]

Sometimes the problem is the failure of the law to keep pace with modern times. A new destroyer of past remains is scuba diving. Peter Throckmorton reports that in 1969 there were only six competent marine archaeologists in the world, while at the same time there were more than four million skin divers. "In 20 years they have done more harm to archaeological sites in the sea than all the forces of nature together in three millennia."[2] Museums and historical societies must

1. *The Daily Idahonian* (Moscow, Idaho), May 27, 1966.
2. Peter Throckmorton, *Shipwrecks and Archaeology: The Unharvested Sea* (Boston: Atlantic-Little, Brown, 1969).

lead in the fight to preserve underwater antiquities and to have adequate state laws passed to protect the public heritage in public waters. James L. Quinn, Director of the Neville Public Museum in Green Bay, Wisconsin, himself an expert diver and diving teacher, was able to coordinate the efforts of many people in the recovery of a sunken schooner and its contents and in the creation of a new museum of Great Lakes maritime history.[3]

Why bother? Because history is important to us. Someone, I do not recall who, said, "Man consoles himself for what he is by what he was." Who is to say that a romantic look backward is not something most of us need? The Kansas Supreme Court said, "History is no longer a record of past events. It is an illuminating account of the expanding life of man in all its manifestations, revealing how each stage of civilization grows out of preceding stages, revealing how the past still lives in us and still dominates us, and enabling us to profit by what has gone on before. So considered, history is inspirational."[4] The study of our history and respect for it is generally believed to have real value for Americans today and for Americans yet to come.

Carl Sandburg said

. . . when a society or a civilization perishes, one condition may always be found. They forgot where they came from. They lost sight of what brought them along. The hard beginnings were forgotten and the struggles farther along. They became satisfied with themselves. Unity and common understanding there had been, enough to overcome rot and dissolution, enough to break through their obstacles. But the mockers came. And the deniers were heard. And vision and hope faded. And the custom of greeting became "What's the use?" And men whose forefathers would go anywhere, holding nothing impossible in the genius of man, joined the mockers and the deniers. They lost sight of what brought them along.

North Americans have no monopoly on such sentiment. People of all ages in many countries are actively engaged in preserving the material evidence of their cultural heritage. In Ireland, the Irish Georgian Society was organized in 1958 to acquire and preserve for the public fine examples of old houses. Artisans receive training in plastercasting and other necessary skills. In 1969, representatives of 19

3. James L. Quinn, "Time Capsule at 19 Fathoms," *Museum News*, 48, No. 7 (March 1970), 14.
4. Elizabeth H. Coiner, ed., *Quotes* (Washington, D.C.: National Park Service, 1966).

European countries, concerned with their common European heritage that transcends national boundaries, resolved at a meeting in Brussels to work together for historic preservation on an international scale.

Historic Preservation Defined

Historic preservation is a well-rounded program of scientific study, protection, restoration, maintenance, and interpretation of sites, buildings, and objects significant in American history and culture."[5] "The purpose of any historic preservation—the one and only purpose—is to communicate the lessons of history, in order that the present and the future may learn from the past."[6] These two quotations describe the nature and purpose of historic preservation.

In its simplest terms, preservation is the rescue from demolition or decay of an old building and maintaining it in good condition for public educational or aesthetic reasons. In some instances, the old houses continue to serve as private homes. In others, the buildings are put to some practical use as museums, libraries, or as headquarters for historical societies or public service agencies. More than 2,000 historic houses in the United States and Canada are being preserved for public benefit as examples of our past culture. It is probable that half of the hundreds of millions of "museum visits" in these countries each year are made to historic buildings and sites. (A historic site may or may not have structures remaining on it. Its educational value may lie in its relationship to surrounding settlements and natural features, its topography, natural vegetation, and so on).

Probably the most difficult question that potential preservationists must face is the philosophical one of what to preserve and what not to preserve. A building is not of value only because it is old or associated with a famous person. The test is the same as for a museum object. Would a museum properly choose to collect it and preserve it if it were the size of a breadbox? Is it significant from the standpoint of either architecture or history? Is it a valuable art object, or will it assist in teaching about life in the past? These are the two main considerations for the society or museum involved in historic preservation; that is, art (chiefly architecture), and history (including the

5. Turpin Bannister, definition adopted by the National Trust for Historic Preservation.
6. Kenneth Chorley, "Historic-House Keeping: A Short Course" (seminar held at Cooperstown, N.Y., 1955).

social and cultural history, which is perhaps more akin to sociology and anthropology).

Notice that nothing is said about saving a house because George Washington slept in it, because it once belonged to a United States Senator, or because it happened to be donated to the county for preservation. For a building to be worthy of preservation it must be capable of being shown to the public—interpreted—as an example of something important. It might be a typical example of a Middle Western farm house of the 1880's; a lower-class cottage on the wrong side of the tracks in the 1920's; a house designed by Frank Lloyd Wright; the home for many years of a person influential in public affairs, complete with the furnishings of those years; a place of business or a school; the list of possibilities is endless. One thing is essential, however. The historic preservation must not simply *be* something; it must be *for* something. Interpretation must be the intermediate aim, and education (or aesthetics) the ultimate.

This brings us to practical considerations. The preservation project must have educational value (not simply private, sentimental, entertainment, or hobby value), and the total cost must be within the capability of the sponsoring agency. There must be no vagueness or uncertainty about the administrative responsibility for the project from the beginning, during acquisition and restoration, and, especially, in perpetuity. (Historic houses, like museums, theoretically have perpetual life, once established.) The location of the project is important. Is it secure and accessible? Can it serve the majority of the public where it is? Will it have to be rescued again and again as the city grows and changes? Finally, there is the matter of authenticity and significance. Is the building an honest representation of what it will be said to be? If it has suffered changes over the years, can these be undone?

Kenneth Chorley lists four principles of historic preservation:

1. To be valid, a historic preservation must center upon a building, object, site, or environment of *substantial* historical or cultural importance. (Not everything is worth saving. Not every town has a building worth saving. Your whole county or part of the state may not have a structure worth saving.)
2. The life blood of historic preservation is research. A great amount of study is necessary to a good job of preservation and interpretation. Workers must become thoroughly familiar with a particular slice of past material culture. This information is not easy to come by. Some details may have been

irretrievably lost. What kind of wallpaper, draperies, rugs, and furniture were used in a certain room at a certain date? Who can answer such a question without research, even for his own childhood home after 25 or 50 years?

3. A historic preservation project, like any other museum, must be clear in its purpose, its possibilities and its limitations.

4. The value of any historic preservation project is determined by the quality of its presentation and interpretation. The greatest collection has no real value unless it can lead to the enrichment of human lives. A perfectly preserved building accomplishes nothing until it is presented and interpreted to the public so that it benefits visitors. Just as museum professionals should have a hand in the planning of museums and museum buildings, interpreters should have a part in the basic planning of a preservation project.

Two excellent examples of historic preservation have been documented in motion pictures. The Corbit-Sharp House in Odessa, Delaware, opened to the public in 1959, is a property of the Henry Francis duPont Winterthur Museum and obviously meets the high standards set by the parent institution. With research and care, one of the finest examples of Late Georgian domestic architecture has been restored to its eighteenth-century appearance.

A discussion of historic preservation could not be complete without adequate mention of the world's greatest example, Colonial Williamsburg, Incorporated. As almost everyone knows, Williamsburg, the colonial capital of Virginia, became the object of interest of John D. Rockefeller, Jr. Since 1926, he and his family have provided about $80 million for the restoration, reconstruction, and refurnishing of more than 500 buildings constituting the heart of the colonial city. The 1970 annual report of the Colonial Williamsburg Foundation reported assets of just under $58 million. The operation continues to expand, accommodating vast numbers of tourists annually. While they undoubtedly enjoy their visits, there is no question that Williamsburg is a serious open-air museum based on sound and meticulous research.

The cover of the leaflet listing the filmstrips made and sold by Colonial Williamsburg bears this statement:

With all of the problems confronting our American way of life, both domestically and abroad, there is no time like the present to reflect upon our political and cultural heritage. This is the very same heritage that gives spiritual strength and understanding to Americans and free people everywhere. Far too often we take our basic freedoms for granted. What thought, if any, is given to the men and ideas of the 18th century? These were the important ideas about human liberty, self-government and the rights of man. Little do we realize how much our planter statesman risked giving up in order to unify the colonies and establish a democratic form of government.

These same feelings of patriotism can be conveyed to students and adult organizations by viewing Colonial Williamsburg filmstrips. Like the entire Williamsburg project, they have been widely heralded for their inspirational and educational value by dramatizing living history in the 18th century surroundings.

But compare this official view of Williamsburg with what others say about it. David Lowenthal, in *Forum*, the Columbia University magazine, said:

There was a day when antiquity was mistrusted because the national mind cherished the newness of the country and was fixed on the future. Even today, obsolescence is planned and the latest edifices vanish unmourned overnight; but more recently, Americans have cultivated a sense of history in the form of narcissistic nostalgia. We protect dinosaur tracks, we put up markers to commemorate the deeds of Billy the Kid, we restore and rebuild Colonial towns. Too often, however, we idealize, museumize, and sanitize the past. Eighteenth century odors in Williamsburg would be such a shock to twentieth century noses that every other impression might be blotted out. But history that is homogenized, cleaned up, and expurgated usually ends as an *entirely artificial recreation of an imaginary past*. Such treatment tends toward a highly selective display of events—selective as to epochs, contents, events, and personalities. History's flow is interrupted, time's continuities are lost to sight. *Historyland remains detached, remote, and essentially lifeless.* (Emphasis added.)

Another example shows that this concern over the accuracy of historic representation by museums is not unique. S. Dillon Ripley, secretary of the Smithsonian Institution, said in his report on the institution's activities for 1968:

It has become apparent that even such a wonderful museum as our own Museum of History and Technology might fall into the preservation trap. Even a curator trained as a research historian can become infected with a special virus that makes him prey to this trap. When objects are preserved they become shiny and new looking. They also become nice. Some might say all gussied up. Everything becomes pretty and nice, and history itself becomes a storybook experience. In this country, everyone in history was romantic and dashing and lived in a genteel manner. A famous example of this perversion was the burning by a zealous librarian years ago of some of George Washington's off-color letters. Many exhibits pander to this myth that all our ancestors were upper-middle-class Protestant whites who lived like ladies and gentlemen. The preservation trap is beautifully illustrated in the average historical restoration projects around the country. From the restoration of colonial cities on to the historic house with formal garden, there is an unfailing tendency for the facts to be tidied up, and everything to be restored to such a degree that reality and truth long since have flown out the window. Public taste accepts this for the most part and seems to appreciate the myth—witness the enormous popularity of towns and old houses or the awed visits to (preferably Eighteenth Century) restoration projects.

That the Smithsonian takes seriously the avoidance of "the preservation trap" is shown by their plan to recreate a slum apartment as an exhibit of American life. Charles Blitzer, director of education and training at the Smithsonian, says, "It's the nasty side of life that we're in danger of losing today." He feared that the nation's upper- and middle-class museum visitors may be losing touch with the seamier side of life. Plans were to keep the exhibit area hot in the summer, cold in the winter, provide it with unpleasant smells and even a resident rat or two. Blitzer said that history museums have a scholarly responsibility to attempt to show the reality of life. "The display of the best of the past characterizes our museums," he said, "but the best of the past is not the way it really was."[7]

Assistance

In recent years the federal government has passed laws that give valuable assistance. Specifically, they do such things as provide financial grants to states to make surveys and plans, expand the National Register of Historic Places (which gives a measure of protection—at least federal money cannot be spent to destroy a building on the National Register), provide matching funds for preservation projects, make the preservation of historic sites national policy (in connection with highway construction, for example), and request the Secretary of Commerce to use "maximum effort to preserve Federal, State, and local government parklands and historic sites and the beauty and historic value of such lands and sites."[8] Some states also

7. "The Smithsonian: More Museums in Slums, More Slums in Museums?" *Science*, 154, No. 3753 (2 December 1966), 1152–53.
8. Public Law 89–574, as quoted in *History News*, 21, No. 12, 238.

have antiquities legislation which protects state property and historic sites and structures designated as state monuments. State-level financial assistance is sometimes available. Organizations with preservation projects should consult their state historical societies as well as the National Trust For Historic Preservation, AAM, and AASLH. Several of the publications listed in the bibliography offer practical advice regarding planning for and organizing a preservation project. Before any local group attempts a historic preservation project they should consult the literature and seek professional advice.

Valuable Considerations Related to Historic Preservation

The following checklist may prove valuable in ascertaining whether a preservation project is worthy of the expenditure of time, effort, and money required for success:

Historic Considerations: Is the structure associated with the life or activities of a major historic person (more than the "slept here" type of association)? Is it associated with a major group of organizations in the history of the nation, state, or community (including significant ethnic groups)? Is it associated with a major historic event (cultural, economic, military, social, or political)? Is the building associated with a major recurring event in the history of the community (such as an annual celebration)? Is it associated with a past or continuing institution which has contributed substantially to the life of the city?

Architectural Considerations: Is the structure one of few of its age remaining in the city? Is it a unique local example of a particular architectural style or period? Is it one of few remaining local examples of a particular architectural style or period? Is it one of many good examples in the city of a particular architectural style or period? Is the building the work of a nationally famous architect? Is it a notable work of a major local architect or master builder? Is it an architectural curiosity or a picturesque work of particular artistic merit? Does it reveal original materials and/or workmanship that can be valued in themselves? Has the integrity of the original design been retained, or has it been altered?

Setting Considerations: Is the structure generally visible to the public? Is it, or could it be, an important element in the character of the city? Is it, or could it be, an important element in the character of the neighborhood (either alone or in conjunction with similar structures in the vicinity)? Does it contribute to the architectural continuity of the street? Is the building on its original site? Is its present setting (yards, trees, fences, walls, paving treatment, outbuildings, and so forth) appropriate? Are the structure and site subject to the encroachment of detrimental influences?

Use Considerations: Is the building threatened with demolition by public or private action? Can it be retained in its original or its present use? Does it have sufficient educational value to warrant consideration of museum use? Is it adaptable to productive reuse? Are the building and site accessible, served by utilities, capable of providing parking space, covered by fire and police protection, and so forth, so that they can feasibly be adapted to contemporary use? Can the structure be adapted to a new use without harm to those architectural elements which contribute to its significance?

Cost Considerations: Is preservation or restoration economically feasible? Is continued maintenance after restoration economically feasible?[9]

The following definitions will suggest different degrees of historical accuracy in representations of structures of the past. A danger lies in the inability of the tourist or visitor always to be able to distinguish between the tawdry or cliche-ridden simulations in commercial ventures, at one extreme, and the painstakingly researched replicas prepared by museums and related organizations and agencies at the other.

Preservation is the keeping of something that exists and the safeguarding of it from any further changes than those which it has already undergone.

Restoration is returning an existing building to its original appearance and condition by removing later additions, replacing missing parts, cleaning, painting, and the like.

Reconstruction is constructing again—building something new as a representation of that which has gone. Buildings are sometimes erected on the original stone foundations of the previous buildings they are representing. "To rebuild" is a synonym for "to reconstruct," but it may also be used in the case of a house being moved from its original site to a new location as at an open-air museum. If the house has had to be largely or entirely disassembled in order to move it, it is then rebuilt on its new site. In this case, though rebuilt, the house is original in the sense that all or most of its components are original. The *original* is the first or initial example from which copies are made. A *replica or copy* is a precise duplicate or close reproduction of the original. An *imitation* is something that follows the style or pattern of the original but is not a close copy. A *simulation* is something that assumes the appearance of the original falsely by imitating its identifying characteristics, usually superficial, and stereotyped like a stage set. To *refurbish* is to clean up and make fresh looking. To *refurnish* is to furnish again, usually with the connotation of duplicating the original furnishings as closely as possible. *Historic* is being, itself, a piece of history—having historic value in its own right. *Historical* is

9. Ralph W. Miner, *Conservation of Historic and Cultural Resources* (Chicago: American Society of Planning Officials, 1969). Reprinted by permission.

being about or related to history. (Thus, Lincoln's rocking chair is historic. A pamphlet describing the chair is historical.)

A cardinal rule is that it is better to *preserve* than to restore; better to *restore* than to reconstruct; better to *reconstruct* than to do nothing.

EXERCISES—CHAPTER 18

The main difference between historic preservation and other kinds of museum work is that of scale. If a historic house were small, it could be added to a museum's collections and stored or exhibited in the museum's building along with other objects. Buildings that are significant within the scope of the museum or historical society should be collected, preserved, and interpreted for public education. As a museum worker, a member of a historical society, or even as a private citizen not belonging to such an organization, you could at any time be asked to jump on the bandwagon as someone or some clique seeks popular support for the idea of preserving a particular old building. People who prefer to act emotionally do not welcome cool heads expressing logic. It is logic, however, that gets the good job done well, and that is what concerns us; that, and the combating of public folly.

1. Discuss the relationship of a preserved building to its contents or use. (Include compatibility of style, public safety, proper use of the building, etc.)
2. Discuss the preservation of buildings by age (modern, Victorian, Colonial, etc.) and by use (store, barn, house, courthouse, etc.) Include your judgment as to relative worth, difficulty of getting public support, and any other aspect that occurs to you. The object here is to get you to think of the entire range of historic preservation and to single out those kinds which you would judge to be of most value, at least in your community.
3. Discuss the issue raised in the examples concerning Williamsburg, pro and con, and the creating of slums and hovels as museum exhibits. Distinguish between an art approach and a history approach.
4. What kinds of historic preservation projects would be appropriate to different kinds of museums? (Imagine yourself in a museum of a certain kind. What type of historic preservation might you be interested in?) Try for at least five different examples.
5. Describe a current preservation project in your own community and evaluate it according to the criteria given in the readings. News clippings may help you but you should also interview the people in charge. What is its stated purpose? What is its *actual* purpose, if different? What are its limitations, its good and bad characteristics, its problems, its prospects?

If there is no actual project in your region with which you can become familiar, you may choose the following alternate assignment: Select a likely candidate for historic preservation among the old buildings of your community. Become sufficiently familiar with it so that you can outline procedures for acquiring, restoring, supporting, and interpreting it to good purpose. Your outline should be realistic enough so that it could be used as a guide by a local art museum or historical society.

19

Philosophy and Public Image

In the United States we place great emphasis on public education. Bazin says that this pedagogical habit which we inherited from England has "metamorphosed into a veritable obsession".[1] Our insistence that our museums educate the public may be our special version of applied museography; that is, the use of museum techniques to achieve specific ends. The propaganda value of museums has been well recognized. Governments today in "underdeveloped" countries have found museum exhibit techniques useful in promoting desired behavior. Illiterate populations can learn the rudiments of sanitation, improved agricultural methods, or perhaps be influenced to support the regime in power. The Communist countries of eastern Europe have sought to demonstrate the importance of the peasant and the urban worker in folk museums and in museums of agriculture and industry. The Soviet government founded 542 museums between 1921 and 1936 to reteach history according to Marxist doctrine. Germany created over two thousand regional museums (Heimatmuseen) between the two World Wars. Their purpose was to restore national pride. The folk museums of Scandinavia (and elsewhere) were created and are still operated, more or less, out of a sense of nationalism.

Political boundaries sometimes seem to supersede cultural boundaries in the interpretation of the collections. For example, the Saxon longhouse of ancient origin, which is still characteristic of the farms of northern Germany, is shown in the open-air folk museums of the Netherlands and Denmark as though it were unique to those countries. Labels and guidebooks do not refer to the use of this house type throughout the area of northern Europe settled by the Saxons. The

1. Germain Bazin, *The Museum Age* (New York: Universe Books, 1967), 267.

International Council of Museums has cautioned against the exploitation of museums for nationalistic purposes and recommends instead emphasis on cultural similarities across political boundaries.

The presentation of an official point of view is more likely where museums are owned and managed by the central government than in the United States, where most museums are locally created and controlled.[2] Our museums may at times suffer from a lack of professionalism, but, on the other hand, they are not stereotyped and propagandistic. The American Association of Museums plays a salient role, through accreditation and through its various informational services, in helping American museums to be efficient though democratic.

Two simple equations may sum up the essentially educational and aesthetic purpose of museums in the United States and Canada:

$$\text{objects} + \text{care} + \text{use} = \text{worth of museum}$$

and

$$\frac{\text{results (education, inspiration, etc.)}}{\text{expenditure (time, energy, money, opportunities)}} = \text{efficiency of the museum}$$

In other words, actual achievement compared with potential achievement indicates how well the museum serves the public within its limitations. A simple listing of services or accomplishments is not enough. Judgment as to what *might* have been done is also necessary.

The characteristics of Western culture—devotion to the ideal of universal education; emphasis on accumulation and dissemination of information; awareness of the importance of reinterpreting history; and public appreciation of art—have led to the concentration of the world's museums in the countries of the Western World. They have created the museums of today and made it an expression of our culture. Museums are not universal, though collecting and exhibiting may well be. A museum is a manifestation of a particular cultural situation.

Dichotomies, or opposing points of view, can help us to understand museums. The changing attitude of museums from aloofness and exclusiveness to a quest for democratic popularity illustrates the dichotomy between the museum for the elite and the museum for the masses. A second dichotomy exists between the amateur viewpoint of

2. Although not all our local museums are free of bias or propaganda intent.

the museum as a place to assemble curiosities, relics, and memorabilia for entertainment purposes and the professional viewpoint of the museum as a repository for significant objects, systematically cared for and used for the purposes of education and aesthetics. The art museum philosophy makes aesthetics the criterion—the objects are use for enjoyment—while other museums make education the criterion—the objects are used as significant specimens of the real world. Art presents another dichotomy; representation for the sake of representation versus art for the sake of art (popular art versus fine art, for example).

In the last century, when the modern museum was becoming an important element in American life, museum professionals became very enthusiastic about the educational potential of the museum. Even art museums shared in this enthusiasm as their directors and supporters maintained publicly that the art museum's function included original research and public education as well as acquisition and preservation. Not all art curators today would agree. A reaction against intellectualism as antithetical to the aesthetic experience has occurred. Intellectualism is of the mind; logical, dispassionate, and impersonal. The aesthetic experience is of the "heart"; emotional, sensory, individual, and not adaptable to scientific description. Some persons criticize art museums for not interpreting more, so that the visitor can gain greater understanding, but art curators generally feel this to be outside their proper function. Some would say that stimulation of the reasoning faculties of the brain might diminish the aesthetic experience. Both sides of the argument have devotees, but it will probably remain undecided.

We must nevertheless be aware that art enjoys a position of prestige today. A successful artist is a respected figure, and people of wealth and social standing attach themselves to art museums with a passion. This vogue permeates such a wide segment of society that it even influences other kinds of museums. Museums of science hold art shows and install their ethnological collections in Halls of (African, Oceanic, Indian, etc.) Art. The staff, collections, and expeditions of a prominent university museum in the East are concerned mainly with anthropology and history, yet the exhibits and other activities are those of an art museum. The Museum of the American Indian in New York City celebrated its golden anniversary in 1966. The news release announcing the celebration used such language as: "archaeological and ethnological treasures . . . to preserve the heritage of the aboriginal inhabitants . . . include . . . remarkable examples . . . crafts expressions . . . finest examples of their type . . . emphasis is placed on esthetic and historic quality . . . balanced cross section of the Indian and his cultural accomplishments . . . Esthetically, the Museum's collection of pre-Columbian objets d'art is outstanding, particularly in terms of its wide coverage of areas and periods of art expression." Yet one would expect this museum to concern itself with the *science* of man, anthropology. My quarrel is not with art curators. They have a right to call attention to the aesthetic qualities of any kind of material—electron microscopes, for that matter. But I am disappointed with curators of history and curators of science who shirk their educational responsibilities and choose the easy, nonintellectual route to the utilization of collections. A curator who wishes to exhibit an American Indian basket can go to a great deal of trouble to explain its function within its particular culture, the techniques used to manufacture it, the instance of culture change which it might exemplify, its stylistic relationships with other cultures, and the like. Or he can put it on a pedestal, shine a spotlight on it, call it "Indian Art," and be finished. I suggest that many "art" exhibits in nonart museums are the result of laziness and faulty museology.

A slovenly attitude toward the distinction between art and ethnology—and especially between art and history—leads to confusion in museums concerning what to collect and how to exhibit the collections. An avowed art museum is not likely to be criticized for not teaching history. On the other hand, the thinking visitor may well be irritated by an art museum approach in a history museum. If museum directors and curators are careless about the distinctions, how can we expect the public to get full benefit from their work? The burden lies on the professional who works in the nonart museum.

Public Image

What is the public image of the museum today? Culture works by stereotypes and prejudgments. We make snap judgments hundreds of times each day, and we have attached bodies of meaning to triggering stimuli. Even such simple things as colors carry meaning. Pink is fine for a baby's dress, but what about the mayor's limousine? Samples of cartoons and articles from newspapers and magazines suggest that the public has such a stereotyped image of the museum. It is regarded as peacefully sleeping—a repository for curiosities of the past—mummies, dinosaurs, suits of armor, and mementos of famous people of yesterday. At the same time, the museum is treated with reverence: some activities that are acceptable elsewhere seem inappropriate in a museum. During Lyndon Johnson's administration an opera ball held in the Smithsonian's Museum of History and Technology to raise money for the John F. Kennedy Center for the Performing Arts shocked some members of Congress. No doubt the idea of drinking and dancing until three in the morning in a museum seemed inappropriate.

The museum's public image cannot be separated from its external appearance. Is it housed in a large stone building with Roman columns on the facade? Is it in a converted automobile garage built of concrete block? Intangibles also create image—grounds, newspaper publicity, school children's impressions, staff activities—all work together to create public opinions about your museum, perhaps even from persons who have no firsthand experience there.

The media also add to the public idea of the museum. A survey made in the early sixties examined the treatment of museums and museum workers in the mass media: motion pictures, theater, television, fiction, newspapers, and cartoons and jokes. It was found that the media presented the museum as hospitable and friendly, but museum workers as "rather stupid but hard-working"; bland and bespectacled, prodding visitors through the museum; shy, neurotic, and unhappy. A scene from "The Lady from Shanghai" was selected to illustrate that "school children in groups, with rather unattractive teachers, are among the relatively few normal kinds of people ever shown in media representations of museums. Ordinary adults are very seldom shown going to museums, unless they are doing something curious or illegal or unusual."[3] Museums and museum personnel seldom figure in fiction, stage plays or jokes, and the museum's usual appearance in the mass media "is as a relatively strange place. Other than children, the nonmuseum personnel who figure in media museum contexts are likely to be marginal people: murderers, soldiers on leave, models, and others whose relationship to the museum is fortuitous. Thus a child who may have had a number of enriching experiences at museums and who may be very favorably disposed toward them, may then as an adult see museums presented in the mass media as bizarre places frequented by bizarre people."[4]

Amused tolerance is not the only public attitude toward the museum. Lately, open criticism has jolted museum people. In "Is the

3. Charles Winick, "The Public Image of the Museum in America," *Curator*, V, No. 1 (1962).
    4. *Ibid*.

Museum a Museum Piece?" Alex Gross wrote, "The real question is whether museums are still necessary to us, at least in their present form. . . . Basically the art museum was (and remains) a place one visits to commune with what are supposed to be the truly meaningful values of life and society, as distinguished from the imperfect poverty-stricken, money-grubbing world outside its walls. The museum was (and is) a place to avoid life rather than to encounter it, a place to congratulate oneself on one's values rather than to doubt them and move on to something better."[5]

Barbara Gold's attack on the museums of Baltimore (mentioned in Chapter 8) and a number of other articles in the public press and even in museum periodicals have questioned whether museums today are doing enough to cure the ills of society. Museums, especially art museums, have been pictured as outmoded playthings of the "Establishment," and, consequently, elitist and racist. They are also sexist, according to the women's liberation movement, being one of the primary bastions of male chauvinism. "The art Establishment is bound by the patronage of the bourgeoisie; by their acquisitiveness and their insistence upon maintaining value judgments which salve their consciences. The art market is kept desirable and chic, since in the bourgeois world everything is viewed first as object, then as property—art, women, etc. Viewing objects as property, the aggressive male ego seeks satisfaction by controlling them. Woman is an object, art is an object, both must be controlled."[6]

Art galleries, art museums, and their patrons have been taken to task for treating lightly the social protest of artists. Even the most heart-rending depictions of human tragedy and injustice are ignored as they form the setting for gallery cocktail parties. Militant spokesmen for minority groups have attacked museums as exploiters of other cultures. American Indians are demanding more and more that artifacts made by their ancestors be returned to them. Many museums have removed their Indian burial exhibits. Museums have been asked to set up "black centers" in the Negro districts of cities. Blacks have said that the purpose of Negro art is to instill pride and identity in black people and demanded that Negro art collections (aboriginal African) have black curators. They have insisted, too, that the racial composition of the museum staff reflect the racial composition of the

5. *The East Village Other*, March 7, 1969.
6. Nancy Spero, "The Whitney and Women," *The Art Gallery Magazine*, (January 1971).

public it serves. Responses to the criticisms have been varied. Museum workers have been indignant; they have been hurt; they have been angry; they have been sympathetic. Upon reflection, the profession generally has agreed to listen and to examine its attitudes and its services. Though the attacks are often emotional, coming from long-frustrated segments of society, the museum response has been, and must continue to be, reasonable. Former AAM President and Director of the Baltimore Museum of Art Charles Parkhurst responded to Gold thus: "I don't feel it's the primary role of the museum to run a school. We have thrust on us a sociological role. We must be careful not to get carried away. Our primary role is collection, conservation, and use. . . . it is important that we play [our role]—to provide pleasure or delectation to anyone who can utilize it. If a museum can afford . . . to go into educational roles in ghetto . . . areas—great. We do not have the resources."

Museums, of course, are not alone; colleges and universities have been attacked on the same grounds. Their spokesmen have responded that institutions of higher learning do not have the funds or the political power to cure social ills. They would accept only a limited role in providing public service to their communities. Theodore D. Lockwood, President of Trinity College in Hartford, Connecticut, said:

[A] development threatening the spirit of free inquiry has been the fervid concern for contemporaneity (or relevance-mongering, as some have called it). Many students and faculty have been justifiably concerned with urgent contemporary issues. Unhappily, this concern has often led to an intense preoccupation with resolving these issues on the campuses. To do otherwise was to be branded irrelevant—a fate worse than death and taxes. In extreme cases there have been insistent demands that colleges become political instruments, dedicated almost exclusively to the eradication of social and economic abuses. No college which cares about its academic integrity can permit this to happen . . . What is needed is to . . . rediscover and reinforce our belief in free and rational inquiry—a belief badly shaken by involvement in emotionally charged issues on and off the campus. Trinity must not become the creature of any ideology or philosophical system; it must retain its academic obligation to search for the truth in a free and open environment, independent of but not insensitive to transient concerns.[7]

Perhaps the true method of determining whether criticisms are justified, however, is to evaluate the effectiveness of the institution. If

7. "The President's Annual Report, 1970–71."

the justification for the art museum is the tenet that important institutions set standards of excellence for society, then we can ask whether the museum is fostering an appreciation for the truly beautiful. In Chapter 8 I noted that "literacy in art" does not rub off on art museum employees. Do we have any better luck with the public at large? Art critics generally say no. They point out that in spite of a great amount of aesthetic education in the schools and a great number of art museums we are still surrounded by ugliness and tastelessness. Our public buildings, our cities, our sprawling commercial developments show no respect for good design, no feeling for form, no sensitivity for cultivated aesthetic values. They would recognize exceptions, of course, but their consensus is that art education and exposure to art result in only an abstract erudition, and that any effect on daily life does not reach the masses of society.

Perhaps the old standards no longer hold, or perhaps they never did apply to our whole society. Certainly, the values of integrity and excellence on which the museum movement is founded appear to be eroding. Colleges and universities are aware of the nationwide inflation of grades, and the awarding of grades may be abolished soon. Our culture is said to be more and more permissive, and authority and laws are not as respected as they once were. Fewer wrongdoers are brought to trial, and fewer are punished. Candidates for high office advocate the abolition of penalties for draft-dodging, and there is growing sentiment for doing away with the dishonorable discharge from military service. Bottled, commercial wine now comes mixed with "the intriguing flavors of tangy pineapple, rich guava, tart lemon, sunny orange and exotic passion fruit." The wrapper on a package of cigars bears this message, "These cigars are predominantly natural tobacco with a substantial amount of non-tobacco ingredients." Matthew Arnold wrote that we can learn two things from history (and therefore, we would add, two things that the history museum has to teach), "one, that we are not superior to our fathers; another that we are shamefully and monstrously inferior to them if we do not advance beyond them." Do we still believe that?

Museologists must ask themselves if the old assumptions regarding the role of the museum in our culture hold true today, or whether it is a whole new ball game. Supreme Court Justice Lewis F. Powell, Jr., speaking to the American Bar Association in August 1972, condemned what he called "the New Ethic," saying that it has become fashionable to question and attack the most basic elements of our society ". . . our institutions and inherited values are no longer respected" by large segments of the population.

While being concerned about the museum's public image we must keep a proper set of values. Museologists from many countries have reiterated in meetings and in their writings the same sentiments expressed by Mr. Parkhurst and the representatives of colleges and universities. If a museum has qualified staff, can spare their time and provide them with funds, then it may with caution take on a social mission. However, above all it must not lose sight of its essential role as a preserver of objects and a conductor of research.

At the very least we must seek to understand our culture and the directions of its changes; to serve society we must know it. More than that, we must be aware of what society understands about museums. Communication is not soliloquy. We have to be sure we are getting through.

Censorship

A sometimes embarrassing point of contact between the museum and society is censorship. It is conceivable that science and history museums in some communities may receive criticism on religious or political grounds, but legal censorship today is mainly concerned with pornography in art, as far as mueums are concerned. A few years ago censorship had more support from law enforcement than it does today. During the summer of 1966 both houses of the New York state legislature passed a statute, sensibly vetoed by Governor Rockefeller, that would have made it an offense for any shopkeeper to permit anyone under 16 (unless accompanied by a parent or guardian) to enter a premise where objectionable literature could be purchased or nude exhibits were displayed. The statute could have been construed as a ban on many literary classics and would have placed most of the art museum directors of the state in jail.

A few years ago the harassment of art galleries on the West Coast was such that the Western Association of Art Museums issued a policy statement: "The Western Association of Art Museums strongly believes that any interference with the professional selection of works of art for exhibition is censorship. The Association is unalterably opposed to official or private invasions into institutional prerogatives or into the professional judgment of duly appointed gallery directors or curators. The Association defends the public's right to know and the selector's right to a free and unfrightened aesthetic and scholarly approach and selection." They went on to make several points including: Works of art hardly fall into the province of laws against urging to violence and inciting to riot; the act of an art director who exhibits a controversial piece in spite of some community opposition would probably be legally defensible; the state must adopt contemporary, as opposed to provincial, standards to determine obscenity; the director should emphasize the right of all the public to see and to know, regardless of the opposition of some individuals or segments of society.

In general, nudity is no longer prohibited if some purpose other than pornography can be shown. Thus, if artists today are painting nakedness, the contemporary art curator has an obligation to exhibit these paintings and the general public has the right to come to see them. Obviously, some communities warrant a more conservative position than others. The museum must not harm itself seriously in order to strike a blow for freedom of expression. Good public relations, of course, are essential to the museum, and its staff will be concerned about its image in the public mind.

As a society changes, its culture must change to satisfy different needs. Those who would strike a new balance call on our social and cultural institutions to rise to the challenge of the times. The museum must evolve in its role and thereby continue to serve society. To maintain its integrity, however, it must not waver from its main purpose. No other institution will preserve significant objects of the past. If this should cease to be the main concern of the museum, the museum will no longer exist; it will have become something else.

EXERCISES—CHAPTER 19

Throughout the book we have touched on the subject of this chapter from time to time. How the museum appears to the public is crucial to its success. Everything the museum does will result from its philosophy; or, to be more precise, the behavior of a museum's staff will be determined by their philosophical understandings. Each will have a concept of why the museum exists, what it should collect, what it should exhibit, and so on. If the concepts of the several staff members are not in accord, confusion and dissension are inevitable.

The following article by Polly Long is a good example of a plausible proposition which hinges on matters of museological understanding and philosophy. Your assignment is to get inside Polly Long's mind to understand what she knows or thinks she knows about museums, and react to it. You may agree or disagree with her point of view, but be aware of her definitions and her museum philosophy.

Why Don't Societies Sell All Their "Junk?"

I have been behind the scenes in many museums and historical societies. Most of these institutions are a sort of cultural iceberg: A great deal of what they have, quantity-wise, is below the surface.

In many instances, for every *quality piece* of art or furniture on view to the public there are 5 to 10 times that number stored in basement rooms or other hidden-away areas.

Recently while walking through the basement of a New England museum to view a certain piece in which I was interested, I passed rack upon rack of American primitive painting—portraits, landscapes and genre—as well as shelf upon shelf of glass and many odd pieces of furniture.

Even if these pieces are catalogued—and in many museums they are on hand for years before any official note is taken of them—they will never be seen except by a few who have access to these treasure rooms.

Museums and historical societies serve the public well as preservers as well as exhibitors. And more often than not, the directors and curators of these institutions have to work against great odds, such as too-small salaries for themselves and their staff, and a general attitude of indifference among the people who control policy and money—the private citizens who are members of the board of directors.

However, it is my feeling that too many well-meaning people wish onto museums pieces that these institutions don't really want.

Particularly with the historical societies and museums in the smaller cities, it is a general practice that rather than hurt the feelings of a well-meaning benefactor who may at a later date be in a position to do much more for the institution, to accept the gifts.

The director, who is expected to maintain—and improve *excellence of the institution*, keeps these gifts in storage.

The tragedy of this policy is that while these objects may be *unworthy of museum display*, they often are highly desirable for individual ownership.

Would it not be appropriate for museums and historical societies to take inventory, at least every 10 years; select those pieces which are *below standard*, and put them up for sale at a public auction? The proceeds from such a sale could be used to buy *top-quality art objects* which could be viewed and appreciated by all.

Can you think of a more pleasant summer afternoon than one spent at an auction on the lawn of any one of the New England historical societies?[8]

---

8. From a newspaper column in the *Baltimore Sun*. Reprinted by permission. Italics added.

1. Write a reply to "Why Don't Societies Sell All Their 'Junk'?" It may take the form of a letter to the editor, a letter to Polly Long, a column similar to hers, or a short essay. But cover all issues she raises, especially the most vital one of what museums of various kinds should be doing.
2. In Polly Long's article there are 5 italicized phrases. What, specifically, does she mean by these terms? What is your reaction to her meaning in view of her speaking of "museums and historical societies"? Does she make a distinction between art museums and history museums?
3. Write a short essay on the subject of the museum of tomorrow. Include the philosophical questions of the museum's role in society and to what extent, if at all, the good museum of the present needs to change to be the good museum of the future.

20

Practical Matters

After all the general remarks have been made, it is time for specific questions regarding immediate problems faced by individuals and their museums. Unfortunately, a brief book of this kind cannot give all the answers, even if all the questions could be anticipated. Solving these problems is the art of museum work, and there is no magic wand that will create a good museum worker in a short time. However, it is the purpose of this book, and of other basic writings in museology, to help to prepare the individual to make wise choices when confronted with alternatives. Several guides or rules-of-thumb should be of help:

1. The amount of floor space devoted to exhibits should probably be no more than one-third of the total floor space of the building.
2. In the daily operation of the museum, the most important consideration is security; the second is cleanliness.
3. The whole purpose of the museum and all its activities is public education. Any expenditure of time, money, or opportunities must ultimately be justifiable as contributing significantly to this end.
4. The properly run museum operation is one whose values and priorities are in keeping with the order of Guthe's "obligations:" a) collections; b) records; c) exhibits; d) activities.
5. Objects in the museum's collections must be significant. That is, they must be useful in teaching facts and illustrating concepts or artistic achievement which are not only within the museum's scope but are worthy of the museum's attention. Relics, curiosities, personal memorabilia, glorification of specific individuals or specific families—as well as unique,

one-of-a-kind objects of no great aesthetic or educational value—do not belong in a public museum.

Another rule might be suggested to the amateur in the small museum—seek professional help. Read and abide by the literature of museology, and call on professionals in larger museums for advice. This is obvious but not automatic. Anti-intellectualism, or at least, non-intellectualism, is a strong force in American culture. It is not limited to the undereducated but extends high up the educational scale. Museum work is still not commonly respected as a profession by the general public; and the need for trained museum workers and professional procedures is not recognized, by and large, even by those leading citizens who are instrumental in founding and operating museums. It is interesting, I think, that only one sixth of the museums and professional museum workers of the United States are members of the American Association of Museums. A few years ago, prominent and active citizens of a medium-sized city established a museum which they expected to have national importance (the word "national" is in its name). In the same city a good museum with several qualified professionals on its staff already existed. These museologists were not invited to give advice during the planning or any other stage of the development and were turned down when they asked to participate. A recent news story from another city tells that those concerned with the establishment of a new museum sought design help from students of a school of architecture, not from museologists. In yet another location a museum director was trying to assist a local group in establishing a noncompeting museum dealing with a different field, but they secretly changed the time of the supposedly public meeting and organized without him.

This attitude is common. Many laymen who are deriving personal satisfaction from the museum's pursuit of their private concerns feel that placing the museum on a professional basis might spoil that satisfaction. The informed citizen could leave them to their hobby, except when their hobby purports to be a public museum operating in the public interest, and especially when it operates on public funds. The issue then is clear. Public funds and public facilities must be used only for the good of the public; and this good, when it comes to museums, requires professional management according to the principles of modern museology. The best of the small museums are founded and run by devoted, public spirited individuals who seek and accept professional guidance and who, themselves, increase their knowledge through all the means at their disposal.

Let me now address the student or young beginner in museum work who is interested in making a career for himself in the museum profession.

Prepare Yourself

Take college courses that will help to prepare you for museum work. Seek to become as broadly educated as possible. The best background for museum directors and curators is a good, broad, liberal arts education. You must be able to write, speak, use the library, and understand museum visitors psychologically and sociologically. Take art appreciation and anthropology. Take any courses in museology and museography that are available. Give serious consideration to public relations, journalism, radio-television, audio-visual arts, office practice, and library science. Courses as diverse as woodworking, social psychology, and outdoor recreation, are pertinent. Art history is indispensable for art museum work as is American history for work with historical societies and regional history museums. Courses in geology and biology are indispensable in many museums. Indeed, it would be difficult to think of college courses that could not be put to use in museum management. Even physics is useful to the curator who must understand such concepts as relative humidity in protecting his collections, and the curator of science can use the concepts of art appreciation in planning and installing exhibits. Many, if not most, museum workers find themselves in situations requiring broad interests and broad educational backgrounds. Especially in the small museum, the generalist rather than the specialist is most needed. This wide scope in museum work holds great appeal for large numbers of museum professionals. Others are attracted by the opportunity to specialize, but specialization (as in Oriental porcelain) is ordinarily possible only in large museums or in those with specialized collections. In addition to a broad education, of course, the student should take as many courses as possible in one or two of the traditional museum fields: art, American history, anthropology, elementary education, geology, biology.

In addition to regular college attendance, consider the special museum training courses (listed in the AAM's museum training directory). Some of these are held for a few weeks during the summer months; others are short workshops held at various times and in various parts of the country. For the worker in a local history museum, for example, attendance at one of the workshop meetings or seminars of the American Association for State and Local History can be a very valuable experience. Of considerable worth are the internships offered by some museums.

Introductory theory courses can carry the beginner only so far. There is no substitute for apprenticeship under qualified professionals in a museum of high quality. Hugo G. Rodeck, Director Emeritus of the University of Colorado Museum, says that no program of museum training can be complete without actual work under supervision in an accredited museum. Work as a part-time volunteer if you cannot get a job immediately; get your foot in the door. Museums can always use the free help of seriously interested individuals. Museum professionals are always willing to help beginners.

My next bit of advice is to become involved in the museum profession. Read books, read the journals, belong to museum organizations, attend meetings, workshops, and seminars. Become acquainted with the people working in museums. The student or amateur is often able, at low cost, to attend a regional museum meeting; either an annual regional conference of the American Association of Museums or the meeting of a state or district association. The people attending will be of all ages, wide-ranging in interests, and universally friendly. Such meetings are excellent opportunities to become acquainted with prospective employers.

How to Get a Job

Museum workers have got their first museum jobs in a number of ways:

1. They have started as volunteers. Having proved themselves useful and likable, they began to receive part-time wages and then stepped into staff vacancies.
2. Through personal acquaintance with museum directors, they have been asked to fill vacancies or have been recommended to the directors' colleagues in other museums.
3. They have qualified in open, civil service examinations for governmental museum positions. Museum people work for national and state park, forest, and recreation departments.
4. They have applied to work at a museum of their choice without knowing that that museum had a vacancy.
5. They have answered advertisements of museum job openings.

Vacancies are listed in museum periodicals, especially newsletters. Some museums send out notices of vacancies to other museums and to college departments. Museum conventions have posted listings of job openings, and the larger conventions (such as the annual meeting of the AAM) have a person designated to receive and give out information from both prospective employers and prospective employees.

Probably the most important regular listing of positions open is in the monthly bulletins of the AAM. Individuals seeking positions may also insert their own advertisements, describing their qualifications and the kind of job they are seeking. A museum director may have a vacancy on his staff or know that he will have one soon. Before he announces the vacancy he may read the "jobs wanted" column in the bulletin. He sometimes finds the employee he wants before the fact that he is looking for someone becomes public knowledge.

Once you and the prospective employer have made contact, you must sell yourself. Usually, his job is the only one you know about that you want, but you are only one of several—perhaps many—that he can hire. In writing a letter of application, be brief and businesslike, but list all qualifications that may have importance to the job for which you are applying. No job can be described completely in the few lines of a short notice. Some of the skills the director or board of trustees is looking for may not be in the job description. You may even be able to convince the employer that you are the person to hire, on the basis of skills and education that he did not know he wanted. For example, the job listing may state requirements of an M.A. in history plus competence in some other field, museum training or experience, public-speaking ability, age under 40, and so on. There might be twenty applications for the job, all from individuals who meet the requirements. How is the employer to decide whom to hire? He will check references, he may compare schools and transcripts, he may be influenced by photographs if he has asked for them, but what will really help him to pull top contenders out of the pile are the additional things the applicants' letters contain. For instance, you may have told him in your letter that you are a good carpenter, a good photographer, and that you spent a summer visiting historic houses in New England. These qualifications may fit into his idea of what your job would entail, and he will, therefore, be especially interested in you. If you have a good voice and are not nervous when speaking on the telephone, a call may raise your stock if you have a plausible reason for calling. On the other hand, if the prospective employer feels that your call was made to pressure him into making a faster decision, he might make one (unfavorable to you) on the spot.

Junior curatorial positions, unless filled by local persons, usually do not involve personal interviews, but most other professional jobs demand one. The top three or four candidates might be asked to visit the museum, meet the staff and the board, and be examined as a potential employee. The interview is a kind of last-minute insurance against a mistake. You can normally expect to have your expenses paid when you travel to be interviewed. If the employer has not specified this in his invitation, you may inquire about it, especially if the cost would be substantial. You may in some instances be willing to gamble. If you feel that you stand a good chance of getting the job but have to pay your own travel expenses in order to have a personal interview, arrange a meeting by telephone. The prospective employer will not let you spend your own money unless you really do have a good chance of getting the position.

In a personal, face-to-face interview you can get a better idea of what the job is, what the working conditions are, and sell yourself in direct relationship to the museum as you see it to be. You can also learn about the climate, the community, and the museum's neighborhood. If you are moving some distance away from home to make a new life for yourself, these things (and others) will be important to you. A good job is not enough. You will have a personal life outside the museum.

In the interview you can present more details of your past education and experience than you put into the letter of application and any forms you had to fill out. Be careful to make a good initial impression. Industrial psychologists have found that the first five minutes of an interview are crucial. If you meet with the board of trustees, remember that they are substantial citizens who are thinking of the museum as it relates to the community. They may be willing to take your word as to your ability to handle the technical details of the position, but they can see for themselves what kind of public representative of the museum you would be. Especially if you are to be the director of a museum that depends on public good will for its support (membership, clubs, volunteers, business gifts, for example), the board will be sure that you can put a simple English sentence together and do not eat your peas with your knife. They may even throw a cocktail party to see how you can handle your liquor. Whatever the test, you must not allow yourself to be overwhelmed, but present yourself in the best possible light.

This advice does not suggest dishonesty, but rather that you show the prospective employer that in manner, appearance, temperament, philosophy, social poise, (and whatever), as well as in skills and education, you can comfortably fit within the acceptable range of variation for the position. Keep in mind, however, that you are not doing yourself or the museum a service if you allow yourself to be hired under false pretences. The real you is bound to surface sooner or later, and if you are really not what you are expected to be, unpleasantness and termination of your employment are sure to follow. The lack of a good recommendation may then be a handicap in getting another job.

The student or beginner should be willing to take a job that is not exactly what he wants for the rest of his life. Any job you can qualify for, that is not completely abhorrent to you, will give you valuable experience and get you started. While you watch and wait for something more to your liking, you will be learning, making contacts, and experiencing the stimulation of daily contact with other museum people with a regular paycheck coming in. As you learn more about museum work, you will be getting a clearer picture of where you would best fit in. Plan on changing jobs more than once before you "settle down." It commonly happens that a museum professional eventually prefers to work in quite a different kind of job from what he had in mind when he first started. Some museum people change jobs a half-dozen times or more during their careers, although some persons stay with the same museum during most or all of their careers, moving up as higher positions become vacant.

I shall not say anything about the normal requirements of an employer. The rules of work apply in museums as they do anywhere. I would point out, however, that museum work is more than a job, perhaps even more than a profession. The quickest way to raise doubts about yourself in the minds of your superiors is to treat your museum employment like a 9 to 5 office job. Lengthy coffee breaks, unexplained absences, gossiping with other members of the staff, and a lack of attention to necessary routine will show that you really belong in some other kind of organization. Museum work is a calling, a public ministry, a commitment to a better world through the enlightenment of the public. It is done through adherence to high standards in the service of truth and quality. If this sounds as though violins, or perhaps even a pipe organ, should be playing in the background, association with museum professionals will bear me out.

Museum people feel that their work has great importance, and consequently it is deeply satisfying. They are often frustrated because they see the need to accomplish more than the limitations under which they work will permit. However, museum professionals are not bored with their work. Museum work can be extremely varied, and it can hardly fail to be stimulating and interesting to most people.

Since new museums are being created each week, since older museums are expanding, and since standards for employees are rising, we can expect an expanding job market for some time. Salaries are generally comparable with the public schools, or, for larger museums, with colleges. There is such a great range in salaries that nothing more can be said without saying a great deal. The interested person should see the AAM's latest *Museum Salary and Financial Survey*.

Getting a Museum Started

Perhaps you are in the position of organizing a new museum or putting one on a sound footing. If you have not yet formed your association, you should consult *Organizing a Local Historical Society* by Clement M. Silvestro. His remarks would apply to the organizing of art and science museums as well. You can also get help from state historical societies and well-established museums in your locality.

In general, you need a broad base of public support. Try to expand outward from the nucleus of the club or historical society which got the program started. A museum that continues to be identified primarily with a small group of people with a narrow, hobby interest will always be struggling for funds. A museum that is truly public in all respects can lay greater claim to adequate public financial support in the form of an annual appropriation from tax funds. Get the local newspapers, service clubs, and radio and television stations involved. And, above all, resolve to operate from the beginning according to sound museological principles. No loans. No two-headed calves. No bricks from the old school house or mementos of prominent families. Get professional assistance in whatever form you can, and hire a professional curator as soon as possible.

All of this applies not only to its beginnings, but to the museum as it continues to grow. A day will come when you will need to step back and evaluate what you are doing. You can use the precepts of this book and other basic writings. One of the simplest tests is to hold up the definition of a museum (Chapter 1). How truly is your operation that of a good, modern museum?

Upgrading Your Museum

The most objective tool yet devised for evaluating museums is the testing for possible accreditation. A precise procedure exists for the examination of a museum which has applied to the American Association of Museums for accreditation, including a visit and on-the-spot detailed inspection by a team of qualified museologists. Accreditation by the AAM is certification by the museum profession that a museum "is carrying on its affairs with at least a minimum level of professional competence."[1] The museum is not graded on a scale of excellence, but if it fails in its bid to become accredited, it is because it is seriously deficient in at least one important aspect of its organization or its operation. The accreditation process is based on the definition of "museum," and here we have come full circle because that was the concern of the very beginning of this book. A museum examining itself, in contemplation of applying for accreditation, asks how well it measures up to the standard of being a permanent institution organized essentially for educational or aesthetic purposes, which has a professional staff, which owns and utilizes tangible objects, cares for them, and exhibits them to the public on a regular basis.

Accreditation improves the profession as a whole by establishing standards, and by focusing attention on all facets of a museum. Nothing is ignored. Accreditation benefits the general public by raising the quality of museums in general, and by pointing out with a kind of "seal of approval" those museums worthy of visitation and support. Accreditation benefits the individual museum by giving it a yardstick for self-evaluation and improvement, by promoting public confidence in it, by assuring other museums that it—being accredited—is trustworthy in the matter of loaned exhibits and objects, and by certifying to supporters and donors—including grant-awarding governmental agencies—that the particular museum is a worthy recipient of financial aid.

---

1. Marilyn Hicks Fitzgerald, *Museum Accreditation: Professional Standards* (Washington, D.C.: American Association of Museums, 1973), p. 27. A very useful publication for self-analysis whether or not the museum is ready to apply for accreditation.

Accreditation applies only to museums; that is, not to the historical society of which the museum may be a part, or to the library, archives, art school, or other peripheral activity of the museum. Science centers, art centers, and visitor centers—not being museums—are not accredited, nor are individuals, though the accreditation of the museum depends on the presence of staff members of high professional qualifications.[2]

The key factor in the procedure is the visit by a team of museologists, normally two in number and not from the immediate locality. The museum that has appeared "on paper" to meet minimum standards may under close scrutiny by outsiders reveal serious flaws. The visiting committee uses a somewhat lengthy and detailed standard checklist to examine the museum's governing authority, board of trustees, staff, membership, finances, physical facilities, collections, conservation and preservation procedures, security, exhibits and exhibitions, programs and educational activities, and its purposes, plans, and probable future course. Museums wishing to be considered for accreditation should ask the AAM for its accreditation brochure.

EXERCISES—CHAPTER 20

The point of this chapter is twofold: (1) to show that a great amount of trial and error, "learning the hard way," and the practical experience of thousands of people over the years has resulted in a system for evaluating the organization and management of museums—a system against which museums can be measured for a professional "seal of approval"; and (2) to show that a museum worker must bring more than intelligence and good will to his job. The employee, the operation, and the product are all evaluated for such things as efficiency, high standards, effectiveness, and the like; any lesser performance is not worthy of the name "museum." "Museum" is a word museum workers respect. If they did not, they could hardly devote their lives to it, as they do.

2. Recently, the Accreditation Commission of the American Association of Museums has moved in the direction of making AAM accreditation available to planetariums, science centers, and other museumlike institutions in keeping with the AAM's liberal policy of embracing them as museums. No compromise is intended, however, as regards public education and professional management.

1. Write a letter of application for a particular museum opening (either an actual vacancy, or one that you can imagine). If you are submitting this letter to an instructor for evaluation, give him a brief description of the job for which you are applying on a separate sheet of paper. You may invent details, if necessary, as you describe your qualifications for the job.
2. On the basis of your knowledge of good museum practice, evaluate a museum as though you were to award or withhold accreditation. Justify your criticisms and make recommendations for improvements. This should be as thorough as possible, depending, of course, on how well you can get to know the museum you are evaluating. If an intimate knowledge of one museum is impossible, evaluate several as well as you can.

Epilogue

As I explained at the beginning, this book is not expected to serve as a complete text for museology. Rather, it is intended to supply what, in my opinion, is missing from the few, easily available publications used by instructors in elementary museology. This is a supplement, as I would teach the course, to what must pass as textbooks at this time. It should be emphasized, too, that my interest has been in the fundamentals of museum theory that underlie all kinds of museum operations. I have not meant to give undue emphasis to any museum fields while slighting others. I have, however, tried to keep in mind the needs of those who are most likely to use this book—students, beginners, amateurs in small general museums, nonprofessional workers in larger museums, volunteers, and public school teachers; as well as museum training instructors and museum administrators seeking help in their teaching or staff improvement programs. Criticism of this book will be welcome, especially from students and instructors who have used it in connection with a museum training course.

This small book is claimed to be, then, only supplementary aid in an *introduction* to museum work. Its emphasis or point of view is based on my contention that technique ought to follow—not precede—theory; museography should come after museology. In my view, the material of this book would normally be supported by reading in other basic texts and in journals. It would be augmented by motion pictures, slides, special assignments, and field trips. This would occupy one-third to one-half the school year. The remainder of a one-year beginning course in museum training could be devoted to techniques and actual practice. Attaching numbers to objects, constructing exhibits, guiding visitors, filing photographs, fumigating animal specimens, etc., would be done under supervision in a functioning museum. Actual work reinforces the student's understanding

191

of museological theory, and the theory gives meaning and purpose to the skills being acquired. The techniques alone, however, cannot be enough for the museum professional. Museum work is not simply an aggregation of skills loosely bound together through the paymaster's office. Directors and curators are forced to learn museology on their own when they do not come to their jobs with such preparation.

No one would claim that one course, whether in a classroom or by correspondence, will produce a finished museologist, any more than one course will produce a chemist, a geologist, or a schoolteacher. An introduction to a field, however, unquestionably facilitates later familiarity by providing a solid base on which to build.

Recommended Resources

An adequate textbook for museology has not yet been developed. Most instructors feel the need to assign readings in a number of books and journals that are available in their campus libraries. I have made reference in this work to several publications which the student may want to consult.

An important source of up-to-date information is the journal of the American Association of Museums, *Museum News*. The student who has decided on a museum career should join the AAM and attend its annual conventions. He should also join and attend the meetings of his regional museum organization. The AAM can supply information concerning these regional conferences. Specialists in American history in whatever kind of museum, library, or historical society, as well as all professional employees in regional historical museums, should belong to the American Association for State and Local History (AASLH). Its meetings, workshops and seminars, its journal, *History News*, its audiovisual "how-to-do-it" kits, and its many other publications provide much benefit.

Museums and museum workers should have their own libraries in museology and museography. Publications can be obtained at reasonable cost from AASLH, (1315 Eighth Avenue, South, Nashville, Tennessee 37203) and AAM (2233 Wisconsin Avenue, Northwest, Washington, D.C. 20007).

Certain motion pictures are of value, especially to those people who cannot visit a variety of good museums. No motion pictures have been made for the teaching of museology. Those listed below are illustrations for a particular topic covered in an introductory course and therefore are most useful at a particular time. An individual student would find renting these films expensive; the costs would not be excessive, however, if several students taking a course together were to share them. In some cases, a museum or historical society might rent one or more films as a program for its members at a time when it would be of value to the student.

Museum: Gateway to Perception, 15 minutes, is a good introduction to what a museum is and how the visitor can get the most out of his visit. *Henry Ford Museum*, 14 minutes, and *Greenfield Village*, 7 minutes, describe a history museum and an open-air collection of historic buildings. They are available to organizations and schools from the Henry Ford Museum, Dearborn,

Michigan 48121. *Through These Doors*, 28 minutes, is probably the best explanation of the work of the natural history museum. *The Leaf Thieves*, 28 minutes, illustrates scientific field work on a botanical expedition. *Animals of the Ice Age*, 16 minutes, an older, black and white film, is still useful for illustrating the field and laboratory work behind the scenes in a museum of natural history. *Museum of Art*, 27 minutes, shows many art museums and their varied activities. *Timeless Treasure* introduces historic preservation as a worldwide concern. *Williamsburg Restored*, 28 minutes, demonstrates the importance of research at the largest restoration project. *Corbit-Sharp House*, 13 minutes, provides an excellent example of historic preservation properly done. Except for the Henry Ford Museum films, these are available from regional film libraries. Other motion pictures of more specific interest to nature study, archaeology, art, pollution control, historic crafts, etc., are available. Those listed above have been found to be of value in a theoretical and philosophical way in the teaching of the principles of museology.

The following publications are suggested as the nucleus of a museology library. The museum worker should add more technical and more specialized books as he needs them. The museum should have, in addition to the titles listed here, reference books for the identification of its collections.

America's Museums: The Belmont Report. Washington, D.C.: American Association of Museums, 1969.
On the nature and condition of museums in the United States.

Bazin, Germain. *The Museum Age*. New York: Universe Books, 1967.
A very readable and excellently illustrated history of museums.

Brawne, Michael. *The New Museum: Architecture and Display*. New York: Frederick A. Praeger, 1965.
A good, attractive, and illustrated description of some recently built or remodeled art museum buildings in various parts of the world. Useful and stimulating essays on technical matters as well as a long introduction on the theory of planning museum buildings.

de Borhegyi, Stephen F., *et al. Bibliography of Museums and Museum Work*. Milwaukee: Milwaukee Public Museum, 1960, 1961.
Thorough listing of articles and publications pertaining to the subject prior to 1961.

Burcaw, G. Ellis. *Museum Training Courses in the United States and Canada*. Washington, D.C.: American Association of Museums, 1971.

Burns, Ned J. *Field Manual for Museums*. Washington, D.C.: National Park Service, 1940.

Chenhall, Robert G. *Museum Cataloging in the Computer Age*. Nashville: American Association for State and Local History, 1975.

Computers and Their Potential Applications in Museums. New York: Arno Press, 1968.

The Conservation of Cultural Property. Museums and Monuments, Vol. XI. Paris: UNESCO, 1968.
Articles by some two dozen authors on the preservation of a variety of materials, monuments, and sites.

Cummings, Carlos E. *East is East and West is West*. Buffalo: Buffalo Museum of Science, 1940.
An evaluation of the New York world fair of 1939 from a museum point of view.

Developing the Self-Guiding Trail in the National Forests. United States Department of Agriculture, Forest Service Miscellaneous Publications 968. Washington, D.C.: U.S. Government Printing Office, 1964.

Dudley, Dorothy H., and Irma Bezold Wilkinson. *Museum Registration Methods*. Rev. ed. Washington, D.C.: American Association of Museums, 1968.
The standard reference on registration, cataloguing, preservation, and related matters.

Fall, Frieda K. *Art Objects: Their Care and Preservation*. Washington, D.C.: Museum Publications, 1967; enlarged and revised version, La Jolla, California: Laurance McGilvery, 1972.
A useful summary of techniques for the preservation and handling of a wide range of materials.

Field Manual for Museums. Museums and Monuments, Vol. XII. Paris: UNESCO, 1970.
An authoritative description of expeditions and field collecting in all the natural history fields.

Fitzgerald, Marilyn Hicks. *Museum Accreditation: Professional Standards*. Washington, D.C.: American Association of Museums, 1973.
Justification and description of the entire museum accreditation process, including a checklist by which a museum might evaluate itself.

Guldbeck, Per E. *The Care of Historical Collections*. Nashville: American Association for State and Local History, 1972.
The best inexpensive guide to the preservation of all kinds of materials.

Guthe, Carl E. *The Management of Small History Museums*. Nashville: American Association for State and Local History, 1959, 1964.
The best single guide for small museums. While the emphasis is on history, the general advice applies to museums of all kinds.

————. *So You Want a Good Museum*. Washington, D.C.: American Association of Museums, 1957, 1973.
Perhaps the best short introduction to museology.

Harrison, Raymond O. *The Technical Requirements of Small Museums*. Ottawa: Canadian Museums Association, 1969.
The best available source on the museum building; planning, lighting, heating, floors, etc.

Historic Preservation Tomorrow. Williamsburg: National Trust for Historic Preservation and Colonial Williamsburg, 1967.
Subtitled "Principles & Guidelines for Historic Preservation in the United States"; inexpensive introduction to the topic, with bibliography.

Kane, Lucile M. *A Guide to the Care and Administration of Manuscripts*. Nashville: American Association for State and Local History, 1960, 1966.

Keck, Caroline K. *A Handbook on the Care of Paintings*. Nashville: American Association for State and Local History, 1965
Useful advice for the small museum.

————, et. al. *A Primer on Museum Security*. Cooperstown: New York State Historical Association, 1966.
A good summary, including physical security, environmental security, insurance, and related matters.

Long, Charles J. *Museum Workers Notebook*. San Antonio: Witte Museum, 1964.
Looseleaf collection of information on museographical techniques and commercial sources of supplies. Very useful for all sorts of museums. Revised periodically.

Luckhurst, Kenneth W. *The Story of Exhibitions*. London & New York: The Studio Publications, 1951.
An excellent source of information on the development of world fairs from their beginning in London in 1851.

MacBeath, George, and S. James Gooding, eds. *Basic Museum Management*. Ottawa: Canadian Museums Association, 1969.
Excellent short survey of museology.

McGrath, Kyran M. *1973 Museum Salary and Financial Survey*. Washington, D.C.: American Association of Museums, 1973.

Miner, Ralph W. *Conservation of Historic and Cultural Resources*. Chicago: American Society of Planning Officials, 1969.
Bibliography and evaluation checklists for historic preservation supplement the text.

Morris, Desmond. *The Biology of Art*. New York: Alfred A. Knopf, 1962.

Murdock, George Peter. *Outline of World Cultures*. New Haven: Human Relations Area Files, Inc., 1963.
Useful for identifying and locating obscure tribal groups; revised periodically.

Museum Studies: A Curriculum Guide for Universities and Museums. Washington, D.C.: American Association of Museums, 1973.
Excellent short guide for instructors and developers of museum training.

Museum Techniques in Fundamental Education. Educational Studies and Documents, No. 17. Paris: UNESCO, 1956.
The UNESCO view of applied museography.

Museums and the Environment: A Handbook for Education. New York: American Association of Museums (Arkville Press), 1971.
The teaching of human ecology by museums through exhibits and activities.

Museums, Imagination and Education. Museums and Monuments, Vol. XV. Paris: UNESCO, 1973.
Twelve articles by 13 authors dealing with education, extension services, "outreach," and applied museography in different parts of the world.

Museums: Their New Audience. Washington, D.C.: American Association of Museums, 1973.

Neal, Arminta. *HELP! For the Small Museum*. Boulder: Pruett Press, 1969.
Subtitled "Handbook of Exhibit Ideas and Methods," offers elementary and practical advice and information regarding exhibit construction.

The Official Museum Directory. Washington, D.C.: American Association of Museums, 1975.
Periodically revised, it is the best source of information about the museums of the United States and Canada.

The Organization of Museums: Practical Advice. Museums and Monuments, Vol. IX. Paris: UNESCO, 1960.
For years, the only thing approaching a textbook in museum training. Articles by museum experts on a variety of topics.

Plenderlieth, H.J. *The Conservation of Antiquities and Works of Art*. London: Oxford University Press, 1966.
The standard reference work on preservation. Should be in every museum library.

Preservation Bookstore Catalogue. Washington, D.C.: National Trust for Historic Preservation, 1972.
A handy source of publications on a wide range of topics; especially useful for architecture and preservation.

Preserving Historic America. Washington, D.C.: Department of Housing and Urban Development, U.S. Government Printing Office, 1966.
Descriptions and illustrations of preservation projects; with guidelines, and advice regarding federal assistance.

Pyke, John S., Jr. *Landmark Preservation*. New York: Citizens Union Research Foundation, Inc., 5 Beekman Street, 10038, n.d.
Has useful summary, "Where to Go for Assistance."

Rath, Frederick L., Jr., and Merrilyn Rogers O'Connell. *Guide to Historic Preservation, Historical Agencies, and Museum Practices: A Selective Bibliography*. Cooperstown: New York State Historical Association, 1970.
Every museum should have a copy.

Rodeck, Hugo G. *Directory of the Natural Sciences Museums of the World*. Bucharest: Council for Socialist Culture and Education, 1971.

Russell, Charles. *Museums and Our Children*. New York: Central Book Company, 1956.
Very detailed guide to educational programs and activities for children in museums.

Shomon, Joseph J., ed. *Manual of Outdoor Interpretation*. New York: National Audubon Society, 1968.
The Nature Centers Division of the National Audubon Society, 1130 Fifth Avenue, New York, New York 10028, also has other related publications.

Silvestro, Clement M. *Organizing a Local Historical Society*. Madison, Wisconsin: American Association for State and Local History, 1959.

Temporary and Travelling Exhibitions. Museums and Monuments, Vol. X. Paris: UNESCO, 1963.
Thorough treatment of the subject by several authors. Good illustrations.

Tilden, Freeman. *Interpreting Our Heritage*. Chapel Hill: University of North Carolina Press, 1957.
A pioneering, illustrated introduction to outdoor, or park, interpretation.

UNESCO Regional Seminar on the Educational Role of Museums. Educational Studies and Documents, No. 38. Paris: UNESCO, 1960.
  Definitions and descriptions of all kinds of museums and their programs.

Wittlin, Alma S. *Museums: In Search of a Usable Future.* Cambridge, Massachusetts: M.I.T. Press, 1970.
  Recommended for the history of museums.

Index

No separate glossary of museological terms has been included in this book because reference to definitions is given here in the index. Merely find in the index the term in which you are interested. The page or pages on which that term has been defined or used in an important way will be given. Lengthy treatments of main topics are, of course, referred to in the table of contents.